SCIENCE, TECHNOLOGY, AND SOCIETY

D0115524

ROBERT E. McGINN
Stanford University

PRENTICE HALL, Upper Saddle River, New Jersey 07458

Library of Congress Cataloging-in-Publication Data

McGinn, Robert E.,
    Science, technology, and society / Robert E. McGinn.
        p.   cm.—(Prentice Hall foundations of modern sociology
series)
    Includes bibliographical references and index.
    ISBN 0-13-794736-4 (paperback)
    1. Science—Social aspects. 2. Technology—Social aspects.
I. Title. II. Series.
Q175.5.M395 1991   90-38403
303.48'3—dc20   CIP

Prepress buyer: Debra Kesar
Manufacturing buyer: Mary Ann Gloriande
Page layout: Joh Lisa

A Pearson Education Company
Upper Saddle River, New Jersey 07458

Printed in the United States of America
10

ISBN 0-13-794736-4

Prentice-Hall International (UK) Limited,London
Prentice-Hall of Australia Pty. Limited, Sydney
Prentice-Hall Canada Inc., Toronto
Prentice-Hall Hispanoamericana, S.A., Mexico
Prentice-Hall of India Private Limited, New Delhi
Prentice-Hall of Japan, Inc., Tokyo
Pearson Education Asia Pte. Ltd., Singapore
Editora Prentice-Hall do Brasil, Ltda., Rio de Janeiro

CONTENTS

CHAPTER 15

SCIENCE, TECHNOLOGY, AND THE FUTURE: NEW MENTALITIES, NEW PRACTICES 258

APPENDIX

THE CURRENT STATE OF THE STS FIELD: A BRIEF OVERVIEW 277

PREFACE

This book is an introductory study of science and technology in society, with particular attention to the contemporary era in the West.

I undertook this project for two reasons, one pedagogical, the other personal. First, in the past two decades a number of undergraduate courses on science, technology, and society (STS) have been established in American, European, and Australian colleges and universities. While scholarly articles pertinent to most areas of the STS field are now readily available, there remains a need for a broad-gauged textbook suitable for use in introductory-level courses with varied student clienteles. The present work is intended to meet that need.

Second, I wanted to contribute to a cause that I have come to regard as vital: enhancing the interrelationships among science, technology, and society in the present and future. The "STS question" is already an important issue for contemporary societies. The ways in which it is posed and answered in a given society will have an important bearing on its future quality of life. Available evidence suggests that achieving a positive resolution of this problem will be a formidable task.

For example, the notion that a basic understanding of the nature and significance of science and technology in modern society is an important part of being both an educated person and a responsible citizen has gained considerable support in recent years. To date, however, social reality lags far behind this ideal. Historically speaking, the situation is no better: The important roles of technology and science in transforming Western (and non-Western) life, from antiquity to the present, have yet to be sufficiently recognized and appreciated, an intellectual failure with recurrent practical consequences.

If the interrelationships among science, technology, and society are to be enhanced in the future, a number of general changes must take place. Problematic as well as beneficial aspects of (what are misleadingly called) the "impacts" of individual scientific and technological innovations on society must be identified and explored. Appreciation of the astonishing material benefits and intellectual liberation that modern technology and science have made possible—something too often taken for granted—must learn to coexist with recognition that the same forces have engendered substantial psychic disorientation and cultural turmoil. The ways in which humans have responded to these developments and to what effects also deserve serious consideration in assessing the significance of science and technology in modern society. A balanced perspective attentive to both the benefits and the problems associated with modern scientific and technological innovations might alleviate the human and social costs of twin ills: facile optimism and resolute pessimism about the social consequences of science and technology.

As we perform this difficult intellectual balancing act, we also need to learn to think comprehensively about the social consequences of science and technology. A disposition must be cultivated to attend to all pertinent aspects of their influence on society: tangible and intangible, direct and indirect, short- and long-term. Further, probing philosophical reflection is needed on a growing number of perplexing ethical issues and value conflicts precipitated by recent technological and scientific changes, including identification of basic cultural assumptions underlying these dilemmas. Finally, serious social debate is needed about what changes in entrenched assumptions, values, and practices might, if adopted, mitigate the science- and technology-related problems plaguing contemporary Western (and world) society.

These convictions animated the writing of this book and are reflected in its structure and content. Were this work to make even the slightest contribution to the fulfillment of any of the aforementioned goals or needs, I would be deeply gratified.

Drawing on experience teaching an entry-level STS course at Stanford University for the past 19 years, I have tried to write a book accessible to the broad spectrum of undergraduates who can, should, and sometimes do take such courses. To that end, although my field of specialization is philosophy, not sociology, anthropology, political science, or economics, I have used important concepts, perspectives, and works from these fields in writing this book. In so doing, my goal was to create a book suitable for students in the social sciences, as well as for those specializing in the humanities, natural sciences, and engineering. This work is not intended as a contribution to the highly specialized field of sociology of science and technology.

PLAN OF THE BOOK

This work is divided into three parts. Part One develops foundational materials useful for analyzing science and technology in society. Part Two explores the influence of science and technology on modern society. Reversing the arrow of influence, Part Three considers the influence of modern society on science and technology.

Part One: Foundations

Chapter 1 explains why science and technology in society is a noteworthy topic and sketches the emergence in recent years of a new academic field: "science, technology, and society," or, as it is sometimes called, "science and technology studies."

Chapter 2 is concerned with untangling different meanings of the elusive terms *science* and *technology* and with characterizing and distinguishing science and technology viewed as forms of human activity. A brief historical survey is then offered of the evolving relationship of these activities.

Whereas Chapter 2 characterizes the *general* natures of science and technology, Chapter 3 discusses some distinctive features of *contemporary* science and technology. These features shed light on why these forces have exerted such a powerful influence on contemporary society.

Chapter 4 argues that adequately understanding the causes and consequences of scientific and technological developments requires seeing them in an appropriately broad, multidimensional context: that of the social-cultural-environmental system. Characterizing this context and illustrating its importance in comprehending the genesis and significance of scientific and technological changes is the twofold task of this chapter.

Chapter 5 is devoted to discussion of influential theories of science and technology in society. Theories discussed include ones purporting to explain the genesis and diffusion of technical innovation and to illuminate the relationship between technical change and social change. Readers uninterested in theoretical concerns may skip this chapter and move directly to Part Two.

Part Two: The Influence of Science and Technology on Modern Society

Chapters 6 through 12 discuss the influence of scientific and technological innovations on modern society, primarily in the twentieth century West. This restriction notwithstanding, comprehensive coverage of this topic is a daunting if not impossible task. Even if feasible, treatment of all noteworthy strands of that influence would be as tedious and unhelpful as it would be long. Realistically, one must be selective.

Each approach to exploring the influence of science and technology on modern society pursued in Part Two takes a "cut" at and illuminates a "slice" of the totality of that influence. Although political-economic changes receive some attention, the primary focus is on notable transformations in society's cultural system, the sectors of which are delineated in Chapter 4.

Specifically, Chapters 6 and 7 examine some ways in which science and technology have altered certain elements of the societal sector of the cultural system: *institutions* and *social groups*. Chapters 8 and 9 explore science- and technology-related changes in elements of the ideational cultural sector: *values and world views* and *ethical ideas and issues*. Chapter 10 is concerned with transformations of an important component of the personality-and-behavior sector of the cultural system: *the behavior setting of everyday life*. Transformations in the material cultural sector are covered in the discussion in Chapter 3 of characteristic distinctive features of contemporary technics and ways of making.

The approaches taken in Chapters 11 and 12 differ significantly from those of Chapters 6 through 10. No area of human activity falls completely within one sector of society's cultural system. Each such area has important ideational, societal, material, and personality-and-behavioral components. Chapter 11 focuses on *the fine arts*, an area of human activity not normally associated with science or technology. The influence of science and technology on that area is illuminated by showing how technical developments engendered changes in ideas, values, institutions, organizations, and behavior patterns associated with the fine arts.

As argued in Chapter 3, it is misleading to treat contemporary science and technology as purely national societal enterprises when their resources, operations, and outputs are increasingly global in character and reach. Chapter 12 examines the ways in which these potent forces have transformed *international relations*; in particular, political, economic, and social relations between and among national societies.

Part Three: The Influence of Modern Society on Science and Technology

In light of issues and problems occasioned by the influence of science and technology on modern society, some of which are discussed in Part Two, the focus of Part Three is on the influence exerted by modern society on science and technology, particularly in the twentieth century West.

Chapter 13 examines the complex structure and expanding scope of the relationship underlying modern Western society's exercise of influence on science and technology. What are the central agents of societal influence on science and technology? What types of influence exercise do they engage in? What kinds of effects do these societal agents have on modern science and technology? These are the central questions considered in this chapter.

Chapter 14 examines what is probably the most important mode of societal influence on science and technology: control. Six of the most important mechanisms by which contemporary Western society exercises control over science and technology are explored in some detail. In that discussion, attention is given to important unresolved issues and problems associated with the various control mechanisms.

Reference to unresolved issues and problems brings us to the book's concluding chapter. Chapter 15 analyzes several obstacles to improved societal management of science and technology in which I have a personal interest. The obstacles considered are largely philosophical-cultural rather than political-economic in nature.

ACKNOWLEDGMENTS

This book could not have been written without the help of many people. Since 1971, past and present colleagues in the Values, Technology, Science, and Society (VTSS) program at Stanford University have been the source of extraordinary intellectual stimulation. To James Adams, Barton Bernstein, Raymond Clayton, Eric Fenster, Barry Katz, William Rifkin, Everett Rogers, Howard Rosen, Nathan Rosenberg, Curtis Runnels, Londa Schiebinger, Paul Seaver, Bernard Siegel, Robert Textor, and Sharon Traweek, my sincere thanks. I am indebted to VTSS faculty members Joseph Corn, Naushad Forbes, Edwin Good, and Stephen Kline for detailed critiques of individual chapters. David Wield of the Open University in England and my former students Benjamin Austin and Rebecca Henderson provided helpful critical comments. With characteristic generosity, my VTSS colleague nonpareil Walter Vincenti read and discussed at length numerous problematic aspects of the entire first draft. I hope I have done justice to at least some of his criticisms. Paul T. Durbin of the University of Delaware, Linda L. Lubrano of the American University, Carl Mitcham of the Pennsylvania State University, and several anonymous referees wrote thoughtful reviews of the penultimate draft and persuaded me to modify the structure of the text. Students in my VTSS classes over the years forced me to clarify, alter, and sometimes abandon favored ideas and theses, for which my gratitude. Stanford University and the VTSS program afforded me a sabbatical in the winter and spring quarters of the 1985-1986 academic year, which facilitated initial progress on this work. My wife, Marguerite Grady, wielded a sharp red pencil and gave me the benefit of her exceptional intellectual and organizational skills. VTSS program assistant Virginia Mann helped with many aspects of this project, not least by being a person for whom fine writing matters greatly. The sensitive professionalism of Nancy Andreola and

CHAPTER 1

WHY STUDY SCIENCE AND TECHNOLOGY IN SOCIETY?

INTRODUCTION

On March 23, 1986, the front page of a large San Francisco peninsula newspaper displayed exactly four news stories. One concerned a tentative $350 million settlement of tens of billions of dollars of damage claims filed against the Union Carbide Corporation. The suits were brought by lawyers for thousands of victims of the largest known industrial disaster in history: the December 1984 toxic gas leak at the company's pesticide plant in Bhopal, India, which took over 2,000 lives and inflicted about 200,000 casualties.

A second item related the detonation the previous day, deep beneath the Nevada desert and in the face of domestic and international protest, of a nuclear bomb roughly ten times as powerful as the weapon that destroyed Hiroshima in August 1945.

A third article described the case of a California man who, since suffering traumatic head injuries in an automobile accident in February 1983, had been in a comatose state in a convalescent home. In the wake of the American Medical Association's then recently adopted policy declaring it ethically appropriate for physicians to withhold or withdraw feeding tubes from hopelessly comatose patients, the article related the efforts of the man's brothers to obtain a court order authorizing the removal of his feeding and hydration tubes so that he could "die."

The fourth story reported the imminent approval by the city of Palo Alto, California, of a contract that would make it and a number of adjacent communities part of what would become at that time the nation's largest subscriber-owned cable-TV system.

These news items have one characteristic in common: They all involve *phenomena of science or technology in society*. While the proportion of front-page newspaper stories with significant science- or technology-in-society components rarely approaches the four-out-of-four level, it is often substantial. It might seem, therefore, that the pervasiveness and importance of science and technology in contemporary society are already widely recognized. However, many writers or

1

readers do not recognize that the twin forces of science and technology lie behind numerous examples as disparate as those just related. Nor do they grasp the many and varied reasons that study of science and technology in society is worthwhile. Let us begin by exploring this question.

THE IMPORTANCE OF SCIENCE AND TECHNOLOGY IN CONTEMPORARY SOCIETY

Military, Economic, and Medical Significance

Science and technology are intimately bound up with three leading concerns of citizens and governments in contemporary societies: military power, economic strength, and medical well-being. Historically speaking, the outcome of World War II depended heavily on the superior scientific and technological capabilities of the United States and its allies. Today those technical resources remain vital to the national security of many governments. One indication of the continuing perceived military importance of science and technology is that in 1988, about three quarters of the approximately $60 billion U.S. federal government research and development budget went for military-related projects.[1]

Regarding national economic strength, consider the following. First, since the conclusion of the Civil War, when the industrialization of the U.S. economy began in earnest, technology has played a major role in increasing the country's productivity,* a factor critical to long-term economic growth and an increasing standard of living. Indeed, technological change is credited as responsible for almost half of the increase in productivity achieved in the United States since World War II, a contribution far greater than those of capital, education, resource allocation, or economies of scale.[2] Second, of the ten U.S. industrial corporations with the highest sales in 1987, seven were science or technology companies:† General Motors (1), Ford (2), IBM (4), General Electric (6), AT&T (8), DuPont (9), and Chrysler (10).[3] Third, high-technology goods—specifically, commercial aircraft and products in the semiconductor, computer, and office equipment sector—were, along with chemicals and crops, among the few bright spots in the troubled U.S. balance-of-trade picture in the 1970s and 1980s.[4] Such facts underscore the central importance of science and technology in the contemporary U.S. economy.‡ Indeed, science-and-technology capability is likely to be an increasingly important factor in national economic competitiveness for the foreseeable future.

These two forces have also played an important role in greatly increasing the scope and efficacy of medical care in this century, from advances in diagnosis and

---

*Productivity here means "amount of output generated per unit of input," where *output* typically refers to goods and services, and *input* typically refers to labor (e.g., labor time) or labor and capital combined.

†By *science or technology companies*, I mean private firms whose main products or services require substantial, ongoing, in-house technical research and development efforts.

‡The pivotal economic role of science and technology in contemporary society has not gone unrecognized in the non-capitalist world. In 1985, the president of the Soviet Union, Mikhail Gorbachev, declared that "The [Communist] party views scientific and technological progress as the main lever for the solution of all economic and social issues" (Erich Bloch, "Basic Research and Economic Health: The Coming Challenge," *Science*, 232, May 2, 1986, 595).

surgery to vaccines, therapeutic drugs, prosthetic devices, and rehabilitative apparatus. On a personal level, my father's quality of life improved markedly as a result of an artificial hip implant; my wife's cholesterol level declined dramatically as a result of taking an anticholesterol drug; and my son's survival, after being born two months prematurely, was due not only to the efforts of highly competent medical professionals, but also to drugs that accelerated his lungs' development *in utero* and to the high-technology equipment in the intensive-care pediatric nursery in which he spent his first three weeks. As with military strength and economic well-being, the substantial individual and public health benefits afforded by technical advances achieved in recent decades are widely recognized and highly valued in contemporary industrial societies, even though they have carried increasingly steep price tags. The conditions that enable such advances to be realized are complex, fragile, and subject to change. Although they are often taken for granted, they should not be; their evolution and problems deserve close study.

It is not just the military, economic, and medical importance of science and technology in contemporary society that warrants study of such phenomena. The unfolding of such developments has raised a number of difficult social issues that also merit careful consideration. For example, to what extent has the domination of many nations' research and development budgets by military-related projects impeded or promoted the growth of their civilian economies? How should scientific and technological research be organized and funded, and what kinds of political-economic incentives should be enacted to promote sustainable, more equitable national and international economic growth? How can societies ensure that cutting-edge advances in medical science and technology are made available to the needy at home and abroad who are neither covered by public health insurance nor able to afford the going market prices? These are but three of myriad complex policy issues that, taken together, strongly suggest that science and technology in society is a subject of vital practical as well as academic importance.

Human Successes and Failures

The forces of science and technology have been centrally involved in many—indeed, in a seemingly disproportionate number—of the episodes widely viewed as notable human (as opposed to merely individual) successes and failures in recent decades. Notable examples of this trend include the landing on the moon, polio vaccines, civilian jet aircraft transportation, the discovery of the double-helical structure of deoxyribonucleic acid (DNA), the Green Revolution, antibiotics, the personal computer, and the confirmation of the big bang theory of the origin of the universe. The failure side of the ledger includes the Bhopal, Chernobyl, and *Challenger* space-shuttle disasters; the pesticide DDT; the Ford Pinto; building collapses and airplane crashes traceable to defective engineering; and various forms of environmental degradation and human disease caused in part by irresponsible scientific and technological practices. Determining the factors contributing to such successes and failures is a worthwhile intellectual endeavor.

While spectacular at the species level, on the individual human level such successes and failures often mean that certain persons and groups reap substantial benefits from such episodes while others fail to realize them, incur serious harms, or are put at risk of incurring harm. This skewed distribution of benefits, costs, and risks has elicited intense study by both friends and critics of the practices and contexts of science and technology in contemporary society and increased public interest in how these forces are exploited and to what effects.

Threats to Human Survival

As suggested by the news story about the underground bomb detonation, the social significance of science and technology in the contemporary era rests to no small degree on threats to human survival posed by development or use of some of their most potent products: nuclear weapons, products designed for chemical or biological warfare, toxic or lethal by-products of manufacturing or energy-generation processes, and products that threaten the viability of the ecosystem. Understanding the conditions that lead to the creation and irresponsible use of such substances and developing means by which their production and diffusion might be restricted or prevented is a task as difficult as it is urgent.

Ethical Dilemmas

The story about the effort of the comatose patient's brothers to secure court permission to remove his feeding and hydration tubes epitomizes yet another reason that the study of science and technology in contemporary society merits attention. Exploitation of advanced scientific knowledge and technological devices and systems has on occasion given rise to situations in which these advances seem to have turned upon their beneficiaries, creating excruciating ethical and legal dilemmas. Application of these technical capabilities has sometimes even had tragic outcomes; an example is the prescription to pregnant women of supposedly therapeutic drugs that actually proved to be carcinogenic or to deform fetuses, such as the antimiscarriage drug diethylstilbesterol (DES) and the tranquilizer and sedative thalidomide. The ethical conflicts posed by such science- and technology-based dilemmas require careful analysis.* The lessons they teach about problematic aspects of established ethical ideas and assumptions and related social practices in the face of rapid, potent scientific and technological change must be absorbed so that appropriate changes can be made.

Disparities in Human Well-Being

Any list of specific science- or technology-based human successes such as that given above lacks at least one crucial item of a more general nature. It is both a major reason that science and technology are held in high esteem in contemporary society and that, at the same time, some scholars and political figures have leveled intense criticism at the international political-economic context of science and technology. On the one hand, these two forces have made possible the possession of a cornucopia of often sophisticated material goods by hundreds of millions of citizens of the industrialized countries of the West and in Japan.

However, millions of people, in both less and more developed countries, have not partaken of this lavish banquet. Some approaches to the alleviation of this problem on the international level will be discussed in Chapter 12. For now, consider Table 1-1. It suggests the magnitude of the gap between the historically unprecedented average levels of material affluence enjoyed in societies in which industrialization is

---

*The sources of some of these ethical conflicts will be explored in Chapter 9.

Table 1-1   Indicators of Material Affluence in Developed and Less-Developed Nations

	TELEVISIONS (1 PER X PEOPLE) (1986)	TELEPHONES (1 PER X PEOPLE) (1985)	AUTOMOBILES (TOTAL IN 1,000S) (LATEST)	PERSONS PER VEHICLE* (LATEST)	GNP PER CAPITA (1985)
United States	1.7	1.3	135,700	1.4	$16,360
West Germany	2.7	1.7	26,099	2.3	10,950
Japan	4.0	1.8	27,844	2.7	11,310
Brazil	3.8	12.0	10,008	12	1,640
South Korea	5.7	5.4	465	43	2,150
Taiwan	3.2	3.9	1,046	13	3,160
Nigeria	196	368	262	241	790
China	15	166	794	341	310
Afghanistan	860	496	31.7	268	230

*Includes trucks, buses, and other vehicles in addition to private automobiles.
Source: "Comparative National Statistics," *Encyclopaedia Britannica, 1988 Book of the Year: Events of 1987* (1988), pp. 740–877.

well advanced and those characterisic of less developed societies. Understanding the genesis of this gap and developing effective strategies for decreasing it are clearly issues of great intellectual and practical importance.

The existence of such glaring disparities and the widespread belief that scientific and technological resources will be required to diminish them provide another reason that these forces have taken on growing social importance.

Social Conflict

The persistent social conflict witnessed in the last quarter-century is not without precedent in the history of the United States. What is new, however, is something that has greatly magnified the social importance attributed to science and technology in the contemporary era. Much social conflict, not reducible to economic or racial differences, has been occasioned by developments in technology and science. For example, in the last two decades such conflict in the United States has swirled around such issues as the location of recombinant-DNA laboratories in or near residential communities, landing rights for the Concorde Supersonic Transport, the Love Canal incident, the Karen Ann Quinlan and Baby Jane Doe cases, the use of laboratory animals in medical research, the Dalkon Shield intrauterine device, the proliferation of high-rise office buildings in urban centers, research on "surplus" embryos, and the neutron bomb, to name but a few. Such struggles have taxed society's capacity for conflict resolution. The adequacy of existing institutional mechanisms for resolving social conflict over developments in science or technology will be explored in Chapter 14.

Social and Cultural Roles

Finally, a less obvious but no less important ground of the social importance of science and technology in the contemporary era lies in various influential social and cultural roles that these forces have assumed.

Science. (1) *Combatting Irrationality.* Beginning in the eighteenth century, science became imbued with a skeptical view of and approach to traditional knowledge claims. It came to be assigned the task of weaning the populace from myth, superstition, and resultant irrational belief and behavior. One may observe science serving this function in the influential mid-eighteenth century classic *L'Encyclopédie* of Denis Diderot and Jean d'Alembert. That social function remains operative today. One clear mission of much twentieth century science—and of many contemporary scientists—is to deflate narcissism and combat assorted noxious claims to inherent superiority associated with various "isms," including racism, sexism, ageism, ethnocentrism, and anthropocentrism.

(2) *Preeminent Source of Cognitive Authority.* In the twentieth century, a new social role for science has emerged. Science has become recognized as the leading source of cognitive authority in modern Western life. For centuries in the West, when there was an important dispute over past, present, or future reality in some area of life, leaders of society often turned to a sacred book or religious sage for assistance in making the necessary determination. In the twentieth century, such a tendency persists in certain religious sub-communities and in many individual lives; witness the popularity of biblical literalism and astrology. However, there is now a relatively firm social consensus about the direction in which to turn in such instances: to science.

In contemporary Western society the situation faced by Galileo has been reversed. Rather than scientists being compelled to renounce their empirical findings because they are not in accord with the a priori positions of some church, mainstream religions conduct their business on an intellectual playing field whose parameters are set by the established findings of modern science. To the extent that a religion refuses to recognize and adapt itself to the existential claims and boundary conditions laid down by this preeminent cognitive authority, it forfeits the support of consistent believers in the knowledge claims of modern science. Scientists are the high priests of the twentieth century, and most of the faithful laity defer to the authority conferred by their specialized expertise.

Confirmation of the powerful cognitive authority of science in contemporary Western society is not difficult to find. In 1981, public hearings were held before a U.S. Senate committee considering whether to adopt a bill declaring the fetus a person from the moment of conception.[5] The point of the proposed legislation was that if the fetus was so declared, then abortion would be outlawed, for the fetus would be entitled to the due process protection guaranteed all persons by the Fourteenth Amendment to the Constitution. It is revealing that both supporters and opponents of the measure called scientists to testify for their respective sides, focusing particularly on the pseudoempirical question "When does human life begin?" Neither side wished the conflict to be perceived as one between its own morality and its adversary's science.

So-called creation science illustrates the same gambit. Instead of the issue of the origin of human life being seen as a conflict between religious and scientific authority, some creationists frame the issue as a dispute between "our science" and "their science." Finally, public disclosure in recent years of a number of cases of scientific misconduct has engendered intense discussion within the scientific community. Responses have ranged from attempts to come to grips with the phenomenon to denials that it constitutes a significant problem. Such reactions are explicable partly because such episodes threaten to undermine modern science's cultural role as the ultimate cognitive authority, something that plays no small role in its ability to attract continuing substantial public financial support.

Technology. (1) *Sustaining the Private Corporation.* Technology has long been important in individual and group survival struggles, whether in hunting-and-gathering or agricultural societies. In more recent times it has become vital in sustaining the life of that pivotal modern social institution, the private corporation. Indeed, outside of government, the dominant role played by technology in contemporary society is that of helping corporations survive and increase their profits, something assumed to translate into substantial benefits for society at large. In the late twentieth century, in most influential circles of the Western world, corporation-controlled technological innovation is regarded as the leading contributor to and sine qua non of continued and enhanced societal well-being.

(2) *Source of Personal Identity.* This socioeconomic role, reflecting the interests of producers and owners, is complemented by a sociopsychological one involving consumers. As religion, race, class, sex, and nationality become less able to serve as compelling sources of individual identity in achievement-oriented post-traditional society, the items of technology a person possesses have, along with work, become increasingly important sources of identity and self-esteem. For people without prestigious positions or meaningful work, such items may well become the primary source of these psychological goods. Reminiscent of philosopher Ludwig Feuerbach's materialist dictum "You are what you eat," in contemporary Western society identity and esteem are increasingly rooted in the individual's personal technological inventory. As personal identity becomes more fragile in modern society, producers suggest that one can secure an identity and garner self-esteem by acquiring and displaying the "right"—read "state-of-the-art, high-tech"—artifacts.

(3) *Social Integration and Stratification.* Finally, modern technology has taken on an important sociological role. It is used in various ways to counteract centrifugal tendencies (e.g., the weakened bonds of family and community) characteristic of large-scale, highly mobile twentieth century societies such as the United States. It carries out this integrative role by promoting shared political awareness, common value orientations, and similar consumption patterns, as well as by facilitating intermittent contact between parties at a distance. At the same time, modern technology also serves as a powerful social stratifier. Desire for possession of or control over the sometimes scarce fruits of technological activity fuels feverish struggles for individual, institutional, and national prestige.

"SCIENCE, TECHNOLOGY, AND SOCIETY": A NEW FIELD OF STUDY

In response to the growing importance of science and technology in contemporary society—and to the increasing recognition of that importance—the last two decades have witnessed the birth and growth of a new academic field: "science, technology, and society," most often referred to simply as "STS." STS does not refer to the kinds of preparatory studies or advanced work in various technical fields pursued by aspiring or practicing scientists and engineers. Rather, it refers to study *about* rather than *in* science and technology. More precisely, STS refers to the study of science and technology *in society*—that is, the study of the ways in which technical and social phenomena interact and influence each other. For example, among the topics studied by STS scholars are the contributions of science and technology to the transformation of social institutions like work and the family, the influence of science and technology on economic growth and international affairs, and ethical and value issues raised by scientific and technological innovations. Other STS scholars, reversing the arrow of influence, study the ways in which science and technology are affected by social factors, such as ideology, political and economic forces, and cultural values.

Besides consideration of the often controversial "external" relationships of science and technology—that is, of their links to social phenomena outside their respective realms—the STS field also encompasses "internal" study of science and technology. *Internal* here does not refer to the inner technical details of scientific and technological work, although that may sometimes be relevant, even essential, to both "externalist" and "internalist" studies. Rather, it refers to studies of phenomena such as the general natures and interrelationships of science and technology, the social structures and reward systems of the professions of science and engineering, and social aspects of everyday scientific and technological activity. The latter category includes the ways in which veteran scientists and engineers initiate and socialize new colleagues, and social factors in the processes by which scientists and engineers adopt or resist proposed changes in theory or practice. This book is primarily concerned with the *external* social relations of science and technology, although modest attention is devoted to internalist matters in Chapters 2, 3, and 4.

Besides their increasing social importance and the growing recognition of that importance, phenomena of science and technology in society are studied by scholars because they are interesting and complex sociocultural phenomena. Surprising though it may seem, the respective natures and functioning of science and technology in society are not yet well understood, especially in the case of technology. The philosophy, history, and sociology of science are fairly long-standing academic specialities. In contrast, the history and especially the philosophy and sociology of technology are still in early stages of development. There is thus considerable room for original scholarly work on intrinsically interesting, intellectually challenging subject matter.*

THE RISE OF CONCERN OVER SCIENCE AND TECHNOLOGY IN SOCIETY: HISTORICAL PERSPECTIVE

One factor in the growth and persistence of concern over science and technology in contemporary society is, then, obvious: These forces are pervasive, potent, and problematic. They do more to shape the character and agenda of modern societies than do most other factors. For an adequate explanation of the *increase* in concern over science and technology in society, however, we must go back at least a half-century.

World War II

Perhaps the most important technical undertaking of the first half of this century was the Manhattan Project, culminating, in August 1945, in the horrors of Hiroshima and Nagasaki. This episode, together with the participation of many German scientists and engineers in the Nazi war effort, raised the issue of the social responsibility of scientists and engineers to a new level of awareness, at least among certain technical

*See the Appendix, "The Current State of the STS Field: A Brief Overview," at the end of this volume.

practitioners. In the wake of the dropping of the atomic bomb, physicist J. Robert Oppenheimer, director of the Manhattan Project, acknowledged the radically altered relationship of science, technology, and society spawned by the atomic age: "The physicists have known sin."[6]

1945–1960

In the years following World War II, between, say, 1945 and 1960, such concerns remained largely dormant. On the whole, the emerging affluence made possible in part by technology and science during this period, and the increasing role of the federal government in funding scientific and technological work, served effectively to suppress public consideration of these issues. However, development of the H-bomb and its deployment for possible use in war with the Soviet Union or Communist China kept the embers of concern from being completely extinguished.

Precipitating Factors: Twin Crises of War and Environment

In the 1960s this situation changed radically. Public awareness of environmental degradation, galvanized by Rachel Carson's classic *Silent Spring*, began to increase. As the decade progressed, social protest over the war in Vietnam also grew in scope and intensity. In both cases "science" and "technology" were implicated. From toxic chemical waste disposal, oil-rig and tanker spillages, and strip mining to agent orange, napalm, and antipersonnel bombs, many untoward occurrences were debited by significant sectors of society to the accounts of advanced technology and science—and their practitioners.

Initial Responses

Society at Large.   In the late 1960s and early 1970s, a number of developments took place in various industrial societies that reflected the growing public awareness of and concern with issues of science and technology in society. In the United States, Congress passed the National Environmental Policy Act of 1969, which mandated the preparation and approval of environmental impact statements before proceeding with public or private projects "requiring planning permission or state funding or any kind of state license, permission or aid."[7] The following year, complementary legislation was enacted resulting in the establishment of a government agency—the Occupational Health and Safety Administration (OSHA)—charged with protecting workers against dangerous or unhealthy work environments. In 1972, Congress passed the Technology Assessment Act, creating an in-house Office of Technology Assessment (OTA) to supply members of Congress with information useful in considering policy issues with important scientific or technological components. In 1973 the United States experienced an "energy crisis" spawned by the Arab oil boycott. This episode fueled discussion about whether society should pursue wind, tidal, geothermal, solar, and other "soft-path" energy technologies so as to conserve energy as well as environmental and financial resources. Finally, this crisis gave new impetus to the ongoing debate about "appropriate technology" for Third World countries, particularly ones hit hard by enormous increases in the prices of petroleum-based products. In sum, by the early 1970s, STS issues had become the focus of heightened governmental concern.

The Academic World.   In American colleges and universities, protest over the war in Vietnam gave rise in the mid- to late 1960s to what was widely seen as an "antitechnology mood" among students. This was an important factor, but not the only one, in the emergence in the late 1960s and early 1970s of programs devoted to study of the social relations of science and technology. Programs were inaugurated at Cornell, Penn State, and the State University of New York at Stony Brook in 1969, and at the Massachusetts Institute of Technology (MIT), the Universities of Washington and Michigan, and Stanford University shortly thereafter.

Motives among the pioneers of such programs were varied. Some early participants wished to subject recent scientific and technological practice to intense, sometimes tendentious critical analysis. Others wished to use such programs as forums in which to defend the existing practice of science and technology in the universities—including, at times, in their own besieged professions, departments, and research laboratories. Such scholars often spoke of the need for "balanced" consideration of the impact of science and technology on society. However, to them this influence was almost always wholly benign, and they sought to impart to their students a keen appreciation of this fact.

Still other scholars became involved out of a belief that the study of STS subject matter could fill an embarrassing intellectual gap in the curricular offerings of the late twentieth century university. Some went further, holding that interdisciplinary study of science and technology in society held the potential for becoming a new and important mode of integrative undergraduate liberal education for the contemporary era. The campus turmoil spawned by the war in Vietnam had as one of its by-products the dismantling of many established general education requirements. Some early STS supporters saw its interdisciplinary courses as an exciting way of linking up in an organic way students' specialized bodies of knowledge with important intellectual and social concerns beyond the purview of their respective majors. STS courses provided an innovative form of liberal education appropriate for the technological era.

Such courses afforded valuable perspectives and imparted needed skills to different sectors of the undergraduate student body. The study of STS, it was believed, would help tomorrow's decision makers in medicine, law, business, education, engineering, science, and journalism grapple more effectively with the real-life STS issues that they would inevitably face with increasing frequency in their future careers.

The emergence of STS courses and programs in American universities in the late 1960s and early 1970s was a welcome if belated attempt by a number of traditionally structured educational organizations to adapt themselves to an aspect of social reality that had become too obvious and important to continue to ignore.

Survival and Consolidation

The 1970s.   With the winding down and termination of the major triggering episode—the war in Vietnam—in the early 1970s, one might have expected STS concern to go the way of other short-lived educational reform movements. This demise would be doubly expectable given the inflation-driven budget crunches faced by colleges and universities in the period from 1973 to 1976. However, in the mid- to late 1970s, in both the academy and society at large, interest in STS matters increased, fueled by a series of controversial scientific and technological developments. Vexing questions raised by technologies such as nuclear power, computers, genetic engineering, and technologies of human reproduction and life prolongation, issues first raised by startling episodes like Three Mile Island, national defense computer system malfunctions, and the birth of the world's first "test-tube baby," demanded serious consideration. STS programs, congressional hearings, and special features in the print and visual media offered arenas in which such discussions could and often did take place.

1980 to the Present.   In the first half of the 1980s there was little opposition in society or in academia to technology and science per se. On the contrary, science and technology tended to be viewed as redemptive, at least as having essential roles to play in America's struggle against economic decline in the face of vigorous challenges from Japan and other newly industrialized countries (NICs) of Asia. However, even in an atmosphere of scientific and technological boosterism, provocative STS issues like the Reagan administration's Strategic Defense Initiative (SDI, the "Star Wars" program), the first artificial heart implants, and increasing unemployment in the manufacturing sector due in part to automation were and have remained the subjects of lively debate, within and outside the academy.

In the mid-1980s, STS concern received new impetus from philanthropic foundation efforts to promote a basic grasp of scientific, technological, and mathematical thinking and methods among nontechnical college and university students. The motivation for this effort was twofold. "Technical literacy" is seen by some as a precondition for enhanced public understanding of technology and science, something essential for realizing meaningful participatory democracy in the contemporary era. The other motive is economic rather than political: The deteriorating levels of mathematical and scientific learning in American society at large are believed to jeopardize future American economic competitiveness.

The late 1980s witnessed the emergence in academia of a small but growing number of autonomous programs and departments devoted to the study of STS at the doctoral level. In the United States, such endeavors were launched mostly at institutes of technology, such as MIT, Rensselaer Polytechnic Institute, and Virginia Polytechnic Institute. Whether such ventures can thrive only in such specialized educational environments or are forerunners of counterparts at leading research universities remains unclear. The outcome is likely to hinge in part on whether STS, or, as it is called at some institutions, "science and technology studies," achieves recognition as a legitimate field of scholarly activity, as did such equally inter- or multidisciplinary enterprises as religious studies, linguistics, and education.

CONCLUSION

We have discussed some reasons that science and technology in society is an important topic and indicated the major factors behind the emergence of the STS field. Widespread concern over science and technology in contemporary society was precipitated by twin crises of war and environment. In the last analysis, however, it is the potency, complexity, and rapidity of development of these forces in contemporary society, coupled with the scope, magnitudes, and often controversial character of the social changes associated with them, that have made STS concern and activity a vital and probably permanent feature of the contemporary social and intellectual landscapes.

Let us now turn to systematic analysis of the natures and significance of science and technology in modern and contemporary Western—especially American—society. The remaining chapters of Part I, Chapters 2 through 5, elaborate basic concepts, frameworks, and theories pertinent to understanding science and technology in society. Parts II and III consider important ways in which science and technology have influenced and been influenced by modern and contemporary Western society (Chapters 6 through 15).

ENDNOTES

1. *New York Times*, August 26, 1988, p. A10.
2. Erich Bloch, "Basic Research and Economic Health: The Coming Challenge," *Science*, 232, May 2, 1986, 595.
3. The other three (Exxon [2], Mobil [5], and Texaco [8]) were oil companies whose business is also research and development–intensive. See *The World Almanac and Book of Facts: 1989* (New York: Pharos Books, 1988), p. 140.
4. Michael L. Dertouzos, Richard K. Lester, and Robert M. Solow, *Made In America* (Cambridge, Mass.: MIT Press, 1989), p. 7.
5. *Congressional Quarterly*, February 28, 1981, p. 386, and April 25, 1981, pp. 729–730. See also *New York Times*, April 24, 1981, p. A16, and April 25, 1981, p. A7.
6. J. Robert Oppenheimer, *The Open Mind* (New York: Simon & Schuster, 1955), p. 88.
7. Ernest Braun, *Wayward Technology* (Westport, Conn.: Greenwood Press, 1984), p. 99.

CHAPTER 2

SCIENCE AND TECHNOLOGY: THEIR NATURES AND RELATIONSHIP

INTRODUCTION

The dominant focus of this book is the formative influences on each other exercised by science and technology on the one hand and modern Western society and culture on the other. However, it will prove useful in what follows to begin by clarifying the natures and functions of technology and science themselves in modern Western society. Confusion about these matters is widespread and nurtures misconceptions that sometimes have regrettable social consequences, such as misdirected funding priorities for enhancing national economic competitiveness. What, then, are technology and science and how are they related? These are the central questions addressed in this chapter. I will argue that, among other things, technology and science are distinguishable forms of human activity and that the relationship between them has changed radically over the centuries from virtual isolation to increasing interdependence.

THE NATURES OF SCIENCE AND TECHNOLOGY

The terms *technology* and *science* are used commonly and unself-consciously in everyday discourse and writing. People who use these expressions take it for granted that they and their listeners or readers have shared unambiguous notions of their respective meanings, as they presumably do with words like *triangle*, *kitchen*, and *dentist*. If, however, the questions "what is technology?" and "what is science?" are posed to students or ordinary citizens, the divergence in replies is always substantial, sometimes astonishing. The situation is no better with the numerous definitions put forth by scholars, be they scientists, engineers, or academic analysts of science or technology.[1] In sum, scrutiny of discourse and writing reveals that *technology* and *science* are deceptive expressions, each of which cloaks multiple unrecognized meanings. (See Figure 2-1.)

Four Meanings of *Technology*

While it would be foolhardy to think that any one account of the semantics of terms used as loosely as *technology* and *science* could be definitive or win general acceptance, one can at least attempt to be clear and consistent in one's own usage. Clarity will be well served in this work by distinguishing four different though related meanings of each of these terms. Let us begin with *technology*.

Technology as Technics.   In what follows, *technology* will sometimes be used to mean and refer to *material products of human making or fabrication*. Borrowing Lewis Mumford's term, I will call such items *technics*.[2] Technics, then, are the material artifacts (to use an anthropological term) or "hardware" (to use an engineering term) produced by a person, group, or society. There are various, sometimes overlapping, subcategories of technics, including tools, devices, machines, implements, instruments, and utensils.[3] Thus, computers, bicycles, contact lenses, hammers, axes, watches, guns, forks, microscopes, and, for that matter, clothing, buildings, pianos, and statues all fall within the general category of technics.

To be precise, as used here, *technic* does not refer directly or primarily to *particular individual* devices, machines, and so on. Rather, it is to be understood as referring to *generic types or kinds* of devices, machines, and so on—to *the* watch, *the* axe, *the* videocassette recorder, *the* dishwasher, *the* personal computer, and *the* knife, rather than to *my watch, your* axe, and so on. My watch and your axe are tokens or specific instances of the technics watch and axe and belong to my and your respective inventories of material goods; the watch and the axe belong to the technic inventories of many societies.

Technology as a Technology.   Consider this use of *technology*: "Great progress has been made in bicycle technology since World War II." Here, unlike in the previous sense, *technology* does not mean or refer directly or primarily to a particular technic itself (namely, the bicycle). Rather, *a technology* refers to *the complex of knowledge, methods, materials, and, if applicable, constituent parts* (themselves technics) *used in making a certain kind of technic* (at a certain point in time). *Technology* in this sense can be used in either the singular or the plural—that is, to refer either to *a technology* or to two or more *technologies*, as in "many technologies are involved in the manufacture of an automobile, such as brake technology, carburetor technology, engine technology, and transmission technology."

Figure 2-1. Four meanings of *technology* and *science*.

TECHNOLOGY	SCIENCE
Technics	Knowledge
A technology	A field of systematic inquiry into nature
A form of human cultural activity	A form of human cultural activity
A total societal enterprise	A total societal enterprise

***Technology* as a Form of Human Cultural Activity.**   In what follows, *technology* will often be used to refer to *a distinctive form or kind of human cultural activity*, just as the terms *art, law, medicine, sport*, and *religion* are often used to refer to distinctive forms of human practice.* In this sense, technology is a type of endeavor of which certain people, technologists—a category including craftspeople and machinists as well as professional engineers—are practitioners, just as artists are practitioners of art and physicians are practitioners of medicine. We will be more specific about the particular nature of the activity-form technology in a moment.

***Technology* as a Total Societal Enterprise.**   "The landing of *Apollo XI* on the moon in 1969 was a great tribute to American technology." Here, *technology* does not refer only to the specific technics and related technologies involved, or to one of the activity forms—technology—through which they were invented or developed. Rather, it refers to the total societal enterprise of technology—that is, *the complex of knowledge, people, skills, organizations, facilities, technics, physical resources, methods, and technologies that, taken together and in relationship to one another, are devoted to the research, development, production, and operation of technics* (at a given point in time in a particular societal unit, be it national or global in scope).

Of these four senses of the word *technology*, the first is the most fundamental, the last the most general and all-encompassing.

Four Meanings of *Science*

Four meanings of *science* can also be distinguished, three of which are analogous to meanings of *technology* just discussed. However, before we undertake to do so, an important distinction must first be made about uses of the term *science*. In its most general sense, one carried by the German term *Wissenschaft*, *science* means "systematic theoretical inquiry." Thus understood, we may immediately distinguish *formal* science, including logic and mathematics, wherein abstract symbols do not necessarily refer to phenomena of the natural world, from what might be called *substantive* science, including physics, biology, psychology, and sociology. In the latter areas, science takes phenomena of the natural world (including mental and social phenomena) as its object. Moreover, key variables and findings in such fields purport to refer to such phenomena and their relationships. Henceforth, unless otherwise indicated, the word *science* should be understood here as referring to the second, substantive branch of *science* in the most general sense. We now turn to four meanings of the term *science*, thus qualified.

***Science* as Knowledge.**   "With his germ theory of disease, Pasteur made a seminal contribution to modern medical science." Here *science* refers to *the organized, well-founded body of knowledge of natural phenomena*,[†] contributions to which have been made by thousands of men and women.

---

*Engineering is one branch of technology viewed as a kind of human activity. In particular, engineering is that professionalized field of technological activity devoted to organizing the design, production, and operation of technics and technical systems in order to meet practical human needs.

†The reader should be aware that much scholarly ink has been expended in controversies over the key words in this seemingly straightforward definition: *organized, well-founded, knowledge*, and *natural phenomena*. Here we will limit ourselves to observing that *natural phenomena* includes not only those that exist or occur spontaneously "in nature," but also those that exist only because of human contrivance. As an example of the latter kind of natural phenomena, the behavior of gases during engine cycles falls within the purview of the science of thermodynamics.

Science as a Field of Systematic Inquiry into Nature. In "physics is the most basic science," _science_ refers to _a particular field or domain of systematic inquiry in which such knowledge_—science in the first sense—_is sought_. As with the second sense of _technology_, _science_ in this second sense can be used in either the singular or the plural ("the science of physics" versus "the social sciences").

Science as a Form of Human Cultural Activity. Corresponding to the third sense of _technology_, _science_ will sometimes be used in what follows to refer to _a distinctive form or kind of human cultural activity_, one practiced by people now called scientists and formerly known as, among other things, natural philosophers and savants.

Science as a Total Societal Enterprise. Paralleling the situation with _technology_, the expression "science" is sometimes used to refer to the total societal enterprise of science—that is, _the complex of knowledge, people, skills, organizations, facilities, technics, physical resources, methods, and technologies that, taken together and in relationship to one another, are devoted to the study and understanding of the natural world_ (at a given point in time in a particular societal unit), the latter understood as including in its domain all human mental, physical, and social phenomena.

In what follows, context will usually make clear which of the foregoing meanings of _technology_ or _science_ is intended in a specific use of either term.

Technology and Science as Forms of Human Activity

Let us now consider in somewhat greater detail the specific natures of technology and science in their third shared sense—that is, viewed as distinctive kinds of human activity. This will lead to a useful way of differentiating between—and relating—technology and science.

One way of characterizing technology and science systematically depends on the fact that many conventional types of human activity can be analyzed in terms of six key aspects or components: their inputs, outputs, functions, transformative resources, practitioners, and processes. In other words, many traditional kinds of human activity, such as medicine, art, education, or law, can be looked at as involving the (intended) transformation or conversion of inputs into outputs via processes with certain stages or phases, in order to serve one or more functions, by practitioners using various resources to effect that transformation.

Technology and science are two such types of activity. Each can be characterized by describing its characteristic inputs, outputs, functions, and so on. Technology and science may thus be differentiated or related by looking at differences and similarities in and relationships between their various aspects. In particular, here we shall differentiate between technology and science by contrasting their respective characteristic outputs, functions, and processes.

Characteristic Outputs of Technology and Science. There are two kinds of characteristic outputs of technological activity: _technics_ and _technic-related intellectual constructs_. The latter term refers to various kinds of mental creations (e.g., procedures, plans, or analyses) that pertain to the design, production, use, or maintenance of technics. Examples of technic-related intellectual products would include a program for the computerized operation of a rapid-transit system, a system for controlling the quality of manufactured goods, or an analysis and assessment of the risk of a proposed design for a new technic.

As for science, its characteristic output or end result is theory-based—or at least theory-*related*—knowledge of nature—that is, of the material world itself, taken here as including humans as well as their individual and social activities and behavior.[4] Of course, some bona fide scientific activity yields sheer data or perhaps a speculative theory as its output, but only as an intermediate, transitional stage. It is the organization, coordination, or explanation of that data with a subsequently confirmed theory, or the confirmation of a speculative theory through an experiment that yields knowledge, which bestows on that episode of scientific activity a sense of closure or brings it to a kind of natural conclusion, albeit perhaps a temporary one.

Root Functions of Technology and Science. Technology arose as a perennial form of human activity because, unaided by technics, most human capacities—that is, perceptual, mental, and physical abilities—are quite limited. These limits render the human vulnerable to harm from various aspects of its environment. Humans therefore attempt through technology to decrease that vulnerability by extending their capacities. The additional power acquired in this way enables the human to survive, sometimes even thrive. Put differently, technology is an attempt to compensate for a central aspect of the human condition: human finitude, including the fact that humans are not omnipotent, immortal, or omnipresent.

But while extension of human capabilities is what much technology is about and may even, if we are right, have given birth to technological activity, the root function of technology is actually somewhat broader in scope. The transistor, one of the decisive technics of the twentieth century, is not plausibly viewed as such an extension. However, like technological extensions of human abilities, the transistor does permit the human to do something otherwise infeasible. Let us say then that the root function or purpose of technology as an activity is *to expand the realm of practical human possibility.*

It is more difficult to say with any degree of certainty what gave rise to the activity of science, even in its "primitive" forms. There are various competing explanations. Aristotle offers a philosophical account: "All men by nature desire to know."[5] The human being is an innately curious creature. Where possible, this primal propensity manifests itself in marvel at the world and attempts to understand it intellectually.

In contrast to Aristotle's reliance on human nature, Friedrich Nietzsche's psychological account attaches primary significance to the human condition. Theoretical inquiry into life is viewed as a sophisticated defense mechanism against the fear and anxiety experienced by vulnerable humans in confronting the awesome phenomena of the natural world. Some disciples of such inquiry believed that understanding the riddles of life through rational thought made the suffering inflicted by Nature bearable. Moreover, through scientific knowledge, the human condition will eventually come to seem less horrific. The individual will then be able to replace an anguished, pessimistic outlook with a "cheerful," affirmative attitude toward life.[6]

More materialist explanations have also been championed. Some scholars hold that even as intellectual an activity as science, albeit in a rudimentary form, arose from the socioeconomic needs of the order that emerged in the ancient world with the discovery of agriculture—namely, a way of life that revolved around the agrarian village. "In order for taxes to be assessed, land to be worked, and the whole complex social machinery kept in smooth working order, various new [intellectual] skills had to be developed."[7]

Given sufficient free time, something made possible by the resultant agricultural surplus, science arose as a by-product of the new intellectual skills.

Another materialist conjecture sees the origin of science as essentially the same as that of technology. Like the latter, science is an attempt to compensate for an aspect of human finitude: the fact that humans are not omniscient. Ignorance of the realities of the natural world makes humans more vulnerable than they would otherwise be. Well-grounded scientific knowledge of the forces and phenomena of the natural world affords new power to its possessors and gives them an advantage over those who lack it.

Still other scholars posit a political explanation. For them, the rise of "the new critical spirit into man's attitude toward the world of nature," something they see as marking the emergence of science, "should be seen as a counterpart to, and offshoot of, the contemporary development of the practice of free debate and open discussion in the context of politics and law throughout the Greek world," a phenomenon of the seventh and sixth century B.C.E.[8]

For whatever ultimate reason it arose, let us say that the root function of science is attaining an enhanced understanding of the natural world. Putting these ideas together, we conclude that:

> Technology is that form of human activity which is devoted to the production of technics — or technic-related intellectual products — and whose root function is to expand the realm of practical human possibility.
>
> Science is that form of human activity which is devoted to the production of theory-related knowledge of natural phenomena and whose root function is to attain an enhanced understanding of nature.

Characteristic Processes of Technology and Science.   Before addressing the question of the relationship between technology and science, let us supplement these two-dimensional characterizations with a brief contrast of their respective characteristic processes—that is, the processes in which the activities of technology and science typically unfold. Note that here we will be discussing technology and science *in general*, not specifically *contemporary* technology and science, the focus of Chapter 3.

Whatever other elements or stages technology processes may include, it is safe to say that whether the technic in question be an axe or a silicon chip, whether it be produced by a traditional craftsperson or on an automated assembly line, technology processes always encompass at least the following, although not necessarily in this order:

1. Identification of a specific need, desire, or opportunity to be met, satisfied, or exploited by means of a projected technic (or related construct);
2. A design phase, however rudimentary;
3. A production phase, however simple or crude; and, usually,
4. A use phase, however ephemeral.

In contrast, the processes in which the activity-form science plays itself out always have at least the following rather different elements or phases, although again not necessarily in this order:

1. Identification of an aspect or phenomenon of nature of interest to the practitioner;
2. Formulation, however crude, of some sort of "this-worldly" intellectual construct—a hypothesis or theory that does not simply attribute the phenomenon to divine intercession—to explain the aspect or phenomenon;
3. Application, however simplistic, of the construct to the aspect or phenomenon;
4. Assessment, however unsystematic, of the adequacy of fit of the construct to the phenomenon; and
5. Adoption or rejection of the would-be explanation or knowledge ostensibly in light of the application and assessment.

With contemporary technology and science it is possible to make these general phase descriptions more specific and recognizable, as well as to add new phases or stages applicable only to the contemporary era. Here, however, the general, contrasting characterizations of the respective processes of technology and science pertain to both the premodern and modern eras.

The qualifier "although not necessarily in this order" inserted before descriptions of the general phases or stages of technology and science processes, and the qualifying phrases "however crude," "however simplistic," "however unsystematic," and "ostensibly" in the descriptions of the phases of technology and science processes may seem superfluous. Here, however, they are absolutely crucial, for they are meant to signal the important fact that the processes of scientific and technological activity have long been idealized by nonpractitioners—scholars included—making them seem more rational, tidy, compartmentalized, uniquely sequenced, and, in general, more uniform than they are in actual practice.

Thus, for example, stage 5 of science processes refers to "adoption or rejection of the would-be explanation or knowledge in light of the application and assessment." The traditional, idealized image of science has long suggested that adoption and rejection of data and related hypotheses, theories, and world views hinges solely on disinterested evaluation of available evidence by individual practitioners. In recent decades, however, sociologists of science, under the influence of historian of science Thomas Kuhn's now classic *Structure of Scientific Revolutions*,[9] have argued that the adoption and rejection of hypotheses are sometimes affected by psychological and sociological considerations—for example, determined resistance by the dominant group of practitioners in the scientific field in question to disruption of their shared, well-ensconced outlook. Kuhn's book, widely regarded as a landmark in science studies, has, in the view of many sociologists, launched a long-overdue *demythologization of science as traditionally represented*. We will return to this topic in Chapter 5.

THE RELATIONSHIP OF TECHNOLOGY AND SCIENCE

With these contrasting characterizations in mind, we now turn to the second major question of this chapter: "How are technology and science related?" The essential point here is that the relationship between technology and science has a history—one which has changed radically over the last two and a half millennia. The central thesis of this section is that this relationship has evolved from one of virtual isolation and mutual independence to one of intimate association and mutually beneficial interdependence.

Technology and Modern Technology

In light of the preceding remarks about the characteristic outputs, root functions, and processes of technology and science, it is evident that technology as an activity existed long before the dawn of the era of modern technology in the mid-eighteenth century. It is therefore remarkable how many people use the word *technology* to refer only to what, upon inspection, prove to be items or ensembles of exclusively *modern* technics. In this way they succumb to and inadvertently foster the misguided view that human history is divided into pretechnological and technological epochs. *Homo sapiens* is not the only species to engage in technological activity, as the work of Jane Goodall and associates on the production and use of elementary tools by chimpanzees clearly shows.[10] Of all the vertebrates, however, *homo sapiens* is the species of which technological activity is most characteristic and definitive. Humans have engaged in (innovative) technological activity in adapting themselves to and transforming their environments as far back as the species has been traced.

One would like to believe that the tendency to (mis)identify *technology* with *modern technology* is merely a linguistic convenience intended to point up the qualitative uniqueness of modern technology by reserving the word *technology* for it. But this is unlikely and, in any event, confusing, for it obscures the important fact that technological progress is normally slow and cumulative. Modern technology evolved gradually out of and is deeply indebted to premodern technology. We will attempt to characterize what is distinctive about contemporary technology in Chapter 3.

Science and Modern Science

The story is much the same for science. The foregoing remarks about the output, root function, and processes of science make it clear that scientific activity existed in Western society long before the sixteenth and seventeenth centuries, the age of the "Scientific Revolution" and the dawn of (early) modern science. In fact, scientific activity, thus characterized, dates back at least as far as the ancient Greeks of the sixth century B.C.E. A number of Greek philosophers, the so-called Ionian cosmologists, attempted to explain the (to them) curious dual phenomenon of flux and change in their everyday experience of the natural world set against the backdrop of a cosmos that exhibited regularity and order. To explain this juxtaposition, a number of them concocted what seem to us crude models that postulated the existence of one or several basic substances (e.g., water [Thales] or air [Anaximenes]), out of which everything in the world was composed. Regularity was due to this underlying substantial unity, while change derived from the fact that the phenomena of everyday life were comprised of different combinations or changing modes or forms of these primary elements or basic stuff of the universe. Each of these speculators presumably tried to "test" his "theory" by seeing how much of the curious dual earthly phenomenon of regularity and change it could plausibly account for. This may be said to be the birth of science as an activity, however rudimentary.[11]

History of the Relationship

With these clarifications in mind, let us now turn briefly to the evolving historical relationship of technology and science.

Antiquity.   In antiquity, science rarely if ever played a role in technological activity.* One possible exception, frequently cited, is the case of the celebrated Greek mathematician and scientist Archimedes. Among his remarkable achievements, Archimedes offered a sophisticated proof for and may also have discovered the "law of the lever." In accordance with this principle, a mathematically calculable weight-lifting leverage can be gained by using a proportionally longer lever. Archimedes allegedly believed that engineering was ignoble in contrast to mathematics and theoretical science. However, he is said to have heeded the call of his king to help defend his native city by using his knowledge of physics to design catapults with which his people tried in vain to repel a Roman invasion in 212 B.C.E.[12]

This possible exception notwithstanding, the interplay of technology and science in antiquity was virtually nonexistent—unless one so relaxes the requirements for an activity to count as science that it does so if only it is done systematically. In this case, technology, since it has always been practiced in at least a minimally systematic manner, would automatically count as science. This gambit, however, would muddy the waters considerably and has not been adopted here.

Even on the basis of what has been said so far, it is already clear that technology is not simply applied science, a claim that continues to exert a powerful grip on the minds of many people, scholars included.[13] In fact, technology was present on the human scene long before the arrival of anything that might plausibly be called science. The making of physical artifacts long preceded this-worldly, theory-related attempts at understanding natural phenomena. It seems reasonable to conjecture that the same is true even if the qualifier "this-worldly" is dropped. That is, technological activity in the form of rudimentary tool-making antedated even "primitive" religious "explanations" of perplexing natural phenomena.

From Antiquity through the Renaissance.   From antiquity to the seventeenth century, the trajectories of technology and science rarely intersected. When they did, the arrow of influence usually pointed from technology to science, albeit sometimes indirectly. In the words of David Lindberg:

> Technological innovation made a prodigious contribution to the development of a prosperous medieval economy capable of supporting universities and theoretical scientific endeavor....[A]dvances in technology surely contributed to the production of scientific instruments — the quadrant and astrolabe of the medieval astronomer, the razors and saws of the medieval surgeon, and the alembic and furnace of the alchemist.[14]

Leonardo da Vinci (1452–1519), "for whom painting was hardly more than a sideline,"[15] is one of the exceedingly rare cases prior to the seventeenth century in which science may have influenced technological practice. Leonardo pursued both kinds of activities, working in scientific fields as diverse as anatomy, fluid mechanics, optics, and acoustics, and engineering specialities such as machine design, architec-

---

*Geometry was used in and influenced the practice of surveying in the irrigation societies of the ancient near east. This is not, however, a counterexample to our thesis, which concerns *substantive* science and sciences. For mathematics, while of great historical and contemporary importance in both science and technology, is not itself a substantive science in the sense of this phrase stipulated in "Four Meanings of Science," earlier in the chapter. While sometimes inspired by and applicable to natural phenomena, mathematics is the systematic study of systems of abstract symbols devoid of empirical meaning, thus a purely *formal* science.

ture, military engineering, and weaponry. Since most of his writings have been lost, it is not possible to make definitive statements.

However, from his surviving notebooks we know that Leonardo studied in detail the behavior and laws of fluids and made numerous scientific drawings of water in motion. He also designed grand hydraulic projects incorporating such structures such as dams, sluice gates, waterwheels, canals, and locks.[16] While no "smoking gun" demonstrating the impact of his scientific studies on his technological pursuits has been found, to suppose that Leonardo's thinking was so compartmentalized that his engineering work on such structures failed to reflect his extensive scientific observations of and reflections on fluids seems implausible. Even if the latter did influence the former, however, Leonardo, a rare combination of curious scientist and visionary design engineer, was an exception to the rule of the day: Science, both the activity and its results, was pursued independent of possible technological applications.

Francis Bacon (1561–1626) grew up in an environment in which a number of impressive technological advances had been made, both immediately prior to and during his lifetime, including: the wedding of gun powder and developments in metallurgy to produce the naval cannon, which altered the practice of warfare; the magnetic compass and improvements in sails, which led to the great European voyages of discovery; and the invention of moveable type. Such progress notwithstanding, Bacon observed that most technological and industrial activity was still of the low-powered artisanal type, being based on trial and error. He conceived the revolutionary, extremely modern idea that if such activity could be grounded on solid scientific knowledge, then progress could be made in improving the human estate. Thus, although technology and science remained in a state of mutual isolation during his lifetime and long after, Bacon anticipated intellectually a time centuries later when science would become an important factor in much technological progress.

Technology and Science from the Seventeenth to the Early Nineteenth Centuries.   When the perennial relationship of virtual mutual independence first changed in earnest, it was not science that began to influence developments in technology, but vice versa. Technology influenced the practice of seventeenth century science in three ways: through provision of scientific instruments, through giving rise to a new world view, and by influencing the research agenda of science.

(1) *Scientific Instruments.*   First, the epochal Scientific Revolution of the seventeenth century owed a good deal to several recent and not-so-recent technics—namely, the clock and the lens. The new science of Newtonian mechanics, which studied relationships between space, time, force, and motion, needed a device to measure time intervals accurately. An adaptation of the escapement-regulated mechanical clock, invented in the thirteenth century, met that need. Galileo's revolutionary astronomical observations of the phases of Venus, Jupiter's satellites, mountains on the moon, and myriad stars not visible to the naked eye, made the reigning Ptolemaic view that the earth was fixed at the center of the universe much less tenable. They also provided circumstantial evidence that the universe might indeed be Copernican. Galileo's observations would not have been possible without the (rudimentary) telescope he made after hearing of the invention of a device by a Flemish optician that made faraway objects seem near.[17]

(2) *A New World View for Science.*   Second, accumulating technological developments from the late thirteenth through the sixteenth centuries exercised a profound effect on science on a completely different level. Coupled with the growing importance and diffusion of the clock, the proliferation of machines in Western Europe during this period changed the way the universe was conceived by a number of scientists and thus, indirectly, the assumptions and approaches of their investigations. The universe, including nature, came to be likened to, even seen as, a vast mechanism—specifically, as a cosmological clockwork.

This likening of the universe to a clockwork is a special case of a new, more general outlook that arose around this time: "mechanistic philosophy." Its adherents likened anything in the universe to some sort of mechanism. They held that the laws in accordance with which the cosmic mechanism operated were of the same sort as those governing technological mechanisms. Thus, to understand nature scientifically, one should proceed just as one does in trying to understand a machine: try to understand its individual parts, how they fit together, and what mechanisms are involved in its coordinated operation. Everything in nature was to be thought of as a well-ordered machine and studied accordingly. "Research, whether into cosmology or physiology, was reduced to the discovery and elucidation of mechanisms."[18]

The approach of regarding natural phenomena as mechanisms became integral to science for two centuries and has borne rich fruit. For example, approaching the human body as a complicated machine with submechanisms focused attention on determining the ways in which the individual parts operate, the nature of the mechanisms by which they are linked, and the ways in which the mechanisms break down and might be repaired. The notion of the heart as a force pump is but one noteworthy example of such an approach, one which remains useful even today.[19]

(3) *Influence on the Research Agenda of Science.*   Third, technology influenced the research topics selected for study in early modern science. One of the disciples of the mechanistic philosophy was the physicist and chemist Robert Boyle (1627–1691). Pioneer of modern chemistry and best known as the discoverer of Boyle's law for ideal gases, Boyle was also one of the founders of that great scientific institution, the Royal Society of London. Founded in London in 1662, the Royal Society was devoted to the advancement of the new empirical thinking and the implementation of Bacon's idea that methodical experimentation and careful observation would lead to new scientific discoveries and valuable technical advances.

Sociologist Robert Merton showed that as far as can be gathered from the research projects discussed at meetings of the Royal Society in the years 1661, 1662, 1686, and 1687—seemingly typical years for which minutes of the meetings are available—58.7 percent of the problems chosen for experimental investigation by members of the Royal Society were directly or indirectly linked to problems of technological practice, primarily in the mining, marine transport, and textile industries.[20] Thus, already in the seventeenth century, technology—more precisely, technological problems in industry—was strongly influencing science by shaping its research agenda. As most of the scientific areas explored by the Fellows of the Royal Society had little theoretical grounding, little came of this Baconian program in the short run. Two centuries later, however, when the physical sciences had been put on a more solid theoretical basis, the fruits of such research proved abundant.

(4) *Scientific Instruments and Scientific Revolutions.* In the late eighteenth and early nineteenth centuries, technology in the form of instruments and devices continued to influence the course of science. For example, the static electrical generator gave rise to the discovery of voltaic electricity and the ensuing "voltaic cell"—a primitive battery—to the discovery of the magnetic field created by a steady electric current in a circuit.[21]

Derek Price goes so far as to claim that most revolutions in the history of science, attributed by Thomas Kuhn to imaginative leaps of bold scientists confronted by data incompatible with existing theory, were in fact engendered by changes in instrument technology. The changes, "often quite slight and innocent in appearance,...provid[ed] new sorts of window for scientists to look from" in conducting their experiments.[22] Both viewpoints have merit. New instruments are sometimes essential for obtaining new data, which may turn out to be troubling and call for theoretical reform or revolution. However, they do not by themselves entail, and are no substitute for, the conceptual breakthroughs and new theoretical syntheses of creative scientists.

(5) *Contribution of Science to Technology in the Eighteenth Century.* On the other hand, the contribution of science to technological progress in the eighteenth century was generally modest. The most notable possible exception, over which disagreement persists, is the important case of the steam engine. The steam engine originated as an attempt to solve the pressing practical problem of draining water from tin and coal mines being sunk ever deeper because of the growing effective shortage of wood fuel in England. The atmospheric steam engine of Thomas Newcomen was introduced in 1712 and remained in use for more than a century. The working, or pumping, cycle of the Newcomen machine made use of the fact that when steam in a cylinder closed at the top with a sliding piston was condensed by introducing a jet of cold water, a vacuum was created and atmospheric pressure drove the piston down into the cylinder. What is still in dispute is whether or to what degree this reliance upon the fact that atmospheric pressure creates a force was taken over from earlier scientific experiments, such as those of Otto von Guerike and Denis Papin in the second half of the seventeenth century.

John Ziman contends that in the long history of the development of the steam engine,

> the only significant contribution *from theory* was the invention of the separate condenser in 1764 by James Watt (1736–1819), who had been an assistant to Joseph Black (1728–1799), professor of natural philosophy at Glasgow University. Black's measurements on latent heat suggested to Watt the importance of avoiding the tremendous waste of heat [involved] in heating and cooling the cylinder of the Smeaton engine [of 1734].[23] (emphasis added)

However, in his own account of how he "contriv[ed]" the idea of the separate condenser, Watt, while acknowledging the utility of Black's latent heat theory for purposes of calculation, denies that that theory led to "the improvements I afterwards made in the engine."[24]

Technology and Science in the Nineteenth Century. (1) *The Rise of Science-Based Industries.* Be that as it may, the nineteenth century marked a crucial turning point in the relationship of technology and science. In the second half of the century there emerged the first so-called science-based industries. Products in these industries would not have come into being without knowledge generated by scientific investigation. The most prominent such industries were coal-tar dye manufacture and electrical power generation and machinery. Even here, though, the ways in which science came to influence technology were interestingly different.

(2) *The Birth of the Industrial Research Laboratory.*   By the mid-nineteenth century, chemistry was rather far advanced in its technological applications, particularly in Germany, where a strong tradition of chemical research and training had emerged in and around the universities after Prussia's humiliating defeat by Napoleon.[25] One area in which applied chemical science had already borne fruit was in the dyestuffs industry, where the Germans overcame early British and French leadership in the manufacture of aniline colors. The German dyestuff manufacturer, often an academically trained chemist himself, originally did his own scientific research. But, as John Beer has written:

> [I]n the two decades that followed the founding of the coal-tar color industry in 1857, as competition between the mushrooming color factories intensified, and as the chemistry of aromatic compounds grew ever more complex, [the manufacturer] found that he alone could no longer master the diversified researches becoming indispensible to the survival of his business. He therefore began to hire help, and in this manner was born the industrial [research] laboratory.[26]

Thus, the way in which science influenced technology in this instance was by marrying the available supply of well-trained academic chemists to emerging technological-industrial problems. The direction of the fundamental scientific research done in the new industrial laboratories was determined by the specific needs of the firm.

In the case of the electrical power and machinery industries, the situation was somewhat different. In this case, the basic scientific discovery of electromagnetic induction in 1831 by Michael Faraday—"the epitome of the pure scientist"[27]—preceded by about 50 years its technical exploitation on a large scale: the construction of the first public power stations. In the early electrical power and machinery industries it was not a matter of structuring the direction of continuing basic research, carried out in a new setting, to serve industrial needs. Rather, the results of prior scientific discoveries made in the academy were adapted to practical commercial requirements.

Although we have been stressing new ways in which science influenced technological practice, it should not be thought that this soon became anything like the norm of the science-technology relationship. The exploitation of Faraday's discovery in the construction of public power systems beginning in the 1880s did make use of the current-generating dynamo, a primitive version of which he developed soon after discovering electromagnetic induction in 1831. However, this exploitation arose from Thomas Edison's desire to replace gas lighting with an independently controlled residential electrical lighting *system.* This system, itself one of Edison's greatest inventions, was made possible by, among other things, his successful development of a suitable incandescent electric light bulb. The latter owed nothing to scientific knowledge, while the former involved far more than developing a huge and much more efficient version of the dynamo, something Edison also achieved.[28]

Technology and Science in the Twentieth Century.   (1) *The Growth of Industrial Research Laboratories.*   The birth in the German coal-tar dye industry of that pivotal modern social institution, the industrial research laboratory, anticipated what was to become an important facet of the science-technology relationship in the twentieth century. At least 139 research laboratories were established in American industry before the turn of the twentieth century, and another 553 were established by 1918.[29] One such facility, Bell Telephone Laboratories (BTL), was the direct descendent of Alexander Graham Bell's laboratory in Boston in the 1870s. In 1929, BTL's Director of Physical Research, H. D. Arnold, indicated a salient reason, besides economic competitiveness, that many technological firms established their own basic scientific research laboratories: scale. American Telephone & Telegraph, BTL's parent company, could not afford the financial and operational risk of making systemwide changes in the national telephone network which were not grounded in solid scientific understanding of underlying principles.[30]

(2) *Technology Not Completely Dependent on Science.* Twentieth century technological activity is much more dependent upon scientific knowledge than ever before. Fundamental research in genetics, physics, and chemistry has been crucial to progress in the genetic engineering, nuclear power, and drug industries. But this unprecedented dependence of technology on science in the twentieth century is easy to exaggerate. Even today, much technological activity proceeds to successful conclusion in the absence of thorough understanding of related underlying scientific principles. Exigencies of politics or economics sometimes require that the technic or technical system in question be produced in a timely fashion, using "seat of the pants," "trial-and-error," and other systematic but nontheoretical bases. For example, the design of airplane propeller shapes in the decade following World War I was carried out empirically, without a complete understanding of the underlying fluid dynamic principles involved.[31] In fact, although it took place in a modern, science-based industry, the replacement of protruding, dome-shaped rivets by newly designed flush rivets in metal stressed-skin airplanes in the 1930s had virtually nothing to do with science.[32]

(3) *Growing Interdependence of Technology and Science.* Thus, any attempt to summarize the relationship between modern science and modern technology as essentially one of an increasingly sophisticated science being applied to develop numerous new and improved technics and technologies is fatally flawed and falls short of being even a half-truth. What is indisputable, however, is that during the past 130 years, that relationship has been one of progressive symbiosis. If instruments were technology's gift to science in the ancient, medieval, Renaissance, and early modern periods, its gifts are considerably more lavish today. Witness the roles of huge accelerators and computers in contemporary particle physics and powerful radiowave-receiving dishes and robotic spacecraft in contemporary astronomy and radioscience. This trend is likely to increase in the future: New technics will be necessary to obtain important scientific data as well as to process and analyze it.

On the other hand, while twentieth century science's main contribution to technology has been the production of well grounded knowledge on which technological activity can confidently build, that contribution seems likely to take on added dimensions in the future. For example, consider recent experimental research on "ballistic transistors," switching devices so small that electrons can traverse them without being slowed down by colliding with impurities or other impediments. Since ballistic transistors can switch on and off one hundred to one thousand times faster than the current generation of transistors, they hold out the hope of greatly increasing the pace at which information can be made to move through computer chips. This in turn creates the prospect of a new generation of computers with greatly increased data-processing capacities. One formidable problem with making ballistic transistors feasible is making them thin enough to prevent collisions. This requires entirely new approaches to semiconductor fabrication, traditionally a *technological* problem.

One approach to this problem has been to try to grow a perfectly uniform, exceedingly thin semiconductor film only a few atoms thick. Finding a material that lends itself to this requirement is an integral part of this effort. At Bell Laboratories, in the late 1980s, the group working to solve this fabrication problem consisted not of engineers but of scientists and was led by the director of the department of chemical physics research. In this instance, in addition to the usual scientific task of generating the necessary new scientific knowledge of suitable materials, scientists were also seeking to develop the fabricative technique, traditionally the domain of engineers.[33]

CONCLUSION

The upshot of this discussion is that the relationship between technology and science has changed markedly over the millenia, from virtual isolation and mutual independence to generally close association and mutually beneficial interdependence. In the late twentieth century, it is increasingly rare to find technical projects of significant scale that do not have both technological and scientific components, be they "technological endeavors" like space shuttle launches or "scientific facilities" like particle accelerator centers. If the former often involve scientific research or experiments and are partly based on scientific calculations, the latter sometimes employ more engineers than scientists and are frequently technology-intensive.

Even a single practitioner's activity can defy simple classification as "science" or "technology." A molecular biologist creating an organism with desired commercial properties may at times function as an engineer, at times as a scientist, and at times as both simultaneously; so too may a mechanical engineer analyzing turbulence. Thus, a technical activity can have a dual, scientific-technological character. Seemingly purely scientific activity is sometimes imbued with technology's root function, as seemingly purely technological activity sometimes is with science's. Modern science and technology are not only interdependent, they overlap.[34]

Yet, forced at the point of a gun to choose between two crude misconceptions, one would have to opt for the heretical notion that "science is applied technology" over the conventional wisdom that "technology is applied science." Remove the technics from the research laboratory and it will be time to close up shop until they are returned or replaced; eradicate the scientific knowledge from the minds and books of the technologists and a substantial amount of technological activity will still be able to proceed, although probably less efficiently, elegantly, and securely.

If, as has been shown here, the *relationship* between technology and science has changed radically over the centuries, so too have the respective characters of technology and science themselves. Contemporary technology and science are far different kinds of activities than their premodern forerunners. In Chapter 3 we will explore in detail what is distinctive about technology and science in the twentieth century, a time when they have had such a profound influence on society.

ENDNOTES

1. See, e.g., Emmanuel G. Mesthene, *Technological Change* (New York: Mentor, 1970), p. 25; John Ziman, *The Force of Knowledge* (Cambridge: Cambridge University Press, 1976), p. 4; Robert S. Merrill, "The Study of Technology," in "Technology," *International Encyclopedia of the Social Sciences* (New York: Macmillan, 1968), vol. 15, pp. 576–577; Charles Singer et al., *A History of Technology* (Oxford: Oxford University Press, 1954), 1, p. vii; Donald A. Schon, *Technology and Change* (New York: Delacorte, 1967), p. 1.

    For a useful discussion by an engineer of misleading ways in which scientists and other scholars construe technology, see Michael Fores, "Scientists on Technology: Magic and English-Language 'Industrispeak,'" in Devendra Sahal, ed., *Research, Development, and Technological Innovation* (Lexington, Mass.: Lexington Books, 1980), pp. 239–250.
2. Lewis Mumford, *Technics and Civilization* (New York: Harcourt, Brace & World, 1963), pp. 3–7.
3. *Ibid.*, pp. 9–12.
4. Raymond Williams, *Keywords* (Glasgow: Fontana, 1976), p. 184.
5. J. A. Smith and W. D. Ross, eds., *The Works of Aristotle* (Oxford: Oxford University Press, 1908), 8, p. 980a.
6. Friedrich Nietzsche, *The Birth of Tragedy* (New York: Vintage, 1967), pp. 42, 95, and 109.
7. L. Pierce Williams, "History of Science," *Cowles Encyclopedia of Science, Industry, and Technology* (New York: Cowles, 1969), p. 2.
8. G. E. R. Lloyd, *Early Greek Science: Thales to Aristotle* (New York: W. W. Norton & Co., Inc., 1970), p. 15.
9. Thomas S. Kuhn, *The Structure of Scientific Revolutions*, 2nd ed., (Chicago: University of Chicago Press, 1970).
10. Jane Goodall, *In the Shadow of Man* (Boston: Houghton Mifflin, 1971), pp. 34–37, 98–99.
11. Lloyd, *Early Greek Science*, Chaps. 1 and 2.
12. Marshall Clagett, "Archimedes," *Dictionary of Scientific Biography*, C. Gillispie, ed. (New York: Scribner's, 1971), 1, p. 213.
13. See, e.g., engineer John G. Truxal, "Learning to Think Like an Engineer," *Change*, 18, no. 2, March/April 1986, 12: "Technology, after all, is simply the application of scientific knowledge to achieve a specified human purpose." For economist Simon Kuznets, the "epochal innovation that distinguishes the modern economic epoch is the extended application of science to problems of economic production," while for biologist Sir Solly Zuckerman, technology is "what we ourselves make of scientific knowledge." See Michael Fores, "Scientists on Technology," p. 240.
14. David C. Lindberg, ed., *Science in the Middle Ages* (Chicago: University of Chicago Press, 1978), p. xii.
15. W. T. Jones, *Hobbes to Hume: A History of Western Philosophy*, 2nd ed. (New York: Harcourt, Brace & World, 1969), p. 69.
16. Ladislao Reti, *The Unknown Leonardo* (New York: McGraw-Hill, 1974), pp. 190–207.
17. John P. McKelvey, "Science and Technology: the Driven and the Driver," *Technology Review*, 88, no. 1, January 1985, 42.
18. A. C. Crombie, "Descartes," *Dictionary of Scientific Biography* (New York: Scribner's, 1971), vol. 4, p. 54.
19. Thomas F. Robinson et al., "The Heart as a Suction Pump," *Scientific American*, 254, no. 6, June 1986, 84–91.
20. Robert Merton, *Science, Technology, and Society in Seventeenth Century England* (New York: Howard Fertig, 1970), p. 204.
21. McKelvey, "Science and Technology," p. 42 and Derek J. deSolla Price, "Notes Towards a Philosophy of the Science/Technology Interaction," in Rachel Laudan, ed., *The Nature of Technological Knowledge* (Amsterdam: Reidel, 1984), p. 111.
22. Price, *ibid.*, p. 110.

23. Ziman, *Force of Knowledge*, p. 25. For an account giving heavier emphasis to the contributions of science to the steam engine, see Milton Kerker, "Science and the Steam Engine," *Technology and Culture*, 2, no. 4, Fall 1961, 381–390.
24. Kerker, "Science and the Steam Engine," pp. 385–386. See also Ronald W. Clark, *Works of Man* (New York: Viking Penguin, 1985), pp. 72–73.
25. W. H. Brock, "Liebigiana: Old and New Perspectives," *History of Science*, 19, part 3, no. 45, September 1981, 201–218, especially 207–210.
26. John J. Beer, "Coal Tar Dye Manufacture and the Origins of the Modern Industrial Research Laboratory," in Thomas Parke Hughes, ed., *The Development of Western Technology Since 1500* (New York: Macmillan, 1964), p. 130.
27. Ziman, *Force of Knowledge*, p. 29.
28. Ronald W. Clark, *Edison: The Man Who Made the Future* (New York: Putnam's, 1977), pp. 87–148.
29. Nathan Rosenberg and L. E. Birdzell, Jr., *How the West Grew Rich* (New York: Basic Books, 1986), p. 247.
30. H. D. Arnold, Preface, in Harvey Fletcher, *Speech and Hearing* (New York: D. Van Nostrand, 1929), pp. xi–xii.
31. W. G. Vincenti, "The Air-Propeller Tests of W. F. Durand and E. P. Lesley: A Case Study in Technological Methodology," *Technology and Culture*, 20, no. 4, October 1979, 712–751.
32. W. G. Vincenti, "Technological Knowledge Without Science: The Development of Flush Riveting in American Airplanes, 1930–1940," *Technology and Culture*, 25, no. 3, July 1984, 540–576.
33. *New York Times*, May 15, 1986, p. 28.
34. In light of this overlap, science and technology can be regarded as Weberian "ideal types," both of which can be manifested in a single concrete technical activity. For Weber on ideal types, see *Weber: Selections in Translation*, W. G. Runciman, ed. (Cambridge: Cambridge University Press, 1978), pp. 23-25.

CHAPTER 3
CONTEMPORARY SCIENCE AND TECHNOLOGY: SOME IMPORTANT CHARACTERISTICS

INTRODUCTION

Science and technology have exercised a broad and deep influence on contemporary Western society. It would be surprising if this were not due in part to characteristics of these activities that have emerged or matured in this century. In Part II we will venture an account of the influence of science and technology on twentieth century Western society. The purpose of the present chapter, however, is to discuss some notable distinguishing features of science and technology in this century.

The rationale for doing so is not purely academic. Debate over issues of science or technology in society can only improve if disputants and decision-makers have a basic grasp not only of the *general natures* of science and technology (Chapter 2), but of *distinctive features* they exhibit in the contemporary era.* Some of these features shed light on why science and technology have been and remain vital factors in twentieth century social change.

The distinctive features of science and technology vary over time. Some that have long been characteristic gradually cease to be, while over time new attributes become increasingly typical. Hopefully, the features examined in this chapter flesh out the intuition that there is something qualitatively and quantitatively distinctive about science and technology in this century, in particular about the kinds of activities and total societal enterprises that science and technology have become in the present era.

IMPORTANT CHARACTERISTICS OF CONTEMPORARY SCIENCE AND TECHNOLOGY

We will discuss six categories of distinctive characteristics of contemporary science and technology. We begin with an important feature of the activities covered by the

*Undertaking to describe these features is not meant to deny that some had roots in the nineteenth century or earlier. Indeed, given the typically evolutionary nature of change in science and technology, it would be surprising if they did not. Nor is this undertaking meant to imply that all twentieth-century scientific and technological activity embodies all the characteristics discussed below.

expressions *contemporary science* and *contemporary technology*. Then we will discuss distinctive characteristics having to do with four dimensions of scientific and technological activities: their products, settings, resources, and practitioners. Finally, we will describe several important distinctive trends in contemporary science and technology viewed as total societal enterprises.

Polymorphism

Although convenient, use of the phrase *contemporary technology* obscures an important fact: Far from being uniform in character, the many technical endeavors subsumable under this expression exhibit significant differences. The same is true of *contemporary science*.

Contemporary technological activity is quite *polymorphous* in character, meaning that it unfolds in many forms.* These include design of a particular technic by an independent inventor; quantitative analysis by an investigator to determine the best or an acceptable way of setting the parameters affecting the operation of a particular technical or sociotechnical system (e.g., a nationwide telecommunications network); and scientific research into the structure and properties of natural or synthetic materials in order to serve a particular technological purpose (e.g., choice of a heat-shielding material for a space shuttle nose cone).

This *polymorphism* is itself an important characteristic of contemporary technology. Just as talk of *postindustrial society* tends to obscure the fact that agriculture and manufacturing have not disappeared from contemporary economic activity simply because information-related and scientific knowledge-generating activities have grown in importance, so too with *contemporary technology*. New kinds of practice continue to be added to the arsenal of contemporary technology—computer-integrated manufacturing, for example. Indeed, some relatively late additions to the arsenal may currently bulk large in the activity as a whole. However, contemporary technology continues to include kinds of practice more characteristic of earlier eras—trial-and-error experimentation, for example. As with economic activity, it is a mistake to characterize contemporary technology as a whole solely in terms of its currently most visible or cutting-edge forms of practice. Unfortunately, the temptation to do so is fueled by the discredited notion that technology is applied science, a confusion which masks the fact that much contemporary technological activity has little if anything to do with scientific research.

The story is much the same for contemporary science. The expression *contemporary science* conjures up images of theory, controlled experiment, and reduction of findings to mathematical form. This suggests in turn that activities having nothing to do with these kinds of endeavor do not or cannot qualify as part of natural science. Upon closer examination, however, it becomes apparent that contemporary science still contains much activity of other sorts. Even in cutting-edge areas, some scientific activity is primarily concerned with the seemingly elementary and pedestrian tasks of observation and description of interesting natural phenomena.

In 1986, for example, during a fly-by of Uranus, the unmanned *Voyager 2* spaceship transmitted data back to earth enabling space scientists to elaborate more precise descriptions of the movement, electromagnetic properties, satellites, and rings of the planet. Similarly, the identification and classification of organisms (taxonomy) is far from being an anachronistic form of inquiry limited to historical biology, chemistry, and

---

Polymorphous is derived from Greek roots meaning "many" and "form."

earth sciences. The vexing issue of how best to classify known "fundamental particles" remains an important part of contemporary nuclear physics.

Several factors foster the overly narrow equation of science with quantitative predictive theory. Historian Walter Pater once wrote that "All art constantly aspires towards the condition of music."[1] By this he meant that music affords its practitioners opportunities for achieving the greatest degree of subjective expression, something painting and the other arts should emulate. Similarly, some scientists believe that all science aspires to the condition of physics, with its unmatched synthesis of mathematically formulated predictive theory and controlled experiment. That dubious claim aside, however, the point is that, like contemporary technology, contemporary science, taken as a whole, is a less monolithic, more multifarious activity than preoccupation with theory, experiment, and mathematically formulated laws with predictive power suggests. Polymorphism is a characteristic of contemporary science that is overlooked or dismissed to our intellectual, and perhaps practical peril.

The Products of Contemporary Science and Technology

The products or outputs of contemporary science and technology exhibit a number of distinctive features sufficiently common to qualify as characteristic of their respective forms of activity. Let us begin with technology.

Technology. (1) *Complexity.* Many twentieth century technics are composed of hundreds, thousands, millions, or billions of parts, many of which are themselves technics or technical systems in their own right. Automobiles today contain about 14,000 parts, while the *Apollo 8* spacecraft had approximately 5.6 million parts.[2] But the classic Steinway concert grand piano produced in the mid-nineteenth century had about 12,000 parts, while the Great Wall of China and some of the great pyramids of Egypt have several millions of parts.[3] Thus, having a large number of parts is by itself insufficient to distinguish contemporary technics from their predecessors. Complexity is a more plausible distinguishing characteristic. Neither the Great Wall, the ancient pyramids, nor even the contemporary Steinway is particularly complex in its structure or operation.

Many contemporary technics, on the other hand, are astonishingly and unprecedentedly complex in structure or operation. Their parts are highly differentiated in nature and function and require extraordinary integration, a key determinant of complexity. The constraints (e.g., reliability, cost, speed) under which they operate often interact, and the operation of such technics is often subject to hierarchically ordered levels of control. For example, the U.S. space shuttle orbiter, one of the most complex machines ever built, has 49 rocket engines; 23 antennas for communications, radar, and data links; 5 computer systems; separate sets of controls for flying in space and in the atmosphere; and electricity-producing fuel cells. All these elements are, of course, hierarchically integrated. Indicative of the vehicle's complexity is the fact that its *Challenger* version had 748 "criticality 1" elements, the failure of any of which would assure loss of ship and crew.[4] Many other contemporary technics and technical systems, from stereo equipment and personal computers to automobiles and nuclear power plants, exhibit similar structural and operational complexity.

(2) *System-Embeddedness.* Whether or not they exhibit internal complexity, many contemporary technics are embedded in complex sociotechnical support sys-

tems on which they depend for their manufacture, use, or maintenance. Dependence on such systems (other than production systems) is scarcely unique to contemporary technics. After all, catapults, roads, and traditional textile machinery depended on various sociotechnical support systems. However, two things are different about contemporary technics in this respect. First, many cannot be used or operated without external support systems over which users exercise little control; electrically powered technics are an example. Hence, the use of the term *embedded* in the heading of this section: It is as if there are invisible umbilical cords linking the technics in question to their respective support systems. Without the "nourishment" provided by the latter, the former could not even be used or operated.

Second, many contemporary sociotechnical support systems are themselves incomparably more complex than those of traditional technics. For example, to acquire a contemporary system-embedded technic such as an automobile or a telephone for personal use is to become enmeshed in a complex web of sociotechnical systems. To undertake to use a car is, in a real sense, to enter into a complex network of road, energy supply, parts distribution, maintenance, registration, insurance, police, toll, and legal systems.

This feature of contemporary technics has been a double-edged development for twentieth century Western life. The support systems in question enable the production and provide for the use and operation of diverse goods and services for large numbers of people unable to generate or use them on their own. Yet this enormous gain is partly offset by the consequences of occasional support-system failures, through, for example, malfunctions, strikes, sabotage, computer viruses, or what Charles Perrow terms "normal accidents."[5] Because of its many system-embedded technics, contemporary society is perched on stilts, able to reach higher and see farther, but vulnerable to being tripped up and thrown off balance by antagonistic forces.

For example, in 1985 and 1986, major segments of the Japanese National Railroad were paralyzed when militants, protesting plans to privatize the system, destroyed signal boxes and cut communications cables, thereby knocking out switching and computerized booking systems.[6] Yet, their vulnerability notwithstanding, the resilience of many such systems should not be overlooked. Technic support systems are often designed with internal backup systems that take over in case of breakdown, while external systems can sometimes be used as alternative ways of performing the tasks carried out by temporarily inoperative systems.

(3) *Production Specialization and Incomprehensibility.*   A third feature of contemporary technics pertains to their specialized character. While the production of technics has long been a specialized activity, dating back at least as far as the Neolithic era, the degree of specialization involved in the production of contemporary technics is unprecedented. Historically speaking, the current situation is the culmination of a long-term trend—away from the perennial arrangement in which a technic's designer, maker, user, and maintainer were often one and the same person, and toward an ever more intensive division of labor under which an individual is an expert on only one category or subcategory of technics—often only on some *phase* in the technic's life cycle (e.g., design or production)—a nonspecialist with respect to all other stages, and a mere user or operator with respect to most other categories of technics.

Consequently, most contemporary technics are *incomprehensible* to the vast majority of their users, most of whom have little idea of how they are made, work, or can be repaired. The internal systemic complexity of twentieth century technics is one reason for this phenomenon; the scientific principles and knowledge—particularly regarding electromagnetism—on which many of them are based is another. This quality of being opaque to most users applies both to personal technics, like compact disc players and digital watches, and to macrotechnics, such as airplanes and power plants. The specialized character of contemporary technics has made everyday life more and more of a "black box" for the average citizen of "advanced" industrialized societies.

(4) *Formalized Technical Procedures.* As stated in Chapter 2, there are two categories of products of technological activity: technics and technic-related intellectual constructs. Thus far, in describing what is most characteristic of contemporary technology, we have focused on technics. However, an increasing portion of the output of contemporary technological activity consists not of technics per se, but of a distinctive kind of technic-related intellectual product: *formalized technical procedures.*

Formalized technical procedures, most often embodied in computer programs, are devised for a variety of purposes, including ones related to the design, production, operation, and maintainance of many contemporary technics and technical systems. For example, industrial engineers create computer-based procedures for inventory and quality control, safety engineers concoct computer programs for automatic train system operation, and electrical and "software engineers" devise software for diagnosing and repairing telephone network transmission problems.

The complexity, cost, potential hazards, computer dependence, and interlocking nature of many modern technics and technical systems have inspired rapid growth in this branch of contemporary technological activity. Regarding cost, the diagnostic software for the telephone network transmission problems just mentioned enables many repairs to be done directly from the local telephone company office, sometimes automatically, thereby yielding enormous savings in time and money in contrast to "house calls." One indication of the recent rapid growth in this kind of technological activity is that about half of the scientists and engineers employed by AT&T Bell Laboratories, a leading telecommunications research and development laboratory, are involved with software research and development, a level far exceeding the one that prevailed as recently as the 1970s.[7]

(5) *Sociotechnical Systems Analysis.* Corresponding to the two major categories of outputs of technological activity—technics and technic-related intellectual constructs—we may say that technology as a form of human activity has two branches: one devoted to the production of technics and technical systems, and the other to devising formalized technical procedures and other intellectual products pertaining to their design, manufacture, use, operation, and maintenance. In the twentieth century, one important subbranch of technological activity devoted to devising technic-related intellectual products has come to be called *systems analysis* (or systems engineering).

In general, *systems analysis* is the quantitative examination of a particular system of interest (e.g., a production system or an international trade system) to determine how it behaves or would behave under certain conditions or assumptions. This analysis is usually carried out with a view to deciding how to structure or restructure the system—perhaps by devising a formalized procedure to be followed in seeking to control its behavior—in order to achieve a desired result in optimal fashion.

Thus characterized, systems analysis is clearly too broad to be completely subsumed under the umbrella of technological activity. For example, the United

States could engage a consulting firm to do a detailed quantitative analysis of the international trading system, with special attention to protective tariffs, import quotas, and the U.S. balance-of-trade deficit, before deciding how to try to restructure that system to serve its national economic interest. Such specimens of systems analysis, however quantitative and well executed, are not plausibly regarded as part of technological activity.

Suppose, however, that attention is narrowed to *sociotechnical systems*—that is, systems with substantial, interacting social and technological components. Factories, city centers, electrical power networks, hospitals, and coal mines can be so regarded, with a view to deciding how to optimize production of goods, traffic flows, power distribution under peak-demand or "brownout" conditions, delivery of healthcare services, and coal extraction. Analysis of such systems is clearly a distinct and vitally important part of contemporary technological activity.

It is distinct because making technics is one thing, deciding how to configure them in technical and sociotechnical systems quite another, and deciding how to structure the operation of such systems yet another. It is important because, given the substantial costs, risks, and expectations associated with such systems, prescribing their modes of operation and margins of safety becomes a matter of considerable consequence.

Let us say, then, that *sociotechnical systems analysis* is a subbranch of contemporary technological activity, one which complements and often works hand-in-hand with that devoted to making technics. Its products—sociotechnical systems *analyses*—are one kind of technic-related intellectual product. Taken together, sociotechnical systems analysis, the analyses produced by its professional practitioners ("systems engineers"), and the systems that embody the conclusions of such analyses constitute an increasingly important characteristic of contemporary technological activity.

Science.   (1) *Abstract and Abstruse Nature.*   The products—or outputs— of contemporary science are distinctive in at least three respects. Much twentieth century scientific knowledge is extraordinarily abstract and abstruse. It often concerns phenomena remote from everyday experience (microorganisms, fossils, nuclei) and sometimes involves concepts that are profoundly counterintuitive (the "relativity" of space and time) or unintelligible ("black holes" in the universe) to all but the initiated. Deriving and understanding such knowledge often hinges on mathematical ideas and methods and scientific theories of extraordinary sophistication or on ingeniously devised experiments of great subtlety. The complexity of such scientific knowledge, as well as of the processes by which it is generated, is such that to the nonspecialist, the opaqueness of modern technics may seem transparent by comparison.

(2) *Theory-Dependence.*   Some scholars contend that *all* scientific knowledge, even that gleaned directly from observation, is implicitly if not explicitly theory-*related*. Thomas Kuhn, for example, contends that there is no such thing as a theory-neutral language of scientific observation.[8] That is, even seemingly neutral descriptions of mundane natural phenomena embody theoretical presuppositions, for such descriptions are couched in terms that presuppose that certain kinds of phenomena are existing *entities* while others are merely descriptive *properties* of such entities. Such theses are highly controversial. What is indisputable, however, is that much twentieth century scientific knowledge is profoundly theory-*dependent*. Much con-

temporary scientific knowledge is attained only at the summit of multi-tiered theoretical constructs.

For example, more precise knowledge of the law of gravity was obtained in the twentieth century only by refining Newtonian mechanics with Einstein's general relativity theory. The key theoretical idea underlying this approach is that the mass of a particle is equivalent to a certain amount of energy, a counterintuitive relationship summarized in Einstein's famous equation, $E=mc^2$. This notion is itself a remarkable product of modern theoretical physics—in particular, of special relativity theory.

In this respect too, the situation in contemporary science parallels that in technology: A kind of multilevel "platform effect" is at work in both. As many contemporary technics exist or work only with the aid of their respective sociotechnical support systems, much modern scientific knowledge is attained and exists only on high theoretical platforms. Moreover, both are difficult, if not impossible, to fathom for the uninitiated individual, to whom they are so many "black boxes."

(3) *Growth of Scientific Knowledge.*   If the number and rate of change of technics in the twentieth century is unprecedented, so too is the amount and rate of production of scientific knowledge. One way of gauging the growth of the latter is by counting the number of scientific journals that existed at various times. Derek Price showed that beginning with the appearance of the *Philosophical Transactions of the Royal Society of London* in 1665, the number of scientific journals has grown roughly exponentially for more than three centuries. Doubling roughly every 15 years, the number of such publications has grown 100-fold every century.[9]

As for individual papers, for every article published in 1665, there were on the order of 100 in 1765; 10,000 in 1865; and 1,000,000 in 1965. Were this rate to continue, there would be about 100,000,000 papers published in 2065. Such a rate of growth—one that, if only because of the costs of journal publication and subscriptions, cannot be sustained indefinitely—has weighty consequences for scientific education, specialization, and epistemological obsolescence. Is this situation merely a matter of more chickens laying larger numbers of smaller eggs? This is an important question, but given the myriad subfields of contemporary science, few experts, if any, are qualified to answer it.

Settings

A third set of characteristic features of contemporary science and technology involves their dominant settings. According to long-standing caricatures, pre-twentieth century scientific and technological activities took place in home attics, basements, and garages, as well as in small shops. However, the housing of scientific research in certain European universities dates from the Middle Ages, while in both Europe and the United States, modest university science laboratories grew considerably in number in the nineteenth century. Similarly, the mid-nineteenth century in western Europe and the late nineteenth century in the United States saw the appearance of the first industrial research laboratories. In the United States, the federal government established a facility for scientific research as early as the mid-nineteenth century (the Smithsonian Institution). These correctives notwithstanding, an important characteristic feature of science and technology in the twentieth century is the *tremendous expansion and consolidation of the housing of scientific and technological activities in an extensive network of firmly established, substantial-sized formal organizations.*

Indicative of the remarkable size and complexity of this organizational network is the fact that in the late 1980s, there were approximately 6,700 university-related and other not-for-profit centers devoted to research in the physical and life sciences and engineering in the United States and Canada. In addition, roughly 10,200 organizations in the United States were active in doing research and development for industry, the great majority owned and operated by private corporations. Finally, about 700 major U.S. federal government laboratories of all sizes were performing research and development work in science and engineering.[10]

In fact, the network of organizations housing scientific and technological activities is even more extensive than we have indicated. Production faciltities aside, many sectors of contemporary scientific or technological activity require other kinds of organizations, such as ones devoted to data collection and analysis, training, planning, operations, and maintenance. For example, the National Aeronautics and Space Administration (NASA) runs an astronaut training center in Houston, while NASA units in Washington, D.C., carry out its planning and policy-making functions. In 1989, United Airlines employed about 600 engineers and technicians and 10,000 machinists at its national Maintenance Operations Center at San Francisco International Airport.[11]

The latter example suggests an important difference in the settings of contemporary scientific and technological activity. It is widely believed that both kinds of activities take place primarily in research and development laboratories. While the laboratory *is* the characteristic locus of contemporary science, contemporary engineering—more generally, contemporary technological activity—takes place primarily in design offices, on shop floors, and in production, operations, and maintenance facilities. Some engineers conduct research, some of which is done in laboratories. However, as a whole, engineering is *not* a research-dominated activity and hence does not share research's or science's characterisic laboratory setting.*

Because most twentieth century scientific and engineering activity occurs in substantial-sized organizational settings, in-house scientists and engineers have access to extensive technical and nontechnical resources without which many of their endeavors would be impossible. The resources in question are those of money, equipment, plant, management expertise, and auxiliary personnel. Consider the cases of NASA, CERN (the Center for European Nuclear Research in Geneva, Switzerland), and AT&T Bell Laboratories. All three organizations have huge budgets, employ large numbers of scientists and engineers, and maintain standing armies of highly skilled technical support personnel.

In 1988, Bell Laboratories employed about 7,100 and NASA about 12,000 scientists and engineers at their respective facilities.[12] As for in-house "standing armies," in 1988 Bell Labs employed about 8,200 "technicians and auxiliaries," while, in 1985, NASA had about 11,000 engineers, technicians, and mechanics at the Kennedy Space Center in Cape Canaveral, Florida, to assemble, prepare for launch, launch, and maintain the space shuttles then in use.[13] These armies sometimes play crucial roles in scientific projects. The 1984 physics Nobel Prize–winning experiments previously referred to were carried out at CERN. In addition to the scientists who

---

*One source of confusion here is a tendency to conceive of engineering solely or primarily in terms of technological *innovation*, a kind of engineering activity properly viewed as mostly laboratory-based research and development. However, this image obscures the overall contours and diverse nonlaboratory settings of engineering and other kinds of technological activity. (The above observations about contrasting settings are due to Walter Vincenti.)

designed and conducted the experiments, over 200 CERN technicians, mechanics, and computer experts—drawn from its in-house support staff of over 3,000 engineers and technicians—were involved in one phase or another of the work.[14] Given the machine- and instrument-intensive nature of contemporary scientific and engineering practice, the spiraling cost of such equipment, and the indispensability of stable bodies of experienced technical support personnel, the continued housing of most contemporary science and technology in well-endowed formal organizations is assured for the foreseeable future.

Nevertheless, the seemingly anachronistic image of "the engineer in the garage" is not completely outmoded. William Hewlett and David Packard began what was to become the Hewlett-Packard electronics firm in a garage in Palo Alto in 1938.[15] More recently, Steven Jobs and Steven Wozniak built the first Apple I personal computer in a garage in Cupertino, California, in 1976.[16] In the 1980s, some undergraduate engineering students ran successful software firms out of their dormitory rooms.

A garage or room may still be the scene of start-up work on a new technological product or business. However, in most areas of contemporary technology, if such a firm is to survive or prosper, the locus of its activity must soon shift to a decent-sized, adequately endowed facility, one able to house and support at least some research and development work and various types of support personnel. Contrast the way their founders began their work with the scale of current research and development activity in the Hewlett-Packard and Apple Computer companies.

The software industry is one of relatively few areas in contemporary technology whose requisites—the knowledge-intensive nature of the labor involved, the affordability of the modest amount of needed hardware, and the relative ease with which opportunities can be spotted and products can be adapted—enable some small-scale, highly specialized, technologically sophisticated firms to coexist with large-scale, centralized, mass-production-oriented enterprises.

The network of organizations in which most twentieth century scientific and technological activity has come to be housed is but one aspect of a broader important and distinctive trend: the institutionalization of twentieth century science and technology. In general, *institutionalization* means a process by which an initially fledgling social phenomenon gradually assumes well-established forms of organization and practice, eventually becoming recognized as an abiding constituent element of the culture in question. While the institutionalization of science and technology in Western societies received an important boost with the emergence of learned societies for promoting scientific research in the late sixteenth (in Italy) and mid-seventeenth centuries (in England and France), it has only reached an advanced stage in the present century. Similar patterns and practices for training scientists and especially engineers in colleges and universities have been widely adopted; a mutually beneficial relation- ship among the federal government, academia, and the private sector has been established and consolidated for the promotion of desired scientific and technological work; the research and development laboratory has become a familiar organizational fixture; and numerous organizational forms and practices have been developed to foster communication between technical practitioners. The latter include associations of technical professionals, periodicals for reporting or abstracting research results, and regularly scheduled scientific meetings organized mostly along disciplinary lines. In short, in the twentieth century, science and technology have attained the status of bona fide sociocultural institutions.

Resources

Many of the achievements of contemporary science and technology would not have come about at all or nearly as early as they did without the *resources* at the disposal of their practitioners. Let us discuss some of the distinguishing characteristics of two quite different general kinds of resources: *input* and *transformative*.

Input Resources.   *Input resources* are supplies of various sorts introduced into scientific or technological contexts to enable or facilitate certain endeavors. Important kinds of input resources for contemporary science or technology include materials, natural phenomena, and money.

(1) *Materials.*   For most of human history, material inputs to technological activity consisted largely of raw materials that had undergone only relatively simple preparatory processes; examples include bones and stones (for tools), straw (for baskets), clay (for pottery), and animal skins (for clothing). About 8,000 years ago, however, some human-made materials were developed in the form of alloys of tin and copper, materials of sufficient human importance to give their name to an epoch: the Bronze Age. Prior to the onset of the Christian era in the West, the Chinese were already making weapons out of sophisicated alloys consisting of as many as 15 elements. Thus, long before the modern era, preparatory processes for technological input materials were sometimes fairly complicated.

In early human times, technological input materials were apt to be obtained locally or from neighboring peoples. However, already in classical antiquity in the West, raw materials were being imported by producers from sources hundreds of miles away, either through trade or force.

Several things are distinctive about material technological inputs in the contemporary era. First, the available stock of such inputs is unprecedentedly large and diverse. Second, of these, many are "designer materials"; that is, they were developed to have specific practical properties using scientific knowledge derived from fields like materials science and organic chemistry. Such is the case with numerous kinds of steel, aluminum, synthetic plastics and dyes, ceramics, rubber, composite materials, and synthetic semiconductor crystals. Third, the processes by which such material inputs are produced are themselves often based on scientific knowledge and the use of sophisticated instruments, techniques, and equipment. Finally, many technological input materials are obtained in what is increasingly a global marketplace, as with U.S. imports of chromium, manganese, and plutonium-group metals from South Africa and the Soviet Union. This *globalization of contemporary technological inputs* parallels the better-known globalization of contemporary technological outputs (technics).

The U.S. space shuttle illustrates some of these trends. It simply would not have been feasible to build this vehicle without specially designed human-made materials. For example, as it re-enters the atmosphere, the shuttle orbiter encounters temperatures of up to 2,500° F. To withstand this inferno, its nose and the leading edges of its wings are protected by a specially designed metal known as "carbon carbon." Seventy percent of the spaceship's aluminum skin surface is covered with heat-resistant tiles composed of silica fiber made rigid by ceramic bonding.[17]

The globalization of contemporary technological inputs is as economically problematic as it is technically impressive. Access to globally obtained resources can become fragile due to political change or instability in an important source country, political differences between source and importing countries, or cartel-like behavior of the countries controlling a desired input. This vulnerability lends impetus to efforts on the part of countries critically dependent on globally obtained inputs to internalize that dependence by developing more stable domestic sources or substitute input materials. For example, during World War II, the United States, deprived of access to countries in Southeast Asia from which it had previously imported natural rubber, developed synthetic substitutes. In the postcolonial era, concern over access to needed technological inputs could spur internalization to the point of disrupting important patterns of interdependence (e.g., exchange of technics and technical know-how for needed inputs of energy and materials). The implications of such disruption for countries providing such input materials, often less developed countries, are potentially devastating.

(2) *Natural Phenomena.* Science in the contemporary era is also characterized by great increases in inputs of various sorts. Thanks in significant part to the incessant development of myriad new or improved technics—including microscopes, computers, and various kinds of imaging machines—the domain of natural phenomena accessible to scientific exploration is constantly expanding. For example, the new Hubble space telescope placed in orbit by the U.S. space shuttle in 1990 will open a much deeper phenomenal window on the heavens for astronomical research.*

(3) *Money.* One indispensible input of most contemporary science and technology is money—in increasingly large amounts. Scientific and technological activities are orders of magnitude more costly to practice than ever before. Given the large number of practitioners of modern science and the amount and rate of production of scientific knowledge, the latter might at least seem easy to produce. However, measured in terms of time, money, and effort invested, breakthroughs in twentieth century science are, on the whole, increasingly difficult and costly to realize. Expensive technology, numerous highly salaried workers, and heavy institutional overhead costs are prime contributors to the steep price of much contemporary scientific research. The situation is no less true in the case of contemporary technology. We will discuss the current situation and some problematic aspects of the funding of contemporary research and development in Chapter 14. For now, suffice it to say that where money for contemporary U.S. science and technology is concerned, most basic science is conducted with federal funding in the major research universities and in government laboratories, whereas most technological development work is done in the private sector with both private and public funding, the mix depending on the technology in question (e.g., national defense versus commercially marketable technologies).

Transformative Resources. *Transformative resources* are ones used in converting inputs of scientific and technological activities into their respective outputs or products. Transformative resources can be divided into two kinds: *first-order*—those *with which* inputs are transformed—and *second-order*—those *in accordance with which* first-order resources are brought to bear on inputs.

---

*Interestingly, machines and instruments originally developed to access new scientific phenomena sometimes give rise to new technological materials. For example, particle accelerators, first developed by physicists for use in experiments aimed at understanding subatomic phenomena, are now used in industry to direct ion beams at objects in order to create micro-alloys with properties (e.g., increased surface hardness) useful for technological purposes.

(1) *First-Order Resources.*   Perennial kinds of first-order transformative resources include technics and technical systems, mathematical techniques, labor power, materials alteration processes, and energy forms—resources which have grown enormously in number and power in the twentieth century. For example, manually operated tools and physical labor power have been largely replaced by electrical machinery and machine tools, while many new change-inducing substances in the physical and biological sciences have been identified or harnassed, such as microorganisms and particle beams. It is, however, on important, less obvious changes in second-order resources that we will focus here.

(2) *Second-Order Resources.*   The second-order resources of science and technology, which have also expanded greatly in the twentieth century, can be divided into two kinds: *methods* and *knowledge.* We will further limit ourselves here to discussion of contemporary technological knowledge.[18]

In general, technological knowledge has several *bases*, or sources. Some such knowledge is based on *direct observation* of and *first-hand experience* working with the ways in which materials and power sources behave under various circumstances. Such was the case with the knowledge of wood properties developed and used by North American Indians in making birch-bark canoes. Such remains the case with some of the knowledge possessed by modern machinists and metal workers.

Other technological knowledge is based on systematic activity—for example, carefully designed (though not scientific) *experiments* and the systematic use of specific *experimental methods.* For example, a scale model of a technic may be devised and tested to see whether a particular design or material is acceptable for a certain technological purpose or specified performance constraint. Examples of such knowledge are not limited to the modern world. The knowledge used in designing some ancient catapults was also based on experiments using systematic empirical methods.

A third source of technological knowledge is bona fide scientific understanding. Such is the origin of some knowledge that goes into the design, development, and manufacture of integrated circuits and lightwave communications cables.

Finally, technological knowledge that may ultimately be certified by experimental methods of science or engineering may have its source in something more elusive: the intuitive insight and imagination of the engineer as to what would be a viable or appropriate way of proceeding with a given technological task, such as design or production. Many technics, from mechanical clocks and cathedrals to rockets and snowmobiles, owe their basic operating principles, mechanisms, or forms to what Eugene Ferguson calls "nonverbal thought" (e.g., thinking in terms of visual images). For example, the designer of a diesel engine must continually use her or his

> intuitive sense of rightness and fitness. What will be the shape of the combustion chamber? Can I use square corners to gain volume, or must I use a fillet to gain strength? Where shall I place the valves? Should it have a long or a short piston? Such questions have a range of answers that are supplied by experience, by physical requirements, by limitations of available space, and not least by a sense of form....Some decisions, such as wall thickness, pin diameter, and passage area may depend upon scientific calculations, but the nonscientific component of design remains primary. It rests largely on the nonverbal thought and nonverbal reasoning of the designer, who thinks with pictures.[19]

Indeed, inventors have sometimes credited visions or dreams as the source of decisive features of their creations, as did the inventor of the electrically controlled antiaircraft gun in World War II.[20]

The importance of intuition and imagination in technological activity is apt to be overlooked or undervalued. Although such intuition depends upon the technologist's past observations and experience, it is not reducible to these characteristics. It is implicit, uncodifiable, and neither scientific nor derivable from scientific understanding, however deep. Its indispensibility in much technological activity is yet another decisive blow to the simplistic reductive notion that technology is merely applied science.

With this four-part taxonomy—observation, experiment, science, intuition—of the bases of technological knowledge in mind, we may now ask, what is it that is most noteworthy and distinctive about contemporary technological knowledge? First, knowledge in contemporary technology rests less and less on the direct observation of nature and more and more on the results of formal scientific and engineering research.

Second, this first characteristic notwithstanding, even in cutting-edge technological activity, empirical methods are still often employed to compensate for a recognized but unacceptable lack of scientific knowledge and understanding. Further, intuitively based knowledge continues to play an important role in contemporary technological practice. Thermoscience may enable the practitioner to understand *how* the internal combustion machine works, but science cannot tell the designer *whether* using a two- or four-stroke engine would be better in an automobile.*

Third, unlike the situation in earlier times, contemporary technological knowledge is not always generated with a particular immediate practical need in mind. The motivation for pursuing it is often more generalized, resting on the belief that in the long run, a particular field of inquiry may prove technologically fruitful.

*To grasp why technological knowledge has not been and will not be completely reduced to scientific knowledge, consider the fact that technological knowledge can be thought of as divided into four kinds: *materials knowledge* (i.e., knowledge of the properties of materials and energy forms used in technological activity), *design knowledge* (e.g., knowledge of the components, mechanisms, structures, and techniques available for use in designing a technic or technical system with the desired characteristics), *production knowledge* (i.e., knowledge of the various methods or techniques able to be used in producing the finished product [e.g., knowledge of how thin a part can be produced, given current production methods, and still retain its desired properties]), and *systems knowledge* (i.e., knowledge of the behavioral properties or tendencies of various kinds of technical and sociotechnical systems [e.g., telecommunications and air transportation systems]).

The design and construction of the 5,989-foot-long, wire-rope suspension Brooklyn Bridge by J. A. Roebling and Son between 1867 and 1884 exemplifies the first three of these four kinds of technological knowledge. Building it required knowledge of the properties of steel cable, wrought iron, masonry, and timber; of what would be a suitable structural configuration and the appropriate number, locations, and dimensions of various components if the desired load were to be supported; and of how to make reliable wire-rope cable efficiently and cost-effectively as well as mastery of the caisson technique used in building the bridge's concrete foundations.

Of the foregoing four kinds of technological knowledge, only the first, materials knowledge, is reducible in principle to scientifically based knowledge. The distinctive polymorphic character of contemporary technological activity in general reflects in part the variety of kinds of technological knowledge pursued and their irreducibility to scientific knowledge.

On the four-stroke engine, see Lynwood Bryant, "The Origin of the Four-Stroke Engine," *Technology and Culture*, 8, no. 2, April 1967, 178–198.

The transistor was invented some years after Bell Laboratories undertook basic research programs in solid state physics, on the hunch that the latter might turn out to be a useful area of knowledge in the future, but in the absence of specific plans for or evidence of practical applicability.

Put differently, contemporary technological knowledge is banked for possible future application. Contributions to this reservoir come from around the world and are in turn widely disseminated through a variety of formal and informal channels and mechanisms. A depositor's contribution to this knowledge bank may eventually yield its most important dividends in an application far removed from initial projected technological uses—if there were any. While the latter phemonenon was probably not absent in earlier times, the formal establishment and ongoing support of a global technological knowledge bank is unique to the contemporary era.

Practitioners

The practitioner can also be regarded as a kind of transformative resource for science and technology. However, as practitioners devise and make use of all other categories of transformative resources, they may reasonably be discussed separately. There are several noteworthy respects in which the practitioner dimension of contemporary scientific and technological activity is distinctive.

Numbers and Density. The number of practitioners of technology and science today is enormous relative to previous centuries. Given modern population levels, that is to be expected. However, the number of engineers and scientists relative to population size is also unprecedentedly large. In 1986 there were an estimated 5.47 million scientists and engineers employed in the United States—2.85 million engineers and 2.62 million scientists. Of the latter, about one third (884,000) were in the physical or life sciences, and two thirds (1.74 million) were in the social sciences, psychology, computer science, or mathematics.[21] Table 3-1 indicates how much and how rapidly the "density" of engineers and scientists in the American population at large has increased in this century.

Table 3-1   Density of Scientists and Engineers in U.S. Population

(1) YEAR	(2) U.S. POPULATION (IN MILLIONS)	(3) TOTAL U.S. SCIENTISTS AND ENGINEERS	(4) RATIO OF (3) TO (2)
1900	76.1	70,000	1 to 1,087
1950	151.3	559,000	1 to 271
1960	180.1	1,104,000	1 to 166
1970	203.3	1,595,000	1 to 121
1980	226.5	3,083,000	1 to 73
1984	236.2	3,995,500	1 to 59
1986	239.4	4,626,500	1 to 52
1988	244.6	5,474,600 (est.)	1 to 45

Source: *Science and Technology Data Book: 1989* (Washington, D.C.: National Science Foundation, 1988), p. 20; *The World Almanac and Book of Facts: 1989* (New York: Pharas Books, 1988), p. 532.

At the time of this writing, the ratio depicted in Table 3-1 shows no sign of stabilizing, a phenomenon which raises a number of intriguing, potentially important questions for research: How much smaller is the denominator—at 45 in 1988—likely to become? Is there any approximate, theoretically imposed limit below which the denominator cannot substantially fall? Does the answer to this last question vary from one industrial society to another? If so, what factors account for these differences?

Collaboration and Teams.   Contemporary scientific and technological activity is increasingly pursued on a collaborative or team basis. The solitary practitioner carrying out an independent investigation has been increasingly superseded by the team of scientists working on an experiment, team of engineers working on a project, or mixed team of scientists, engineers, and technicians working on either a scientific experiment or a research and development project.

One indicator of the increasing prominence of teamwork in science is the historical rise of joint authorship of scientific papers. In a study of a sample of professional journals in the natural and biological sciences, Harriet Zuckerman showed that between 1900 and 1959 the percentage of articles with two or more authors grew from 25 percent in the period from 1900 to 1909; to 31 percent, 49 percent, 56 percent, and 66 percent in the next four decades; and to 83 percent in the period from 1950 to 1959.[22]

This trend continues unabated. Although not typical, the following example is suggestive. Results of the experiments for which Carlo Rubbia and Simon van der Meer were awarded the 1984 Nobel Prize in physics were reported in two articles in the journal *Physics Letters* published in 1983. The investigations were carried out by two experiment teams, "The Collaborations," as they called themselves, and the articles were published under the names of 59 and 138 joint authors, respectively.[23]

The team nature of contemporary scientific and engineering research and development has affected the character of advanced technical education. For example, it is not unusual for a Ph.D. student in the physical or life sciences to be accepted on a team of investigators that has been working on an experiment for a long time. The "rookie" is unlikely to be awarded the Ph.D. until "veterans" ahead of her or him on the "queue" have done sufficient work on the experiment—often on only one aspect of the work—to be allowed to write up the results and present them as their theses. Thus the traditional educational ideal of an original thesis done by a single individual is in tension with the protracted, team character of much contemporary scientific and technological activity. Conversely, insofar as higher technical education reinforces traditional patterns of invidious competition among students, skills conducive to effective participation in team-oriented contemporary technical work may go undeveloped.

Management Skills.   One consequence of this development is that in the twentieth century, being an effective scientist or engineer is more likely to require management skills than ever before; scientists and engineers will need to have fund-raising, interpersonal, and organizational skills. Indeed, in 1988, of the estimated 5.47 million scientists and engineers employed in the United States, slightly more were engaged in management activity (1.5 million, or 27.4 percent) than in actual research and development work (1.49 million, or 27.2 percent).[24] The scientist or engineer heading a project may be responsible for supervising hundreds or even thousands of "line" technical practitioners.

Large-scale technological projects require the efforts of a relatively new breed of scientist or engineer: the *technical project administrator*. Although not doing "hands-on" work on one or another technical aspect of the project, such individuals are responsible for important project-related decision making, such as setting personnel levels, allocating tasks to competing units, selecting a way of satisfying all design constraints, certifying testing, and meeting schedules.

As the inquiry into the 1986 space shuttle *Challenger* disaster made clear, management decision making on such matters can be critical. Selection at the outset of a cheaper, and hence more fundable, shuttle design; discharge over the years of 70 percent of the 1,689 reliability and quality assurance personnel working for NASA in 1970; decisions to launch the shuttle in the face of repeated evidence of problems with critical shuttle systems; a gradual shift in organizational attitude from requiring "proof of no danger" to accepting "no proof of danger" regarding the safety of launch conditions, including weather—all such phenomena demonstrate that the quality of technical administrative decision making in contemporary technological activity can be as crucial to project success as the quality of the technical work of line engineers, scientists, and technicians.

Individual Practitioner Reaffirmed.   Although the importance of the team and of management skills in twentieth century technological and scientific practice has grown greatly, the role of the individual has by no means been eclipsed. Individual practitioners are sometimes the key sources of ideas for inventions, innovations, or experiments, and may make crucial differences in fund raising, in the design of prototypes or experimental apparatus, in marketing, or in theoretical breakthroughs. *It is the synthesis of the individual, social, and institutional components of contemporary scientific and technological activity that is responsible for much of its distinctive and potent character.*

Training and Specialization.   The situation of the contemporary technical practitioner is also historically unprecedented, as regards both the duration of formal preparatory study and the degree of specialization within the general fields of engineering and science.

(1) *Training.*   In 1986, 24.2 percent (529,100) of the 2.186 million scientists employed in the United States held master's degrees.[25] In engineering, a field in which formal educational training became the norm much later than in the case of science, the proportion was about the same: 23 percent (561,300 of 2.44 million practitioners). However, in the same year, the number of scientists in the United States who held Ph.D.s far exceeded the number of engineers with doctorates: 511,200 to 105,500. This disparity, although revealing, should be seen in the context of a noteworthy recent development.

The number of engineers employed in the United States expanded by 10.2 percent between 1984 and 1986. However, the number with doctorates rose by 61 percent, from 65,400 to 105,500. This reflects, among other things, the growing role of scientific knowledge in contemporary engineering activity. Thus, in a two-year span, the portion of engineers in the United States with doctorates increased from 2.95 to 4.32 percent. A similar trend existed among U.S. scientists between 1984 and 1986: their overall ranks grew by 22.7 percent while the number with doctorates rose by 63.5 percent, from 312,600 (17.6 percent) to 511,200 (23.4 percent). Thus, in the U.S. in the mid-1980s, the density of Ph.D. degree recipients increased significantly in *both* engineering and science.

A second development influencing the average length of training for contemporary U.S. engineers and scientists lies in the fact that, for a combination of internal intellectual and external financial and employment reasons, the Ph.D. degrees held by increasing portions of technical practitioners are, on average, taking longer to complete. The median *total registered time*—the total amount of time during which students are registered in school—between receipt of the bachelor's degree and conferral of the doctor's degree increased from 5.7 years in the physical sciences in 1977-78 to 6.6 years in 1986-87. The corresponding figures for engineering also reveal an increase, from 5.6 to 5.9 years.[26] Comparable increases have also occurred in the median *total time*—including time not registered as a student—between the baccalaureate and the doctorate. The upshot is that in recent years greater portions of U.S. scientists and engineers possess doctorates that on average are taking longer than ever to complete.

(2) *Specialization.*   Indicative of the extraordinary degree of specialization in contemporary science, the "Physics and Astronomy Classification Scheme" published in 1985 by the American Institute of Physics divides the "joint disciplines of physics and astronomy" into no fewer than 1,000 subfields.[27] The situation is much the same in the major disciplines of engineering. For example, in 1989, members of the American Society of Mechanical Engineering were organized into no fewer than 36 general divisions, each of which subsumes numerous subareas of specialized research.[28]

Salient Characteristic Trends in Contemporary Science and Technology

Our sixth and final category of distinguishing characteristics of contemporary science and technology consists of four salient trends exhibited by these enterprises during this century: increasing scale, internationalization, rationalization, and symbiotic interdependence.

Increasing Scale.   Much that is important and distinctive about contemporary science and technology is summed up in the phrases *Big Science* and *Big Technology*.* Besides connoting the large amount of technical apparatus increasingly used in both activities as well as, in many instances, its large size, *Big* also suggests the unprecedented magnitudes of various other aspects of these activities: the quantities and rates of production of their outputs, the numbers of their practitioners, the sizes of their budgets, the average sizes of the organizations in which they are housed, the amounts of material and organizational resources required to sustain their practice, and the power of the special interests that control them and shape their practices to serve their respective, sometimes parochial, interests. As we will see in Part II of this book, contemporary science and technology are "big" in yet another important respect: the magnitude of the

---

*Donald Kennedy has proposed an interesting criterion for "Big Science": when "[t]he capital cost of the equipment and special facilities...become[s] larger than the capital value of the endowment necessary to yield the faculty member's salary" ("Government Policies and the Cost of Doing Research," *Science*, 227, February 1, 1985, 481).

influence they exert on society and the rates with which they have transformed and are transforming contemporary life.

International Character.   Viewed as total societal enterprises, contemporary science and technology continue to take on an increasingly international character, a trend fueled by the twentieth century revolutions in telecommunications and transportation. On the informational level, practitioners publish in internationally distributed journals and are linked by international telecommunications networks, including computer nets and facsimile machines. Flows of technical personnel have also been internationalized: International conferences and scholarly exchanges are routine and numerous, while thousands of students and practitioners of science and engineering study and work abroad. For example, in 1986, the ranks of scientists and engineers working in the United States included almost 150,000 citizens of other countries.[29]

Individual research facilities are becoming increasingly international in character. For example, the Stanford Linear Accelerator Center (SLAC) in Stanford, California, is a major center of experimental particle-physics research. Between August 1985 and August 1986, 43 foreign nationals were employed by SLAC as full-time research associates; 165 others, paid by their home institutions and countries, were formally appointed as "visiting scientists" and engaged in collaborative research with SLAC scientists; still 80 others were granted "user" status and employed SLAC facilities to conduct their own research; and hundreds of others paid short visits to SLAC to exchange scientific ideas and information. Under bilateral exchange agreements between the United States and countries such as the Soviet Union, West Germany, and the People's Republic of China, foreign scientists are afforded opportunities for short- or long-term study visits and internships at SLAC.[30]

The enormous costs (and complexity) of many Big Science projects have provided impetus for expanding the internationalization trend into the areas of funding and facility construction. For example, the European Southern Observatory (ESO) decided in 1987 to build a "very large telescope" in northern Chile. Not only is the project's $198 million cost to be borne collectively by ESO's eight European member nations, but the construction of the telescope will also be an international venture, with different member nations assigned responsibility for different telescope parts or construction processes in order to use their respective technological strengths.[31]

The increasingly international character of contemporary science and engineering is an important phenomenon essentially unique to the twentieth century.

Rationalization.   We have noted the increasing importance of the results of scientific research in the knowledge base of twentieth century technology, the growing importance of formalized technic-related procedures, the increasing use of systematic methods such as systems analysis, and the growing, highly specialized practice of modern technology in hierarchical groups housed in large bureaucratic organizations. What unites such seemingly disparate phenomena is that they exemplify the potent general trend that Max Weber referred to as *the rationalization of modern life*.[32] Let us explain Weber's contention as applied to the sphere of technological activity.

Paralleling developments in other spheres of modern life, approaches to the production of technics and related systems that had long been based on "tradition, sentiment, and rule of thumb" have greatly diminished in importance in this century. On the other hand, ones based on "explicit, abstract, and intellectually calculable knowledge, rules, and procedures" have become considerably more important.[33] One notable outcome of this rationalization process has been the transformation of numerous fields of engineering (e.g., audio engineering) from predominantly craft-based enterprises to mature professional fields grounded increasingly in scientific, mathematical, and advanced engineering methods and knowledge.

However, to avoid an idealized portrait of contemporary technological activity, a complementary pattern must also be emphasized. The continuing importance of intuitively based technological knowledge, the nonscientific (albeit more or less systematic) nature of technological methods such as risk analysis and parameter variation, the thriving of a significant amount of contemporary technological activity in small-scale, relatively nonbureaucratic organizational settings, and politicoeconomic distortions of technological practice must also be recognized as important aspects of the anatomy of contemporary technological activity. They must not be dismissed as anachronistic residues or transient lapses of good judgment. This point is closely related to the one made earlier in this chapter: that contemporary technological activity is quite polymorphic and not reducible simply to those of its facets that have undergone Weberian rationalization in this century. A similar story holds for contemporary science.

Symbiotic Interdependence.   Finally, contemporary science and technology continue to exhibit an unmistakable trend towards increasing symbiotic interdependence. Stripped of their contributions to each other in this century, each would be virtually unrecognizable and both would be much less effective. Technics and related intellectual constructs (e.g., software) play an ever more influential role in the process of acquiring scientific knowledge and attaining a better understanding of nature. Conversely, the knowledge thus generated often makes possible or facilitates the development of new, more potent or efficient technics and related technical and sociotechnical systems. This iterative feedback relationship is sufficiently widespread to qualify as an important distinguishing characteristic of contemporary science and technology.

CONCLUSION

We have tried to flesh out the intuition that there is something different and unprecedented about contemporary science and technology by describing a number of important distinctive characteristics of these influential activities and their respective total social enterprises. Looked at as wholes, contemporary science and technology are unprecedentedly polymorphic in character; their products are singularly voluminous, complex, and dependent on complex sociotechnical and intellectual support systems; they are housed in an extensive network of well-established, substantial-scaled, hierarchically structured formal organizations; the latter make available to science and technology unprecedentedly abundant, diverse, and well-developed material, capital, epistemological, and personnel resources; and, finally, as science and technology have attained the status of cultural institutions, their enterprises have become increasingly international, "rationalized," "Big," and interdependent. These characteristics underlie many of the important influences of science and technology on contemporary society explored in Part II.

ENDNOTES

1. Walter Pater, "The School of Giorgione," in *The Renaissance: Studies in Art and Poetry*, Donald L. Hill, ed. (Berkeley: University of California Press, 1980), p. 106.
2. *Washington Post*, May 26, 1986, p. A10.
3. Michael Lenehan, "The Quality of the Instrument," *Atlantic Monthly*, August 1982, p. 34.
4. *Washington Post*, May 26, 1986, p. A10.
5. Charles Perrow, *Normal Accidents* (New York: Basic Books, 1984).
6. *New York Times*, November 30, 1985, p. 1. For more detailed discussion of the vulnerability of contemporary technology, see Ron Westrum, "Vulnerable Technologies: Accident, Crime, and Terrorism," *Interdisciplinary Science Reviews*, 11, no. 4, 1986, 386–391.
7. Estimate provided by AT&T Bell Laboratories, Murray Hill, N.J., 07974.
8. Thomas Kuhn, *The Structure of Scientific Revolutions*, 2nd ed. (Chicago: The University of Chicago Press, 1970), p. 206.
9. Derek J. de Solla Price, *Little Science, Big Science* (New York: Columbia University Press, 1963), p. 9.
10. P. D. Dresser and K. A. Hill, eds., *Research Centers Directory*, 13th ed., (Detroit: Gale Research, 1989), vol. 1; P. D. Dresser, ed., *New Research Centers: Supplement to the 13th Edition of Research Centers Directory* (Detroit: Gale Research, 1989); and *Directory of American Research and Technology: 1988*, 22nd ed. (New York: R. R. Bowker, 1987), p. vii. The federal laboratory figure was provided by the Division of Science Resource Studies, National Science Foundation, Washington, D.C., 20550. According to NSF, the figure of 700 is only a rough estimate, since data permitting an exact count do not currently exist.
11. Estimate provided in May 1989 by Kirke Comstock, United Airlines' Maintenance Operations Center, San Francisco International Airport.
12. *Directory of American Research and Technology: 1988*, p. 51; and *New York Times*, March 6, 1989, p. A11.
13. *Washington Post*, May 25, 1986, p. A9.
14. *New Scientist*, October 25, 1984, p. 11.
15. Jane Morgan, *Electronics in the West* (Palo Alto: National Press Books, 1967), p. 121.
16. Paul Freiberger and Michael Swaine, *Fire in the Valley* (Berkeley: Osborne/McGraw-Hill, 1984), p. 213.
17. *New York Times*, April 7, 1981, p. C4, and April 13, 1981, p. A14.
18. Similar points can be made about scientific knowledge. For insightful discussion of the development of the *methodological* resources of contemporary technology, see W. G. Vincenti, "The Air-Propeller Tests of W. F. Durand and E. P. Lesley: A Case Study in Technological Methodology," *Technology and Culture*, 20, no. 4, October 1979, 712–751.
19. Eugene S. Ferguson, "The Mind's Eye: Nonverbal Thought in Technology," *Science*, 197, no. 4306, August 26, 1977, 827–828.
20. M. D. Fagen, ed., *A History of Engineering and Science in the Bell System: National Service in War and Peace (1925–1975)* (Murray Hill, N.J.: Bell Telephone Laboratories, Inc., 1978), pp. 134–136.
21. *Science and Technology Data Book: 1989* (Washington, D.C.: National Science Foundation, 1988), p. 20.
22. Robert K. Merton with Harriet Zuckerman, "Age, Aging, and Structure in Science," in Robert K. Merton, *The Sociology of Science* (Chicago: University of Chicago Press, 1973), p. 547.
23. See, e.g., *Physics Letters*, 122B, no. 1, February 24, 1983, 103.
24. *Science and Technology Data Book: 1989*, p. 23.
25. Except where indicated, all figures used in this subsection are drawn or derived from *ibid.*, p. 24.
26. National Center for Education Statistics, *Digest of Education Statistics: 1989*, 25th ed. (Washington, D.C.: U.S. Department of Education, 1989), pp. 271–272.

27. *Physics Today*, 37, no. 12, December 1984 (suppl.), 1–32.
28. Information provided in 1989 by the American Society of Mechanical Engineers, New York, 10017.
29. *Science and Technology Data Book: 1989*, p. 21.
30. Information (to be regarded as estimates) provided in 1986 by Scientific Personnel Office, Stanford Linear Accerator Center, Stanford University, Stanford, California, 94305.
31. *International Herald Tribune*, September 15, 1989, p. 8.
32. For Weber on rationalization, see *Weber: Selections in Translation*, W. G. Runciman, ed. (Cambridge: Cambridge University Press, 1978), pp. 331–340. For discussion of the bureaucratic form of rationality, see *ibid.*, pp. 341–354.
33. Dennis Wrong, "Introduction," in D. Wrong, ed., *Max Weber* (Englewood Cliffs, N.J.: Prentice-Hall, 1970), p. 26.

CHAPTER 4
CONTEXTS
OF SCIENCE
AND TECHNOLOGY

INTRODUCTION

Science and technology never exist in a vacuum. On the contrary, they always unfold in a definite context. However, studies of science and technology in society are sometimes led astray by conceiving the surrounding circumstances of technical developments in too narrow a fashion. Consequently, noteworthy contextual factors are sometimes overlooked, resulting in deficient understandings of two key aspects of particular scientific and technological developments: their *causes* and *consequences*.

Regarding causes, employing a narrow concept of context may give rise to futile attempts to reproduce an existing technical development under circumstances lacking important, overlooked causal factors. Such oversight can undermine even the most well-intentioned efforts to transfer technology from industrialized to less developed countries. As for consequences, analyzing a particular scientific or technological development in too narrow a context may lead to underestimation of its overall societal influence. This can impair the quality of both decision making and policy making about such developments. Thus, conceptualizing the context of technical developments in an appropriate way is vital for practical as well as theoretical reasons.

Part II of this book is devoted to exploring the consequences of scientific and technological developments in modern Western society. If important kinds of consequences are not to be overlooked, such developments must be viewed and analyzed in an appropriately comprehensive context. Therefore, let us elaborate a suitable concept of context. In the model of context put forward here, special attention is paid to an element that often receives less than its due in discussions of science and technology in society: culture. Use of the conceptual lens that we will call the *social-cultural-environmental system* fosters systematic, comprehensive, and perceptive thinking about science and technology in society.

TWO KINDS OF CONTEXT: MICRO AND MACRO

The contexts of scientific and technological activities may be roughly divided into two general kinds. Internal, or *micro*, contexts are ones closely related, either geographically or logically, to the conduct or evaluation of such activities. For example, the micro context of a scientific experiment might be taken to consist of the sociotechnical setting of the laboratory in which it is carried out. The experimentalist's professional peer group whose members assess the validity and value of the work in question may be looked upon as comprising another micro context of the same activity. External, or *macro*, contexts are more comprehensive, typically extending far beyond the geographical locus of the activity or its reference peer group to encompass, say, an entire regional, national, or world society.

The notions of micro and macro contexts are, of course, relative. What is regarded as a micro context under one set of circumstances for one purpose may be properly regarded as a macro context under different circumstances or for a different purpose. For example, an entire corporation may seem an appropriate micro context for a scientific or technological activity undergoing federal scrutiny, while it may be plausibly viewed as comprising a macro context in relation to the specific laboratory in which the work is being carried out. Whether something is viewed as a micro or macro context of a scientific or technological activity depends not just on the inherent features of the situation but on the interests of the analyst doing the viewing.

Micro Contexts

Consider the group, firm, or organizational setting in which some scientific or technological activity or phenomenon unfolds (e.g., a tribe, household, university research laboratory, or company factory). Situational aspects such as the composition and social structure of the group of practitioners involved; the resources, philosophy, and policies of the group or supporting organization; and the physical characteristics of the environment in which the work is carried out are elements of one plausible microcontext of the scientific or technological development in question.

The microsocial context of a scientific and technological activity is sometimes vital for understanding the causes or consequences of a scientific or technological development or phenomenon (e.g., the factors involved in its inception, course of development, completion, or outcome). For example, AT&T's Bell Laboratories is generally recognized as one of the world's premier industrial research laboratories. For obvious reasons, there has been considerable interest in trying to explain—that is, understand the causes of—the fact that for over half a century its level of scientific achievement has been so high. While factors like the quality of its technical personnel and facilities and the size of its budget surely play important causal roles, study has been directed at the characteristics of the internal organizational context created over the years at Bell Labs. The belief underlying such investigations is twofold: first, that specific characteristics of this context play some causal role vis-à-vis the overall quality of the research and development work achieved within its confines; and, second, that if the pertinent microcontextual aspects can be identified, they may be able to be replicated in the design of other facilities, thus enhancing their prospects for success.[1]

Macro Contexts

In recent years, micro contexts of scientific and technological activity, long neglected by scholars, have been analyzed by a modest number of sociologists and anthropologists of technical communities.[2] *The primary focus in this book, however, will be on what might be termed the external, or macro, contexts of science and technology.* More global in scope, these contexts subsume specific scientific and technological activities and their respective micro contexts. They incorporate the general aspects of society, whether on the national or international level, such as its societywide political, economic, and environmental dimensions. As we will see shortly, macro social contexts are also essential to understanding adequately the causes and consequences of specific scientific and technological developments.

FIVE KEY DIMENSIONS OF THE CONTEXT OF SCIENCE AND TECHNOLOGY

Whether focusing on a micro or a macro context of a particular scientific or technological development, sound analysis of its causes and consequences requires consideration of factors having to do with five constituent dimensions or components of the context in question: the practitioner, the technical, the political-economic, the environmental, and the cultural. Let us discuss each of these dimensions separately.

The Practitioner Dimension

Understanding a particular scientific or technological development sometimes requires attending to factors having to do with the specific practitioner or practitioners involved. In accounting for the phenomenon in question, the motivations that impel the practitioner to undertake a particular project may be pertinent, as may the number and competence of the practitioners involved. Thus, Alexander Graham Bell's wish to develop a device to aid the hearing impaired is relevant to understanding the birth of the telephone, while the hundreds of outstanding scientists enlisted to work on the Manhattan Project during World War II is no less germane to understanding the development of the atomic bomb. In such cases, practitioner-related aspects of a situation can be considered contributory causal factors of the technical development in question.

In assessing the consequences—and thus the significance—of a particular technical development, practitioner-related factors may be no less germane. A fruitful technical development may alter the methods employed or directions taken by subsequent activity on the part of some practitioners, whether involved in the initial development or not. Thus, for example, breakthroughs in scientific theory and instrumentation, such as quantum mechanics and the electron microscope, made substantial differences in the approaches and research directions subsequently taken by many scientists. The same is true for engineers in relation to influential inventions such as the wind tunnel and the digital computer. Such practitioner-related changes must be considered as part of the overall significance of the developments in question.

The Technical Dimension

Pursuit of a technical innovation sometimes arises from the fact that a preexisting technical system or preadopted technical goal has or is projected to have certain needs or requirements that the sought-after innovation is intended to help meet or satisfy. Thus, an organization may foresee that a currently operating technical system for which it is responsible will have to undergo significant changes if it is to be able to meet a projected growth in demand for its products or services or to realize a technical performance improvement that has been set for it as a goal. Such technical considerations may launch intense, sometimes protracted searches for appropriate innovations.* For example, AT&T's Bell Laboratories did not undertake the long-term program of fundamental research that culminated in 1948 in the invention of the transistor—the device which launched the contemporary microelectronics revolution—primarily for reasons of profit. Rather, in the words of Ernest Braun and Stuart Macdonald, "[Bell Laboratories' Director of Research Mervin] Kelly felt that one day the mechanical relays in telephone exchanges would have to be replaced by electronic connections *because of the growing complexity of the telephone system and because much greater demands would be made on it*" (emphasis added).[3] Hence, a key factor in launching the research project that yielded the transistor was the requirement that the telephone system remain viable in the greatly changed market situation projected for the future.

Similarly, an adequate account of the consequences of realizing a technical innovation must include its subsequent bearing on related technical systems and goals, including the very ones whose continued technical viability, improvement, or pursuit may have launched the quest for the innovation. Thus, a related system may achieve important increases in product output, handling capacity, or qualitative performance as a result of the sought-after innovations; similarly, a hitherto elusive goal may now come within reach, or a radically new one be adopted.

The Political-Economic Dimension

The most familar dimension of the context of scientific and technological developments, one at the heart of most accounts of the causes and consequences of such developments, is the political-economic. In heeding this contextual dimension, attention is usually focused on *the prevailing constellation of political and economic forces and interests* that played a role in the genesis of the development in question or that were influenced by its achievement and implementation.

On occasion, political considerations are decisive causal factors in the occurrence of technological developments. For example, the genesis of the U.S. government's Apollo program, which culminated in the moon landing of July 1969, lay in national political concerns of the day. The surprise, successful launch of the Russian *Sputnik* satellite in 1957 was held in U.S. government circles to pose a potential military threat to the United States. Also, the Russian achievement was widely seen as a blow to the international prestige of the United States. The ensuing American venture into space, a development that engendered numerous technological innovations, was prompted by and intended to alleviate these political concerns.

More often, traditional economic concerns such as profit play a dominant role in the genesis of technological innovations, as was the case with the development of consumer electronic technics such as the home video cassette recorder and video camera by Japanese companies in the period from 1965 to 1985.

---

*It is important to note that this kind of factor is distinguishable from the more familiar kind of economic considerations (e.g., profit maintenance or growth) that provide the rationale for pursuing many technological developments. See the next section.

The origins and courses of some scientific developments are also traceable to political-economic considerations. Witness the growth in the 1980s of private corporate financial support for certain areas of scientific research in universities (e.g., in microelectronics and genetics). While corporate influence on academic science is a relatively recent development, the phenomenon of economic interests affecting scientific research is scarcely new. Recall from Chapter 2 that in the seventeenth century, economic interests of industrialists influenced the scientific research agenda of the Royal Society of London.

In the twentieth century, politics has come to exercise a substantial genetic influence on scientific activity—for example, in the area of public health. Societal consensus about the desirability of government support for or conduct of research into various human diseases has provided impetus for a variety of scientific endeavors, from the launching of a "war on cancer" to the rapid increase in government funds devoted to research on the AIDS virus.

Sometimes—seemingly with increasing frequency in the contemporary era—political and economic interests merge to provide the impetus for a scientific development. For example, the 1988 decision by the U.S. government to build a multibillion-dollar particle accelerator (the Superconducting Super Collider [SSC]) was largely due to the political interest of the federal government in sustaining American scientific prestige, the political influence mobilized and exercised by the American particle-physics community on behalf of its interest in continued scientific advancement, and the economic interests of the firms and local governments that stand to benefit from the SSC's construction and operation.

In assessments of the consequences of technical developments, factors related to the political-economic context sometimes bulk large. For example, the possession of nuclear weapons by the United States and the Soviet Union since the early 1950s exerted a decisive influence on international political affairs in the post–World War II period. More recently, some accounts of the consequences of Japanese technological prowess in the 1970s and 1980s have included a broad political-economic dimension, including claims that Japan is now obliged to render substantial economic assistance to poorer, less developed nations. In sum, adequate accounts of the causes or consequences of scientific and technological developments must often incorporate elements related to their respective political-economic contexts.

The Cultural Dimension

Attempts to understand the cause of a scientific or technological development that focus on the specific actions and motives of particular individuals and organizations, on the specific resources and strategies employed by the protagonists, or on the political, economic, or other social circumstances of the day are emphasizing proximate, or *foreground*, factors as the cause of the development in question. We will call the context comprised solely of such proximate factors the *immediate social context* of science and technology. Since such factors often interact and affect each other in important ways, we will speak of the *immediate social system* (ISS) context associated with a scientific and technological development.

As we have seen, foreground factors *are* often important contextual elements, in both micro and macro contexts, and such a particularistic approach to the determination of the cause of a scientific or technological development is fine as far as it goes. Unfortunately, it does not go nearly far enough to ensure a sound understanding of the phenomenon under study.

For example, suppose one is trying to explain the following technological development: the termination of the effort to develop an American supersonic transport (SST) airplane. One might point to the specific congressional votes in March and May of 1971 that denied further government funding for development of such a plane by private industry. One might seek to determine who voted against providing such money and why, what current political-economic forces were at work, and whether any important specific events had occurred (e.g., a test crash, prior budget overrun, or schedule delay) that made congressional approval less likely. Such foreground factors are indeed relevant ingredients of a satisfactory explanation. However, there is more to the causal story than reference to such factors suggests.

By the late 1960s, protest movements against environmental degradation and the war in Vietnam had generated a significant level of social concern over technological products, processes, and practices believed to be harmful to the environment or antithetical to humane values. One effect of this movement was to call into question for the first time since the dropping of the atomic bomb the deeply rooted cultural assumption that technological progress is always socially benign. This transformation in social attitudes opened the door for a challenge to those who held that the technological advance represented by the SST was something that society should definitely pursue. The long-standing societal presumption in favor of pursuing all affordable technological advances was weakened. It was now possible for society to think the previously unthinkable: seriously consider not going forward with a feasible technological advance. It was in this new social climate that the dispute over the SST was fought out.

Thus, in addition to foreground factors of the day, ones usually easily discerned and susceptible to relatively rapid change, there are apt to be equally if not more important *background factors* that must also be taken into account. Such factors are often harder to discern and of a relatively more abiding nature.

To see more precisely what is meant by *background factors*, the concept of a society's *cultural system* must be introduced. Like the scientific or technological development in question, the specific motives and actions of parties involved with the development at issue do not crystallize or unfold in a vacuum. Rather, they do so in a particular society, which, like any society, comes equipped with a backdrop that serves to help the society and its members fulfill their respective needs. This backdrop is the society's culture.

The *culture* of a society is meant here in the broad, anthropological sense—that is, as referring to "*the grand total of all the objects, ideas, knowledge, institutions, ways of doing things, habits, behavior patterns, values, and attitudes which each generation in a society*" *receives and passes on—often in altered form—to its successor* (emphasis added).[4] Put differently, a society's culture (at a given time) is *the total way of life* it inherits from preceding generations, presents as a backdrop for life in the current generation, and transmits, usually in altered form, to the next generation.

Since elements of this complex interact and influence each other, we shall speak of the *cultural system*. The cultural system of a society influences the actions and motives of members of that society in various ways and is in turn sometimes affected by them. Specific foreground factors of the sort just mentioned may *precipitate* certain scientific and technological developments, but the way for their doing so is often paved by background factors in the form of various elements of the society's cultural system. *Foreground factors may be the causal match or seed, but cultural background factors are often the causal gunpowder or fertile soil.* No matter how long the match, how hot the flame, or how strong the seed, it may prove useless unless the powder is dry and explosive or the soil is fertile. This is why any account of the cause of some scientific or technological development that fails to take into account the role of cultural background factors is bound to be superficial. As we shall see in a moment, the same is true of accounts of the consequences of such developments. We will look more closely at the components of a society's cultural system shortly.

The Environmental Dimension

If we are to think systematically and comprehensively about the causes and consequences of technical changes, a fifth kind of factor must also be borne in mind. Not only do such phenomena not take place in a social vacuum, they also do not unfold in a physical vacuum. Besides social and cultural contexts, there is always a *natural environmental* context for scientific and, especially, technological developments. As with the cultural context, the elements of the environmental context often interact with and influence each other. Hence we may speak of the *environmental system* context.

Environmental context is sometimes crucial to what happens in science and technology. The character of its natural environment often affects the inventory of technics a society evolves to enable its members to cope with that environment (e.g., snowshoes or air conditioners). Similarly, perplexing or troublesome aspects of a society's natural environment may engender scientific inquiries aimed at explaining or overcoming them. Conversely, the natural environment is sometimes seriously affected by scientfic and technological practices: Biological species may be endangered or rendered extinct, climate may be altered, and ecosystem processes may be disrupted—effects that may in turn elicit alteration of the very technical practices that gave rise to them.

The Cultural-Environmental System

Combining the cultural system and environmental system contexts gives us a society's total *cultural-environmental system* (CES). As depicted in Figure 4-1, the cultural system (CS) of a society is represented by the area inside a rectangle CS. The various elements of the cultural system, are represented by points inside the rectangle. The natural environment (E) of the society is represented by the interior of the curvilinear figure E encircling the rectangle. (Enclosing CS in E is meant to suggest that the entire cultural system of society has a natural environmental envelope or context with which it interacts.) Following a standard anthropological approach, the

Figure 4-1. The Cultural-Environmental System (CES) of a society.

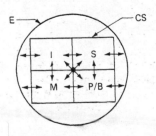

cultural system comprises four major subsystems: the ideational (I), societal (S), material (M), and personality-and-behavior (P/B) realms.[5] Each such subsystem is represented by one of the four smaller rectangles making up the larger one. The arrows pointing from one realm to another represent possible influence relations between phenomena in the respective subsystems.

Since cultural causes and consequences play an important role in Parts II and III of this book, we will now look closely at each of the five CES subsystems: I, S, M, P/B, and E.

The Ideational Subsystem. The ideational realm of a society's cultural system consists of its *characteristic mental phenomena*, such as its

> core ideas,
> world views,
> recognized body of knowledge,
> core beliefs,
> central values, and
> behavioral norms

and its characteristic

> tastes (aesthetic and otherwise),
> styles,
> attitudes,
> expectations, and
> aspirations.

In short, the ideational realm consists of society's characteristic attitudes and belief systems. An idea, value, or attitude held by only one or a negligible number of people in the society is typically not regarded as part of its ideational cultural matrix. For a specific ideational element to be part of a society's culture (at a given point in time), it must be held and transmitted by at least a significant number of people in that society. Hence, individual eccentric beliefs and attitudes do not automatically count as part of a society's ideational culture.

The ideational realm of modern Western society includes phenomena such as the ideas of success and democracy, the body of currently accepted scientific knowledge, the values of freedom and justice, prevailing attitudes toward work and nature, and world views such as those of Christian fundamentalists and secular humanists.

In important respects, science itself belongs to the ideational realm. For example, the currently accepted body of scientific knowledge, the idea of what counts as bona fide scientific activity, and the reigning norms of scientific practice are all parts of a society's ideational cultural realm at a given point in time. In other respects, however, science is *not* part of this realm. Various essential scientific resources, such as experimental apparatus, belong to other realms of the cultural-environmental system.

The content of or changes in a society's ideational-cultural realm are often intimately intertwined with developments in science or technology. For example, the core modern Western value of *progress* has given impetus to and been reinforced by the continuous, generally successful drive during the last two and a half centuries to enhance scientific understanding and technological performance and bring the latest science and technology to bear on all areas of human endeavor and inquiry. In Parts II and III of this book, we will explore some ways in which the ideational realm of modern Western culture has been transformed by developments in science and technology. For example, how have science and technology affected traditional human values and world views (Chapter 8)? What kinds of ethical conflicts and issues are being engendered by scientific and technological innovations (Chapter 9)? Conversely, in Chapter 15 we will consider what kinds of ideational-cultural changes (e.g., changes in reigning values or world views) might, if effected, enhance the influence of science and technology on contemporary society.

The Societal Subsystem.   The societal subsystem of a society's cultural system consists of the *characteristic non-mental forms and structures* that it has evolved to regulate or facilitate social interaction, survival, and evolution, such as its

> institutions,
> groups,
> organizations,
> classes,
> social structure (e.g.,differentiation and stratification systems),
> roles,
> statuses,
> rituals,
> processes (e.g., of evaluation, control, socialization, and change), and
> type of economy.

The societal-cultural realm of contemporary Western society includes *institutions* such as the family, school, work, stock market, and church; *groups* such as families, communities (geographical and cultural), political parties, labor unions, and parishes; *movements*, such as the environmental and women's movements; *roles*, such as parent, student, judge, politician, scientist, and engineer, and their respective *social statuses*; *organizations*, such as IBM, the Roman Catholic Church, the U.S. Supreme Court, and Stanford University; *classes*, such as the "underclass" and the "middle" class; and *rituals*, such as those associated with Christmas, Superbowl Sunday, and the Fourth of July.

The societal realm often steeply influences and is influenced by scientific and technological developments. Entrepreneurs (a group) and research laboratories (tokens of a type of institution) are responsible for much modern Western scientific knowledge and technological innovation. Conversely, developments in communications and transportation technology (e.g., television and the private automobile) have greatly influenced the family and leisure (institutions). In Chapters 6 and 7 we will explore some ways in which selected institutions and groups in contemporary Western society have been significantly affected by developments in science and technology.

The Material Subsystem.   A society's material-cultural subsystem consists of the ensemble of its

> material artifacts (technics),
> technologies,
> ways of making things, and
> human-made or "built" environments.

Regarding its technics as an integral part of a society's cultural system suggests a number of intriguing questions. For example, what are the implications for other elements of the cultural-environmental system (e.g., values, ideas, and institutions) of the fact that modern Western society possesses such a cornucopia of sometimes potent personal technics? We will address aspects of this question in Chapters 6, 8, and 10.

As with science vis-à-vis the ideational realm, it is tempting to view technology as being completely included in the material-cultural realm. This, too, would be a mistake, for while technics do belong to this subsystem, other aspects of technology as an activity do not. For example, the raw material resources of technology belong to the environmental realm, a given society's reservoir of technological knowledge belongs to its ideational-cultural realm, and the institutions that serve as important technological resources in the contemporary era are part of the societal-cultural realm.

The Personality and Behavior Subsystem. The personality-and-behavior subsystem consists mostly of *personality traits and behavior patterns*—linguistic and otherwise—characteristic of at least a substantial portion of the members of the society in question. The two parts of this realm are not as unrelated as they might seem, for personality traits are dispositions to behave in certain ways under certain kinds of circumstances and are often reliably inferred from observed behavior patterns.

Even the personality-and-behavior realm is related to scientific and technological activity. Modern science and technology have engendered or altered a number of important cultural behavior patterns, including those of courtship, childrearing, dieting, sexually explicit speech, and interaction with nature. They may also be linked to certain personality traits. For example, students attracted to or repelled by the study of mathematics, natural science, and engineering tend to have distinctive personality traits. Conversely, involvement in these specialties may foster or reinforce the development of certain personality traits and behavioral patterns, such as introversion, diligence, and a "problem-solving mentality."

In addition to characteristic personality traits and behavior patterns, there is a third important dimension of this cultural subsystem, one closely related to but distinguishable from the society's material-cultural realm. Let us call this the *behavior setting* of everyday life in the society in question. In general, the behavior setting of an environment refers to *the constellation of physical objects and material artifacts deployed in that environment that serve as a backdrop for, and sometimes affect, the behavior that unfolds against it*. For example, the behavior setting of a school classroom includes the specific objects (desks, chairs, flags, windows, signs, and so on) and lighting in the room, and, equally important, *the way the objects are arranged*, something which can have a subtle or not-so-subtle effect on the behavior of occupants of the room. The behavior settings of contemporary industrial societies are often complex and dynamic. As we will see in Chapter 10, they have significantly affected the behavior and character of everyday life.

The Environmental Subsystem. The natural environmental realm includes the physical features of the area in which the society in question is located; such features include its topographical and geographical properties, characteristic weather patterns, and air, land, plant, mineral, and water resources. Also included within a society's environmental system are its resident human and nonhuman animal populations, with respect to both their respective demographic features and general organismic health and well-being. Since these elements of the environmental realm interact continuously, it is reasonable to speak of the society's environmental system or subsystem.

If we now combine the immediate social system (ISS) and the cultural-environmental system (CES) into one comprehensive, overarching system, we arrive at an appropriate context in which to view and analyze the causes and consequences of scientific and technological developments: the total *social-cultural-environmental system* (SCES) of the society in question. This context embraces both foreground (ISS) and background (CES) factors. Popular discussions of the genesis of scientific and technological innovations and of their "impacts" on society tend to limit themselves to foreground factors belonging to the immediate social system (e.g., political, economic, and medical considerations). To compensate for this misleading preoccupation, considerable attention will be given in what follows to less obvious but equally important background factors—namely, to elements of society's cultural-environmental system. This emphasis should not be read as denying the importance of attending to factors belonging to the ISS context, however. Let us now turn to several examples that illustrate the usefulness of the SCES concept for understanding the origins and consequences of scientific and technological developments.

UNDERSTANDING THE CAUSES OF SCIENTIFIC AND TECHNOLOGICAL DEVELOPMENTS

The notion of a society's total cultural-environmental system helps one understand better *the causes*—put differently, the genesis—of scientific and technological developments. It does so by directing attention not just at the various foreground factors at work in a particular situation but also at pertinent background factors belonging to the cultural-environmental system. Since thinking in terms of background cultural causal factors is not a common mode of thought (outside anthropological circles), we will illustrate the use of this conceptual framework by discussing two famous examples: the Scientific Revolution in sixteenth and seventeenth century Europe and the Industrial Revolution in Britain.

EXAMPLE 1 : The Scientific Revolution in Seventeenth Century Europe

The Scientific Revolution is traditionally used to refer to the towering intellectual achievements of sixteenth and seventeenth century European astronomy and physical science. A new mechanistic theory of nature triumphed over both the traditional Aristotelian world view that held sway in the Middle Ages and the tradition of hermetic natural magic that flourished in the Renaissance. In short, the Scientific Revolution marks the emergence of modern science.

Suppose one were interested in understanding the cause or genesis of this epochal development, one Herbert Butterfield termed the most important landmark in history since the rise of Christianity.[6] One could, of course, focus on the remarkable achievements of the specific individuals involved, from Copernicus and Bacon to Descartes, Galileo, and Newton. While the individual talents and skills of these and other illustrious practitioners clearly played important roles in the genesis of their achievements, there is more to the causal story than concentration on such foreground factors would suggest.

Invoking the cultural-environmental system concept, one should immediately inquire: Were any ideational, societal, material, personality-behavioral, or environmental background factors at work preparing the cultural soil for these achievements? Did such factors serve as preconditions or facilitating factors for the ensuing crucial scientific accomplishments or pave the way for their diffusion, reception, and eventual adoption? In recent years scholars have pointed to various cultural background factors that supposedly contributed to the emergence and success of the Scientific Revolution.

Some have pointed causal fingers at certain *ideational* phenomena. For example, during the revival of interest in classical thought and art in fifteenth century Italy, humanist scholars translated numerous Greek and Latin works, including scientific treatises. The empirical and mundane, rather than other-worldly, interest in humanity and the natural world that resulted was a key ingredient of the spirit of the new science. Another pivotal aspect of modern science, the role of mathematics, also derives partly from the Renaissance classical revival. Rediscovery of the works of Plato and the Pythagorean school of philosophy, in which mathematics was of central, indeed metaphysical, importance, led to renewed interest in mathematics as supposedly providing the key to solid knowledge about the real world.[7]

Robert Merton has argued that another important aspect of the (late phase of the) Scientific Revolution, the widening of interest in scientific activity, was fostered by the values of Puritan religion. Through scientific study of nature, the human being acquires ethically valuable mental discipline. The human's appreciation of and praise for God's powers is enhanced by coming to know his marvelous world. In short, Calvinistic Puritanism legitimized and thereby facilitated the diffusion of the new empirical science.[8]

As for causal factors related to the *societal*-cultural realm, that seminal medieval social institution, the university, was the setting for a good deal of both critical analysis of the then-dominant Aristotelian world view as well as the gradual progress in science which culminated in the Scientific Revolution, especially in anatomy, astronomy, and the theory of motion. Further, the economic aspirations and endeavors of the emerging, dynamic middle class, especially in sixteenth and seventeenth century England, provided motivation for the selection and study of many problems addressed by the new empirical science.

Regarding the *material*-cultural realm, we mentioned earlier the role of the proliferating technology of the Renaissance in engendering a mechanistic view of the cosmos and its processes, one which undergirded and informed much of the new science. Also noteworthy was the role of the printing press, which, by making it possible to produce inexpensive books, facilitated the spread of the fruits of bold scientific inquiries and the transformation of educated common sense from belief in a geocentric, enchanted cosmos to a heliocentric, mechanistic universe.

None of this, of course, is intended to dismiss or depreciate the contributions of individual "natural philosophers," particularly with regards to what might be termed the cognitive side of science—its new objects, concepts, methods, and procedures. Rather, background factors of the sort just discussed are best seen as *complementary contributory causal factors*.

EXAMPLE 2: The Industrial Revolution in Britain (c. 1750–1850)

The phrase *industrial revolution* usually refers to "that complex of technological innovations which, by substituting machines for human skill and inanimate power for human and animal force, brings about a shift from handicraft to manufacture and, in so doing, gives birth to a modern economy."[9] Many would agree with Eric Hobsbawm that the industrial revolution, which began in earnest in the eighteenth century, was "the most fundamental transformation of human life in the history of the world recorded in written documents."[10]

The first manifestation of this process took place in England. The first phase of the Industrial Revolution in Britain (IRB) occurred between 1750 and 1850. It consisted of four major techno-economic changes: (1) the development of better power sources to drive production (ultimately, the coal-fueled steam engine), (2) the progressive mechanization of human work, (3) the development of improved processes for transforming raw materials into states more suitable for manufacturing, and (4) the introduction of a more efficient mode of organizing production: the factory system.[11] The upshot of this revolution was that by 1850, Britain had become the "workshop of the world." As David Landes observed, "It was a moment of [world] dominance without parallel before or since."[12]

As in the case of the Scientific Revolution, to understand the cause or causes of the IRB, one could choose to focus on pertinent foreground factors such as the names of pivotal inventors and innovators, their technological inventions and innovations, their motives, and their respective political and economic supporters.

However, an adequate causal analysis must also attend to various important background factors present in the country's cultural-environmental system. For example, certain aspects of the *environmental* realm played a notable causal role. Britain's oceanic position gave it easy access to overseas markets and suppliers. Its modest size and indented coastline placed most of the country within ready reach of easy and inexpensive water transport. The country possessed in abundance those natural resources that proved important for the new power technologies, especially water and coal.

One other phenomenon pertinent to the environmental system is sometimes viewed as a cause of the IRB. Some note the rapid rise in English population beginning around 1740 and view the IRB as a successful though far from inevitable response to the *challenge* posed by the need to feed, clothe, house, and provide essential goods for the rapidly expanding populace.[13] Debate continues, however, over the degree to which this increase was a cause, effect, stimulant, or mere concomitant of the IRB. One thing is clear, however: Industrial revolutions have occurred in some countries in the absence of such increases and failed to occur in others in their presence.

In the *ideational* sector, as against their French counterparts, many British aristocrats evidenced no cultural attitudes of disdain toward involvement in industrial activity and commerce. There was also in British society a general interest in and enthusiasm about developments in science and technology. The predominance at the time of a laissez-faire, or "leave-alone," philosophy of governmment-economy relations was also conducive to the take-off phase of the IRB.

As for the *societal*-cultural realm, some scholars have pointed to the causal roles of certain British social institutions. For example, unlike many countries, Britain had evolved a capitalist, private-profit-oriented market economy, including a patent system for manufacturing processes that offered significant material incentives to risk-taking entrepreneurs. Further, with its national banking system, capital made in agriculture and commerce could be readily moved and invested in nascent industrial enterprises. Moreover, if the greater efficiency of the new economic system were to be exploited, there had to be a sufficiently large middle class to purchase the volume of products now capable of being produced. That this was the case was tacitly acknowledged by Napoleon in referring contemptuously to Britain as "a nation of shopkeepers."

Regarding the *material*-cultural realm, many inventions and innovations at the heart of the IRB pertained to the mining of coal and its use as a fuel, the development of power technologies (initially the waterwheel, later the steam engine), the production of iron and steel, and the spinning and weaving of textiles. Although the inventions and innovations involved belonged to the material-cultural realm, it is essential to point out that elements of that same realm served as important background factors— namely, the prior technologies constituting the existing state of the art in the coal, power, iron, and textile industries. That is, the new inventions did not spring suddenly into existence in a technological vacuum, but were typically improvements on—and thus stood on the shoulders of—earlier technics or ways of doing things that served as the material-cultural contexts for these improvements.

The material-cultural realm in Britain was an important causal factor in a second way. Britain had or developed efficient technical "support" or "infrastructure" systems—for example, ones related to transport, such as harbors, roads, bridges, tunnels, and especially canals and (later) railroads. While these were not directly productive, they were essential to the efficient distribution of the industrial economy's rapidly expanding output.

Finally, regarding the cultural subsystem of *personality-behavior*, the IRB witnessed the emergence of a new type of business person: the industrial entrepreneur. Originating mostly in the lower and middle classes, people like John Wilkinson, Richard Arkwright, James Watt's partner Matthew Boulton, and Josiah Wedgwood, although doubtlessly in quest of profit, were also motivated by desires for seeing through large, complex, generally daunting industrial undertakings to successful conclusions and for making a discernible impact on the world through their personal efforts.

The point of presenting these two examples in some detail is to underscore and elaborate the contention that attempts to understand satisfactorily the causes of scientific and technological phenomena must proceed on several levels, taking into account both pertinent foreground and less obvious but equally germane background factors, including ones falling into any of the five realms of the society's cultural-environmental system.

Questions about the "causes" of cultural phenomena are notoriously tricky ones. The factors that have played a contributive causal role may be "causes" in any one of at least four different senses. They can be *enabling factors* which make the phenomenon in question possible; *pull factors* which exert an attractive force on the phenomenon from without; *push factors*, which impel or exert a driving force on it from within; or *facilitating factors*, which, while neither necessary nor sufficient for the occurrence of the phenomenon or development in question, make it easier for it to come to pass. All such background factors may be involved in setting the stage for one or more foreground factors (such as specific inventions or innovations) whose appearance is then (and only then) sufficient to trigger the occurrence of the development in question.

UNDERSTANDING THE CONSEQUENCES OF SCIENTIFIC AND TECHNOLOGICAL DEVELOPMENTS

Of equal intellectual, and perhaps greater practical, interest than the issue of understanding the causes of scientific or technological developments is that of understanding *the consequences*—and thus the larger significance—of such developments. How might one approach this problem?

First, one might undertake to ascertain what difference the discovery, theory, invention, or innovation made in the subsequent growth of the scientific or technological field or fields in question. In addition, one might try to determine what practical effects, if any, the development in question had on people's lives. Such effects would include various economic and medical ones (e.g., ones affecting wealth, employment, health, and longevity) as well as ones altering the availability and expenditure of various resources (e.g., free time, labor power, information).

Such relatively clear-cut aspects of the influence of a scientific or technological development on people's lives might be termed *first-order*, or direct, effects. However, any account of the consequences of such a development that stopped there would be incomplete and superficial, for sometimes—indeed, seemingly increasingly—scientific and technological developments effect marked changes in elements of the total cultural-environmental system of the society in question. Such changes often have consequences that go far beyond short-term effects on the lives of people directly affected by first-order consequences.

For example, a pivotal idea in the culture might be undermined or a particular social institution might become dysfunctional in the face of new circumstances engendered over time by the development; a traditional way of doing things (e.g., the long-standard method for making a certain product) might be rendered obsolete; or a perennial behavior pattern or environmental relationship might be disrupted or severed. Such aspects of the development's "impact" transform the society's inherited/transmitted way of life—that is, its cultural or cultural-environmental system. Let us call such aspects structural, or *transformative*, consequences. Compared to first-order consequences, transformative ones are often intangible in nature, sometimes occur indirectly, and typically appear only in the intermediate to long term. While not an easy thing to do, either prospectively or retrospectively, they too must be taken into account in attempting to understand adequately the consequences or overall significance of scientific or technological developments. Let us revisit our two earlier examples and bring two new ones into the picture to illustrate this approach.

EXAMPLE 1: The Scientific Revolution

The Scientific Revolution profoundly influenced developments in several scientific fields, especially physics and astronomy. Newtonian mechanics held sway over and bore abundant fruit in Western science for over a century. On the other hand, the Scientific Revolution had negligible practical impact on people's lives prior to the mid-nineteenth century, when discoveries in fields indebted to that revolution were finally wed to technological concerns and developments.

However, the Scientific Revolution did exercise a powerful influence on one aspect of the cultural-environmental system of Western Europe, one still in evidence to this day. The world view of educated Europeans was decisively transformed. In the words of Brian Easlea:

> In 1500 educated people in western Europe believed themselves living at the center of a finite cosmos, at the mercy of (supernatural) forces beyond their control, and continually menaced by Satan and his allies. By 1700 educated people in western Europe for the most part believed themselves living in an infinite universe on a tiny planet in (elliptical) orbit about the sun, no longer menaced by Satan, and confident that power over the natural world lay within their grasp.[14]

From the traditional belief that nature was "a living organism, a connected structure linked by a web of hidden active powers," by around 1700, educated people had come to conceive of the universe as a dead, "mechanical structure like a clock."[15]

The contemporaneous and subsequent establishment of scientific societies and academies aside, the Scientific Revolution did not have any appreciable transformative effect on the societal-cultural realm. Nor did it have any significant impact on the material, personality-and-behavior, or environmental realms. This, however, is not surprising, for unless scientific discoveries and theories, however novel and challenging, are embodied in technological projects or products that are used in important ways or diffused widely in society, their influence on a society's cultural-environmental system is apt to be limited (in the short to intermediate term at the least) to the ideational realm (e.g., changes in values, world views, or ideas). Darwin's theory of evolution by natural selection is a rare exception to this generalization.

If, on the other hand, scientific developments *are* given technological expression and are used in important ways or diffused widely in society, the entire cultural-environmental system may be transformed. Such was the case both with early twentieth century theories and discoveries in nuclear physics that subsequently found application in the atomic bomb and with the scientific research that culminated in the invention of the transistor, a science-intensive device which made the computer age possible.

EXAMPLE 2: The Oral Contraceptive

The example used to illustrate the problem of adequately understanding the consequences of scientific developments—namely, the Scientific Revolution—is actually a *cluster* of scientific achievements. Although this cluster did not exert a ripple effect throughout the whole cultural-environmental system, it might be thought that only a cluster of such discoveries and theories could do so. In order not to leave the impression that our approach is applicable only to clusters of scientific developments, let us briefly examine a *single* scientific development that has had a wide variety of important ramifications. Here, too, the point is that its consequences, to be soundly understood, must be analyzed in the context of the total cultural-environmental system. The example we will consider is the steroid oral contraceptive, better known as "the pill."

After considerable chemical research and clinical trials—in, be it noted, Puerto Rico and Haiti—the U.S. Food and Drug Administration approved the first birth-control pill in May 1960.[16] It is estimated that worldwide in the mid-1980s, over 60 million women of child-bearing age used oral contraceptives, roughly equal to the total number who have used it in the past.[17]

An initial step in understanding the consequences of this scientific development would be to determine its first-order effects. These effects would be primarily medical in nature, including both its efficacy in preventing conception as well as its much-publicized short- and long-term physiological and psychological side effects. However, equally important—more important for present purposes—are the pill's effects on the cultural-environmental systems of societies in which it enjoys wide use, such as the United States.*

Given the nature of the subject, claims about the pill's nonmedical influence are not easy to confirm. Nevertheless, any account of the consequences of the pill that

---

*A 1982 study estimated that of 33.4 million American women then practicing contraception, about 10 million used the pill (*Family Planning Perspectives*, 15, no. 4, 1983, 162).

omitted its effects on the cultural-environmental system would greatly underestimate its overall societal significance. A satisfactory account of the pill's consequences would include propositions such as the following.

In the *ideational* realm, the pill helped shatter the mental linkage between intercourse and procreation, thus paving the way for the influential contemporary idea of sex for pleasure per se. The concept—as well, of course, as the practice—of family planning has become an important fixture in the outlook on life of most members of developed societies.[18] The diminished risk of pregnancy effected by the pill has contributed to the decline of the long-standing Western-cultural belief that sex before marriage is morally wrong. A 1985 survey revealed that for the first time this has become a minority belief in the United States.[19] Conversely, due in no small measure to the pill, in society at large chastity has come to be regarded as "unnatural," and sexual activity before marriage has assumed the status of a norm. By reducing fear of unwanted pregnancy through sexual activity, the pill gave rise to the cultural expectation that sex should be enjoyable for women as well as men. In short, the pill helped bring about a sexual revolution in the ideational-cultural realm, albeit one partly offset in recent years by the spread of AIDS.[20]

Societally speaking, the pill has contributed powerfully to the establishment of new roles for women. By facilitating female reproductive control, the pill afforded sexually active women the options of a childless professional career and of a life combining work and child bearing. Equally important, the pill has also given rise to altered societal and sexual roles for men. For example, they no longer necessarily have to assume the role of sole family breadwinner.[21] The efficacy of the pill has also contributed to the flourishing of the relatively new social institution known as the family-planning center. Roughly 1.2 million women were provided with contraceptive services by 191 Planned Parenthood affiliates in the United States in 1981. Of first-time clients who sought reversible contraception, 61 percent chose the pill.[22]

As for the personality-and-behavior realm, the pill seems to have altered patterns of sexual behavior, facilitating greater spontaneity and offering women options for more initiatory sexual behavior.

Finally, regarding the environmental realm, by contributing to significantly lower fertility rates in countries in which it is widely used, the pill has helped raise the mean age of the populace, a topic to which we will return in Chapter 7.

Besides such specific changes in the cultural-environmental system, since its introduction the pill has been a significant factor in engendering—for good and ill—a general climate of greater openness about sexual matters in Western society. As contraceptive-pill research pioneer Carl Djerassi has noted, "the fact that contraception has become an accepted form of dinner conversation—something the condom never inspired" is due primarily to the pill.[23]

EXAMPLE 3: The Industrial Revolution in Britain

Few technological developments have had as profound an influence on society as a whole as the first phase of the industrial revolution, that in which largely agricultural societies became predominantly industrial in character. Having used the IRB to illustrate the issue of understanding the *causes* of a technological development, let us use the same example to illustrate the fact that understanding the *consequences* of such developments also requires grasping the ways in which they transformed the total cultural-environmental system of the society in question.

The first-order consequences of the IRB were, not surprisingly, momentous. Many individuals and private firms acquired enormous wealth; the British government's military power and political influence increased greatly; and British engineers and entrepreneurs seeking to exploit the opportunities opened by the early IRB markedly expanded their inventive and innovative activities.

However, the consequences of the IRB for Britain's cultural-environmental system were numerous and at least as important. *Ideationally*, the IRB fostered the concept that nature is a raw material "out there" to be tamed, exploited, consumed, and improved upon by using technology. With the success of the IRB, and contrary to the opinion of many British Romantic poets in the late eighteenth and early nineteenth centuries, a societal consensus began to emerge that "natural" is not always better. The idea of progress became more deeply rooted in people's minds, affected their personal expectations, and, as technologies were measurably improved, took on an increasingly quantitative cast.

Societally, the new industrial order engendered an urban way of life. Industrial life increasingly unfolded in rapidly growing cities located around or near large factories. The new industrial order also transformed the institutions of work and family. The old artisanal mode of work, with its variable rhythms and relative autonomy, yielded to the new organizational and temporal disciplines of factory production. It became harder for spouses and their children to continue to work together as co-producers in family-run cottage industries and farms. Industrial work opportunities for women were seen as so demeaning by prosperous middle-class men that they invented a "cult of domesticity" to justify the nonparticipation of their spouses in the public work sphere. The female servant became a fixture in the middle-class family to spare the "lady of the house" grimy private as well as public labor.

Regarding the *material*-cultural realm, the IRB was responsible in large part for the creation and diffusion of a historically unprecedented array and volume of technics: from clothing, furniture, and toys, to railroad equipment, bicycles, and industrial tools and machinery. New ways of making and doing things proliferated.

Environmentally, the IRB inflicted a nasty scar on the English landscape. The aggressive mining of coal, the sprawl of industrial cities, and the operation of pollution-spewing factories gave a substantially different, often depressing look to the physical environment of the country that D. H. Lawrence fondly called "Merrie England."

Few aspects of the British way of life remained untouched by the IRB. The ideas, values, institutions, roles, everyday technics, patterns of behavior, and environmental condition of nineteenth century British society all underwent profound changes. Comprehension of the full range of such transformative impacts is imperative if a sound assessment of the significance of this and future revolutions is to be realized.

EXAMPLE 4: The Snowmobile in Finnish Lappland

As we did with science, let us consider an example of a *single* technological invention that substantially transformed the cultural-environmental system of the society in which it was unleashed.[24] The Skolt Lapp people of northern Finland traditionally used reindeer sleds for transportation. Reindeer were also a source of meat, and their skin was used to make clothing. Older Skolt men were repositories of knowledge and wisdom for the young on the care and use of reindeer and reindeer sleds.

The snowmobile, introduced into Skolt Lapp society in the early 1960s, rapidly displaced the reindeer sled. Its first-order consequences were predictable. It substantially cut the time required to go between the main trading post across the border in Norway and the Lapp settlements. Moreover, it offered improved access to better health care and more varied diets and recreational activities. However, the snowmobile also brought a number of unforeseen transformations in the Skolt Lapp cultural-environmental system.

Societally, although older Skolt males could still drive reindeer sleds, they lacked the strength and muscular dexterity to drive snowmobiles over rough terrain. Consequently, they rapidly lost their traditional social role and prestige. Their accumulated reindeer knowledge was no longer essential for the education of the young. The Skolts' relatively egalitarian, self-sufficient, subsistence economy became an increasingly stratified cash economy dependent on the outside world (e.g., for fuel and spare parts).

Environmentally, the unfenced reindeer herds, with which the Skolts had long lived in symbiosis, were "de-domesticated" by the noise of the snowmobiles, and the number of reindeer calves born declined substantially. Finally, the snowmobile significantly altered the traditional Lapp personal *behavioral* style. In the days of the reindeer sled, everyday life focused on the age-old struggle between self and nonhuman environment. The traditional Skolt personality type thus did not include "any strong element of aggressive competition with other persons." The Skolts who have emerged as successful in the snowmobile regime exhibit "considerable flexibility of personal behavior, a self-confidence in individual task performance, and a high level of personal initiative in the accomplishment of economic work."[25] As the snowmobile enables herders to spend more time with family and friends, social interaction has increased. Thus, over time, a more interpersonally competitive and gregarious Skolt Lapp personality type is likely to emerge.

The Skolt Lapps did not anticipate the disruptive transformations that their cultural-environment system underwent. Consequently, many were distressed, and some suffered unnecessary hardship. As newcomers to rapid scientific and technological innovation, they understandably envisioned the consequences of introducing the snowmobile narrowly—largely in terms of the beneficial first-order effects of greatly improved transport efficiency and the saving of time. The broad context of the cultural-environmental system elaborated above suggests an agenda of concerns that, if scrutinized, could lessen the chances and diminish the costs of such myopia.

CONCLUSION

In this chapter we have addressed on a theoretical level the issue of setting science and technology in appropriate social context. Our general position is threefold. First, for an account of the causes or consequences of a scientific or technological development to be adequate, its pertinent micro and macro contextual factors should be scrutinized, individually as well as in terms of the possible influence relationships between them. Second, whether analyzing a micro or a macro context, attention should be given to two kinds of factors: the often subtle and relatively abiding cultural background features (e.g., enabling and transformative factors) of those contexts as well as more obvious and ephemeral foreground features (e.g., precipitating and first-order factors). Third, along with political-economic contextual factors—usually, but not always, foreground features—as well as ones having to do with the practitioners and technical systems involved, the conceptual framework of the cultural-environ-

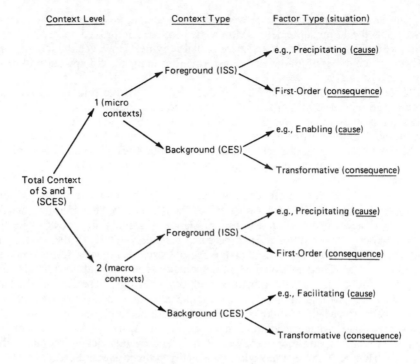

ISS = The foreground, or "Immediate Social System"
CES = The background, or "Cultural-Environmental System"
SCES = The composite "Social-Cultural-Environmental System," resulting
    from combining the ISS and the CES

Figure 4-2. The context of science and technology.

mental system provides a useful checklist of important background factors. Scrutiny of these factors is imperative for adequate comprehension of the genesis and consequences—and, for that matter, the nature and larger significance—of scientific or technological developments. Figure 4-2 summarizes the foregoing analysis of the context of science and technology.

ENDNOTES

1. One feature that has received attention is Bell Labs' long-standing organizational policy of interpreting broadly what counts as research "relevant" to its telecommunications mission. This gives its researchers greater latitude in choosing and pursuing projects—including ones that fall under what the firm calls "fundamental research"—and affords them occasions for considerable interaction with academic scientists, factors which seem to enhance employee morale and facilitate recruitment and retention.
2. See, for example, the study of life among biologists by sociologists Bruno Latour and Steve Woolgar (*Laboratory Life: The Social Construction of Scientific Facts* [Beverly Hills, Cal.: Sage Publications, 1979]); sociologist Sherry Turkle's study of communities of computer programmers and users (*The Second Self: Computers and the Human Spirit* [New York: Simon & Schuster, 1984]); and anthropologist Sharon Traweek's examination of high-energy particle-physics communities in Japan and the United States (*Beamtimes and Lifetimes: The World of High Energy Physicists* [Cambridge, Mass.: Harvard University Press, 1988]).

3. Ernest Braun and Stuart Macdonald, *Revolution in Miniature*, 2nd ed. (Cambridge: Cambridge University Press, 1982), p. 36.
4. Alex Inkeles, *What Is Sociology?* (Englewood Cliffs, N.J.: Prentice-Hall, 1964), p. 66.
5. See, e.g., David Kaplan and Robert A. Manners, *Culture Theory* (Englewood Cliffs, N.J.: Prentice-Hall, 1972), pp. 88–161.
6. Herbert Butterfield, *The Origins of Modern Science* (New York: Free Press, 1957), p. 202.
7. P. M. Harman, *The Scientific Revolution* (London: Methuen, 1983), pp. 8–9.
8. "Motive Forces of the New Science," in Robert K. Merton, *Science, Technology, and Society in Seventeenth Century England* (New York: Howard Fertig, 1970), pp. 80—111.
9. David S. Landes, *The Unbound Prometheus: Technological Change and Industrial Development in Western Europe From 1750 to the Present* (London: Cambridge University Press, 1969), p. 1.
10. Eric Hobsbawm, *Industry and Empire* (Hammondsworth: Penguin, 1969), p. 13.
11. David S. Landes, "The Industrial Revolution," in *Encyclopaedia Britannica*, 15th edition (Chicago: Benton, 1979), Macropaedia, vol. 6, p. 229.
12. *Ibid.*, p. 233.
13. See T. S. Ashton, *The Industrial Revolution: 1760–1830* (Oxford: Oxford University Press, 1968), p. 111.
14. Brian Easlea, *Witch-Hunting, Magic, and the New Philosophy* (Atlantic Highlands, N.J.: Humanities Press, 1980), p. 1.
15. P. M. Harman, *The Scientific Revolution*, p. 1.
16. *Family Planning Perspectives*, 13, no. 6, 1981, 254.
17. A. D. G. Gunn et al., *Oral Contraception in Perspective: Thirty Years of Clinical Experience With the Pill* (Park Ridge, N.J.: Parthenon, 1987), p. 45. Also see John A. Ross, ed., *International Encyclopedia of Population* (New York: Free Press, 1982), vol. 1, p. 109.
18. *Family Planning Perspectives*, 13, no. 6, 1981, 256–261.
19. *Family Planning Perspectives*, 17, no. 4, 1985, 186.
20. *Family Planning Perspectives*, 13, no. 6, 1981, 261.
21. *Ibid.*
22. *Family Planning Perspectives*, 15, no. 1, 1983, 136.
23. Carl Djerassi, "The Making of the Pill," *Science 84*, 5, no. 9, 1984, 127.
24. Pertti Pelto, *The Snowmobile Revolution: Technology and Social Change in the Arctic* (Menlo Park, Cal.: Cummings, 1973).
25. *Ibid.*, p. 161.

CHAPTER 5

THEORIES OF SCIENCE AND TECHNOLOGY IN SOCIETY

INTRODUCTION

Thus far, our treatment of science and technology has been short on theory. The discussion in Chapter 2 of the general natures of science and technology and our criticism of the notion that technology is just applied science are borderline exceptions to this generalization. The account in Chapter 3 of important distinguishing characteristics of contemporary science and technology has some theoretical implications, but the account itself is essentially descriptive. Although it provides a useful conceptual framework, the model of an appropriate context for analyzing technical developments elaborated in Chapter 4 is not a theory. With this shortage in mind, let us examine some influential *theories of science and technology in society*, in particular ones that supposedly shed light on the ways in which these forces develop in and affect society. The reason for such an examination at this juncture is not that theoretical analysis is an end in itself. Rather, the theoretical conclusions reached in this chapter inform the discussion of the interplay of science, technology, and modern society contained in Parts II and III of this book.

We will begin by considering the influential theory that technology has a life of its own—that is, the idea that it develops independently of outside attempts to promote or restrict it. Then, having rejected that claim, we will inquire into the factors that help explain technological and scientific innovation, a key feature of contemporary Western society. Next, we will explore another influential theory about technology—namely, that technology and technological change "determine" social change and structure. Finally, having found that theory inadequate, we will attempt to clarify on a theoretical plane the complex relationship between technical and social change.

AUTONOMOUS TECHNOLOGY

Humans like to think of themselves as having their hands firmly on the steering wheel and their feet ready to depress or release the accelerator and brake pedals of

72

the modern technological enterprise. However, many people, ordinary citizens and scholars alike, have the uneasy sense that technology develops autonomously. In a number of respects, the process of technological change in the modern world seems juggernaut-like, an irresistible force moving relentlessly forward but no longer controllable by humans. This process seems to many to be animated by a built-in force. It seems to' feed on itself, growing ever larger and gathering increasing momentum. Moreover, that growth and forward march seem unstoppable and irreversible. In short, the process of modern technological change presents itself to many observers as inherently dynamic, self-augmenting, and ineluctable.

Others find this view anathema and exert themselves to discredit it. For Glenn Seaborg, "Technology is not a juggernaut; being a human construction it can be torn down and modified at will."[1] Such individuals see the process of technological change as proceeding along a path consciously and more or less rationally chosen by human beings, one that is, moreover, alterable if appropriate decisions are taken. Is there, then, any validity to the influential notion of *autonomous technology*? Let us consider the views of the two thinkers most closely associated with this idea: Jacques Ellul and Langdon Winner.[2]

Despite his reputation, Ellul does *not* in fact believe that the directions, increasing momentum, and ever-expanding scope of the process of technological change are inevitable in any absolute sense. He purports only to be *describing* the way in which the process has been developing and predicting the way it will continue to develop—unless humankind can bring itself to intervene forcefully in the process: *"[I]f* man does not pull himself together and assert himself (or if some other unpredictable but decisive phenomenon does not intervene) [against the modern technological phenomenon], *then* things will go the way I describe."[3] Thus, for Ellul, although the process of technological change *appears* to be—and for some time has been and still is—autonomous in character, it is not *inherently* so.

Its perceived autonomy is due, for Ellul, partly to the fact that humans have abdicated their responsibilities to direct that process in more humane ways, and partly to important but contingent truths about modern Western society and culture. These truths, although recent historical arrivals, have already assumed the status of eternal verities: that Westerners (and, increasingly, non-Westerners) are predisposed in favor of technological innovation; that research and development have been institutionalized in the form of myriad competitive organizations devoted to the incessant creation and rapid dissemination of technical innovations; and that with the aid of huge, ever-growing reservoirs of knowledge, technics, materials, and techniques, technical innovations can be developed relatively systematically and rapidly. Nevertheless, however well entrenched these phenomena are in modern life, they could in fact be otherwise, although it might take a major military or economic catastrophe, profound transformation in cultural attitudes, or decisive religious intervention to effect that change.[4] This potential for change, however unlikely its realization, suffices to show that its autonomous character notwithstanding, the process of technological change is not inherently so.

Ellul's observations about the apparent inherent autonomy of the process of technological change suggest a further question: What additional factors help make the process of technological change, including the incessant creation and rapid diffusion of technological innovations, *seem as if it were intrinsically self-augmenting and ineluctable*—a perception which makes even selective opposition to this phenomenon seem futile to some tempted to intervene in it?

According to Robert Heilbroner, in the eighteenth and nineteenth centuries, the heyday of the British Industrial Revolution and its spread to continental Europe and the United States, not only "the initiation of technical improvement but its subsequent adoption and repercussion throughout the economy was largely governed by market considerations. As a result, both the rise and the proliferation of technology assumed the attributes of an impersonal diffuse 'force' bearing on social and economic life."[5]

A factor currently contributing to the sense of technological change as autonomous is the existence of intense national and international competition, be it political, economic, or social in nature. On the international level, such competition is sometimes compounded and fueled by distrust or insecurity. In North America, Western Europe, Japan, and the newly industrialized countries of the Far East, control over scientific and technological innovation is, to a significant degree, multipolar. Yet the outputs of these activities are unprecedentedly mobile. Thus, as survival and "thrival" are explicit or implicit values of all competitors, the attainment by one of an innovation that affords it a military, economic, or social advantage over its rivals virtually compels the latter to match or compensate for it. Similarly, decision by a nation to forego developing or using an innovation that it views as a mixed blessing is made difficult by the likelihood that some of its rivals will pursue it.

This dual situation greatly strengthens the impression that the process of modern technological (and, for that matter, scientific) change is ineluctable. Yet this state of affairs, however unlikely to change in the foreseeable future, might well be radically different. Such would be the case if there were a world political or economic authority entitled to decide which research projects to support at what funding levels and which innovations to accept and reject, and empowered to impose those decisions on all parties concerned. Under such circumstances the impression that the process of technological change is inherently autonomous would quickly fade.

Barring such an unlikely governmental reorganization, it is difficult to specify a set of plausible developments that would destroy once and for all the notion that the process of technological change, taken as a whole, is an ineluctable force unto itself. However, because of growing recognition of the unprecedented potency of contemporary science and technology and concern over the magnitude and scope of their influence, the problem of the social control of these forces has gained new visibility and urgency in recent decades.

Consider these statements: "Where will science and technology take us in the remaining years of this century?" and "We cannot understand all that the sciences...do to us without recognizing that only just before and during the Second World War did they begin to deliver the sorts of rewards we now require of them—and the dangers we have learned to dread."[6,7] Combatting the passive point of view reflected in such autonomistic questions and comments in the popular and semipopular media and intervening in the process of technological change on behalf of general societal well-being are, for some writers, vital tasks. Thus, for Ezra Mishan, "[T]he new way of thinking predicates itself on free will to the extent of reversing this logical sequence. We are to ask, that is, first what sort of society do we *wish* to establish, after which the consequences for science and technology are to be determined."[8] We shall return in Chapter 14 to the important topic of the social control of science and technology.

For Langdon Winner, autonomous technology encompasses all aspects of the process of technological change that are not products of "conscious decision" or under "intelligent control."[9] With this expanded notion, he delineates several noteworthy respects in which modern technology can be said to be autonomous or effectively "out of control." We will now briefly discuss three of these.

Fully aware that the dynamic modern technological enterprise reflects conscious decisions made by thousands of individual practitioners, Winner argues that, *taken as a whole*, its increasing specialization, complexity, scope, and rate of technical progress—phenomena he collectively dubs *technological evolution*[10]—are nevertheless not realistically subject to individual or societal control. No human agent can seriously hope to substantially affect any of these aspects of technological evolution. Even seminal contributions made by outstanding individual practitioners do not fundamentally alter the course of modern technological development, for the same achievements would have been realized by other parties in short order. For all practical purposes, in the above respects the modern technological enterprise evolves autonomously.

Second, Winner observes that to a great extent the result of modern technological change is an *accumulation of unintended and unanticipated consequences*, something which, remarkably, society makes minimal effort to control and to which it makes maximal effort to adapt. With respect to this phenomenon of *technological drift*,[11] modern technology is again effectively out of control, although, Winner suggests, it need not and should not be.

A third kind of technological autonomy analyzed by Winner arises from the embeddedness of contemporary technics in complex, unintelligible sociotechnical systems (Chapter 3). While recognizing the practical benefits such systems afford those with access to them, Winner is more concerned with the fact that these systems strongly condition and constrain the total way of life of contemporary industrial society, including its characteristic thought and behavior patterns, as well as its social and environmental relationships. This they do in many, sometimes subtle ways, often to problematic effect. Moreover, the extensive network of such systems confronts people born into twentieth century industrial society not as something that they may freely choose to adopt if they wish, but as an *imposed given* imbued with great inertia, a situation that makes effecting substantial change in the character of life virtually impossible. For Winner, the "loss of [human] agency" which results in an environment pervaded by complex, recalcitrant technological systems is a central, profoundly disturbing feature of contemporary industrial life.[12]

In sum, the notion of "autonomous technology" is an accurate and useful one for describing some important, contingent aspects of twentieth century technological development taken as a whole. However, that phrase is misleading when it is used to make claims about the supposed *inherent* character of the process of technological change and harmful insofar as it induces people to acquiesce in states of affairs that concern them but that, because of the phrase, they wrongly deem beyond their control.

THEORIES OF SCIENTIFIC AND TECHNOLOGICAL INNOVATION

If, as we have argued, technological and, by similar reasoning, scientific change are not inherently autonomous, how is the phenomenon of technical innovation to be explained? Let us examine some influential theories of technological and scientific innovation, arguably the most important source of social change in modern Western life.

It is essential to recognize at the outset that the term *innovation* is used in two different senses. It sometimes refers to "an idea, practice, or object that is perceived as new by an individual or other unit of adoption," such as a group or a whole society.[13] In this singular/plural or *product* sense of the term, one may speak of or refer to one or more innovations.

On other occasions, the word *innovation* is used to refer not to one or more new products or techniques but to a *process*—namely, that by which an innovation (in the first sense) comes into being and is distributed in a social system. In this section we will explore some of the leading theories put forth to explain four aspects of the total phenomenon of technical innovation. These four aspects result from considering two phases or stages of innovation life cycles—*creation* and *diffusion*—for two kinds of innovations—*scientific* and *technological* (see Figure 5-1).

The Creation of Innovations

Technological Innovation.   Over time, technological activity yields a variety of outcomes: Inventions are conceived, designs are formulated, new data are obtained, and new knowledge is generated. Some such changes appear to hold considerable potential for the creation of new or improved products, materials, systems, or techniques. Changes so viewed may undergo complicated, costly processes of development. If successful, they may yield technological innovations of one type or another, such as the videocassette recorder, a new heat-resistant ceramic material, a new computerized air-traffic-control system, or a mechanized automobile body welding or painting technique.

Innovation creation is often a complicated process. A good deal is known about factors that foster innovation and push or pull it in certain directions. In contrast, our understanding of the *nature* of innovation, while much improved in recent years, remains in need of further development. Readers are therefore cautioned to keep their theoretical expectations on a leash. With this caveat, we now turn to theories of innovation creation.

Not every innovation requires a new invention. Many involve only changes in design or materials. On the other hand, not all inventions become innovations. Many are set aside as impractical or inferior to existing alternatives. However, invention is unquestionably a leading source of innovation. We therefore begin this section by looking at theories of invention.

Figure 5-1. Aspects of the phenomenon of technical innovation.

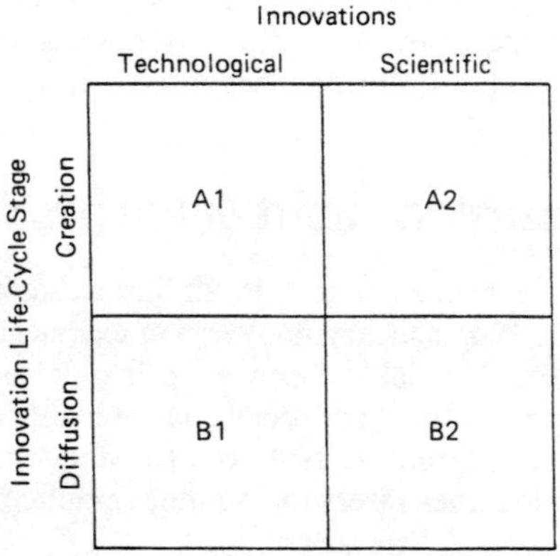

(1) *Invention.*   Inventions are devised by independent inventors as well as by individuals or teams of workers in university, government, or industrial facilities. In contemporary industrial society, most patents are awarded to organizations. However, the traditional independent inventor remains an important force. In 1988, some 77,924 patents were awarded by the U.S. Patent and Trademark Office. Of these, 14,264 (18.3 percent) went to independent investigators and the great bulk of the remainder to corporations.[14] The relative decline in the importance of the independent inventor and the institutionalization of invention in the research and development institution are major features of twentieth century inventive activity. Our treatment will therefore emphasize invention in institutional settings. We begin with factors affecting invention.

Factors that help to explain invention in modern Western society include (1) external pressures exerted by social and natural environments, (2) motives of inventors and related decision makers, and (3) flexibility in the face of chance discoveries.[15]

The directions in which inventive activity is pursued are often strongly influenced by *external pressures.* The origins of such pressures include scarcities in society's available resources, its military needs (particularly during wartime or states of heightened international tension), and governmental regulatory decisions that constrain or unleash private firms. In addition, as Dennis Gabor has pointed out, in contemporary society the direction of inventive activity is often affected not just by the desire to fulfill "primary needs or...archetypal wishes," but by the need to overcome problems associated with the implementation of prior technological inventions, as was the case with the invention of the air bag to protect passengers in car crashes.[16]

A second set of factors affecting invention involves the *motivations of inventors and other decision makers involved in inventive activity.* Inventors' motivations are heterogeneous. Far from always being economic or profit-oriented in nature, they may involve phenomena as diverse as difficult personal circumstances, aesthetic reactions, and curiosity. For example, Joseph-Armand Bombardier, the inventor of the "Ski-Doo" snowmobile, the first successful one-person snow vehicle, was prompted by personal circumstances to develop a machine that could travel rapidly over the snow, even under the most adverse winter conditions: His sick child had died while being taken to the hospital when snowdrifts made the journey by horse-drawn sled fatally slow. Felix Wankel's pursuit of what came to be called the rotary engine was ignited by the fact that he considered "the shaking and the pounding of the reciprocating piston engine unaesthetic compared with the running of a turbine or electric motor."[17] As for curiosity, one day in 1941, while he was walking in the woods near Geneva, Switzerland, Georges de Mestral's clothes became entangled in a patch of burrs. This led him to wonder what made the burrs cling so tenaciously to his clothing. Thus began a process of research and development that culminated in 1948 with the introduction of the revolutionary nylon fastening material, "Velcro."[18] Indeed, some people pursue inventive activity almost for its own sake—i.e., for its intellectual and organizational challenges.

The dominant motive of noninventor decision makers involved with inventive activity in private institutions is usually profit enhancement, sometimes short term, sometimes intermediate to long term. Managers tend to support areas of inventive activity that they deem likely to yield financial returns to their firms and thereby to advance their careers. Executives in large private firms sometimes support such activity because they believe it essential to the long-term survival of their firms or because they believe that such activity helps develop or preserve a progressive image useful for recruitment purposes.[19] At bottom, however, these motivations too are economic-competitive and commercial in nature. Their public-firm counterparts are typically motivated by the desire to promote the broad economic, military, and social welfare policies of the state, thereby enhancing their personal career prospects.

A third set of factors affecting the direction and rate of inventive activity has to do with *flexibility in the face of chance discoveries and experiences*. Invention is usually viewed as a highly planned activity, moving gropingly but resolutely from clear-cut market and technical needs or opportunities to inventions that help meet or exploit them. This is indeed often the case in large-scale firms. However, such needs and opportunities are not always discernible. Successful research and development organizations recognize that inventive activity can be kept on too tight a leash. Bell Laboratories, a fertile incubator of inventions in the twentieth century, has a tradition of allowing some of its researchers to pursue interesting phenomena discovered serendipitously in the course of mission-oriented research, even if such discoveries currently lack any visible economic-payoff potential.

In Donald Schon's words, the process of invention sometimes involves exploiting a phenomenon that "pops up" while someone is trying to do something else. Invention, "often pictured like a race, is more like exploring an unfamiliar coastline in a fog."[20] The process of innovation in institutional contexts may be optimized only if it retains a degree of flexibility sufficient to permit selective pursuit of unexpected, intriguing findings. Invention is as much the mother as the child of necessity. Witness, for example, the invention of the airplane early in this century.

The significance of these three kinds of influence factors should not be misinterpreted. They do not explain what is involved in *the actual occurrence* of invention, only why invention takes some directions rather than others and sometimes yields unanticipated results. Nothing said thus far bears on the important "internalist" question of *how* invention occurs when it does. For that we must consider selected theories of the *nature* of invention.

An illuminating account of technological invention in this sense is Abbott Payson Usher's theory of *cumulative synthesis*.[21] Since inventions involve insight, Usher puts at the base of his multilevel theory a model of "the emergence of novelty in the act of insight." He formalizes the individual act of inventive insight as "a genetic sequence of four steps" or phases: (1) the inventor's *perception of a problem*, the latter conceived as "an incomplete or unsatisfactory pattern" of relationships; (2) the *setting of the stage* for solving the problem (i.e., the making available to inventors, sometimes through little or no effort of their own, of all the ingredients required for achieving a solution); (3) *the occurrence of the critical act of insight* by which a problem solution is found; and (4) *critical revision*, the phase during which the solution—a new, now completed pattern—is "studied critically, understood in its fullness, and learned as a technique of thought or action." For Usher, both *discontinuities of thought and action* and *progressive intellectual synthesis* characterize the inventor's traversal of these four stages of insightful novelty production.

Although creative intellectual synthesis is essential to technological invention, dwelling on it is potentially misleading. Doing so tends to reinforce the entrenched "heroic theory of invention," according to which inventions are due to sudden breakthroughs by solitary individual geniuses. As against this potent stereotype, Usher defends the idea that an invention is best viewed as the outcome of *a social process*.

For example, the Wright brothers are generally credited with the invention of "the airplane" in 1903. However, while not without foundation, this attribution obscures several crucial facts. The process of invention for manned, powered, directionally controlled flight extends back at least to the early nineteenth century, to the pioneering theoretical and experimental work of Sir George Cayley. It also includes cumulating contributions by numerous other aeronautical researchers, such as Alphonse Pénaud, Clement Ader, and Otto Lilienthal.[22] In Usher's terminology, the "setting of the stage" for an ensuing invention is typically accomplished not by the ultimate inventor her- or himself but through a distinctly social process.

Indeed, crucial contributions to setting the stage for some inventions are sometimes made by investigators in fields far removed from and with no apparent relationship to the inventive activity in question. The Wright brothers embarked upon systematic study of manned, powered, directionally controlled flight in 1899. By then, Gottlieb Daimler's and Wilhelm Maybach's invention of a gasoline-fueled carburetor enabled the production of a practical internal combustion engine with a power-to-weight ratio sufficient to make powered flight possible.[23] Successful invention is sometimes partly fortuitous.

To underscore the fact that many inventions depend heavily on multiple instances of prior inventive activity, Usher adds a second level to his theory. He notes that the process through which each invention comes into being is one of "cumulative synthesis." Such a social process encompasses "a sequence of *strategic* inventions which draw together many different individual items of novelty as well as many familiar elements."[24] As a whole, the cumulative social process by which an invention such as the airplane—that is, a fixed-wing, heavier-than-air flying machine—or the reciprocating steam engine is realized also involves traversing Usher's four genetic stages, here on a macro level. Reaching any of these stages typically depends on a number of individual insightful contributions by other practitioners (e.g., prior strategic inventions).* *Each* such contribution is *itself* the outcome of some practitioner's having traversed Usher's four stages on some lower, micro level.

Thus, for Usher, while technological invention may in principle involve only a single four-stage process traversed by a single practitioner, it is typically a *cumulative social process*. This is particularly true in modern Western society, where inventive activity has largely been institutionalized in research and development facilities. In Usher's theory, technological invention has a multilevel, nested quality, involves the four genetic stages of novelty production *at each level*, and unfolds via "cumulative synthesis" of multiple strategic inventions.

In recent years, a related but more radical theory of the nature of invention has emerged. Inspired by a similar approach to the study of phenomena in everyday scientific activity, some sociologists have developed a *social constructivist approach* to the study of technological phenomena. Trevor Pinch and Wiebe Bijker, leading advocates of this approach, have analyzed what they call the "Social Construction of Technology."[25] Social constructivist approaches to the study of science stress the role of social factors in the "construction" of supposedly purely naturalistic scientific phenomena, such as particular facts and discoveries. Similarly, social constructivist approaches to the study of technology stress the role of social factors in the "construc-

*For example, Thomas Newcomen's atmospheric steam engine and James Watt's low-pressure steam engine are two of at least five strategic inventions synthesized in the reciprocating steam engine (Abbott Payson Usher, *A History of Mechanical Inventions* (Cambridge, Mass.: Harvard University Press, 1954), p.68).

tion" of supposedly purely objective or single-event technological phenomena, such as specific inventions and designs.

For example, Pinch and Bijker consider the case of the "invention" of the safety bicycle in the late nineteenth century. Using their approach, the authors disclose that, as in the case of the airplane, the invention of the bicycle was not an "isolated event" in 1884, but the outcome of a long(1879–1898), complex, multidirectional, conflict-laden, social developmental process. In the initial stages of that process, a number of *variants* of distinctly different design competed for adherents. Each variant presented one or more *problems* (safety, dress problems, vibration, increasing acceptance and use) to *relevant social groups* interested in it (women cyclists, elderly men cyclists, tourist and sports cyclists, anticyclists). For each such problem, various *solutions* were proposed (lower front wheels, trousers, air tires, ridicule and sabotage). In the wake of various *conflict-resolution processes*, each proposed solution was incorporated into a revised design, modified, or abandoned. This gradual selection process eventually culminated in the *stabilization* of the artifact.

> [While] at the beginning of this period the relevant groups did not see the "safety bicycle," but a wide range of bi- and tricycles...[b]y the end of the period, the word "safety bicycle" denoted a low-wheeled bicycle with rear chain drive, diamond frame, and air tyres. As a result of the stabilization of the artifact after 1898, one did not need to specify these details: they were taken for granted as the essential "ingredients" of the safety bicycle.[26]

The Social-Construction-of-Technology approach to invention "brings out the interpretive flexibility of technological artifacts and the role which different closure mechanisms may play in the stabilization of artifacts."[27] This approach helps explain the nature of technological invention by showing both that it is typically a (nonlinear) social process, not an event, and that *the very content and structure* of technological inventions of apparently "natural" or "logical" design is sometimes at least partly socially constituted—that is, influenced by conflicting social interests and the process by which they are resolved.

(2) *Innovation in General.*   We now turn to technological innovation proper. What are the most influential theories that have been put forward to explain the crucial phenomenon of technological innovation?

Recall the dual meaning of *innovation*: either a new product (e.g., an object, idea, or practice)—an innovation—or a process aimed at achieving an innovation—an innovation process. Technological innovations take the form of new or substantially modified technology-related products (e.g., technics, technic-related intellectual constructs, or materials), processes, and services (e.g., electronic funds transfer). These innovations are the outcomes of the creation or transformation of combinations of some or all of the following: inventions, discoveries, ideas, data, analyses, and bodies of knowledge. When complete, a technological innovation must be operationally practical; that is, it must be ready to be put to work.

The process of technological innovation is sometimes defined quite broadly; it has been described, for example, as "the set of actions that leads to actual adoption in practice of a device, machine, process or system."[28] This definition leads to the conclusion that "if no market (or use) exists for a product, [then] innovation, by definition, will not occur."[29] In contrast to this approach, I prefer to speak of two major phases of the life cycle of the products of technological innovation: *creation* and *diffusion*. The creation phase is that in which combinations of inventions, analyses, discoveries, knowledge, data, ideas, and the like are transformed into technological innovations ready to be put to work—whether or not they wind up actually being put to use. The creation of innovations is the central topic of this subsection.

The diffusion stage, which we will consider in greater detail later, encompasses everything having to do with getting technological innovations "out the door" and "into the hands" of end-users. This view allows one to speak of technological innovation as having occurred as long as such an innovation has in fact been *created*, even if its diffusion is negligible or nonexistent (i.e., even if it is a market failure). Although it has found a niche, given its enormous development costs, the Anglo-French *Concorde* supersonic transport airplane was a relative market failure. It cost its sponsoring countries hundreds of millions of dollars to develop, not one plane has been sold to another country, and profits from the few currently operated by British Airways and Air France do not even begin to recover prior outlays. The Bell System "Picture Phone" of the 1960s is an innovation that never even reached the marketplace. One may thus distinguish between innovation processes that are successful only from a technical point of view and those that are successful from both the technical and economic points of view.

As before, since contemporary innovation, even more than invention, is "a product of organized enterprise, not just of the individual with an idea,"[30] we will focus our discussion on industrial innovation.

What factors influence the process of technological innovation? For many scholars, the most important factor influencing industrial innovation is *market pull*. The phrase "market pull" is usually used as shorthand for the claim that by offering enhanced profit prospects, current or projected market demand for a new product (or new version of a current product) activates technological innovation aimed at realizing those prospects. More generally, innovations are seen by many analysts as "in some sense 'called forth' or 'triggered' in response to demands for the satisfaction of certain classes of 'needs.'"[31]

While scarcely denying the important role of market demand in the innovation process, and after scrutinizing a number of empirical studies purporting to confirm the decisiveness of this factor, Nathan Rosenberg concludes that "the now widely accepted bit of conventional wisdom concerning the primacy of 'demand-pull' forces in the innovation process is lacking in any persuasive empirical support."[32] For Rosenberg, "the role of demand has been overextended and misrepresented, with serious possible consequences for our understanding of the innovation process and of appropriate government policy alternatives to foster innovation." Rosenberg stresses the importance of a different societal factor: "the underlying, evolving knowledge base of science and technology." This plays a "central role" in innovation, meaning innovation activity as a whole. Indeed, "the supply of applicable science and technology" influences "the nature of the problems posed for innovative solution in the first place."[33] The importance of *technical-knowledge push* in relation to *market* or *demand pull* varies from one technological innovation to another. However, the relative importance of the knowledge-push factor appears to have increased in contemporary technological innovation as a whole. Whether it has achieved primacy is an open question.

At the *organizational* level, several factors play important roles in the creation of innovations. The existence of high-quality in-house research and development expertise appears on the surface to be a necessary condition for successful technological innovation. However, it is not. A firm with sufficient financial resources can purchase access to selected fruits of the research efforts of other, perhaps smaller firms not directly competing with it. What *is* necessary is *access to* a suitably rich and pertinent scientific and technological knowledge base, whether "imported" or developed "domestically." Of course, if it is imported, there must still be sufficient in-house capacity to absorb the foreign knowledge and turn it to productive account in the process of creating desired innovations. Thus, competent in-house development expertise is a bona fide requisite of successful industrial innovation.

Some scholars who recognize the important role of technical expertise in technological innovation place strong emphasis on "a successful marketing approach."[34] (I will reserve remarks on the marketing factor for our later discussion of the innovation diffusion stage.)

Donald Schon has stressed a different element within the firm as sometimes crucial in successful technological innovation: a "product champion."[35] This is an individual (or group) that so commits itself and its prestige to the cause of a proposed innovation that it overcomes neglect, competition from alternatives, managerial skepticism about feasibility or desirability, and general reluctance to proceed, so that its product eventually attains the status of a fully developed innovation.

Such individuals typically possess the intellectual ability to make nonobvious links between the nature or qualities of the proposed innovation and the structure of latent or future market demand. They must also possess attributes of intellect and personality sufficient to persuade management to sanction development of and assign adequate resources to the innovation project. Finally, they must possess organizational and personal skills adequate to mobilize and motivate the workers assigned to or enlisted for the project. The vital role of the "project champion" is vividly illustrated in Tracy Kidder's *Soul of a New Machine*, an account of the struggle in the Data General Corporation over a proposal to develop a new microcomputer. While not a necessary prerequisite for technological innovation in general, the "product champion" is an internal push factor that may be of particular importance when evidence of a suitable market is marginal at best or when the proposed innovation requires the firm to move in a new commercial or technical direction.

With the widespread concern in recent years over economic competitiveness, the problem of the *nature* of innovation, i.e., what is involved in the innovation process, has garnered increased attention. Industrial innovation has often been implicitly if not explicitly conceived as a linear process—one beginning with research, then proceeding to development, then marching on to production, and concluding with marketing. This *linear model* greatly oversimplifies the complexity of technological innovation.[36] It also has unfortunate policy consequences. These consequences flow from the erroneous belief that the only way to improve technological innovation and hence industrial competitiveness, is to foster the activity that the model wrongly suggests is its sole source—namely, "research," usually understood to mean *basic scientific* research.

In contrast, S. J. Kline's *chain-linked model* of industrial innovation better reflects the complexity and variability of that process.[37] His model contains seven elements: (1) market finding (assessment of the marketability of possible new products or new product features), (2) invention and analytic design, (3) detailed design and testing, (4) redesign and production, (5) distribution and marketing, (6) knowledge, and (7) research. These elements are linked via a complex pattern of *feedback and reciprocal influence relationships*. For example, market reaction to a diffused innovation often affects subsequent design, testing, and production activities. These relationships, "essential to effective innovation," are omitted in the linear model. Thus, technological innovation unfolds not along a single line, as suggested by the linear model, but via multiple, sometimes roundabout innovation "pathways" connecting the model's elements.

As against what the linear model implies, innovation does *not* typically begin with "research." Rather, Kline contends, it starts with invention or analytic design work and with calls on the "*totality of cumulated human knowledge*" for answers to open questions stalling progress in such work. Innovation initiates new research efforts—in process, production, and systems research as well as in scientific research—only when calls on the existing "storehouse of knowledge and systems" prove unsuccessful. Indeed, "[m]uch innovation proceeds with little or no input from current research." While research is critical for innovation as a whole, the existing "cumulated knowledge base and the systems built from it ...provide the primary *direct* inputs to current innovation."

Besides providing a better *descriptive* model of the process of industrial innovation, Kline's model suggests strategies conducive to *successful* technological innovation, such strategies include resisting investing all resources in basic scientific research and supporting (sometimes nonscientific) research in pertinent engineering activities as well (e.g., invention, analytical design, and production).

Among the most comprehensive and compelling causal explanations yet offered of Western technological innovation in general is Nathan Rosenberg's concept of the innovation system. For Rosenberg, the explanation of the modern West's remarkable record in technological innovation, a key ingredient in its level of economic development, has two parts. First, modern science has contributed handsomely to the creation and growth of the aforementioned knowledge.

> Western basic science created explanations of nature that possessed unprecedented potentialities for practical application—an achievement one may credit partly to the genius of Western scientists and partly to the constraints of the experimental method, which held their explanations closer to reality than the more freewheeling explanations of other societies.[38]

Second, "the West bridged the traditional gap between science and the economic sphere and translated scientific explanations into economic growth." It did so by developing

> what amounted to a *system for innovation*, first at the level of the firm and then at the level of the economy as a whole. The bridge was anchored at one end in industrial research laboratories invented to apply scientific methods and knowledge to commercial problems and, at the other end, in consumer purchase and use of a product or service embodying that knowledge. The West was unique in combining the manufacturing and marketing functions of the traditional business firm with centers of scientific knowledge under common management and with common goals and incentives.[39]

Although technology—and one of its key supportive social institutions, the industrial research laboratory—is "vitally important" to innovation in the modern West, it is "not the sole responsible agent." Rosenberg's model is particularly valuable for its integrated emphasis on four important social and cultural factors rarely brought together in explanatory accounts of technological innovation.*

---

*It is therefore congenial to our emphasis in Chapter 4 on setting science and technology in the context of the total sociocultural-environmental system (SCES) of the society in question.

First, the growing technical knowledge base could not have been transformed into innovations, and ultimately into continuing economic growth, if not for ideational cultural receptivity to the products of technological innovation and readiness to adopt them for everyday use. Second, innovators in the West enjoyed "a degree of freedom from political and religious interference that was unusual among major societies, if not unique." Third, the practical power to innovate was decentralized, a situation made possible by a Western economic institution: "the freedom to form new enterprises and change old ones, in whatever sizes and shapes seemed best adapted to the task at hand." And fourth, through its basic economic institution, the market, "the West conferred great rewards on those who innovated successfully and penalized those who did not." Thus, to summarize, while the evolving technical knowledge base was and is vital to technological innovation, a matrix of external social institutions and cultural attitudes provided a powerful incentive for expanding and applying that knowledge in pursuit of ongoing innovation.[40]

Scientific Innovation.   Much scientific activity is devoted to the generation of raw scientific data, preliminary formulation of hypotheses, conceptions of new possible ways of approaching a problem, or proposed experimental techniques for obtaining elusive desired data or physical conditions. Such outcomes may be usefully distinguished from other, more developed or mature results of scientific activity. These include well-founded knowledge of the existence of specific entities such as atomic particles, microorganisms, and celestial bodies; quantitative laws and models for which abundant confirmation is available; and techniques that have taken their place in the standard repertoire of scientific practice.

Discovery.   When first achieved, these and other established outcomes of scientific endeavors would seem to merit being regarded as genuine innovations in science. Perhaps the most important category of scientific innovations is that of scientific discoveries. "Discovery," asserted Norwood Russell Hanson, "is what science is all about."[41] In this section we will examine some important theories that have been advanced to explain scientific discovery. As we did with technological invention and innovation, we will attend both to factors deemed important in fostering efforts at scientific discovery and to factors supposedly involved in their actual achievement.

We will begin with the question of the *motivation* for pursuing scientific discovery. The one certain conclusion here is that the motives in question are many and varied, including curiosity about the natural world, response to intellectual challenge, and a wish to attain the degree of autonomy supposedly enjoyed by practitioners of basic scientific research.

In recent years, however, sociologists of science have focused attention on various more earthly, less "pure" motives: concern for social or occupational prestige, envy of competitors, wish to help meet an urgent need of society, desire for pecuniary rewards, memorial tribute to a deceased esteemed teacher or colleague, determination to preserve one's reputation, and the like. "The scientist," contends Bernard Barber, "is in no sense a 'selfless' creature above and beyond the influences of his social role."[42] Even within one person, multiple motives may be at work, their order of importance depending on, among other things, the individual's professional role.

Various *external factors* foster the development of science, thereby indirectly promoting scientific discovery. However, no single such factor, or unique weighted combination of same, accounts for the growth of science in all cases, for much scientific discovery has in fact been driven simply by one or more of the motives just noted.

Nevertheless, certain cultural value systems are clearly more conducive to the development of modern science than others. For Barber,

> [T]he high value the modern world puts on rationality as against traditionalism, on this-worldly activities as against other-worldly activities, on libertarianism as against authoritarianism, on active striving as against passive adaptation to the world, and on equality as against inequality—all these values support the development of the several components of science.[43]

Like technological innovation, social need, whether in military, health, or agricultural matters, has become an increasingly important impetus to scientific activity in this century. For example, the U.S. National Institutes of Health support an enormous scientific research effort aimed at understanding phenomena associated with public health problems, such as cancer and AIDS. As noted in Chapter 2, the relevance of scientific research to commercial endeavors was clearly recognized as long ago as the seventeenth century. However, the rise in the late nineteenth century and the enormous expansion in the early and mid-twentieth century of "science-based industries" has made business—hence economic concerns—as well as government prime factors in the growth of scientific activity, "basic" as well as "applied."

The growth of science was also facilitated by several social structural developments in the modern world. To begin with, a two-dimensional process of role differentiation took place. First, over time there emerged a specifically scientific—as against a philosophical or theological—realm or enterprise. Science, once called "natural philosophy," eventually became a realm unto itself. No longer was it a branch of a superior, more comprehensive, more ethereal enterprise. The importance of this development is that, in Barber's words,

> [t]he more that values, ideologies, aesthetic ideas, and philosophical ideas are distinguished both from one another and from substantive scientific ideas, the easier it is to see the special problems of each and to develop each and all of them.[44]

Not coincidentally, the word *scientist* was not coined until about 1840 (by the Reverend William Whewell), a development which tacitly recognized the acccomplishment of this role differentiation.

Second, role specialization also took place within science itself. This process, along with increases in sympathy for and resources devoted to training scientists in institutions of higher education, produced a greater number of researchers able to focus on a wider array of problems in a growing number of fields and subfields, something which could only heighten the volume of scientific discovery. This result would have been less consequential but for the gradual increase in Western society of social mobility and emerging commitment to equal opportunity. These developments allowed the growing number of institutionalized scientific roles to be increasingly occupied by individuals of demonstrated talent or promise from varying social origins.

An influential and provocative historical thesis relating changes in social structure to the rise of modern science, thereby fostering scientific innovation, is that of the German philosopher Edgar Zilsel. For Zilsel, the social structure of late medieval Europe effectively segregated the carriers of formally systematized rational modes of thought—university scholars and humanistic literati—from the repositories of experimental and observational techniques—groups of "superior artisans," including artist-engineers, surgeons, and makers of nautical, astronomical, surveying, gunnery, and musical instruments. As Zilsel notes, before 1600, "methodical training of intellect was preserved for upper-class learned people, for university scholars, and for humanists; experimentation and observation were left to more or less plebeian workers."[45] This gulf reflected the social elites' traditional attitude of disdain toward manual labor. With the coming of early capitalism, however, this polarization began to fade, particularly in city centers of capitalist production.

> About 1550, however, with the advance of technology, a few learned authors began to be interested in the mechanical arts, which had become economically so important, and composed Latin and vernacular works on the geographical discoveries, navigation and cartography, mining and metallurgy, surveying, mechanics, and gunnery. Eventually the social barrier between the two components of the scientific method broke down, and the methods of the superior craftsmen were adopted by academically trained scholars: real science was born.[46]

The intermingling of these modes of theory and practice bore rich fruit, as evidenced in the work of people like Gilbert, Bacon, and Galileo. For Zilsel,

> [t]he whole process [of synthesis] was imbedded in the advance of early capitalistic society, which weakened collective-mindedness, magical thinking, and belief in authority and which furthered worldly, causal, rational, and quantitative thinking.[47]

The Zilsel thesis leads directly to another "external" factor that early on gave (and still gives) great impetus to scientific discovery: the existing arsenal of technological devices. At the dawn of modern science the available arsenal was due in significant part to the efforts of Zilsel's artisanal class. The importance of the achievements of clock and lens makers in making possible the seminal work of Galileo, Snell, and Newton cannot be overemphasized. Similarly, the ever-expanding array of increasingly sensitive, efficient, accurate, and powerful instruments and machines—from spectrographs, automatic titration devices, high-frequency tissue homogenizers, and electronic scales, to Geiger counters, particle accelerators, computers, and scanning tunneling microscopes—has bulked large in many scientific discoveries attained in the modern and contemporary physical and biological sciences.

While these "fostering" and "enabling" factors help one understand the growth of scientific activity and progress, once again they shed no light on what is involved in the actual processes in which scientific discoveries are realized. Many theories purporting to explain scientific discovery in this sense fall into one of two types: mentalist and culturalist.[48]

Mentalist accounts of scientific discoveries represent them as outcomes of prior mental events or conditions that are held to be their decisive naturalistic causes. In many first-person accounts of scientific discovery, scientists relate dreams or dreamlike or abnormal states of mind in which key insights occurred to them. For example, the hexagonal structure of benzene molecules became apparent to Friedrich August Kekulé while he was staring, half asleep, into his fireplace. Imagining that the flames were snakes, he "saw" one bite its own tail, forming the hexagonal ring.[49] Such accounts indicate that the process of scientific discovery is not always rational. However, they do not disclose the mechanism by which such discoveries are achieved—only the unusual circumstances under which the mechanism may be activated.

Perhaps the most influential, basically mentalist account purporting to shed light on the nature of the mechanism of scientific discovery is that of Thomas Kuhn. For Kuhn, a scientific discovery is not a single event that happens to an individual at a specifiable time and place. Rather, a scientific discovery is the culmination of a social process that begins with a scientist doing "normal science"—that is, science carried out within the confines of and in the manner prescribed by the reigning "paradigm" in her or his field.* An example of such a paradigm would be Newtonian physics in the field of classical mechanics. In the course of doing normal science, a scientist may sometimes make an observation or reach a conclusion that is deeply at odds with the reigning paradigm (i.e., one which runs counter to what the paradigm would lead the practitioner to expect).

Examples of influential paradigm-disrupting phenomena include (1) the results of experiments showing that the current induced from a metal emitter is proportional to the intensity of the incident light (the "photoelectric effect"), a finding that revealed the inadequacy of the classical electromagnetic theory of light for atomic physics and gave rise to the photon theory of light; and (2) the 42-seconds-of-arc-per-century deviation in the perihelion of Mercury, which violated the expectations of scientists adhering to the paradigm of Newtonian physics and paved the way for Einstein's general theory of relativity, which explained the observed deviation.

Occasionally, such a troubling phenomenon stubbornly resists all efforts to dismiss or explain it in terms of the existing paradigm, albeit perhaps in refined form. It then achieves the status of being a bona fide "anomaly" to the now-threatened paradigm and precipitates a search, at least by some scientists, for a radically new conceptual model—part of the revolutionary new paradigm-to-be—which accommodates the anomaly. To Kuhn, who limits scientific discoveries worthy of the name to conceptual advances, discoveries originate with the recognition of paradigmatic anomalies. For that to occur, the scientist must possess sufficient "skill, wit, or genius to recognize that something has gone wrong in ways that may prove consequential."[50] Given sufficient development of scientific instruments and concepts "to make the emergence of anomalies likely and to make the resultant anomaly recognizable as a violation of expectation,"[51] it is the aforementioned intellectual capacity that holds the key to the occurrence of scientific discoveries.

In contrast to mentalist accounts, culturalist theories represent scientific discoveries as culturally determined—that is, as caused by aspects of social or cultural growth. Mental phenomena, crucial to the first family of explanations, are viewed here as being of only incidental importance to the achievement of discoveries. In their

---

*By *paradigm* here, Kuhn means the "disciplinary matrix" or ensemble of intellectual commitments common to most practitioners of the discipline in question at a given point in time. The elements of this matrix include the formalized or readily formalizable "'symbolic generalizations' ... deployed without question or dissent by group members," be they expressed in symbolic form (f = ma) or word form ("for every action there is an equal and opposite reaction"); shared beliefs in particular models, literal or heuristic; shared values regarding the practice of the discipline and the evaluation of theories; and "exemplars," concrete problem solutions encountered by students in their science education and even by advanced practitioners in their postdoctoral research and early careers. These exemplary problem solutions (e.g., solutions to inclined plane, conical pendulum, Keplerian orbit, and elementary Schrodinger equation problems) "show them by example how their job is to be done" (Thomas S. Kuhn, *The Structure of Scientific Revolutions*, pp. 182–187).

heyday in the early twentieth century, purely cultural theories of scientific discovery served as a useful counterweight to earlier theories stressing the primacy of the heroic genius in scientific discovery.

Scholars in the cultural-theory tradition support their approach indirectly. They cite evidence supposedly showing that numerous scientific discoveries were actually made independently and simultaneously by multiple researchers. (Robert Merton argued that *all* discoveries were "in principle" multiple.) It is then held that it would be singularly implausible to explain this pattern of multiple discovery as the result of the coincidental expression of genius or any other mental attribute. Hence, it must be that for each such discovery, its time had come. A certain stage in cultural growth or maturation had been reached, something which, "given a certain level of mental ability," made the discovery "virtually inevitable as certain kinds of knowledge accumulated in the cultural heritage and as social developments directed the attention of investigators to particular problems."[52]

In this view, both intellectual capacities and immediate social concerns are regarded as being, at best, immediate precipitating or enabling factors. The society's or culture's accumulated knowledge base is deemed the decisive background condition. However, while scientific discovery, like technological invention, surely requires an appropriate multidimensional base of knowledge, technics, techniques, and so on, the presence of such a base is by no means sufficient for the achievement of scientific discovery. Moreover, in the absence of solid evidence of what *proportion* of scientific discoveries in, say, the last few centuries are bona fide multiples, the relevance of mentalistic factors cannot be so readily devalued or dismissed.[53]

Physicist and historian of science Gerald Holton has elaborated an interesting semimentalist–semiculturalist model of scientific discovery. He argues that crucial to a number of seminal scientific discoveries has been the existence of "themata." Themata are "pre-theoretical suppositions about nature: for example, that it is mathematically harmonious, that it is composed of fundamental units, or atoms, that it is mechanically integrated like a clock, that natural forms are symmetrical, inherently aesthetic, etc."[54]

Such primal suppositions are brought by scientists *to* their work, not derived *from* it. Holton notes that essential to Einstein's formulation of special relativity theory was not the empirical work of Lorentz and Michelson but the fact that the asymmetry of Maxwell's equations violated the thema that natural forms are symmetrical and inherently aesthetic, something that should be reflected in equations purporting to accurately describe physical reality.

These themata are not part of the evolving scientific knowledge base that in some culturalist theories makes scientific discoveries virtually inevitable. However, these notions are part of an evolving stock of nonscientific, culturally generated and transmitted notions; in other words, they are part of a society's cultural heritage. However, mentalist concerns would seem to enter in here as well. Surely Einstein's mental abilities were crucial in discerning the conflict between one or more of these subtle themata and the asymmetric form of Maxwell's equations, to mention nothing of the effort involved in elaborating an alternative theory reflecting these presuppositions.

A more mundane but undeniably important factor in scientific discovery is chance or accident. For example, in 1856 the British chemist William H. Perkin set to work to learn more about chemical reactions that might prove useful in synthesizing natural organic compounds, such as the medicinal and tonic quinine. Using aniline as a starting point and employing "the then popular additive and subtractive method,"[55]

Perkin produced, not quinine, but a black sludge. The exploratory addition of alcohol, however, produced a deep violet solution that, he discovered, could dye silk a brilliant mauve. This accidental discovery launched the coal-tar-based synthetic dye industry and led to Kekulé's aforementioned discovery of the hexagonal structure of benzene.

The last account of scientific discovery we will consider is an ingenious and subtle extension of work in the 1970s by British sociologists of science on "cognitive" elements of science. Known as *social constructivism*, this approach to the sociology of science parallels the more embryonic social constructivist view of technology illustrated earlier in Pinch and Bijker's analysis of the invention of the safety bicycle.

Social constructivists scrutinize the actual theories, decisions, practices, and other internal cognitive aspects of science that are of everyday interest to working scientists. Their general objective is to see what factors of a social nature are involved in the constitution of such phenomena (and their being regarded) *as* scientific theories, decisions, practices, or discoveries. Consider, for example, the social constructivist approach to the last item: scientific discoveries. Rather than accepting talk by scientists of their discoveries at face value, as if it were straightforward and referred solely to certain kinds of claimed findings by scientists, social constructivist Augustine Brannigan's "attributional model of scientific discovery" treats scientific discovery as "social production"—that is, as a profoundly social process.[56]

The key question for Brannigan is not, as in naturalistic accounts, how the events associated with scientific discoveries come to pass. Rather, it is how certain scientific innovations come to acquire the quite different, more elevated status of (being regarded as) scientific discoveries. For Brannigan, a scientific discovery is not such on its own or in and of itself, but only as the result of a certain kind of social process. In particular, a scientific innovation is accorded the status of a scientific discovery in a social group only when dispute in the group has been resolved to a point where there is general agreement that (1) the innovation was achieved in a research context, (2) the claims about nature associated with it are true, and (3) no competitor plausibly claiming precedence exists. "[Scientific] discoveries do not occur as discrete, causally explicable events. [They] are *context-dependent categorizations* made by groups of participants *in pursuit of their own practical objectives*."[57] The concept of scientific discovery, like the concept of prestige, is allegedly a "community concept"; in other words, it cannot sensibly be applied to a solitary individual in a social vacuum. Rather, it has a built-in subtle reference to a social group.[58] However, we objectify the essentially social construct of the scientific discovery until it "comes to *appear to be* a natural fact of life" like the genuinely naturalistic events, processes, and acts to which it purports to refer.[59]

This radical sociological account is a useful counterweight to the mentalist, culturalist, and hybrid models discussed earlier. It sheds considerable light on one element of scientific discourse usually viewed "in straightforward positivist fashion" as utterly unproblematic: the phenomenon of scientific discovery. However, to acknowledge that what a scientific or lay community recognizes as scientific discoveries are so partly because of the outcomes of often conflict-laden processes is not to deny that certain investigators "really do" make bona fide discoveries regardless of whether or not society acknowledges them as such. The concept of scientific discovery is not a *pure* community concept as the concepts of face and prestige are.

More generally, the conceptual framework offered by any single discipline in the natural or social sciences is unlikely to provide a fully adequate explanation of the occurrence of any complex social phenomenon. A multidisciplinary approach is needed to compensate for the often fruitful selective blinders employed by each single disciplinary or subdisciplinary approach. A plausible model of scientific discovery should therefore include mental and social aspects as well as the element of chance, recognize the role of processes of social recognition, and stress that the importance of each kind of factor varies from one discovery situation to another.* Emphasis on the nature of the mechanism(s) of discovery need not obscure the importance of motivation, intellectual capacity, external enabling conditions, and push or pull forces as complementary causal factors. Given the richness and variability of scientific discovery, it is unrealistic to expect a single universally valid theory, much less one entirely enclosed within the confines of a single traditional discipline. What can and should be done is to ensure that all major factors and mechanisms that play important roles in scientific discovery, whether as fostering or enabling factors or in the actual discovery-making or discovery-constituting process, are clearly identified and carefully elaborated.

Diffusion of Scientific and Technological Innovations

The second major phase of the life cycle of (many, but not all) scientific and technological innovations is that of *diffusion*: "the process by which an innovation is communicated through certain channels over time among the members of a social system," such as a city, profession, group, or national or international society as a whole.[60]

Everett Rogers specifies four "main elements," or variables, in this definition: the innovation itself, the communication channels through which its diffusion takes place, time, and the social system in which the process takes place.[61] Let us briefly discuss each of these elements, and then consider how they apply to the diffusion of scientific and technological innovations. Again we will see that there is no tidy, universally valid theory or model of innovation, scientific or technological. However, a number of factors whose relative importance varies from situation to situation affect the natures and outcomes of diffusion processes, including their rates, directions, and scope.

Certain characteristics of *the innovation itself*—or characteristics closely related thereto—can powerfully affect the diffusion process. These characteristics include (1) the degree of improvement it offers over the idea, product, or process (if any) it is bidding to replace; (2) its cost (and thus its affordability); (3) its perceived complexity of understanding or use; (4) its "revocability" (i.e., the degree to which it may be adopted experimentally on a trial basis, rather than only totally and irreversibly); and (5) its "observability" (i.e., the degree to which an in-place innovation or its results are visible to others yet to adopt it).[62]

Among the features of *the communications channel(s)* that may affect diffusion processes are the scope of the audience reachable in a given time period through the channels used and the nature of the message realistically transmittable through the

---

*Kuhn, who, as noted, put considerable emphasis on mentalist prerequisites—"the individual wit, skill, or genius" to recognize anomalies — also recognized the importance of cultural considerations: "anomalies do not emerge from the normal course of scientific research until both instruments and concepts have developed sufficiently to make their emergence likely and to make the anomaly which results recognizable as a violation of expectation" (Kuhn, "Historical Structures of Scientific Discoveries," *Science*, 136, June 1, 1962, 763). This development of instruments and concepts is clearly a cultural outcome or product.

chosen channels (e.g., commercials on mass media channels versus face-to-face conversations "over" interpersonal channels). Closely related to the nature of the communications channels employed is the nature of the relationship between the message sender and recipient. Is the sender someone who has previously adopted the innovation or is represented as having done so? Is the claimed prior adopter merely recognized by or personally known and trusted by the potential adopter?

The element of *time* is a significant aspect of diffusion processes in several ways. Temporal duration is an important aspect of the "innovation-decision process": that process through which an individual passes from first knowledge of an innovation to confirmation of a preceding decision to adopt or reject it. Time is also crucial in assessing an individual's innovativeness, or how relatively early or late the individual adopts an innovation compared with other members of the social system in question. Time is an essential variable in assessing the rate of adoption and penetration of an innovation in a social system, something measurable by determining either the absolute number or the percentage of individuals in the system who have adopted the innovation by the conclusion of a given time period (e.g., 50,000 or 10 percent in the first year).[63] The speed with which an innovation is adopted and diffused throughout a social system is often an important determinant of its sociocultural consequences.

Finally, *the social system*, or, as we dubbed it in Chapter 4, the total social-cultural-environmental system (SCES) of the group or society in question, is an important variable affecting the nature and outcome of diffusion processes. For various historical, social, cultural, economic, and environmental reasons, certain societies as wholes and some groups in a given social system are decidedly more receptive to adopting innovations than others. For similar reasons, perhaps ones having to do with varying distributions of innovation-related personality traits, the same is true of certain subgroups within a given group.

Now let us consider how these factors apply to technological and scientific innovations.

Diffusion of Technological Innovations.   The diffusion of technological innovations in modern Western societies depends critically on a number of economic, sociological, and political features of the total SCES. Diffusion is greatly fostered by the existence of formidable corporate marketing divisions, societywide distribution, sales, and service organizations and networks, and mechanisms for extending consumer credit. These relatively recent institutional innovations of capitalist enterprise were virtually required by the unprecedented productive capacity and cost of modern systems of mass production. Without such organizations and mechanisms, the operation of such systems could not have been sustained.[64] The determined effort of marketing divisions to find or, if necessary, create new or expanded markets for the never-ending procession of technological innovations, partly by designing messages for targeted audiences and delivering them through mass media channels, is a salient, characteristic facet of the diffusion process in contemporary Western society. Numerous strategies, often based on extensive psychological research, are used for cultivating or exploiting consumer dissatisfaction. These include stoking the embers of envy ("the Jones effect"), proliferating felt needs, and attempting to insert new products between psychic itches and scratches.[65]

Technological diffusion also often hinges critically on a number of sociological considerations. For example, recruitment of prestigious individuals or corporate entities as early adopters of an innovation may set off a "learning process" in which numerous others take their cues from these "opinion leaders." Thus, some companies opt for an innovative technology or system to no small degree because firms perceived as technological leaders have already done so.

A second sociological factor is that of "value compatability." The diffusion of innovations like the motorbike and the "Walkman"-type personal stereo is greatly facilitated by the fact that they are perceived to be consistent with established values of the social setting in question; such values might include mobility, individualism, and convenience. Conversely, diffusion is hindered to the degree that an innovation is perceived to be antithetical to reigning social values, as a technic like the oral contraceptive pill is in certain predominantly Roman Catholic countries.

A feature of contemporary Western culture that is critical to the diffusion of technological innovations is the existence of a powerful ideational cult of the new. According to this notion, newer, like bigger, is better. Any adopted innovation supposedly has only a limited lifetime before it becomes hopelessly out of date and inferior to newer, currently available models. It is common knowledge that this mentality is promoted intensively by corporate marketing divisions as well as that many private firms reinforce this idea by building "planned obsolescence" into their products. While the socioeconomic motivation for this strategy is apparent, less evident is the fact that promotion of this predilection for the new is also driven by a technical consideration: the ability of an advanced technological system of mass production to turn out on an annual (or more frequent) basis myriad units of "new, improved" models of numerous products. Were such a system used to turn out far fewer nonobsolescent products, productive capacity would not be sufficiently used, investment would not be quickly recovered, and profits would probably plummet.

The diffusion of technological innovation sometimes depends critically on considerations of domestic or international politics. A government may decide to attempt to *limit* the export of certain kinds of innovations, particularly those believed to have great military or economic significance. In attempting to preserve its competitive edge, from the late eighteenth to the mid-nineteenth centuries England forbade the export of any of its innovative textile machines (as well as machine plans and skilled craftsmen) to the United States. For reasons of politics, the U.S. government has for years attempted to prevent the export of certain kinds of high-technology products to East European countries, while its Soviet counterpart severely limited the diffusion of personal computers in the Soviet Union.*

Diffusion of Scientific Innovations.   The diffusion of scientific innovations is a function of, among other things, their nonmaterial character (ideas, data, knowledge, models, laws) as against the material character of many, if not most, technological innovations. It is not clear, however, whether, all things considered, the diffusion of scientific innovations is easier because of considerations of reproducibility, portability, and the tradition in science of open exchange, or more difficult because it is sometimes easier to keep information secret than it is to keep material items secret.

Notable in the case of scientific innovations is the complex network of communications channels through which they are diffused. These channels include not only formal vehicles such as scientific journals, professional meetings, abstract services,

---

*Conversely, innovation diffusion is sometimes vigorously *promoted* by governments for domestic or international political or economic reasons. For an example, see Chapter 13.

and publication preprints, but also informal channels, such as professional grapevines (facilitated by the telephone and the facsimile machine).

There are, of course, countervailing factors that hinder the diffusion process. These often involve aspects of the total SCES in which the diffusion process is unfolding. For example, vested economic and political interests, reflected in terms like *trade secrets, proprietary knowledge,* and *classified research* often, perhaps increasingly, serve to retard the diffusion of scientific innovations, albeit on grounds of protecting "the national interest."

Sociologically, one of the more interesting analyses of barriers to the (rapid) diffusion of scientific innovation is due to Kuhn. As noted earlier, he argues, in effect, that the diffusion process is sometimes impeded by the intense commitment of communities of scientists doing "normal science" to the reigning disciplinary paradigms in their respective fields.[66] Exposure to the innovation being diffused, even if buttressed by apparently strong evidence, is often insufficient to ensure a short "*innovation-decision period.*"[67] (Kuhn does not lament this phenomenon. He merely identifies and explains it by reference to the reigning paradigm and social psychological considerations.)

As with technological innovation, the nature of the total social system into which a scientific innovation is introduced is often crucial to the course and outcome of the diffusion process. Such was the case with Darwin's theory of evolution, perceived as incompatible with core Christian beliefs and values, and the over-300-year period that elapsed before the Catholic Church accepted the validity of Galileo's heliocentrism. On the other hand, the commitment of mainstream modern Western culture to the core Enlightenment beliefs that scientific knowledge is a good thing and that the more widely it is diffused the better for the individual, society, and humanity in general has long encouraged the diffusion of scientific innovation and served as ammunition against attempts to restrict that process.

The growing tension between cultural spurs to and political-economic brakes on the diffusion of scientific ideas is vividly reflected in a contemporary controversy unfolding in American universities. The cherished tradition of free scientific inquiry and unrestricted public access to its results is being put to the test. Pressure has grown in recent years to place limitations on access to the results of selected university research projects funded by industrial or governmental groups.

TECHNOLOGICAL DETERMINISM

Having examined some factors involved in the genesis and diffusion of technical innovation, the following question naturally arises: To what extent is society determined by its technology? More precisely, to what degree does the existing structure of a society depend on its technological base, and to what degree does the nontechnical change that occurs in a society depend on its existing technology and on prior technical change that unfolds in that society? The most famous—to some, noxious—answer to these questions is provided by the theory of *technological determinism* (TD). Whereas autonomous technology is a notion focusing on technological change per se, TD concerns the relationship between technology and society. In particular, it bears on the issue of "the influence of the machine on social relations."[68]

At the outset, a critical distinction must be made. The theory of TD is interpreted in at least two ways. First, some construe it as the strong claim that the technical base of a society "determines"—that is, causally sets the form or configuration of—social existence. This point of view is often ascribed to Karl Marx* because of famous statements of his such as the following:

> In acquiring new productive forces men change their mode of production, and in changing their mode of production they change their way of living—they change all their social relations. The hand-mill gives you society with the feudal lord; the steam-mill, society with the industrial capitalist.[69]

More recently, historian R. J. Forbes expressed a similar viewpoint:

> Technology can no longer be viewed as only one of the many threads that form the texture of our civilization. With a rush in less than half a century it has become the prime source of material change and so determines the pattern of the whole social fabric.[70]

In Marxism, innovations in the forces of production shape social relations. Thus, this first, strong version of technological determinism is one aspect of the Marxist doctrine of historical materialism.[71] In this version, technological change is viewed as both a necessary and a sufficient condition determining all other social change, a doctrine sometimes called *hard technological determinism* (HTD).

The second, weaker version of the theory of technological determinism is that "changes in technology are the single most important source of change in society."[72] This version allows that there are or may be sources of social change other than changes in technology, but contends that they are less important than the technological sources, perhaps because technological changes *catalyze* or *precipitate* the social changes in question. Some proponents of this version, or qualified variants thereof, add that without such admittedly less important sources or factors, the social change in question would not have occurred (at least not when it did). Here technological changes are viewed as necessary but *not* by themselves sufficient conditions for the occurrence of the related social changes, a doctrine sometimes called *soft technological determinism* (STD).

What truth, if any, is there in the notion of TD, in either of its versions? Regarding HTD, it simply is not true that identical technological changes by themselves effect the same social changes or result in the establishment of the same social relations in all societies in which they are introduced. Two societies with the same or similar technological bases can and sometimes do nonetheless differ significantly in their basic attitudes, values, artistic styles, and legal and political systems. New technologies that emerge in a society *do* determine the *range* of options for changing the parameters of the field on which the game of life is played in that society.[73] However, which of those possibilities are actualized depends, among other things, on the prior reigning matrix of values, traditions, social structures, and political forces in the society in question. This matrix differs from society to society and typically varies over time.

Put differently, the possibilities that are adopted by a particular society are a function of *both* the technological changes in question *and the specific "initial conditions" that obtain in the particular society under study*. The United States, Norway, and Japan have roughly the same technological base, in the sense that the sets of technologies that they use or to which they have access do not radically differ.

---

*In recent years this attribution has been challenged. See, e.g., Donald MacKenzie, "Marx and the Machine," *Technology and Culture*, 25, no. 3 (July 1984), 473–502.

However, they are very different societies; that is, their respective sets of social relations differ markedly—which is not to say that they do not overlap in significant ways. Hence, the introduction of the same technological innovation in the three societies is apt to have different consequences, as, for example, in the case of technologies of workplace automation.

Setting certain "high-cultural" aspects of society aside (e.g., aspects having to do with artistic and philosophical expression), Robert Heilbroner argues for the considerably more limited thesis that

> the prevailing level of technology imposes itself powerfully on the structural organization of the productive side of society....We cannot say whether the society of the computer will give us the latter-day capitalist or the commissar, but it seems beyond question that it will give us the technician and the bureaucrat.[74]

However, even this more limited thesis leaves open the possibility that *not all* aspects of the productive side of society are strictly determined by the "prevailing level of technology." While certain general features of the production system may be "determined" (required) by the technology adopted, a measure of indeterminacy may remain in certain other, more specific features. The outcomes that emerge in different production situations using the same technological base may hinge on the differing mixes of historical, cultural, or political factors present. Japanese-style worker "quality circles," however desirable, are not "determined" by contemporary advanced production technology.

As for STD, the thesis that "changes in technology are the single most important source of change in society," some qualifications and caveats are in order. First, while technological changes have exerted a powerful influence on society throughout history, there have been other nontechnological changes that have done likewise; take, for example, the rise, spread, and conflict of religious and political ideals such as Christianity, Islam, Marxism, and democracy, and the occurrence of plagues and climatic and demographic changes. The STD thesis seems most plausible if restricted to twentieth century Western society. Second, as we will see in Chapters 6 through 12, *scientific* as well as technological changes have played an increasingly important role in engendering social changes in the twentieth century West. Let us posit that *technical change* has been the most important factor in social change *in the last century in the West*, perhaps even as early as 1800. Third, even when thus qualified, the STD thesis is not susceptible to firm empirical confirmation; judgment about the relative influence of technical and other factors inevitably comes into play.

None of the foregoing should be taken as an argument that technological change, while a crucial element in the process that has radically transformed the contours of modern society, was ever or is now independent of social factors. On the contrary; as we have seen in this chapter—and will stress throughout this book—technological activity, especially in the modern period, is itself a *profoundly social phenomenon*. Its directions, pace, priorities, methods, resources, design specifications, successes, and failures depend on, among other things, extant or projected political-economic incentives or disincentives, as well as on the evolving (partly cultural) "initial conditions" that obtain in society. For example, as we noted in Chapter 4, the rise of capitalism fostered the development of industrial technology in eighteenth century England. Similarly, the shortage of nonfarm labor spurred technological innovation in the nineteenth century United States. More recently, the 1986 U.S. Tax Reform Act's elimination of investment tax credits, decrease of depreciation allowances for plant and equipment, and failure to include comprehensive tax write-offs for research and development expenses constitute disincentives to private-sector technological development in the United States.

Belief that technological and, more recently, scientific-cum-technological changes have been perhaps the most powerful driving forces for social change in the last century is compatible with recognition that the process of technical change is itself conditioned by social factors. A *complex, iterative feedback relationship* exists among scientific, technological, and social changes in modern times. But for its existence, any hope of achieving real societal control of science and technology would be futile—not that that truth is by itself any evidence of the feasibility of that goal.

As with autonomous technology, technological determinism—the general notion that machines are determinants of the shape of society—has in the minds of many taken on the status of an eternal verity. It is more accurately seen, in Heilbroner's words, as "peculiarly a problem of a certain historic epoch—specifically that of high capitalism and low socialism—in which the forces of technical change have been unleashed, but when the agencies for the [public] control and guidance of technology are still rudimentary."[75]

Let us summarize. First, if we restrict ourselves to certain general relationships directly concerned with the process of production itself, ones having to do with, for example, the general occupational composition of the labor force and the general hierarchical organization of work, we agree with Heilbroner that "the technology of a society imposes a determinate pattern of social relations on that society."[76] This means nothing more mysterious than that the adoption and use of such technology gives rise to or requires the pattern in question. Beyond the realm of production, however, technology often exercises an important, but not determinative, influence. This is the quite limited (but still important) element of truth in HTD. Second, STD is a plausible thesis if and only if it is qualified as above. However, even then, it is destined to elude definitive confirmation.

As with the idea of autonomous technology, however, in neither STD nor HTD, qualified or not, is the technical change in question independent of social considerations: The activities and products of science and technology on the one hand and society on the other reflect each other's influence in many ways and on many levels.

THE RELATIONSHIP BETWEEN TECHNICAL CHANGE AND ENSUING SOCIAL CHANGE

The theory of technological determinism seriously misrepresents the relationship between technical and ensuing (nontechnical) social change. That social change is a *joint* product of the technical change in question *and* the "initial social conditions" under which the technical change is introduced. However, that conclusion, though valid, is too general to be of much use in clarifying thinking about the technical-change/ensuing-social-change (TCESC) relationship. The task of this section, therefore, is to see what of a more specific nature can be said on a theoretical plane to shed light on this obscure but important relationship.

To this end, we will first describe a general heuristic model that helps explain how the initiating technical change and the initial social conditions combine to produce the eventual social change outcome. Then, we will explore a second heuristic model. This model incorporates specific aspects of the concrete change process that mediate the initial technical change and the ensuing social change and that are affected by the initial social conditions. Effecting changes in these mediating aspects is the way in which the initial social conditions help to bring about the social change outcome.

The Equilibrium–Disequilibrium Model of Technically Induced Social Change

For convenience, we will focus our attention here on the cultural-environmental system (CES), with its five component subsystems (the ideational, societal, material, personality and behavior, and environmental sectors). Similar remarks apply to the more complex SCES.

Prior to the introduction of a technical change into a society, the elements of the society's CES typically exist in dynamic equilibrium. Usually they have previously worked out some form of more or less peaceful coexistence. The entrance of a scientific or technological development onto the social scene typically opens up *new behavioral or intellectual possibilities* for its users or adopters. In contrast, users or adopters may also be subject to *new behavioral or intellectual requirements*. These changes—requirements as well as possibilities—may well be consonant with the CES, as, for example, in the case of the audiocassette recorder. Often, however, these changes are in tension with elements of the CES. If the tension engendered is significant and persistent enough, the CES may be destabilized; put differently, it may be thrown into disequilibrium.

If so, one of two things tends to happen: Either the CES succeeds in rejecting the innovation in order to regain its prior stable state—an increasingly rare occurrence—or, more likely, it transforms itself so as to accommodate the development with which it has been confronted. In the latter case, *changes take place in one or more cultural subsystems*. For example, ideas, institutions, roles, or behavior patterns may undergo change so as to be more compatible with the new possibilities and requisites of the innovation. Often such accommodation works, in the sense that system tension abates, a new equilibrium state is attained, and life proceeds more consonantly against the backdrop of the altered CES.

Sometimes, the cultural changes made in the adoption-accommodation process may, while ushering in a new, perhaps ultimately improved way of life, exact a steep psychic toll of uncertain duration. Under certain circumstances, "attempts" to compensate for the disruption of the CES precipitated by the introduction of a technical development can fail miserably, and the cultural system may disintegrate.

For example, Lauriston Sharp has described and analyzed the transformation in the 1930s of the culture system of the Yir Yoront, an aboriginal bush people of northeastern Australia. The stone axe had long played an important role in many sectors of the CES of Yir Yoront society. Besides its everyday utility as a chopping tool, the stone axe was central to trading relations with neighboring tribes (including annual fiestas organized around trade relations), totemic clan activities, sex-role definitions, initiation rites, and intrasocietal authority relations. For example, women and children were permitted to use stone axes only at the leave of older men—who alone obtained axe heads and produced finished axes—and only for specified purposes.

Anglican missionaries' indiscriminate and widespread distribution, especially to women and children, of "improved" steel axes profoundly disrupted Yir Yoront society. The perturbation elicited changes in the Yir Yoront CES aimed at regaining system equilibrium. Some males adopted other ready-made Western artifacts and practices. Others resorted to stealing toothpaste, in hopes of establishing new cults enabling them to recapture their authority. Yet others became demoralized and fell into protracted states of depression.[77]

In sum, the general heuristic model described here involves traversal of six stages: initial CES equilibrium, introduction of a technical development, behavioral and intellectual changes, consequent tension within the prevailing CES, transformation of the CES, and attainment of a new CES equilibrium state.

The equilibrium–disequilibrium model emphasizes the dynamic interaction of the initiating technical change and society's CES as crucial to the eventual social change outcome. However, it sheds no light on how the *general, background* CES influences the *specific, concrete* process linking the particular technical change and ensuing social change under scrutiny. To address this issue, we turn to a second heuristic model.

The IDUAR Model of Technically Induced Social Change

The "initial social conditions" that obtain when a technical change is introduced into society comprise the social *context* existing at the time—what we called in Chapter 4 the prevailing SCES. The importance of this context is that the initiating technical change does not bring about the ensuing social change directly or by itself. Rather, it exercises an influence on society only indirectly, via its interaction with the reigning SCES context. Put differently, it does so only by activating a *complex transformer*: the SCES. Conversely, serving as a transformer is how the SCES exercises *its* influence on the ensuing social change outcome. Let us say then that the SCES *mediates* the relationship of the initiating technical change and the ensuing social change (Figure 5-2).

The SCES transformer influences the social change outcome initiated by a technical change by affecting certain *intermediary variables*. These variables refer to specific features of concrete, technical-change-initiated processes of social change. These features "come between" the initiating technical change and the ensuing social change and represent the "points" in specific TCESC processes at which the general, background SCES brings its transformative influence to bear. Taken together, the changes in these features produce the eventual social change outcome.

The key intermediary variables influenced by the SCES are five in number: (1) innovation, (2) diffusion, (3) use, (4) adaptation, and (5) resistance (IDUAR). Let us discuss each of them separately.

The Innovation. A technical change (e.g., an invention or discovery) typically travels a long road before attaining the status of an innovation ready for dissemination. As it travels this road, many aspects of the innovation-to-be are subject to SCES influence: its design features and performance specifications, the price at which it is offered, the "meaning" of the innovation (what it is seen as), and the "gain" it is perceived to offer to prospective users. Of course, as we have discussed, prior to

Figure 5-2. Mediation by the SCES of the relationship between technical change and ensuing social change.

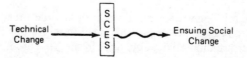

influencing developments along the path from technical change to innovation-to-be, the SCES often influences *which* technical changes are pursued in the first place. (Thus, Figure 5-2 should not be interpreted as meaning that the initiating technical change or, for that matter, the ensuing social change transpires "outside" the SCES.)

The Diffusion Process.   Many aspects of the process by which an innovation is diffused in society are subject to SCES influence. For example, the *mechanism* of diffusion may be the free market or some mode of government-controlled or government-subsidized distribution. The *character* of the diffusion process depends on whether strict or permissive government regulation is exercised and on the marketing plan put into effect. The *speed* of the diffusion process is a function of, among other things, available disposable consumer income, which is in turn dependent on the country's economic health.

The Pattern of Use.   Whereas the first two SCES-influenced variables are *stimuli* in the overall TCESC process, the last three are SCES-influenced *responses* to these stimuli. Our first response variable is use. The SCES often influences *which* uses are made of an innovation, *how much* and *how widely* it is used, and the *composition* of the user group. For example, amniocentesis is a diagnostic technique used primarily to detect fetal genetic abnormalities. In some countries, certain cultural values have impeded or effectively barred access to this procedure for offspring sex-selection purposes. Other cultural values have fostered gender-imbalances in innovation user groups (e.g., the personal computer in the industrialized West and the private automobile in Saudi Arabia).

Adaptation.   Use of a diffused innovation may require no significant change in a society's SCES. Sometimes, however, adoption and use of the innovation will require that significant adaptations—behavioral or intellectual—be made to accommodate it. How much of an adaptation and which specific adaptations will be required depends on the prevailing SCES. For example, the diffusion and use of the snowmobile required different and much greater adaptations in the society of the Skolt Lapps than it did in American society. Those differences reflected the societies' different prevailing SCES contexts and were reflected in the fact that markedly different social changes resulted from the same innovation.

Resistance.   The diffusion of an innovation in a society may engender resistance to some or all of the personal or societal uses made of it. Whether it does and the degree to which it does will depend on the prevailing SCES—for example, on its ideology or social structure. The resistance elicited helps determine what social change eventuates.

For example, the introduction of the gun—specifically, the matchlock musket—into Japan in the mid-sixteenth century transformed traditional warfare in that country.[78] This change gave rise to so much resistance in Japanese society that gun manufacture was gradually phased out, and firearms played no role in Japanese life until the late nineteenth century. Several features of the Japanese SCES fueled this resistance. Of these, social structure and ideology were crucial. The status of the Samurai warrior was jeopardized by the ability of the lowly gun-toting peasant to destroy him. As Samurai comprised about 8 percent of the society, they were able to bring great pressure to bear on the central Tokugawa government to abolish firearms.

Regarding the ideational realm, the sword had powerful symbolic significance in Japan. It was the embodiment of the bearer's honor. Moreover, respected aesthetic norms of elegant body movement governed Samurai sword use. The musket, on the other hand, required body movement deemed inelegant by Samurai.

This model of the TCESC relationship is (infelicitously) called the *i*nnovation/*d*iffusion/*u*se/*a*daptation/*r*esistance, or IDUAR, model. It is represented in Figure 5-3.*

The IDUAR model shows that talk of the "impact" of scientific and technological changes on society is profoundly misleading. This "impact model" of causality, evoking the image of a collision of two billiard balls, erroneously suggests that the social outcome of a scientific or technological innovation depends solely on its inherent characteristics and momentum of introduction. It implies that the effect of scientific and technological changes on society is, like a billiard ball collision, direct and immediate, and that society is a *passive* party to the impact occurrence, simply absorbing the momentum of the "incoming" innovation and being moved accordingly. Transferring talk of "impacts" from the realm of Newtonian physics to the realm of society is not only seriously misleading; it also aids

Figure 5-3. The IDUAR model of the technical-change/ensuing-social-change (TCESC) relationship.

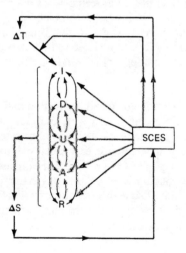

Δ = A symbol indicating a change in the variable to its right
ΔT = A technical change (e.g., an invention or discovery)
I = A technical innovation based on a ΔT
D = The process of diffusion for the I in question
U = The pattern of use of the diffused I
A = The changes made by users and/or society in adapting to the U of the diffused I
R = The individual and/or societal resistance to U and A
ΔS = The ensuing social change outcome resulting from the above
SCES = The society's Social-Cultural-Environmental System
⟶ = A possible directional influence relationship

*Figure 5-3 is by no means a fully adequate representation of the complex TCESC relationship. For example, it does not incorporate the role of pertinent *social actors* — inventors, entrepreneurs, and "product champions"—who may exercise considerable influence on the technical change, intermediary variables, or SCES in question by, for example, effecting some organizational or policy change.

and abets the pernicious notions of autonomous technology and (strong) technological determinism and obscures the interactive, dialectical character of the science-technology-society change relationship.

In contrast, the IDUAR model highlights the fact that the eventual social change outcome attributed to a technical change is a function of at least five SCES-influenced intervening variables: I, D, U, A, and R.

To conclude this section, consider an example involving all five intermediary variables. The notable American social change attributed to the telephone was due not just to the space-transcending and other technical capacities of the instrument and its support systems; it also depended on the easily mastered requisites of telephone use (nature of the innovation), the market character of the American economy of the day and the evolving marketing strategies of the competing telephone companies (type of diffusion process), the different patterns of phone use by men and women and by rural and urban residents (pattern of use), the willingness to use the phone in lieu of or to supplement face-to-face interactions (adaptation); and consumer opposition to early phone company campaigns against "frivolous" use of the phone for purposes of mere "sociability" (pattern of resistance).* All five of these intermediary variables were influenced by the reigning American SCES.†

CONCLUSION

In this chapter we examined some influential theories put forward to explain various phenomena of science and technology in society (STS). We identified what is valid, misleading, and erroneous in the concept of autonomous technology and the theory of technological determinism. Using the SCES and IDUAR models, we sought to shed light on important STS phenomena and issues, such as the causes of modern scientific discovery and technological invention, the diffusion of technical innovations, and the genesis of social changes initiated by developments in science and technology. A critical conclusion that emerges from this chapter is that accounts of technological development and of technological change as a "cause" of social change *must* take on board the fact that the activities of science and technology exist and unfold in rich social contexts. These contexts contribute powerfully to the development of these twin forces and interact with them and their products in an ongoing process of sociotechnical transformation.

ENDNOTES

1. Glenn T. Seaborg and Roger Corliss, *Man and Atom* (New York: Dutton, 1972), p. 265.
2. Jacques Ellul, *The Technological Society*, J. Wilkinson, trans. (New York: Knopf, 1967); and Langdon Winner, *Autonomous Technology* (Cambridge, Mass.: MIT Press, 1977).

*For details on some ways in which the social change outcome initiated by the telephone hinged on mediating SCES-influenced variables, see Claude S. Fischer, "'Touch Someone': The Telephone Industry Discovers Sociability," *Technology and Culture*, 29 , no. 1, 1988, 32–61. See also the same author's "Gender and the Residential Telephone, 1890–1940: Technologies of Sociability," *Sociological Forum*, 3, no. 2, 1988, 211—233.

†In Chapter 4 we explored four examples of scientific and technological developments whose consequences included significant transformations of the SCESs of the societies in question. These examples may be fruitfully revisited with the IDUAR model of technical-change-initiated social change in mind. Similarly, while they need not be, the discussions in Chapters 6 through 12 of the societal influences of modern scientific and technological innovations may also be read in light of this model.

3. Ellul, *Technological Society*, pp. xxxi, xxxiii.
4. *Ibid.*, p. xxx.
5. Robert L. Heilbroner, "Do Machines Make History?" *Technology and Culture*, 8, no. 3, 1967, 344. By permission of the University of Chicago Press.
6. *New York Times*, September 30, 1986, p. 28.
7. Horace Freeland Judson, "Century of the Sciences," *Science 84*, November 1984, p. 42.
8. Ezra Mishan, "On Making the Future Safe For Mankind," *Public Interest*, no. 24, 1971, p. 60.
9. Winner, *Autonomous Technology*, p. 56.
10. *Ibid.*, pp. 57–73.
11. *Ibid.*, pp. 88–100.
12. *Ibid.*, pp. 279–305.
13. Everett Rogers, *Diffusion of Innovations*, 3rd ed. (New York: Free Press, 1983), p. 11.
14. U.S. Department of Commerce, Patent and Trademark Office, Office of Documentation Information, "Technology Assessment and Forecast Report: All Technologies Report, 1/1963–12/1988," April 1989, p. A2; and "Technology Assessment and Forecast Report: Independent Inventors By State By Year, 1975–1988," May 1989, p. 2.
15. These remarks draw on Robin Roy and Nigel Cross, *Technology and Society* (Milton Keynes: Open University Press, 1975), pp. 30–34.
16. Dennis Gabor, *Innovations: Scientific, Technological, and Social* (London: Oxford University Press, 1970), p. 9.
17. Ray and Cross, *Technology and Society*, p. 31.
18. *New York Times*, February 13, 1990, p. B 16.
19. Ray and Cross, *Technology and Society*, p. 32.
20. *Ibid.*, p. 33.
21. Abbott Payson Usher, *A History of Mechanical Inventions* (Cambridge, Mass.: Harvard University Press, 1954), pp. 56–83.
22. Ronald W. Clark, *Works of Man* (New York: Viking, 1985), pp. 238–246.
23. *Ibid.*, p. 245.
24. Usher, *A History of Mechanical Inventions*, p. 68.
25. Wiebe Bijker and Trevor Pinch, "Social Construction of Facts and Artifacts," *Social Studies of Science*, 14, 1984, 399–441.
26. Bijker and Pinch, "Social Construction," p. 416.
27. *Ibid.*, p. 419.
28. Stephen J. Kline, "Innovation Is Not a Linear Process," *Research Management*, 28, no. 4, July–August 1985, 36.
29. *Ibid.*
30. Nathan Rosenberg and L. E. Birdzell, Jr., *How the West Grew Rich* (New York: Basic Books, 1986), p. 258.
31. Nathan Rosenberg, *Inside the Black Box: Technology and Economics* (New York: Cambridge University Press, 1982), p. 194.
32. *Ibid.*, p. 235.
33. *Ibid.*, p. 195.
34. K. Norris and J. Vaisey, *The Economics of Research and Technology* (London: Allen and Unwin, 1973), quoted in Roy and Cross, *Technology and Society*, p. 35.
35. *Ibid.*, p. 36.
36. The phrase *linear model*, quoted in Kline, "Innovation," p. 36, is due to William J. Price and Lawrence W. Bass, "Scientific Research and the Innovative Process," *Science*, 164, no. 16, 1969, 802–806.
37. Kline, "Innovation," pp. 36–45.
38. Rosenberg and Birdzell, *How the West Grew Rich*, p. 243.
39. *Ibid.*, pp. 243–244.
40. *Ibid.*, p. 264.
41. Augustine Brannigan, *The Social Basis of Scientific Discoveries* (Cambridge: Cambridge University Press, 1981), p. 1.

42. Bernard Barber, "The Sociology of Science," Part III of article on "Science," *International Encyclopedia of the Social Sciences*, Vol. 14 (1968–1979), p. 97.

43. *Ibid.*, p. 94.

44. *Ibid.*

45. Edgar Zilsel, "The Sociological Roots of Science," *American Journal of Sociology*, 47, 1942, 553.

46. *Ibid.*, pp. 554–555.

47. *Ibid.*, p. 544.

48. The following remarks on scientific discovery draw heavily on A. Brannigan, *Social Basis*, Chaps. 1 and 2.

49. *Ibid.*, p. 2.

50. Thomas S. Kuhn, "Historical Structures of Scientific Discoveries," *Science*, 136, June 1, 1962, 763.

51. *Ibid.*

52. Robert Merton, "Singletons and Multiples in Science," in *The Sociology of Science* (Chicago: University of Chicago Press, 1973), p. 352.

53. Brannigan, *Social Basis*, p. 51.

54. *Ibid.*, p. 8.

55. Clark, *Works of Man*, p. 197.

56. Brannigan, *Social Basis*, p. 70.

57. Michael Mulkey, quoted in Brannigan, *Social Basis*, p. ix.

58. Robert E. McGinn, "Prestige and the Logic of Political Argument," *Monist*, 56, no. 1, 1972, 103.

59. Mulkey, quoted in Brannigan, *Social Basis*, p. x.

60. Everett Rogers, *Diffusion*, p. 5.

61. *Ibid.*, p. 10.

62. *Ibid.*, pp. 15–16.

63. *Ibid.*, pp. 20–24.

64. Alfred D. Chandler, *The Visible Hand: The Managerial Revolution in American Business* (Cambridge, Mass.: Harvard University Press, 1977).

65. Cf. Karl Marx, "Economic and Philosophical Manuscripts," in T. B. Bottomore, ed. and trans., *Karl Marx: Early Writings* (New York: McGraw-Hill, 1964), pp. 168–69.

66. Thomas S. Kuhn, *The Structure of Scientific Revolutions*, pp. 77–91.

67. Rogers, *Diffusion*, p. 21.

68. Heilbroner, "Machines," p. 342.

69. *Ibid.*, p. 340.

70. Quoted in Roy and Cross, *Technology and Society*, p. 26.

71. W. F. Bynum et al., eds., *Dictionary of the History of Science* (Princeton: Princeton University Press, 1984), p. 412.

72. Langdon Winner, *Autonomous Technology* (Cambridge, Mass.: MIT Press, 1977), p. 76.

73. I owe this idea and metaphor to Walter G. Vincenti.

74. Heilbroner, "Machines," p. 342.

75. *Ibid.*, p. 345.

76. *Ibid.*, p. 340.

77. Lauriston Sharp, "Steel Axes for Stone Age Australians," in E. Spicer, ed., *Human Problems in Technological Change* (New York: Sage Publications, Inc., 1963), pp. 69–92.

78. Noel Perrin, *Giving Up the Gun* (Boulder, Colo.: Shambhala, 1980), especially Chaps. 4 and 5.

CHAPTER 6
SOCIAL INSTITUTIONS

INTRODUCTION

Innovations in modern science and technology have helped bring about profound changes in most of the central cultural institutions of industrialized societies, including education, government, law, religion, sport, and family. In this chapter, we will focus our attention on two such institutions: work and leisure.

Why work and leisure? Besides being the established form of social activity through which individual and societal survival are realized, work is important in various noneconomic ways. For example, it shapes workers' patterns of social interaction and affects their senses of identity and self-esteem. In the last century and a half, a series of far-reaching techno-economic changes has transformed the institution of work in both its economic and noneconomic roles.

Leisure warrants attention because, as an institution, it is peculiar to the modern industrial era and, in less obvious ways, it has become crucial to the development of industrial society. Leisure is a natural cultural institution to pair with work because transformations in the latter have repeatedly elicited significant changes in the former. The understanding of each is enhanced by appreciating the vicissitudes of the other.

WORK

Historical Perspective

Occupational Profile of the Workforce. The occupational profile of the U.S. workforce has shifted dramatically in the nineteenth and twentieth centuries. "As recently as 1850 farmers made up 64 percent of the labor force in the U.S."[1] With the acceleration of industrialization in the post–Civil War period, the number and percentage of workers involved in manufacturing rose rapidly. Early in the twentieth century the number of "blue-collar" workers first surpassed the number of farm workers. The 1910 census reported 14.2 million manual workers and 11.5 million farm workers, the latter by then comprising only about 30 percent of the workforce.[2]

By 1986, another milestone in the evolution of this profile appeared on the horizon. Blue-collar workers (30.3 million) accounted for 28.5 percent of the workforce, compared with about 40 percent in 1910. As this percentage fell, what took up the slack? Not agricultural employment: By 1988 the percentage of the workforce involved in farming had declined to 2.5 percent (about 3 million workers). It is, rather, the so-called service sector. Employment in trade (including sales and finance) aside, this sector now accounts for about 55 percent of the workforce. Even more strikingly, about half of the service sector is comprised of highly educated professional, technical, and managerial workers. These workers numbered 29.6 million in 1986—remarkably, only .75 million fewer than the number of blue-collar workers—compared with 7.5 million fewer in 1980.[3]

Technical changes played a major role in this transformation. Reapers, threshers, combines, new seeds, fertilizers, herbicides, and other advances in agricultural science and technology led to enormous productivity increases, enabling progressively fewer farm workers to produce more and more food for an ever-expanding population. Improvements in manufacturing technology, including new materials, processes, and machines, enabled that growing population to be provided with an ever-widening array of material goods without anything like a comparable increase in the number of (domestic) manufacturing operatives and laborers. Without the computer, the growth of the professional, technical, and managerial domain of the service sector seen in the last two decades is unlikely to have occurred with the speed and to the extent that it has.

These epochal macro changes reflect myriad micro changes, in many of which scientific and technological changes have bulked large. In the past century, inventions, discoveries, and innovations have given rise to thousands of new kinds of jobs, including those of pilot, air traffic controller, radio announcer, assembly line worker, auto mechanic, computer programmer, laboratory technician, and genetic scientist. Other jobs, of course, have been virtually eliminated. The third edition (1965) of the *Dictionary of Occupational Titles* listed 21,741 jobs, 6,432 of which were not contained in the second edition (1949). The fourth edition (1977) continued this trend: It listed 2,100 jobs not included in the 1965 edition. However, by 1977, 3,500 jobs listed in the 1965 edition had disappeared from the occupational rolls.[4] While there have been significant science- and technology-based increases in the numbers of people in positions of certain types (e.g., sales), significant technically based contractions have occurred in the numbers and percentages of people in certain other jobs (e.g., farmer, coal miner, printer, autoworker, telephone operator, and bank teller). (We will return to the question of technological unemployment in a moment.)

Locus, Content, and Process.   Hand in hand with the science- and technology-based transformation of the occupational profile of industrial society have gone important changes in the locus, content, and processes of work. The farm, the workshop, and the mine first gave way to the factory. Later, all yielded ground to the office and laboratory. That development, as we shall see shortly, proved more important for the institution of work than a mere change of physical spaces.

Job content has changed too. Direct manipulation of nature with simple, hand-operated tools in farming and mining was superceded by indirect manipulation using farming and mining machinery and displaced by manipulation using the machinery of industrial production. In recent decades, manipulation of symbols and information has gained in prominence. The intellectual activities involved in the latter kinds of manipulations are far removed from the content of traditional agricultural or industrial jobs.

Technology was and is involved in all three kinds of manipulations. Work activity may be seen as involving one or more of the following three general components: the *power* by which the activity in question is carried out; the *control* exercised over the work process; and *intellectual analysis and decision making* pertaining to work goals, means, and processes.[5] The power component of work activity has largely been technologized. Industrial energy-generating technologies replaced animal and human physical power with inanimate sources of energy, thereby putting the human at additional remove from direct physical involvement with the work process. Processes of control have also undergone mechanization, as with Jacquard looms, integrated-flow assembly lines, computer-assisted manufacturing systems, and remote-sensing devices and related control systems. To a significant degree, control over work processes is now exercised via technological means. In recent years, even the conceptual-intellectual component of work activity has begun to undergo mechanization. Computer-based programs and procedures have been developed to assist in product and system design, as have computer-based "expert systems" for medical diagnosis and financial, industrial, and military decision making. The degree to which the cerebral dimension of work activity can be mechanized is a matter of dispute and remains to be seen.[6]

In general, technology has played a pivotal role over the past two centuries in making work activity less physical and more perceptual-mental in content. This trend is reflected in diverse occupations, from that of miner (using picks and shovels versus using robotic coal claws and computerized processing equipment) and fisherman (using manually versus automatically operated nets and processing procedures) to that of factory worker (using hand-operated lathes versus using computer-controlled machine tools) and engineer (building and testing physical models versus using computer-aided design techniques).

Time.   A less obvious influence of modern technology on work involves a profound change in time orientation. In preindustrial days, much work was artisanal in character. Independent craftspeople set their own paces and production goals. Alternating between intermittent bouts of intense work and sometimes extended periods of nonwork, preindustrial work was not normally carried out on a regular daily schedule. Artisanal work was executed on what E. P. Thompson calls a "task orientation" basis: One worked as long and as hard as it took to get the required job done. Thompson contrasts this with work done on the more familiar industrial "time orientation" basis, whereby (overtime aside) one works a fixed number of hours per day whether or not one has enough work to do or has finished one's assigned work.[7]

The transition from a "task" to a "time" orientation at work was an important outcome (and ingredient) of the industrialization process. As Thompson makes clear, Calvinist religion and considerations of private profit played noteworthy roles in bringing about this change. However, technology was also a significant factor, for the substantial capital investment involved in establishing the large technology-intensive industrial factories encouraged the drive to convert the workforce from an artisanal, time-orientation to a more regular, regimented, industrial one. Persistence of artisanal "indolence" was viewed as incompatible with the new ability of expensive factory machinery to work continually. Transformation of work time consciousness was imperative if the huge investments by capitalists in expensive technological plants were to be recovered quickly.

In the United States, during the period from 1880 to 1900, Frederick Winslow Taylor, a pioneer of industrial engineering, elaborated and promoted the influential philosophy of work known as "scientific management." Taylorism can be viewed as a response to the conjunction of expensive new production technology and a workforce imbued with traditional artisanal time consciousness. Taylor divided work into microtasks, each of which was to be carried out in a prescribed way at a prescribed pace by a carefully chosen and trained worker. The way and pace were to be experimentally determined by management representatives (industrial engineers) in such a way as to maximize output. The objective of this "scientific" approach was to eliminate waste. This "waste" resulted in part from using a workforce rich in recent immigrants ingrained with "promiscuous" Old World artisanal time consciousness in the large, expensive new factories of the steel and other industries.[8] Taylorism went a long way toward inculcating a new time orientation in American industrial workplaces.*

The Modern Business Firm.   Technological change exercised an important twofold influence on the organizational context of work in industrial society. Up until the 1830s, such industrialization as had occurred in the United States (e.g., in the textile industry) took place in small, single-unit, informally run, family-owned and -managed firms. Beginning around 1840, new technologies of communication and transportation, such as the railroad, telegraph, steamship, and cable, began to make possible unprecedented increases in the speed of distribution. This in turn stimulated the development of new methods of mass production to take full advantage of the new possibilities. While these technical changes did not by themselves determine a change in the nature of the firms doing the production or distribution, their effective operation and the importance of coordinating input acquisition, production, marketing, distribution, and, later, research and development made an appropriate transformation in the structure of the business firm essential. Otherwise, the potential offered by the new technologies would remain unexploited and the competitiveness of old-style firms would be jeopardized. Thus, technological advances prepared the ground for the gradual emergence of a new form of business enterprise in the United States: *the large-scale, multi-unit, horizontally and vertically integrated, professionally managed, hierarchically organized firm.* The latter emerged as a response to the stimulus provided by the new technologies. Put differently, new technology exercised an elicitive influence on the modern business organization.[9] The evolution of the business enterprise in the United States in response to mid-nineteenth century technological innovations was, in Heilbroner's words, "part of an organizational revolution that was an essential component of the industrial revolution."[10]

Unions.   A second important influence on the organizational context of work exercised by the industrial revolution was the rise of unions. Several factors underlay this development. Physical conditions at the new industrial workplace were often grim

*Interestingly, the onset of the information era has led to a modest revival of the task orientation approach to work. In the computer industry, some companies allow their technical employees considerable latitude in their work habits—for example, in duration and scheduling—as long as they satisfactorily complete their assigned tasks.

and dangerous. Later, intensification of the division of labor and the rise of the assembly line increased the tedium of work. The breakdown of relatively personal relations between the preindustrial "boss" and his workers in old, smaller-scale firms and the rise of impersonal iron discipline characteristic of the new, large-scale factories led to increased worker-management estrangement. Such factors stimulated a new institutional response by workers aimed at redressing the imbalance of power between management and labor in industry and at achieving concrete improvements in their work situations. First in Great Britain and on the European continent, and later in the United States, unions were organized and thrived, initially among skilled workers, and later among unskilled laborers. According to Heilbroner, "unionization was ... labor's response to the problems of technology and large-scale organization."[11] We will return to the relationship between technology and labor unions below.

Work Week.   A central objective pursued by unions was a shortening of the work week. The length of the work week in manufacturing industries in the United States decreased from about 67 hours in 1860 to about 42 hours in 1950, and has remained roughly constant since then.[12] It cannot be baldly claimed that technological changes "caused" this decline. Nevertheless, unions, however powerful, would not have been able to extract concessions in the form of a progressively shortened work week unless technological advances had so enhanced productivity as to make it possible for firms to operate profitably with shorter work weeks and without decreasing wage levels. Thus, as an enabling condition, technology was a contributory causal factor in the shortening of the average industrial work week.

Recent Issues

Let us now look briefly at several recent work issues that supposedly arose from the influence of technological change.

Technological Unemployment.   Microelectronic technologies and systems, such as robotic manipulators and vision systems and flexible and computer-integrated manufacturing systems, have in recent years helped give currency to the term *technological unemployment.* While technology can and does play an important role in the elimination, as well as the creation, of jobs, it is important to be clear about precisely what that role is. Technological change per se cannot simply be said to be the "cause" of such unemployment as may occur in the wake of its implementation. To make such a claim is to succumb to a version of technological determinism, as if the technological change in question made the ensuing unemployment inevitable.

Unquestionably, technological changes sometimes enable fewer workers to do what it took more to do under a prior technological regime, as in the cases of the data-processing technology used by bank tellers and the switching and voice-synthesis technologies supporting telephone operators. What new technologies sometimes do in such cases is to offer opportunities for savings in manpower. But this is not the same as saying that the technology is the cause of the unemployment that may ensue, for the employment consequences of introducing a new technology depend critically on the policies of the firm in question (e.g., lifetime employment, in-house retraining and reassignment for employees affected by new technologies, or letting the size of the employee pool decrease by attrition). They also depend on the mode of introduction of the innovation (e.g., phased or all-at-once). It is only the contingent fact that most companies have traditionally tended to dismiss employees when they adopt labor-saving technologies that has made the concept "technological unemployment" seem plausible.

When the specter of technological unemployment is raised, a popular rebuttal consists in claiming that a new technology creates more jobs than it eliminates. The a priori nature of that claim aside, it is often made disingenuously: Even if it is true, the individuals who get the newly created jobs that may emerge are not always—and are perhaps rarely—the same as those whose jobs are eliminated by the technology in question.

Deskilling.   Another controversial issue in recent debate over the influence of technology on work is whether new technology is effecting a deskilling of the workforce. Many critics of "the impact of technology on work"* argue that the skills built into new technologies mean that workers no longer have to exercise some skills that they were previously using, and that such skills as they may have to exercise with the new technology are in some sense "lower" ones (e.g., less complex).

The deskilling debate can be made more fruitful if several important points are kept in mind. First, new technologies can "enskill" as well as deskill. Carrying out the work processes associated with them may require new skills which, individually or on average, might be "higher" in some sense than those called for by the old technology. While, as Wallace and Kalleberg found, skill levels in the printing industry have declined significantly with the introduction of computerized typesetting technologies, Adler found that the skill levels required by the automation of teller work in a large French bank increased, in spite of management's expectation that they would decline.[13,14] The deskilling debate should therefore be stripped of its polarizing a priori character and become rooted in sensitive, empirical, case-by-case study.

Second, the skills involved in many microelectronic technologies are sensory and intellectual ones, such as monitoring, data entry, and system status assessment and decision making. More physically demanding traditional work skills, including neuromuscular skills, may well be rendered redundant by such technologies. Mentalist prejudice aside, however, it is far from clear why physical skills should be ranked "lower" than intellectual ones. Hence it is difficult to ascertain the *on-balance* skill consequences of such technologies and thus to determine whether they are reasonably regarded as calling for workers who are more or less skilled than their predecessors.

Third, to whatever extent it makes sense to say that a given microelectronic technology does deskill, that is not to be "blamed" on the technology per se, but on those who commission it, determine its design parameters, and approve its mode of implementation.

*This phrase reflects the error discussed in Chapter 5—that of assuming that the social change outcome of a technical change is a function solely of the nature of the initial technical change. In contrast, the innovation-diffusion-use-adaptation-resistance (IDUAR) model of the technical-change-ensuing-social-change (TCESC) relationship emphasizes the important role of intermediary variables influenced by the social-cultural-environmental system (SCES), namely, I, D, U, A, and R, in determining the social change outcome. A useful case study illustrating the important role of such intermediary variables in determining the workplace consequences of a technological innovation is Robert E. Kraut, Susan T. Dumais, and Susan Koch, "Computerization, Productivity, and Quality of Work-Life," *Communications of the Association for Computing Machinery*, 32, no. 2, February 1988, 220–238.

Fourth, even when it turns out in a particular case that the work done under a new technological regime can reasonably be said to have "enskilled" rather than "deskilled" the workforce, it remains to be determined on a case-by-case basis whether the *number* of employees at work under the new regime is more, less, or the same as were employed under its predecessor. It could turn out in certain or even in most cases that the introduction at the workplace of new technologies of a certain type requires the employment of *fewer* workers albeit with *higher* average skill levels. The debate over deskilling should not be concluded until the verdict is in on the extent to which new work technologies are contributing to "fewer, better jobs"—as a function of, among other things, type of technology and sector of work.

The Decline of Unions.   Ironically, technology, the same force that provided a great impetus to the rise of the institution of worker unions, has in recent years become an important factor in their decline. Unionization of the American workforce, which reached its historic high point of about 33 percent in 1954, had fallen to 16.4 percent of the workforce in 1989.[15] While a number of factors are responsible for this precipitous decline, several involve technological change.

With the revolutions in communications and transportation technology and the ability to quickly install highly mechanized production facilities almost anywhere in the world, the "global factory" concept has become feasible. A production facility need no longer be located in the same region or country as the market in which its products will be sold. Taking advantage of low overseas wage rates, thousands of higher-paying jobs in industries with high rates of unionization (e.g., the garment industry) have been "exported" overseas.

Second, for reasons having a good deal to do with technological change, employment in manufacturing, traditionally a union bastion, has fallen relatively and absolutely. In contrast, the service sector has expanded rapidly. Yet, the government worker and transportation and utilities areas aside, unionization in the service-producing sector stood at only 5.7 percent in 1989.[16] While considerations of status play an important role—"unions are only for blue-collar workers"—the less grimy, less overtly dangerous nature of most service-sector workplaces removes factors that historically fueled union sympathy and enrollment.

Third, unionization has declined substantially even in the anemic manufacturing sector; it reached 21.6 percent in 1989.[17] The work of William Form sheds light on this trend. Studying automobile factories in four countries of differing degrees of industrialization—the United States, Italy, Argentina, and India—Form found that the more complex the production technology, the lower the density of factory work stations. This led to less opportunity for worker interaction on the job and, as a consequence, less extra-factory contact. Form concluded that "insofar as working-class solidarity is stimulated by work contacts, it should decrease with advancing industrialization because cleavages along skill lines are greater in the most industrialized societies."[18]

In a word, advancing technology seems to promote blue-collar stratification rather than solidarity. Herb Mills reached a similar conclusion in his study of the transformation of San Francisco waterfront longshoring operations. The movement from the old, relatively egalitarian regime of work "gangs" using grappling hooks to the new one of containerization, with its huge electric winches and noisy forklifts being driven into and out of ships' hulls, engendered decreases in social contact on and off the job, splits between workers of different skills and statuses, and a significant weakening of traditional union solidarity.[19]

Health and Safety.   Advances in modern science and technology have led to sharp disagreement over the level of workplace safety in the contemporary era. Some writers plausibly represent modern technology as bringing about safer workplaces, through, for example, robotic automation of dirty and dangerous tasks previously done by workers. To other writers, no less plausibly, contemporary workplaces are, if anything, more dangerous, for in addition to the risk of a disabling accident—the rate was 2.4 per 100 workers per year in 1980[20]—many workers are exposed to serious threats of disease.

The primary source of disease is the thousands of industrial chemicals and other human-made materials used in modern workplaces, many of which are known or suspected to be carcinogenic. Every work day, over 25 million workers, almost a fourth of the American workforce, are exposed to potentially hazardous chemicals. An estimated 17,000 of them die each year from cancer caused by that exposure. As a result of growing recognition of this threat, the Occupational Safety and Health Act was passed by Congress in 1970. A new federal regulatory agency was created to implement the act, whose declared purpose is "to assure as far as possible every working man and woman in the Nation safe and healthy working conditions and to preserve our human resources."[21] Clearer perception of the threat to health and safety at the workplace posed by use of the fruits of modern science and technology has given rise to a new ideational construct: the basic right of the worker to be informed of what hazardous substances are present in the workplace. In 1987, this right was made operational for almost every major category of worker and workplace, manufacturing and nonmanufacturing alike.[22]

The leading cause of occupational injuries in contemporary workplaces is repetitive motion, typically at high speed. Repetitive-motion disorders, many of which require surgical correction, include carpal tunnel syndrome (an injury to the hand and wrist), tendonitis, arthritis, and sprains. Meat packers, poultry workers, and pianists have long been at risk for carpal tunnel syndrome. However, this disorder has mushroomed along with the proliferation of computers in the workplace. Whereas repetitive-motion disorders accounted for only 18 percent of workplace injuries reported by U.S. private industry in 1981, by 1988 that figure had reached 48 percent.[23] Computers and chemicals have helped redraw the risk profile of contemporary workplaces: fewer fatal accidents and more disabling diseases and debilitating injuries.

Work Aspirations and Expectations.   Technology has had an indirect enabling influence on one other important work-related ideational change: the embryonic notion that the worker has a right to *meaningful* work, not just to some kind of job. In the years of mass immigration into the United States in the late nineteenth and early twentieth centuries and during the years of the Great Depression, workers were satisfied to find any kind of work that would keep food on the table. With the affluence and relatively low unemployment of the post–World War II era, developments dependent upon many scientific and technological innovations, the notion could and did emerge that the individual was entitled to work that was intrinsically satisfying, over and above its extrinsic rewards (wages and benefits). Studs Terkel's classic of the 1970s, *Working*, documents the profound, culturally nurtured dissatisfaction of many securely employed individuals with the character of their work.[24]

LEISURE

The influence of science and technology on leisure is, in some respects, less obvious than in the case of work. Once again, let us begin with some historical perspective on that influence and then turn to some noteworthy contemporary issues.

Historical Perspective

The Creation of Leisure.   The industrial revolution exerted a powerful influence on the institution of leisure: In a sense, it created it. It is not as if free time or play was absent in the preindustrial world. On the contrary, "in medieval Europe over 100 saints' and feast days were recognized. Notwithstanding the influence of Puritanism, in 1761 the Bank of England still closed on 47 bank holidays."[25]

However, in the preindustrial world, recreation was inextricably interwoven with community life, religious festivals, family life, and work, particularly seasonal agricultural activities. Industrialization unraveled this seamless garment and compartmentalized life into distinct work and leisure sectors. Leisure eventually became an established, structurally differentiated sphere of social activity with its own evolving values (relaxation, self-development) and forms (the annual multiweek vacation, the three-day holiday weekend).

The Industrial Revolution and Leisure.   The decline of the traditional custom of taking Monday as a holiday (Saint Monday) was fueled by the regular, synchronized work patterns required to fully exploit the centrally driven power technologies of the new factory system. The determination of factory owners to keep production systems going for extended periods without interruption initially led to *increases* in the length of the work week. In the words of Krishan Kumar:

> Factory workers in 19th century Europe worked a 70 and even 80 hour week. It took a hundred years for them to return to the working hours roughly equivalent to that of the guildsmen who were their medieval forebears.[26]

In the early phase of the Industrial Revolution in Britain, say from 1750 to 1825, capitalist entrepreneurs and their representatives linked up with puritanical clergy in a vigorous campaign to discredit traditional popular recreational pursuits characteristic of the patriarchal agricultural society of the seventeenth and early eighteenth centuries. More than ever, work was trumpeted as the key to success now and to salvation beyond; idleness, or leisure, was the path to financial and spiritual ruin.[27]

The Commercialization of Leisure.   As industrialization and urbanization grew in the nineteenth century, leisure began to be culturally rehabilitated. Entrepreneurs began to recognize that profits could be made by producing after-work leisure experiences for the growing numbers of people simultaneously disgorged by urban factories and ready, willing, and able to pay for their leisure activities. The late nineteenth and early twentieth century development of the commercialization of leisure could not have occurred without the technology of the industrial revolution. A mass entertainment industry required a concentrated urban population to provide a large pool of consumers of new leisure products, be they in the form of music-hall shows or moving pictures, professional sports, or mass-circulation newspapers. The centralized power technologies of the industrial revolution had conveniently brought that about, as well as making possible (along with union activity and reform legislation) a state of affairs in which more and more workers had sufficient disposable income and time to spend on the new leisure products.

The mass entertainment sector of the industry was facilitated by the development in the late nineteenth century of urban public transportation systems (e.g., trams and underground railways) which could move people between their city or suburban residences and the urban leisure centers.[28] One profound effect of the commercialization of leisure made possible by the industrial revolution was a shift from the substantial self-generation of leisure activity by the working class in the preindustrial period to the purchase and consumption of leisure experiences and products designed, marketed, packaged, and delivered by capitalists.[29]

The Importance of Leisure to Industrial Society. If the modern institution of leisure and some of its particular forms, such as mass entertainment and the vacation, could not have come into existence without the techno-economic advances of the industrial revolution, it is also true that leisure has taken on an important new function beyond that of relaxation from the rigors of work. Through the novel, specifically industrial institution of "shopping," leisure time is now the designated time for perusal, purchase, and consumption of the *nonessential* goods and services able to be produced by the expanding industrial system. The institution of leisure has been socially reconstructed to make it seem natural and legitimate that significant amounts of free time be devoted to shopping for nonessentials which *must* be sold because they *can* be produced. The enormous capacity of the economic system, a function of the mass-production technology it employs, makes it mandatory that those goods be sold if economic expansion is to be realized. The institution of leisure has therefore been permanently mobilized for that task.

Contemporary Issues

Technologization of Leisure. From bicycling, listening to the radio, going to the movies, and reading mass-circulation newspapers, to pleasure driving, "working out" at a fitness center, and listening to recorded music, technology has played an increasingly important direct role in leisure activity during the last century. This trend has continued, seemingly at an accelerated pace, to the present day, most recently involving the videocassette recorder, that extraordinarily popular marriage of moving pictures, the tape recorder, and television. A 1983 survey of a 1,000-person cross-section of the American public confirmed the extent to which contemporary leisure activity is technology-intensive. The four most popular leisure activities, judged by the percentage of interviewees who engage in them every day or almost every day, are (in order of decreasing popularity): watching television, reading a newspaper, listening to music at home, and talking on the phone with friends or relatives.[30]

The technologization of leisure is sociologically significant in several ways. It bears on the degree to which people's leisure-time activity enhances sociability or promotes personal development rather than merely affording "relaxation" or recuperation from tedious or exhausting work. It may lead to shortchanging activities that are "fixed by *rules and traditions*" in favor of increased attention to amorphous fashionable pursuits; it may induce people to settle for passive technological anesthesia rather than "*go to the world* for direct and new experiences."[31] In short, the increased potential leisure time available in the twentieth century and its progressive technologization have made the issue of the quality of that time more poignant.

Television. As we have noted, the contemporary leisure-time activity—technology-based or not—to which Americans devote by far the most time is watching television. The sociological significance of this fact has been the subject of a good deal of research and much speculation. Let us first consider several important facts about contemporary leisure pursuits.

The most obvious influence of television on leisure is a direct one: the portion of the total leisure-time budget allocated to "watching television." After sleep and work, watching television is the primary activity to which Americans devote the most time each day. By the mid-1980s, almost every American home had one or more televisions and had a set on for the astonishing figure of slightly over 7 hours per day. As "television viewing" is a discontinuous, often interrupted, and frequently nonexclusive activity, and as different people in the same household often watch television at different times, the 7-hour figure by no means represents the mean amount of time that an individual actually watches television, either as a primary activity or as an accompaniment to doing something else, such as homework, eating, or housework.

The average amount of television watched by people in their own homes differs little from one Western industrialized country to another. However, the amount of television watched by an individual varies significantly as a function of the viewer's life-cycle stage: children and the elderly tend to watch considerably more than adolescents and young adults. In 1965, a study of 44 American cities revealed that the average amount of daily television viewing per individual among viewers watching in their own homes was 142 minutes, during 101 of which watching television was the primary activity. In the United States, where television watching is the most popular leisure pursuit and where people watch the highest number of minutes per person per week, Americans spend up to 40 percent of their total leisure time with television.[32] In short, quantitatively speaking, television dominates leisure activity in industrial societies.

Apart from the sheer amount of leisure time allocated to watching television, what are the effects of that amount of viewing on other leisure activities? In their classic *Television and Human Behavior*, Comstock and colleagues observe that recording how people behave when television is present in a society "does not permit inferences about how that behavior differs from what it was before television—except in the obvious sense that television viewing and such behavior as conversing about television represent changes. What is needed, but hard or impossible to obtain now, are data reflecting behavior before television or without television."[33]

Fortunately, Williams and co-workers carried out and analyzed the results of a "natural experiment," which yielded just such data.[34] To probe the influence of television, the researchers studied a Canadian town, dubbed "Notel," which happened to be located in a geographic blind spot, both prior to and two years after the introduction of television (one channel: the CBC). Two control towns with television, one ("Unitel") with a single channel (CBC) and the other ("Multitel") with four channels (CBC and the three major American commercial networks), were also studied both before and after Notel introduced television. Thus the Notel results were controlled for both the number of channels and such content differences as existed (in the mid 1970s) between Canadian and American television.

Several major findings of this seminal study are pertinent to assessing the influence of technology on leisure in contemporary society. First, while the introduction of television in Notel did not have any appreciable influence on the number of community activities available for leisure activity, it had a noticeable negative effect on the degree of participation in those activities. Significant decreases were detected in a number of activities not able to be "time-shared" with television, such as sports (especially among youth), dances, and club activities. Two years after the introduction of television, Notel adults older than 56 evidenced significant declines in both the number of community activities attended and the number of sports activities in which they participated. The age-segregation implications of this situation are troubling. In short, television displaced community leisure activities to a significant degree.

Second, television probably slows down the acquisition of reading skills by children. It does so by offering a less demanding alternative to the often difficult activity of decoding involved in learning to read. To the extent that children fail to become fluent in decoding texts, their future private leisure-time profiles are likely to be skewed away from difficult-to-navigate print activities. Thus television can inaugurate a vicious circle, leading a child to become a "print dropout."

Third, the children of Notel obtained significantly higher creativity scores on standardized tests before the introduction of television than did their Unitel and Multitel peers. Two years later their scores were similar to those of students who had grown up with television from the start. Similarly, pre-television Notel residents outperformed their Unitel and Multitel peers in creative problem-solving. They solved nonobvious problems much faster and, when unsuccessful, kept trying longer, a result replicated two years later. "[T]his seems to be the first empirical evidence demonstrating that television may, over the long term, affect concentration or persistence by adults."[35] Thus, television may exercise an indirect long-term influence on leisure by biasing future leisure activity profiles against endeavors requiring the very mental traits or skills it seems to diminish.

Leisure at Risk.   The increased leisure time promised by the historical decrease in the average manufacturing work week has not fully materialized. In 1981, of every 1,000 Americans with full-time nonagricultural jobs, 192 worked 49 or more hours per week. By 1989, 235 of every thousand did. The occupational categories most heavily populated with such workers are "executive, administrative, and managerial" (33.1 percent), "professional specialty" (29.4 percent), and "sales" (33.9 percent). Workers in the first two categories, comprising only 28.7 percent of the full-time nonagricultural workforce, accounted for 40.5 percent of those working 49 or more hours a week.[36] Ironically, one factor contributing to the above trend is technological innovation. Personal computers, modems, multifunctional telephones, and fax machines enable work to be done away from the office. As per the IDUAR model, the diffusion of these innovations in the competitive business world has fostered their use for incremental extraoffice work. Indeed, such use is fast becoming a corporate cultural norm. The growth in the proportion of "49 hours or more" workers is not cost-free: the mean weekly leisure time taken by American adults has fallen from 19.2 hours in 1980 to 16.6 in 1987.[37]

The proliferation of personal technics in everyday life has also diluted leisure time, through the increasing time spent on their purchase, use, and maintenance. Consequently, the time available for "cultivation of mind and spirit" and for "idleness," both foreseen as beneficiaries of technological progress, has dwindled. Moreover, the technoeconomic rhythm of contemporary work conditions the character of leisure time: Activity aimed at meeting nonwork (e.g., family) obligations tends to be speeded up. Obsession with time saving vitiates or precludes forms of pleasure that require substantial relaxed time to unfold, such as friendship, contemplation, and appreciation of certain kinds of books and music. The upshot is what Staffan Linder calls a "paradox of affluence": the emergence of a "harried leisure class."[38]

Technology, Work, and Leisure in the Future.   Unemployment associated with technological advances, the neglect of worker retraining, and the relative scarcity of meaningful work in a society that affirms it as central are factors promoting the grounding of self-esteem, personal identity, and the hope of meaningful everyday life on the quality of leisure activities. Yet, to date, negligible societal attention has been paid to fostering creative rather than dissipative or vegetative uses of leisure time. On the contrary, the commercialization and technologization of leisure, via books, newspapers, films, professional sports, and television, has created a situation in which the bulk of mass leisure opportunities are designed to cater to the existing tastes of the public rather than to challenge, elevate, or refine them.

CONCLUSION

The influence of science and technology on the institutions of work and leisure in the last two centuries has been manifold and profound. Their ideational, societal, material, and behavioral contexts have been transformed, a process which continues apace. Even as work becomes physically less demanding for most, financially rewarding for many, and intellectually challenging for some, the rapidly changing occupational profile, the vulnerability of workers to technological change, and the bifurcation of the "service sector" into dead-end and advanced sectors pose serious economic and ethical challenges to contemporary industrial societies.

   Similarly, while potential leisure time and the range of leisure opportunities have increased greatly in this century, the mean quantity of net available leisure time and the quality of de facto leisure-time experience have fallen substantially short of expectations and hopes. The unprecedented opportunities for individual development afforded by the industrial revolution have in many cases been turned to good account. To a large extent, however, this cultural potential has been dissipated as the institution of leisure has been co-opted and made to serve the imperatives and interests of large-scale techno-economic systems, capitalist and socialist alike.

ENDNOTES

1.   Wayne D. Rasmussen, "The Mechanization of Agriculture," *The Mechanization of Work* (San Francisco: Freeman, 1982), p. 15.
2.   *New York Times*, August 15, 1986, p. 26.
3.   *Ibid.*
4.   U.S. Employment Service, *Dictionary of Occupational Titles*, 4th ed. (Washington, D.C.: U.S. Government Printing Office, 1977), pp. xiii–xiv.
5.   This notion was first brought to my attention by John Celona.
6.   For a sophisticated philosophical critique of the claim that artificial intelligence can in principle produce systems equalling or improving upon any kind of human mental ability or activity, see Terry Winograd and Fernando Flores, *Understanding Computers and Cognition: A New Foundation for Design* (Reading, Mass.: Addison-Wesley, 1987).
7.   E. P. Thompson, "Time, Work Discipline, and Industrial Capitalism," *Past and Present*, no. 38, 1967, pp. 56–97.
8.   Frederick Winslow Taylor, *Principles of Scientific Management* (New York: W. W. Norton & Co., Inc., 1967).
9.   Alfred E. Chandler, "Technology and the Transformation of the Industrial Organization," in Joel Colton and Stuart Bruchy eds., *Technology, Economy, and Society* (New York: Columbia University Press, 1987), pp. 56–82.

10. Robert L. Heilbroner and Aaron Singer, *The Economic Transformation of America: 1600 to the Present*, 2nd ed. (New York: Harcourt Brace Jovanovich, 1984), p. 226.
11. *Ibid.*, p. 226.
12. Wassily W. Leontief, "The Distribution of Work and Income," in *The Mechanization of Work*, p. 103.
13. Michael Wallace and Arne L. Kallenberg, "Industrial Transformation and the Decline of Craft: The Decomposition of Skill in the Printing Industry, 1931—1978," *American Sociological Review*, 47, June 1982, 307—324.
14. Paul Adler, "New Technologies, New Skills," *California Management Review*, 29, no. 1, Fall 1986, 9–27.
15. U.S. Department of Labor, Bureau of Labor Statistics, USDL 90-59, February 7, 1990, Table 1, p. 5.
16. *Ibid.*, Table 2, p. 6.
17. *Ibid.*
18. William Form, *Blue Collar Stratification* (Princeton: Princeton University Press, 1976), p. 258.
19. Herb Mills, "The San Francisco Waterfront: The Social Consequences of Industrial Modernization I: The Good Old Days," *Urban Life*, 5, no. 2, July 1976, 221–250; and "The San Francisco Waterfront: The Social Consequences of Industrial Modernization II: Modern Longshore Operations," *Urban Life*, 6, no. 1, April 1977, 3–32.
20. Paul C. Rohan and Bernard Brody, "Frequency and Costs of Worker Accidents in North America," *Labor and Society*, 9, no. 2, April–June 1984, 167.
21. Bernard Rifkin and Susan Rifkin, *American Labor Sourcebook* (New York: McGraw-Hill, 1979), Section 4, p. 95.
22. *New York Times*, August 21, 1987, Section II, p. 5.
23. *New York Times*, November 16, 1989, p. A12.
24. Studs Terkel, *Working* (New York: Ballantine, 1985).
25. Kenneth Roberts, *Leisure*, 2nd ed. (London: Longman, 1981), p. 12.
26. Krishan Kumar, "The Social Culture of Work: Work, Employment, and Unemployment as Ways of Life," *New Universities Quarterly*, 34, no. 1, Winter 1979/1980, 9.
27. Robert W. Malcolmson, *Popular Recreations in English Society: 1700–1850* (Cambridge: Cambridge University Press, 1973), pp. 89–117; and Sidney Pollard, "Factory Discipline in the Industrial Revolution," *Economic History Review*, 2nd Series, 16, 254–271, especially 267–270.
28. Asa Briggs, *Mass Entertainment: The Origins of a Modern Industry* (Adelaide, Australia: Griffin Press, 1960), p. 9.
29. V. T. J. Arkell, *Britain Transformed: The Development of British Society Since the Mid-Eighteenth Century* (Harmondsworth: Penguin, 1973), pp. 44–50.
30. J. C. Pollock et al., *Where Does the Time Go?* (New York: Newspaper Enterprise Association, 1983), p. 30.
31. Max Kaplan, quoted in Stanley Parker, *The Sociology of Leisure* (London: George Allen and Unwin, 1976), p. 39.
32. George Comstock et al., *Television and Human Behavior* (New York: Columbia University Press, 1978), p. 147.
33. *Ibid.*, p. 152.
34. Tannis MacBeth Williams, ed., *The Impact of Television: A National Experiment in Three Communities* (Orlando, Fla.: Academic Press, 1986).
35. *Ibid.*, p. 403. See also pp. 121 and 372–375.
36. U. S. Department of Labor, Bureau of Labor Statistics, "Employment and Earnings," vol. 37, no. 1, January 1990, Table 34, p. 201.
37. Louis Harris and Associates, cited in *New York Times*, June 3, 1990, sect. 4, p. 3.
38. Staffan B. Linder, *The Harried Leisure Class* (New York: Columbia University Press, 1970), pp. 1, 12, 14, and 15.

CHAPTER 7
SOCIAL GROUPS

INTRODUCTION

The preceding analysis of one component of the total influence of science and technology on modern society obscures an important fact: That influence is far from uniform across social groups. If the *structure* of the societal influence of a technical change is to be revealed—thus better enabling comparative social justice to be done—one must disaggregate that influence and determine its varying effects on the interests and lots of different social groups, whether defined by age, ethnicity, class, gender, or other sociological variables. Let us therefore look at some ways in which science and technology have affected and are affecting the situations of four important social groups: blacks, children, the elderly, and women.

BLACKS

The influence of modern and contemporary science and technology on black people in the West has been decidedly mixed. However, any account of that influence must begin by recalling the fateful use by Europeans in the seventeenth and eighteenth centuries of military and transportation technologies and expertise to forcibly relocate tens of thousands of African natives to South America, the West Indies, and what was to become the United States of America. There, they and their descendants were compelled to live as slaves to their white "owners."

A technological development that profoundly influenced the ensuing lot of black people was the invention by Eli Whitney in 1793 of the cotton gin. With it, the lint of short-staple cotton could be efficiently separated from the seed for shipment back to English textile factories. The bottleneck in cotton production thus shifted from processing to cultivation and harvesting. The problem was met, according to James Street, by greatly increasing the amount of imported African slave labor.

Although slavery had long been a part of American colonial life, it was the expansion of cotton acreage which provided the great stimulus to the slave trade and the subsequent strenuous efforts to preserve the institution. In 1790, there were 697,697 slaves reported in the entire country. By 1860 there were 3,953,760, of whom the overwhelming number were confined to the South. The estimates ... make clear that by far the bulk of this labor came to be used in the cultivation of cotton.[1]

Hence, the social importance of the cotton gin for blacks: It gave powerful impetus to the expansion and consolidation of the Southern slave-based plantation system.

The previously mentioned post–Civil War revolution in American agriculture affected blacks differently than it did whites. "Emancipation" left roughly 4 million former black slaves "free" but propertyless. In contrast, white Southerners had property but were cash-poor. The labor system that emerged from this state of affairs was "sharecropping": The landowner provided the black laborer with "small plots of land, tools, seed, and work animals. The sharecroppers provided the skill and muscle needed to grow the crop" and turned over between one half and two thirds of the harvest to the landlords.[2]

As a result of the unproductive sharecropping system of small farms, black farm workers, three quarters of whom were still sharecroppers or tenant farmers as late as 1900, remained virtually propertyless as long as they remained in agriculture.[3] The days of the sharecropping system, however, were limited. As a wave of revolutionary agricultural innovations, such as reapers, combines, and tractors, swept across the United States in the 1880s, it became increasingly difficult for small farms to compete. Many small white-owned farms were consolidated into larger units able to realize the economies of scale offered by such innovations. Consequently, sharecropping blacks were driven out of agriculture in huge numbers.

Between 1865 and 1929, millions of blacks left the South, most of them for city life in New York or elsewhere. During the 1920s alone, 600,000 blacks moved north, many of them to Harlem.[4]

Unlike whites, who were also driven out of agriculture in huge numbers, black migrants to Northern cities, as former sharecroppers, had little money or property. Even more important, they possessed little of the knowledge and training that were to prove increasingly essential to success in the industrial work world of twentieth-century science and technology.

In the cities, the blacks provided an underlayer of cheap labor that served the economic needs of the growing industrial metropolis. Black males became the city's day laborers, its casual dockhands, its dishwashers, hallmen, bellboys. The black female workers became its servants, laundresses, cleaning women.[5]

Given the substantially greater material, financial, and human capital resources possessed by whites, black men were relegated to low-paying blue-collar jobs to a much greater extent than whites. This trend persisted over time. By 1977, about 50 percent of the employed workforce in the United States were in white-collar occupational groups (professional and technical; managers, administrators, and nonfarm proprietors; clerical; and sales). However, less than half that percentage (23 percent) of black *men* were so employed, compared with 42 percent of white males. On the other hand, almost three fifths (58 percent) of employed black men were in the shrinking blue-collar sector, compared with about two fifths (42 percent) of employed white men. Thus, in the words of Harold Vatter:

[I]n the two main occupational categories, white collar and blue collar, black males remained locked into the nineteenth century pattern ... [T]he revolution in American occupational structure [initiated by industrialization in America] tended to bypass black men.[6]

In the 1950s and 1960s, technology exerted a radically different kind of influence on American blacks: It gave impetus to the black liberation movement. Without television, the United States would not have witnessed Sheriff "Bull" Connor unleashing police dogs and high-pressure fire hoses at blacks demonstrating for equal access to public accommodations in Selma, Alabama, or followed the drama of James Meredith being escorted by federal troops into the University of Mississippi. Without television—and the transportation revolution—the nation would not have been moved by Martin Luther King's address to 1 million black and white people about his dream of racial justice on the occasion of the historic, technology-intensive "march" on Washington in 1963. In short, technological revolutions in communications and transportation made possible and facilitated the crystalization of a *national* black consciousness of racial discrimination and deprivation. This in turn helped engender a national civil rights movement. Television and the print media also fostered the recognition by mainstream white society of the injustices still being visited on black people. These changes in black and white consciousness helped bring into being ideational and institutional prerequisites of such socioeconomic progress as blacks have achieved in the last three decades.

In recent years, television has begun to convey to millions of black and white viewers images of black workers in professions other than entertainment and sports. More generally, blacks are no longer forced to consume diets of all-white programming. While the influence of such a phenomenon is difficult to gauge, it seems likely to have contributed to a heightening of black aspirations, a growing sense of legitimacy for black participation in mainstream society, and an increasing recognition that the social aspirations of blacks and whites largely overlap.

The recent influence of technology on black people is not always specifically focused on blacks as such. However, it has affected them as a group constituting a disproportionate percentage of the semi- or unskilled workforce. Relatively prosperous skilled or semiskilled black workers have been negatively affected by the increasing automation or "emigration" of industrial work processes to other parts of the "global factory," a trend which has resulted in an absolute decline in the 1980s of the number of jobs in the U.S. manufacturing sector. Numerous unskilled blacks have found low-paying, dead-end jobs in the service industry, such as the fast-food business, with its semiautomated production and service processes (e.g., computerized cash registers). The increase in the number of blacks in the technical professions, including engineering and science, has been impressive relative to earlier baseline figures of black participation. However, even with such growth, the proportions of technical professionals who are black remain miniscule. Between 1976 and 1986, the percentage of scientists who are black rose from 2 percent to 3 percent; of engineers, from 1 percent to 2 percent.[7]

Most disturbing, the analytical and quantitative skills needed for jobs available in the sector of the economy with the most promising future, the computer-based, information-intensive sector, are precisely those at which blacks, on average, have yet to realize their potential. In the absence of a serious societal commitment to develop the human capital resources of this social group, future technological change is likely to widen the gap between the many successful whites and relatively few blacks with the skills required by work in the new information order, and a growing "underclass" of black and other poor seemingly beyond the point of acquiring such skills. Lacking such a commitment, the ongoing revolution in information technology is likely to result in further stratification of the workforce along essentially racial-economic lines.

The fate of blacks under nineteenth and twentieth century American industrialization is a particularly compelling example of a central thesis advanced in Chapter 5 and throughout this book—namely, that the influence of a technical change on society (here, on a specific social group) depends critically on the "initial social conditions" that are in place when the innovations are unleashed. Pervasive and persistent discrimination against them aside, the meager human capital resources of "emancipated" blacks pertinent to the emerging industrial order relegated them at the outset to the bottom of the new economic totem pole. A variation of that tragedy may be in the process of being acted out in the context of the developing information economy.

CHILDREN

The situation of children has been profoundly affected by technology, from the agricultural societies of the Middle Ages to the contemporary electronic and computer society. In the Middle Ages, childhood, as modern industrial society conceives of it, did not even exist. There was no culturally shared idea of young people between birth and, say, 12 years of age as traversing a period of life requiring special treatment, such as being sheltered from certain kinds of labor or particular secrets, such as ones concerning sex, violence, and death. Western society in the Middle Ages was largely an oral, agricultural world. By the age of 7, young people had the skills to function in the adult work world: They had command over speech and could labor in the fields. Hence, prior to the sixteenth century, people as young as 7 years of age were regarded and treated as mini-adults.[8]

The invention of the printing press using moveable type and the growth of literacy in the late Renaissance not only undermined the authority of the Catholic Church; it transformed childhood. Over time, childhood was invented as a distinctive stage of life bridging infancy and adulthood. It began with the task of learning how to read and continued until that task was completed, at about 13 years of age. School was the institution created in order to teach people how to read. It took the young, who had mastered speech, and segregated them from infants and adults, for in that way reading could be taught efficiently and become an unconscious reflex. Over the next few centuries the special educational regimen deemed appropriate for people in this "natural" (actually technologically engendered) stage of life was elaborated into beliefs that there were special things children should know and not know, and special ways children should think, talk, dress, play, behave, and be treated, all different from adults. The socially constructed idea of childhood as a distinct life-stage—and the cultural institution of school—was rooted in the fact that since reading has a complex symbolic grammar, it took time (childhood), effort (discipline), and help (school) to master.

The new specialness of children was reflected in a number of important changes in the lot of children in the industrial era. Legislation was eventually passed that forbade full-time childhood work and banned outright certain kinds of dangerous work as incompatible with childhood specialness and its central literacy task. Both directly, through expanding productivity, and indirectly, through engendering the notion of childhood as special, and hence warranting the prescribing and proscribing of certain kinds of intellectual and physical treatment, technology has made the lives of children in industrialized societies physically easier.

Some writers contend that twentieth century electronic media are contributing to the erosion of the valuable traditional dividing line between childhood and adulthood. Books vary greatly in syntactical and lexical complexity, a feature long utilized in attempting to keep children from premature exposure to certain kinds of highly charged, potentially disturbing knowledge. Unlike books, however, television does not possess any formal grammatical prerequisites that must be mastered prior to gaining access to the material it offers; hence that material is relatively equally accessible to adults and children. Children may not be able to read and grasp books suitable for adults but they can watch television programs with "adult" subject matter. If, by affording differential access to sensitive subject matter, print media helped sustain the line between childhood and adulthood, the electronic media seem to be eroding that distinction, a development of uncertain psychological significance.

While provocative, this argument, advanced by Neil Postman and Joshua Meyerowitz, is somewhat speculative.[9] There is, however, abundant solid evidence about the influence of television on children. In the study by Williams and colleagues, cited in Chapter 6 in connection with the transformation of leisure, television was determined to have a number of significant influences on children. It retards the development of children's reading skills, produces lower scores on standardized creativity tests, intensifies the sex-typing of children's sex-role attitudes (i.e., beliefs about appropriate and typical behavior for girls and boys), and gives rise to heightened persistent aggressive behavior—verbal and physical—in both girls and boys.

Both the relative ease of accessing television (as compared to books) and the nature of television role models played important causal roles in these findings. The role-model issue, however, requires clarification. Unlike the findings associated with television's ease of access, the conclusion about the sex-typing of sex-role attitudes is attributable more to the socially shaped content of the medium than to its inherent nature. Were the models presented differently than they are, television might well diminish such sex-typing.

There is some evidence that two other modern technics, one "high" and one "low," may be exerting subtle but important influences on children: the computer and the high-rise apartment building. Sherry Turkle has identified three stages in children's relationships with computers.[10] Very young children exposed to computers are apt to go through a "metaphysical stage" in which they exhibit intense interest in whether the computer thinks, feels, or is alive. Their early experience with computers affects how they construct such central concepts as animate and inanimate, and conscious and nonconscious.* Subsequently, elementary school children enter a "mastery phase," during which they are mostly concerned about exercising effective control over the computers with which they come into contact, initially by playing video games, later by learning in school how to program computers. Third, the personal computer colors many adolescent children's views of themselves. Those who adopt the computer as their major activity choose a distinctive way to traverse their "identity" phase, one that may offer reliable companionship without emotional demands. For such children, computers induce self-creation and self-reflection through use of the programs they write.

*One is tempted to speak in such contexts of the sociotechnical construction of reality.

Although interested in the ways in which the computer influences childhood psychological development, Turkle's study has a broader purpose. She is also interested in shedding light on the character of the emerging computer culture. How will the ways in which children are affected by the computer be reflected in the emerging adult computer culture? Turkle suggests that the three childhood relationships to the computer prefigure the respective characters of three of the most important communities of adult computer users: the artificial intelligence community, whose members pursue metaphysical philosophical interests in whether it is possible to create machines capable of human intelligence; the hacker community, whose members delight in composing programs that can carry out complex tasks of mastery and control; and the community of home computer users, whose members ground parts of their identities in the ownership and use of personal computers.

While interested in learning "how the computer affects children," Turkle is aware that the computer's influence is not determinative but elicitive. Moreover, the "impact of the computer on children" is really a product not only of the nature of the computer itself but of initial social and psychological conditions: the nature of the human mind in general, the individual psychological history of each child user, and the structure and content programmed into the machine that confronts the child.

Surprisingly, the high-rise apartment building also seems to influence children's lives: Living in such structures may deleteriously affect psychosocial development. Between the ages of 2 and 7, a major developmental task for children is to achieve a satisfactory balance of autonomy and dependence in everyday experience. Completion of this task is important if the child is to gradually attain a sense of competence and independence. An important way in which small children develop an embryonic sense of autonomy is through excursions and explorations without the presence but within the sight of parents, followed by return to the safety of the parent. Initially, this may take the form of wandering a few feet away from the parent in a backyard or playground, but later it involves unsupervised play episodes, including exit from and return to the family residence. Such episodes are made viable where the caretaking parent can readily glance out a window of the residence, see the child playing, and be poised to intervene if necessary. The high-rise apartment building is strongly biased against this possibility. Young high-rise-bred children, writes Alice Coleman, "cannot cope with the stairs or lifts alone, nor is it safe to leave them alone on shared lawns open to strangers or to roads with traffic. Yet parents cannot be constantly supervising passage in and out of the block on the short time-scale of the toddler's attention span."[11] What results is, in Roger Hart's words, "an all-or-nothing approach. Either the parents relinquish care and let their children play anywhere they wish or they take the overprotective route of keeping them inside the apartment all of the time."[12] Since women in high-rise buildings also have less "neighboring contact" than those in low-rise units—a cause of depression for some young mothers who have previously worked—so do their children. A study of children living in New York City high-rises found that most were not allowed out to play by themselves until they were 10 years old.[13] To date, evidence of the negative effects of such isolation on children is as suggestive as it is disturbing. For example, Coleman states that high-rise-bred children, having been "more cooped up indoors" and having missed a "crucial stage in the development of self-confidence, ... seem [to be] more vulnerable to peer pressure and gang behavior."[14] Such claims and the continued proliferation of high-rise buildings make the influence of high-rise life on children a topic warranting further research.

THE ELDERLY

Developments in science and technology have transformed the situation of the elderly in contemporary society in a number of ways. We will focus here on three aspects of that situation in contemporary American society.

First, iatrogenic illness and industrial occupational diseases notwithstanding, as a result of improvements in nutrition, sanitation, and health care, people are living much longer lives on the average in the late twentieth century than ever before. In 1986, the average life expectancy for Americans was 74.9 years, compared with 47 years in 1900. Not coincidentally, the density of elderly people in the populations of the industrial nations of the world is increasing. Nine of the ten nations with the highest percentages of people over 65 years of age are industrial societies. Sweden leads the list with 17.8 percent, while the United States stands at eighteenth. About 12.2 percent of the American population in 1987 exceeded 65 years of age.[15] By 2030, it is estimated that 21.1 percent, or slightly over one in five Americans, will be over 65.[16]

However, this remarkable achievement has not been an unmixed blessing. Consider the situation with life-sustaining medical technology. More than half of all patients who receive cardiopulmonary resuscitation and tube feeding and about a third of patients who receive mechanical ventilation, renal dialysis, and total parenteral nutrition (TPN, an intravenous feeding procedure) are over age 65.[17] Such dramatic advances give hope for extended life to people with conditions that only a few years ago would have meant certain death. However, as resort to such technologies has increased, concern has grown about their use for patients who do not benefit from them or whose suffering may be prolonged. For example, it is estimated that in 1986, about 10,000 Americans were being sustained by technological means in irreversible vegetative comatose states, a development that has exacted enormous financial and psychological costs.[18]

The impressive achievement of greatly increased life expectancy also has problematic sociological aspects. The twentieth century transport revolution enables people in the United States to live at great distances from, and to visit periodically with, their elderly parents. Even where children do not live at great distances from their elderly parents, the growth of the two-career family and the single-parent mother—the former a phenomenon promoted by the women's movement (itself made posssible by a series of technological changes)—has lessened the extent to which children provide personal care for their elderly parents. This, together with the availability of sufficient disposable income, has created a situation in which many elderly are consigned to "nursing homes," an institutional innovation of the industrial era. In such homes, the elderly are segregated from youth and younger adults, are apt to atrophy intellectually, and serve little or no meaningful social function. As we saw earlier, when television is available, adults over 56, more than any other age group, tend to decrease both the number of community activities in which they participate and the degree to which they participate in them. Yet research has shown that active leisure pursuits help the elderly to age more successfully than do passive ones.[19]

A second dark social side of the longevity increase stems from the rate of technological change in contemporary society. Longer-living elderly run the real risk of being perceived as obsolescent, otiose, and even parasitic on society. The rapidity of technological change is an important factor in this cultural devaluation. However, the prevailing "initial social conditions"—the absence in industrialized countries of substantial institutional provision for helping or encouraging the elderly to stay abreast of technical changes—also contribute greatly to their being perceived as socially useless. The phenomenon of a "generation gap" is possible only in a society of considerable longevity and rapid social change.

In his aforementioned study of the effects of the introduction of the snowmobile into the reindeer sled–based society of the Finnish Skolt Lapps in the 1960s and 1970s, Pelto found that whereas elderly Lapps were able to drive their reindeer sleds well into their 70s, they did not possess sufficient strength or muscular dexterity to use the snowmobile much beyond the age of 60. Consequently, they rapidly lost the status and prestige they had enjoyed under the reindeer sled regime. The latter had been based on the fact that the elderly were the experts in reindeer matters and transmitted their hard-won experiential knowledge to the next generation. The old were rapidly displaced by the young, who could easily operate the snowmobile and now had little to learn in this regard from their elders.[20]

The triangular relationship of the elderly, the young, and the snowmobile may well prefigure that involving the computer in contemporary American society. Similar vitiation of the respect accorded the elderly by computer-literate youth and young adults seems likely. Enacting a law prohibiting mandatory retirement at age 65 or 70, as the United States has done, may prove economically useful to many elderly. However, it is unlikely to materially affect the negative way in which they are perceived and valued by younger members of society. Intergenerational conflict is technically rooted in at least two phenomena: (1) the central, productive involvement of youth and young adults and the negligible, unproductive involvement of the elderly in contemporary science and technology, and (2) the fact that the nonelderly must foot the mounting bill for the technology-intensive medical care of the growing, longer-living elderly population. Barring some imaginative societal intervention to generate for the elderly a productive and meaningful role in contemporary technological society, conflict between young and old adults seems likely to intensify for the foreseeable future.

WOMEN

Technological change has had a deep, complex influence on women since 1800. Prior to the onset of industrialization in the United States, most women worked at home as co-producers with their families in the predominantly agricultural economy. After 1800, women sometimes supplemented their seasonal farm labor by doing paid piecework in the home, usually in the textile industry (then organized on a putting-out or cottage-industry basis). With the coming of industrialization, initially in the period from 1820 to 1840 and in earnest after the Civil War, an increasing number of young women were induced or compelled to work outside the home. While some became teachers, kept boarders, did needlework, set type, or worked in bookbinding, most went to work as domestic servants to the emerging middle class or as operatives in large factories doing work reminiscent of what they had previously done at home (e.g., clothes making, textile and millinery work, and food processing). Indeed, in the 1830s and 1840s these were the seven major occupations open to women outside the home.[21]

Given the nature of the work then available to and permitted to women, paternalistic male attitudes being what they were, middle class men did not want their wives to work outside the home. Indeed, while in 1870 about 15 percent of all women 16 and over worked for wages outside the home, most of them were young and unmarried and disporportionately poor or nonwhite or both.[22] Middle-class male attitudes engendered a cult of domesticity. The proper woman's place was the home. The emerging fateful industrial equation of "work" with "paid employment," meant that the supposed proper sphere of the woman was the private one of nonwork.

In the period from 1870 to 1900, as industrialization in the United States moved into high gear, a spate of inventions and innovations, such as the telephone, the steel-framed office building, and the typewriter, provided new employment opportunities for women. For example, between 1870 and 1900, the number of women working in offices increased by 2,700 percent, from 19,000 to 503,000. Many of these women worked as typists. Women made inroads in retail sales—selling the products produced by the nation's rapidly expanding industrial system—and in telecommunications. Some of these jobs quickly became typed as women's work and were thus associated with meager remuneration and negligible chances for professional advancement. For example, while telephone operators were originally all men, they were quickly displaced by lower-paid women who offered companies the bonus of more "courteous" behavior toward customers. Almost as dramatically, whereas in 1870 there were only 350 female telegraph operators, by 1907, of the roughly 80,000 telegraphers, all but 3,500 were women.[23]

Thus, in the period from 1800 to 1900, particularly after the Civil War, new technology opened the door for substantially increased paid employment of women outside the household, albeit primarily in a limited number of sex-typed occupational fields. Middle-class white women, however, were not greatly affected. Nevertheless, this development was significant in three ways. First, it offered many women their first (although often temporary) exposure to an alternative to traditional female home work. Second, the machine gradually eliminated differential physical strength as a factor upon which to base male and female work roles.[24] Third, the new employment opportunities generated by technologies introduced toward the end of the nineteenth century gave many working women options to the occupation of domestic servant. The number of women employed in this position, which still amounted to almost 2 million in 1910, dropped steeply thereafter, even as the number of households rose rapidly. This helped foster a new technological revolution that affected women.

This revolution, which unfolded in the period from 1910 to 1940, took place not in the factory but in the home. A host of technological innovations was introduced that radically changed the nature of household work carried out by millions of women, partly as a response to the declining supply of domestic servants. The industrialization of the household took several forms: the appearance of a new technological infrastructure (running water, electricity, gas, and sewerage), "labor-saving appliances" (the washing machine, dishwasher, electric vacuum cleaner, electric iron), "convenience foods" (canned, concentrated, and frozen goods, the latter made possible by the refrigerator), and the expansion of "market-sector services" for work traditionally done in the home, such as restaurants and laundromats. Technology, it was believed and thought, would liberate women from the drudgery of housework, thereby releasing them into the public world of paid employment outside the home.[25]

More recent scholarship has challenged this liberation thesis. Ruth Schwartz Cowen has argued that while new household technologies often made existing work easier or able to be done more quickly, several factors effectively dissipated the benefits women might have been expected to derive. The radical decline in "household assistants" and the emigration of daughters from the home and into newly created industrial positions meant that many individual women had to do household tasks previously done by several people. Technological advances thus enabled women homemakers only to keep from being overwhelmed. Second, in order to promote the purchase of new mass-produced industrial products, the increasingly potent institution of advertising projected new components and higher standards of home and child care for women. Ideology succeeded in inducing women to devote the technology-based time savings that they gained into meeting the demands of a radically expanded job description: the "housewife" or "homemaker" as dietician, sanitary engineer, home economist, and chauffeur.[26]

The introduction of technological infrastructure utilities like hot and cold running water, electricity, and convenience foods did reduce the time and labor required by some forms of work, such as water heating, clothes washing, and food preparation. However, while the proliferation of new small, single-task electrical appliances made possible by such utilities increased the standard of living, it also expanded women's work in living it. Increased time was required for shopping for, cleaning, and seeing to the maintenance and repair of these innovations.[27] Here, too, middle-class women are seen as having been sold a revised, expanded bill of household goods. Bose and colleagues argue that for middle-class women, "the greatest influences on time spent on household work have come from nontechnological changes, changes in household size and in paid employment of women."[28]

While there is considerable truth in this critique of the household-technology-as-women's-liberator thesis, it underestimates the role of technology in altering women's situation. For example, the two changes highlighted by Bose and co-workers were made possible in considerable part by changes in technology (and science): ones at the base of new technological industries and those underlying the increasing efficacy, production, and diffusion of contraception in the twentieth century. Together with the fact that machine-based production rendered male-female strength differences increasingly irrelevant, the radical decline in infant mortality rates, the increasing ability of women to control reproduction, and the increased exposure to the world of paid employment occasioned by the widespread work of women in industry during World War II helped pave the way for the women's movement of the last two decades.

The cultural-environmental system (CES) Equilibrium–Disequilibrium explanation of this important phenomenon (see Chapter 5) is that new behavioral possibilities were unleashed by these technical changes, options which were at bottom incompatible with the perpetuation of the old middle-class female roles and traditional restricted patterns of access to key work institutions, including universities, unions, and the "learned" professions. Determined, resourceful, even heroic efforts of feminist writers and activists notwithstanding, the cultural changes associated with the women's movement were and are to a great extent adaptive ideational, institutional, and behavioral responses to the tension in the CES between the new behavioral (including work) options made available to women by scientific and technological changes and the attempts by vested, typically male-dominated, interest groups to sustain mentalities, roles, and practices adapted to an earlier scientific-technological order.

Critics of the technology-as-women's-liberator thesis argue correctly that technical change per se did not bring about the changes associated with women's altered situation in contemporary Western society. Capitalist-inspired advertising, by projecting expanded job descriptions for homemakers, dissipated the gains afforded by individual household technologies. Nevertheless, technological changes, while not sufficient, helped prepare the cultural soil for the changes in women's situation that ensued. Powerful episodic dislocations like World World II, social trends such as the increasing divorce rate, and the economic needs and interests of one- and two-career families aspiring to post-World War II affluence also played causal roles of various sorts in bringing about women's changed situation. A complex, evolving set of technical enabling conditions and an array of ideological and societal factors, some promoting and others retarding significant change in women's situation, remain locked in struggle to this day with uncertain outcome. Nevertheless, without the technological and scientific changes of the last hundred years, the greatly changed cultural and economic situation of women in contemporary Western society would in all likelihood not yet have come to pass.

CONCLUSION

There is no way of neatly summarizing the substance of our discussion of the influence of technology and science on the social groups considered in this chapter. It may be worth stressing once again, however, that thinking and speaking of "the influence of technology and science on society" obscures the cardinal fact that that influence is apt to vary from one social group to another and, further, that the influence exerted by technology and science on a particular social group depends critically on the initial social conditions prevailing (in society at large and in the group itself) when the technical innovations are unleashed.

ENDNOTES

1. James H. Street, *The New Revolution in the Cotton Economy: Mechanization and Its Consequences* (Chapel Hill: University of North Carolina Press, 1957), p. 7.
2. Robert L. Heilbroner and Aaron Singer, *The Economic Transformation of America: 1600 to the Present*, 2nd ed. (New York: Harcourt Brace Jovanovich, 1984), p. 136.
3. *Ibid.*, pp. 136–137.
4. *Ibid.*, p. 256.
5. *Ibid.*
6. Harold Vatter, "Technological Innovation and Social Change in the United States, 1870–1980," in Joel Colton and Stuart Bruchey, eds., *Technology, Economy, and Society* (New York: Columbia University Press, 1987), p. 40.
7. *Science and Technology Data Book: 1989* (Washington, D.C.: National Science Foundation, 1988), p. 27.
8. Neil Postman, *The Disappearance of Childhood* (New York: Dell, 1982), p. 13.
9. Joshua Meyerowitz, "The Adultlike Child and the Childlike Adult: Socialization in an Electronic Age," *Daedalus*, 113, no. 3, Summer 1984, 19–48.
10. Sherry Turkle, *The Second Self: Computers and the Human Spirit* (New York: Simon & Schuster, 1984).
11. Alice Coleman, "High Rise," *Science and Public Policy*, 15, no. 2, April 1988, 102.
12. *New York Times*, September 10, 1987, p. 19.
13. *Ibid.*
14. Coleman, "High Rise," p. 102.
15. *San Francisco Chronicle*, July 15, 1987, p. 6.
16. U.S. Congress, Office of Technology Assessment, *Life-Sustaining Technologies and the Elderly* (Washington, D.C.: U.S. Government Printing Office, 1987), p. 77.
17. *Ibid.*, p. 11.
18. *New York Times*, August 18, 1986, p. 9.
19. Tannis MacBeth Williams, ed., *The Impact of Television: A Natural Experiment in Three Communities* (Orlando, Fla.: Academic Press, 1986), p. 184.

20. Pertti J. Pelto, *The Snowmobile Revolution: Technology and Social Change in the Arctic* (Menlo Park, Cal.: Cummings, 1973), pp. 74–75, 139–140, 170.
21. Heilbroner and Singer, *Economic Transformation*, p. 230.
22. *Ibid.*
23. *Ibid.*, pp. 231–232.
24. For a useful case study of continuing attempts by men to exclude women from traditionally "male occupations" even when technologies were introduced into the workplace that rendered differences in physical strength irrelevant, see Ava Baron, "Contested Terrain Revisited: Technology and Gender Definitions of Work in the Printing Industry, 1850–1920," in Barbara Drygulski Wright et. al. eds., *Women, Work, and Technology: Transformations* (Ann Arbor: University of Michigan Press, 1987), 58–83.
25. Christine Bose, Philip Bereano, and Mary Malloy, "Household Technology and the Social Construction of Housework," *Technology and Culture*, 25, no. 1, 1984, 53.
26. Ruth Schwartz Cowen, "The 'Industrial Revolution' in the Home: Household Technology and Social Change in the 20th Century," *Technology and Culture*, 17, no. 1, 1976, 13.
27. Bose et al., "Household Technology," pp. 65–66, 74, 80.
28. *Ibid.*, p. 81.

CHAPTER 8

WORLD VIEWS
AND HUMAN VALUES

INTRODUCTION

The influence components examined in Chapters 6 and 7—namely, those involving changes in institutions and social groups—pertain to the *societal* sector of the cultural system. In this chapter we will explore the influence of modern science and technology on phenomena belonging to a different sector of that system: the *ideational* realm. As noted in Chapter 4, the elements of this sector are mental: society's characteristic values, norms, ideas, beliefs, knowledge, philosophies, world views, tastes, attitudes, feelings, and expectations.

Few if any mental elements of modern Western culture have gone untouched by the continuing scientific and industrial revolutions which began in Europe in the seventeenth and eighteenth centuries. However, our discussion of the ideational influence of modern scientific and technological change will focus on several kinds of mental elements. We will begin by exploring the influence of science and technology on modern Western world views. Next, we will consider the bearing of technical changes on selected modern Western ideas, beliefs, and attitudes. Finally, a number of central modern Western values affected by developments in science and technology will be discussed. Since relatively little systematic empirical study has been devoted to identifying specific value changes attributable to scientific and technological developments, our discussion of this topic will be correspondingly speculative. Besides exploring noteworthy substantive changes in selected mental elements of modern Western culture engendered by advances in science and technology, we will also be interested in characterizing some of the *mechanisms* by which technical developments eventuate in cultural value change.

WORLD VIEWS

A *world view* is a descriptive-interpretive mental model of the universe and its phenomena. World views encompass beliefs about various fundamental matters, such as what things are real and what are illusory in the world; the origins, natures, and destinies (if any) of things that exist; the primary forces at work in the world; the purposes (if any) built into the world and manifested in what transpires in it; and how human life ought to be lived. Among other things, world views help their subscribers find meaning in otherwise unbearable suffering, give direction to their lives, and spur them to overcome opposing forces.

The Scientific Revolution and the Rise of a Mechanistic World View

The first great influence of science and technology on world views in modern Western culture was the transformative one wrought by the scientific revolution of the seventeenth century. A radically new world view emerged and eventually achieved primacy, at least in educated circles. In it, as noted in Chapter 2, the universe was seen as a mechanism akin to a clockworks. In the words of P. M. Harman:

> By around 1700, educated men conceived the universe as a mechanical structure like a clock, the earth was regarded as a planet revolving around the sun, and the mysteries of nature were supposed to be open to investigation by means of experimentation and mathematical analysis. These new attitudes to the natural world contrast strikingly with the traditional conception of nature: that the earth was immobile and the center of the cosmos, the cosmos itself being envisaged as a structure of crystalline spheres enveloping the central earth like the layers of an onion; nature was conceived as a living organism, a connected structure linked by a web of hidden active powers.[1]

The emergence of this heliocentric-mechanistic world view left a place for the deity as designer and winder of the cosmological clockworks. During the next two centuries, however, further scientific developments posed new challenges to the revised world views of educated religious believers. Advances in paleontology and geology in the nineteenth century, culminating in Darwin's theory of purpose-less, directionless evolution by natural selection, and Freud's account of human behavior as driven most powerfully by unconscious instinctual urges for survival and sexual pleasure, wrote new chapters in the scientific assault on human narcissism. Many educated people thus felt compelled to make further major revisions in their world views.

Most Westerners had long seen themselves as superior to "animals," partly because of their supposedly characteristic rationality and partly because they were supposedly specially created by God. Moreover, it was widely believed that human life had inherent purposes and directions. The upshot of the aforementioned changes was that to many educated modern Westerners, science seemed to call for greater intellectual humility, perhaps even agnosticism or atheism. The human being had been dethroned and human life decentered: The human is also an animal, and human life is not at the "center" of the universe—if such a concept even makes scientific sense. Nineteenth and twentieth century science has challenged Westerners to develop world views compatible with the modern belief that there are no scientifically credible, pre-existing "grids" into which a human being may plug in order to imbue his life with objective cosmological meaning, value, and purpose. Beliefs that such grids did exist had characterized Western world views at least since the days of the ancient Greek, Egyptian, and Near Eastern peoples. Now such beliefs are regarded, at least by the great majority of Western intellectuals, as increasingly problematic if not incredible.

Twentieth Century Developments in Science

Even people who had successfully adapted their world views to these disturbing changes in the earth and biological sciences found developments in nineteenth and twentieth century physics difficult to grasp and internalize. Prior to the acceptance of Maxwell's electromagnetic theory, the mechanistic explanation of the natural world in terms of interactions between particles, each modeled on the lines of a miniature billiard ball or ballbearing, held sway. In 1931, on the occasion of Maxwell's centenary, Albert Einstein observed:

> Since Maxwell's time, Physical Reality has been thought of as represented by continuous fields, and not capable of any mechanical interpretation. This change in the conception of Reality is the most profound and the most fruitful that Physics has experienced since the time of Newton.[2]

At least as perplexing were the implications of two other towering achievements of twentieth century physics. Einstein's theory of special relativity discredited the time-honored, seemingly unimpeachable notions of absolute space, time, and mass. In their place it put forward the esoteric notions of a space-time continuum and a surprising thesis affirming the interconvertibility of matter and energy, as represented in the fateful equation underlying the atomic bomb, $E=mc^2$. In 1927, physicist Werner Heisenberg formulated his indeterminacy principle, according to which achieving absolute precision in determining simultaneously both the position and the momentum of a single subatomic particle was impossible. For many intellectuals, this principle delivered a crushing blow to the venerable Enlightenment ideal of attaining absolute certainty about the physical world. With these and other puzzling developments in twentieth century physics, contemporary intellectuals and educated lay people have been confronted by science with a universe of unimaginably counterintuitive character that seems to defy or render absurd many perennial, psychologically comforting human assumptions, concepts, and beliefs.

Abstract Science, Rapid Technological Change, and Contemporary World Views

One by-product of this cultural development has been that traditional religious world views have become increasingly suspect. In the twentieth century West, religious believers have tended to react to this challenge in one of three ways. Most have remained ignorant of the findings of twentieth century physics (and biology) and have retained intact their traditional anthropocentric and anthropomorphic religious world views. Some have tried to forge world views synthesizing certain traditional religious elements with the ever more abstract and arcane views of the universe propounded by modern scientists. Thus, for example, God is seen by some religious believers as having created the universe by instigating the recently confirmed big bang. A few intellectually inclined believers have felt compelled to adopt more thoroughly abstract world views in hopes of doing justice to the abstractness of the latest scientific view of reality.

Regarding the first option, rapid technical change has challenged the credibility of traditional anthropomorphic world views. Some hunting-and-gathering Native American tribes may have been comfortable with a conception of afterlife as a happy *hunting* ground, an obvious projection of the techno-economic character of their own societies. However, with the increasingly abstract character of the-world-according-to-contemporary-science, it is increasingly problematic for the world views in, say, the Judeo-Christian tradition to continue to incorporate anthropomorphic religious conceptions—"God the Father," "the wrathful Jehovah"—understood as literally true.

The same crisis of credibility applies to immutable world views conceived in terms of specific technologies characteristic of a relatively static phase of cultural development. For example, are bows and arrows still used in the "happy hunting ground," or has the afterworld also been agriculturalized or industrialized? If the latter, does St. Peter still secure the entrance to the afterworld—a place or a condition?—by using gate keys, or has a state-of-the-art, remotely operated electronic security system been installed?

A difficult dilemma has thus emerged for intellectually conscientious believers. On the one hand, only world views of a sufficiently abstract character and content—thus ones not couched in terms of particular technologies and technological processes—are immune to seeming increasingly implausible in a rapidly changing scientific-technological society. On the other hand, to the extent that a world view is made more abstract in order to render it so immune, it loses its ability to touch the individual on a deep psychospiritual level. Either the deity becomes an uninspiring impersonal force, or the continued attribution to it of anthropomorphic qualities, such as humanoid thoughts and feelings, seems gratuitous and arbitrary in such a setting.

IDEAS AND IDEALS

Many key ideas and ideals in the mental matrix of modern Western culture, such as those of human nature, the human mind, the good life, community, democratic government, property, and sex roles, have been profoundly influenced in various ways by developments in modern science and technology.

Progress

Consider, for example, the pivotal Western idea of progress. For Sidney Pollard,

The idea of progress is, in this modern age, one of the most important ideas by which men live, not least because most hold it unconsciously and therefore unquestioningly. It has been called the modern religion, or the modern substitute for religion, and not unjustly so. Its character, and its assumptions, have changed with time, and so has the influence exerted by it, but at present [1968] it is riding high, affecting the social attitudes and social actions of all of us.[3]

The idea of progress has been construed in several different senses. First, many have taken it to mean continued improvement in "knowledge of the environment of man, in the natural sciences, and, more recently, ... in technology derived from them."[4] Second, almost all who believe in progress in this sense also believe that this technological improvement will lead in the future to "improvement in the material conditions of life."[5] Third, of those who believe in progress in both of these senses, many "would feel equally persuaded that the tendency of the past, to be continued into the future, includes the improvement of social and political organization, and that human societies will become better governed, more just, freer, more equal, more stable or in other ways better equipped to permit a higher development of the human personality."[6]

Let us call this latter understanding "societal progress." It is this sense of "progress" that is the focus of our interest here.

The notion of societal progress did not emerge in a vacuum. Rather, it crystallized in response to a narrower but unmistakable technical trend. Beginning in the early sixteenth century, growing awareness of a number of impressive recent inventions and advances in technology and science planted the seeds of the idea of progressive improvement in matters technical in the minds of several thinkers, including Francis Bacon.* The wedding of gunpowder and an improved cannon, the invention of printing with movable type, and the magnetic compass ("the true rudder") and improved sails (which together made possible the great European voyages of discovery)—these technical improvements and the gains they made possible occurred just prior to or during Bacon's lifetime. Given this development—technical progress—and the substantial social gains that it made possible for some Europeans, it is perhaps not surprising, at least in retrospect, that Bacon, while using the term explicitly only to refer to progress in knowledge, clearly grasped the idea of societal progress as a goal to be pursued in certain specific ways.

Bacon believed that grounding future technological activity on systematic science, instead of on artisanal trial and error, would yield more solid knowledge in increasing amounts. This would permit increased control over nature in order to, in his words, "relieve and benefit the condition of man."[7] Animated by his awareness of recent progress in science and technology, Bacon was the first major Western thinker to envision the possibility of overcoming the traditional attitude of resignation and pessimism that had long held sway in Western culture regarding humankind's ability to substantially improve its earthly lot.

Many eighteenth century French Enlightenment thinkers wrote explicitly of societal progress. This often meant a general improvement in social and political life as construed by the prosperous and increasingly influential middle class. Such thinkers usually grounded their belief that such progress was likely—in Condorcet's case, inevitable—in the recognizable, accelerating technical progress then being made in the mechanical arts and sciences.[8] Ironically, the ambiguous legacy of the twentieth century wedding of science and technology, particularly in the field of weaponry but also in regard to industrial pollution, has, in the minds of many people, sundered the previously conflated notions of technical and social progress. Living with ever more potent, accurate, and widely diffused nuclear weapons has made technical progress seem neither a guarantor nor even a generally reliable index of societal progress.

Happiness

One of the most striking changes in the ideals of modern Western society is the emergence and widespread diffusion of an ideal of happiness based heavily on material consumption—in short, a consumptional ideal of happiness. As the productive system spawned by the industrial revolution moved into high gear, people's lives were increasingly organized around the conditioned desire to acquire, display and consume industrial products in sufficient amounts and qualities. This new orientation coexisted, sometimes uneasily, with periodic, often perfunctory bows in the direction of tradi-

---

*This growth in awareness of advances in science and technology was linked to the proliferation of books around this time, a development in turn attributable to the invention of the movable-type printing press. On this point, see Elizabeth Eisenstein, *The Printing Press as an Agent of Change* (Cambridge: Cambridge University Press, 1979).

tional ascetic religious and work ideals. The crucial point here—and in the treatment of several human values that we will discuss shortly—is that the changed nature of the reigning cultural ideal of happiness reflected the new socioeconomic need to ensure sufficient demand for the greatly increased supplies of goods that the new industrial system was now capable of producing. In this way, the potent new technologies of production influenced society's ideal of happiness. Reminiscent of the aforementioned transformation of leisure in the late 1800s, the societal ideal of happiness gradually accommodated itself to the new profusion of material goods by devaluing ascetic denial and celebrating affluent consumption.

BELIEFS AND EXPECTATIONS, ATTITUDES AND FEELINGS

A number of important beliefs and attitudes long associated with modern Western life have been undermined by developments in science and technology. In some instances, substitutes have arisen to take their places. For example, in the era of global transportation and communication, traditional beliefs about the alleged inherent superiority or inferiority of one or another people, race, gender, or way of life have, in many educated people's minds, come to be recognized as parochial and culturally conditioned. In the post–World War II period, such crude, self-serving beliefs have begun to yield either to relativistic views—no people, race, gender, or cultural way of life seen as inherently better than any other—or to case-by-case, comparative judgments of particular people or of specific aspects of lifeways, where such judgments are subject to periodic reassessment based on empirical evidence.

Once-familiar expectations of parents living on after death through their children, about children following in parental occupational footsteps, and about retaining a job, spouse, residence, or community for much or all of one's life have to a significant degree become casualties of twentieth century scientific and technological developments. In contrast, science and technology have helped engender many new cultural beliefs about the future, such as the "revolution of rising expectations" of material wealth and the widespread Western expectations of living a long and "successful" life and of frequent foreign travel.

As for attitudes, the twentieth century revolution in mass communications has contributed to the weakening of traditional xenophobia and fostered greater tolerance of groups once effectively excluded from mainstream life, such as homosexuals and the handicapped. At the same time, developments in science and technology have engendered disturbing new feelings in modern Western culture. Apprehensiveness over the fragility of peace, fear of the carnage of nuclear war, and, more recently, anxiety over environmental degradation now seem ongoing and sufficiently widespread to qualify as characteristic of contemporary Western culture.

HUMAN VALUES

Many people regard human values as purely matters of individual choice. However, even such personal preferences are often influenced by, among other societal phenomena, prior or concurrent scientific and technological trends and achievements. Indeed, a number of the most important characteristic values of contemporary Western society have been strongly affected in different ways by scientific and technological developments during the past two centuries. With this in mind, let us explore the following important modern Western values:

knowledge	self-realization
technology	cosmopolitanness
science	peace
progress	environment
efficiency	justice
novelty	authority

Knowledge, Technology, Science, and Progress

Empirical *knowledge*, material *technology*, systematic *science*, and societal *progress* have long been four of the cornerstone, mutually reinforcing values in modern Western culture. They held sway among most members of the intellectual and economic elites in Enlightenment France, England, and the United States and, by and large, continue to do so to this day. These values were at the heart of the work that, more than any other, embodied and promoted the neo-Baconian spirit of the French Enlightenment: *The Encyclopedia*, edited by Denis Diderot.

In a seminal article ("Encyclopedia") in Volume 5, Diderot makes explicit the centrality of these four values in his work. On one level, he states, its purpose is to bring together in an organized way all knowledge pertaining to human beings and nature. Of special importance to Diderot in this connection were comprehensive knowledge of the natural world and, surprisingly, given the long-standing prejudice of many intellectuals against the "mechanical arts," of inventions and technological processes as practiced in shops and factories by secretive craftsmen. Using careful "observation," "experimental science," and "rational philosophy," "all things must be examined,...winnowed and sifted without exception and without sparing anyone's sensibilities." If the resultant body of empirical knowledge that has survived critical scrutiny is "transmit[ted] to those who come after us," it will have a most "useful effect": "The general education of mankind" will be advanced, ignorance and superstition will be undermined, and people will thereby be made "more virtuous and happier." A new chapter will have been written in "the forward march of the human spirit" (read: societal progress).[9]

These four values eventually became deeply ensconced in the mental matrix of a broad cross-section of people in twentieth century Western societies, not just among intellectual and economic elites. This happened largely because advances in science and technology helped deliver the economic and medical goods to large numbers of people in those societies. Moreover, they gave undeniable evidence of a continuing, indeed increasing, ability to do so.

Efficiency

Let us look in greater detail at a value that in this century has become a fixture in Western culture: *efficiency*.* To ascertain how efficiency attained this status requires consideration of this concept's long and complex career, one whose definitive cultural history has yet to be written. Nevertheless, even cursory examination of the evolution of this concept reveals that developments in science and technology have been pivotal in its rise to the status of a central Western cultural value.

---

*Although it has several different meanings, depending on the kind of item under consideration, in general we will understand *efficiency* to refer to the relationship of the "outputs" of a system to its "inputs" or to its defining parameters.

Roughly speaking, the concept of efficiency has traversed six distinguishable, sometimes overlapping evolutionary stages.

The Perennial Technical Stage.   Achieving improvements in technics and technical systems is something humans have done for millenia. Although ancient peoples seem not to have had the word *efficiency* or its equivalent, many such improvements (e.g., in technics like catapults and plows and in technological processes like spinning and smelting) amounted to gains in what would today be called efficiency. The perennial quest for and receptivity to improvements in efficiency may be said to be a "natural" disposition for humans, for they typically have limited amounts of valuable resources at their disposal (e.g., time, materials, and strength). Efficiency improvements offering savings in such resources often bestow on those with access to them considerable adaptive advantage vis-à-vis their natural or social environments.

The Modern Technical Stage.   The eighteenth century marked a new stage in the career of efficiency as a value. Around the middle of the century, British engineer John Smeaton carried out *systematic* studies of energy technics such as windmills and waterwheels. His goal was to determine which designs would yield the most efficient operation of the respective technics. Smeaton's method was to introduce a series of slight variations in *one* of the variables characterizing the technic in question (e.g., blade angle in relation to wind or water stream) while holding the values of *all other* defining variables constant (e.g., number or weight of blades, interblade distance, or shape of blade element). For each set of parameter values chosen, Smeaton would determine the output—here, power—of the corresponding device. Each device-defining variable would eventually undergo gradual variation while the others would be held constant, and output measurements for the corresponding devices would be obtained. After measuring the output for all combinations of the variables defining the device under investigation, Smeaton would select the design characteristics yielding the maximum efficiency: maximum output—here, power—for a given input—wind or water current.[10]

In the nineteenth century, the explicit, systematic pursuit of efficiency as a technical value expanded from the realm of mechanics into that of thermodynamics. French physicist and engineer Sadi Carnot carried out theoretical research on steam engines. His aim, however, was quite practical: to ascertain whether there was "an assignable limit to the motive power of heat, hence to the improvement of steam engines."[11] Using a number of abstract concepts, several of which he took over by analogy from earlier work of his father's on mechanical devices, Carnot analyzed a specific cycle of an ideal heat engine ("the Carnot engine") and concluded that the "maximum thermal efficiency of a heat engine," the work it puts out divided by the heat it absorbs from a hot reservoir, "depends only upon the temperatures of the reservoirs between which it runs, and not at all upon the nature of the gas inside it."[12] Thus, in the eighteenth and nineteenth centuries, through systematic empirical and theoretical scientific work, efficiency became an explicit, central technological value pursued in both empirical engineering and theoretical scientific research.

The Modern Human Stage.   In the eighteenth century, French physicist and engineer Charles Augustin Coulomb carried out systematic experiments on human work. His aim was to determine how to increase the efficiency and thus the output of the individual worker's labor. In 1799 Coulomb published a memoir, "Results of Several Experiments Aimed at Determining the Amount of Work that Men Can Furnish by Their Daily Labor, According to the Different Manners in Which They Employ Their Strength." It was based on his earlier work in Martinique as engineer in charge of several hundred laborers and responsible for constructing a huge fort.

Like Smeaton, Coulomb also employed the method of "parameter variation." He identified and systematically varied one at a time the variables characterizing the work being studied in order to maximize "the ratio of effect to fatigue." Conclusions such as "frequent rest periods during certain tasks produce higher overall output" and "maximum daily work results from seven to eight hours' labor for heavy tasks and ten hours' labor for light tasks" marked the debut in earnest of efficiency as an explicit, systematically pursued value in a new area: human labor.[13] Coulomb's study was far in advance of its time, however. Systematic attention to the complex relationship between the tools, tasks, and methods of human labor on the one hand and resultant output on the other did not become a central topic of engineering interest until the mid-nineteenth century.

The Modern Sociotechnical Stage.   With the rapid expansion of the factory system in nineteenth century Europe and the United States, and the coming together of large numbers of workers and expensive machinery in large-scale workplaces, the stage was set for the emergence of a new kind of technical professional: the industrial or efficiency engineer. The aim of such engineers was to determine how to train workers and organize and orchestrate the operations of people, technics, materials, and capital so as to maximize industrial output in relation to the resources employed in producing it. This is the concept of economic efficiency, which now became an explicit value pursued vigorously by managers and owners.[14] This movement received powerful and influential expression in Frederick Winslow Taylor's notion of "scientific management," in effect, a set of rules, practices, and procedures for enhancing the efficiency of industrial activities, in construction as well as in the factory (see Chapter 6).

The Modern Institutional Stage.   Taylor was prompted to formulate his principles for efficiency enhancement by what he saw as the rampant waste in industrial settings. However, in his classic *Principles of Scientific Management*, Taylor argued presciently that

> [T]he same principles can be applied with equal force to all social activities: the management of our homes; the management of our farms; the management of the business of our tradesmen, large and small; of our churches, our philanthropic institutions, our universities, and our governmental departments.[15]

He believed that interest in efficiency enhancement was on the verge of spreading beyond the confines of the factory and embarking on a long march through the full spectrum of large-scale institutions of twentieth century industrial society. Taylor thus anticipated the emergence of the most recent stage in the career of efficiency as a value: everyday life.

The Contemporary Stage of Everyday Life.   As scientific and technological development accelerated in the twentieth century, everyday life became more complex, at least for individuals in urban and metropolitan areas. The increasing demands made on the individual, coupled with the expanding array of attractive ways of expending available time, resulted in growing pressure to do things more efficiently. Consequently, millions of people were induced to alter the ways in which they went about doing mundane things in everyday life. Activities that consumed considerable amounts of time or labor were natural targets for efficiency enhancement; hence the proliferation of phenomena like speed reading, food processors and microwave ovens, word processors, communicating by phone instead of letter, and appliances that automate or speed up household cleaning tasks.

In sum, efficiency began its career as an implicit "natural" human goal; became an explicit, systematically pursued value of modern engineering; entered the shop and factory, where it took on human and economic dimensions and was systematically pursued as a cardinal organizational value; was extended to the office and various noneconomic institutions, and finally, in the twentieth century, attained the status of a central value promoting the reformation of practices of everyday life in Western culture. Thus did developments in science and technology pave the way for the relentless "efficiency-ization" of contemporary Western life.

Novelty, Self-Realization, Cosmopolitanness

Novelty, self-realization, and *cosmopolitanness* are important Western values of more recent vintage. Like the consumptional ideal of happiness, novelty as a cultural value is also unique to industrial society. It owes its existence and vitality primarily to the capital-intensive nature and enormous annual generative power of Western production systems. Firms with large capital investments in mass-production machinery could not survive or thrive if inconsiderate consumers persisted in being satisfied with what they already had. The emergence of novelty as a cultural value and complementary culturally fostered disparagement of "old-fashioned" models helped forge concepts of consumer virtue and vice well suited to what producers regarded as techno-economic necessity.

The important post–World War II value of *self-realization* could have emerged only in social circumstances in which the material needs of most citizens were securely and more than adequately met. This being the case, qualitative considerations about self-realization could emerge, assume center stage, and command attention. More generally, post–World War II affluence in the West, a phenomenon made possible by the enormous capacity and productivity of its industrial system, has given rise to a cluster of self-realization values, such as self-fulfillment, self-expression, meaningful work, and creative leisure. These and similar values have been dubbed "postmaterialist" values or elements of a "postmodern syndrome."[16] The expressive "release" values of the postmodern syndrome are sometimes contrasted with the suppressive "control" values of the modern syndrome, the latter incorporating both the aforementioned Enlightenment values and the values of the Protestant ethic, such as frugality, abstinence, work as a good in itself, self-discipline, and postponement of gratification.[17]

While the latter syndrome dominated the ideational cultural realm in the era during which industrialism grew to maturity in the United States, say the period from 1860 to 1960, an issue currently under debate is whether the very productivity of the science- and technology-based industrial system is spawning from within a new syndrome of values at bottom incompatible with the system that engendered it. Some scholars maintain that this is indeed what is happening. For Daniel Bell, the deepest and most serious threat to contemporary capitalist society "in the longer run" lies in a "disjunction" between industrial values—"efficiency, least cost, maximization, optimization, and functional rationality"—and the "hedonistic," "anti-cognitive," "anti-intellectual," and "anti-rational" modes of behavior favored by the value orientations of many contemporaries and "promoted by the marketing system of business."[18] Others hold that, driven by revolutionary developments in computers and telecommunications, the information-based character of the postindustrial economy is actually quite compatible with—may even require—the postmodern value syndrome with its self-realization emphasis.

The prominence of other distinctive contemporary cultural values, such as *cosmopolitanness* (in experience, taste, and outlook), reflects the quicker, easier, immensely broader access to information about and experience of the different societies of the world and their cultures made possible by modern communications and transportation technologies. While cosmopolitanness is a value which reflects the emerging global society, being *au courant* is one which celebrates the rapidly changing environments of contemporary industrial societies.

Peace, Environment, Justice, Authority

As we have seen, some important modern Western cultural values (e.g., efficiency) flourished in this century because, as ideational echoes of powerful techno-economic trends, they offered adaptive advantages to their subscribers. Other values (e.g., novelty) flourished because, by helping attune consumer demand to the expanded generative capacity of modern production systems, they served producer economic interests. Efficiency achieved its central status as a cultural value through what might be dubbed a "spillover-adaptation" mechanism, from the techno-economic realm to society at large. In the case of novelty, the mechanism could be termed one of "making a virtue out of necessity"—here, techno-economic necessity.

The important post–World War II values of *environmental integrity* and *peace* became more fervently and widely held in the twentieth century via a different mechanism. They blossomed because of mushrooming revulsion at certain disturbing science-and-technology-related states of affairs: the threat of nuclear war and manifestations of various modes of environmental decay, phenomena perceived as posing unacceptable dangers to the public interest. The mechanism by which these values rose to prominence might be termed "reactive crystallization," for the attitudes embodied in them probably would not have crystallized (risen to explicit consciousness) as long as the circumstances that their subscribers now seek to promote were not perceived as endangered.* The degree to which the promotion and spread of such values has served to overcome or prevent the worsening of the phenomena that gave rise to them is a bone of contention between activist proponents of these values and their opponents.

Like peace and environment, the new-found strength of the value of (economic) *justice* is reactive in origin. The demand for fairness in allocating ever larger pots of enticing material goods was intensified by the dawning recognition that the material

---

*For example, clean air was long taken for granted and did not become the basis of a cultural value until it was widely perceived as threatened. The values of community and intimacy owe their vitality in recent years to the same mechanism: belated recognition that something worthwhile is at risk, spawning attempts to reverse the situation by underscoring its importance as a value.

fruits of the contemporary scientific and technological order flaunted in the mass media were inaccessible to large groups of disadvantaged citizens.

Finally, of traditional Western cultural values, one that has been profoundly shaken by the new behavioral options and intellectual horizons opened to people, especially youth, by developments in science and technology (e.g., the automobile, television, the pill) is that of *authority*. By this is meant submission to the dictates or deference to the judgments of individuals in established powerful societal roles or positions. Such individuals include parents, teachers, employers, and religious, government, or military superiors. The wave of religious fundamentalism witnessed in recent years bespeaks a yearning in certain quarters of society for the clear-cut, comforting epistemological certainties and predictable social patterns associated with the exercise of and respect for traditional authority. However, attempts to undo the effects on values like authority of the turbulent cultural currents unleashed by twentieth century science and technology and the social changes that followed in their wake are likely to be no less futile than King Canute's legendary efforts to reverse the tides.

CONCLUSION

It is hard to imagine what contemporary ideational culture might be like absent the scientific and technological changes of the last two centuries. Through the wider intellectual horizons and expanded realms of practical possibility they opened up, innovations in science and technology fostered the emergence of new values reflecting those new horizons and possibilities. They also hastened the demise of existing values grounded in the more limited knowledge, technics, and systems of an earlier era.

This having been said, sophisticated interdisciplinary research aimed at illuminating the relationship of technical changes and ensuing changes in human values in twentieth century industrial societies is sorely needed. Technical developments may *enable* or *require* the formulation of certain human values and *engender* the projection of others as antidotes for unpalatable effects of technical developments or practices. However, whether and the degree to which developments in twentieth century science and technology have, on balance, fostered or undermined certain long-cherished human values—considering both the degree of *realization* of such a value and the breadth and depth of the *support* it enjoys in a particular society—remain, in many instances (e.g., friendship, community, freedom, civility, privacy, and fidelity), matters of controversy pending sensitive empirical investigation.

Nevertheless, the central importance of the world views, ideas, and values discussed in this chapter, be they old and surviving or new and thriving, and the widespread failure to recognize that these mental elements have been strongly conditioned by developments in science and technology, is by itself sufficient reason to include this particular influence component in an account of the difference that science and technology have made in modern Western society.

ENDNOTES

1. P. M. Harman, *The Scientific Revolution* (London: Methuen, 1983), p. 1.
2. Quoted in R. V. Jones, "How Far Has Twentieth-Century Physics Changed Man's Concept of the Universe?" *Proceedings of the Fifth International Conference on the Unity of the Sciences* (New York: International Cultural Foundation Press, 1977), p. 917.
3. Sidney Pollard, *The Idea of Progress* (Harmondsworth: Penguin, 1971), p. 13.

4. *Ibid.*, p. 11.
5. *Ibid.*
6. *Ibid.*
7. Francis Bacon, *The New Organon*, in Sidney Warhaft, ed., *Francis Bacon: A Selection of His Works* (New York: Odyssey Press, 1965), LXXIII, p. 351.
8. Pollard, *Idea of Progress*, pp. 88–93.
9. Denis Diderot, "Encyclopedia," reprinted in Denis Diderot, *Rameau's Nephew and Other Works*, Jacques Barzun and Ralph H. Bowen, trans. (Indianapolis: Bobbs-Merrill, 1964), pp. 277–307.
10. For discussion of what one scholar calls the method of "parameter variation," see Walter G. Vincenti, "The Air-Propeller Tests of W. F. Durand and E. P. Lesley: A Case Study in Technological Methodology," *Technology and Culture*, 20, no. 4, October 1979, 712–751, especially 740–746.
11. James F. Challey, "Nicolas Leonard Sadi Carnot," in Charles C. Gillispie, ed., *Dictionary of Scientific Biography* (New York: Scribner's, 1971), vol. 3, p. 81.
12. Bruce R. Wheaton, "Heat and Thermodynamics," in W. F. Bynum, E. J. Browne, and Roy Porter, eds., *Dictionary of the History of Science* (Princeton, N.J.: Princeton University Press, 1984), p. 180.
13. C. Stewart Gillmor, "Charles Augustin Coulomb," in *Dictionary of Scientific Biography*, vol. 3, p. 442.
14. See, e.g., Daniel Nelson, *Managers and Workers* (Madison: University of Wisconsin Press, 1975), especially pp. 55–78.
15. Frederick Winslow Taylor, *Principles of Scientific Management* (New York: W. W. Norton & Co., Inc., 1967), p. 8.
16. See Alex Inkeles, "Convergence and Divergence in Industrial Societies," in Mustafa O. Attir, Burkart Holzner, and Zdenek Suda, eds., *Directions of Change: Modernization Theory, Research, and Realities* (Boulder: Westview Press, 1981), p. 13.
17. For discussion of the tension between cultural "control" and "release," see Philip Rieff, *The Triumph of the Therapeutic: Uses of Faith After Freud* (New York: Harper & Row, Pub., 1968), pp. 233–241.
18. Daniel Bell, *The Cultural Contradictions of Capitalism* (New York: Basic Books, 1976), p. 84.

CHAPTER 9
ETHICS

INTRODUCTION

For at least the last two decades, many of the most divisive ethical issues debated in Western societies have been precipitated by developments in science and technology, including advances in reproductive, genetic, weapons, and life-prolonging technologies. The adoption and alteration of public policy for regulating science- or technology-intensive practices, such as the provision of access to exotic medical treatment, the disposal of toxic waste, and the invasion of individual privacy, have also raised perplexing ethical issues. This chapter is devoted to analysis of such conflicts.

There is no universally shared criterion for deciding when a conflict of values falls within the province of ethics rather than, say, law. However, the issues and conflicts discussed in this chapter involve values widely regarded as integral to the enterprise of ethics in contemporary Western societies; such values include freedom, justice, and human rights such as privacy. Disputes over whether an agent's freedom should be limited prospectively or its prior exercise punished, whether justice has been denied or done to some party, or whether someone's human rights have been protected or violated, are widely regarded in Western societies as specifically *ethical* disagreements, thus marking them as human value issues or conflicts of special importance in these societies.

As a prelude to analysis of science- or technology-based ethical issues, we will describe a quartet of basic considerations centrally involved in judgments about and the playing out of such conflicts. We will then characterize and analyze a number of important *kinds* of ethical issues and conflicts associated with contemporary science and technology. Where appropriate, we will indicate noteworthy sociocultural factors that, in concert with the technical developments in question, help generate the issue or conflict. All this will pave the way for a key conclusion reached in this chapter: that developments in contemporary science and technology are calling into question the adequacy of traditional ethical thinking. A more comprehensive and sensitive kind of ethical analysis is now required, one more

adequate to the complexity and consequences of contemporary scientific and technological processes and products.

CLARIFICATION OF ETHICAL ISSUES AND CONFLICTS

Ethical issues and conflicts, whether or not they are associated with developments in
science and technology, can often be usefully clarified if four kinds of considerations
pertinent to ethical decision- and judgment-making about controversial actions, practices, and policies are kept in mind.[1]

The Facts of the Matter

One consideration is that of determining, as scrupulously as possible, the facts
of the situation underlying or surrounding the conflict in question. Doing so may
require ferreting out and scrutinizing purportedly factual assumptions and allegedly
empirical claims made by disputants about the conflict situation in question. It may
also require ascertaining whether any persuasive accounts of the facts of the matter
have been developed by neutral parties. In such efforts, important concerns include
unmasking pseudo-facts and factoids posing as bona fide facts, ensuring that the
credibility attributed to an account of the facts reflects the reputation and interests
of its source, and setting the strength of the evidence required to warrant acceptance
of an account of the facts at a level proportional to the gravity of the issue or conflict
in question.

Affected Patients and Their Interests

A second kind of clarificatory consideration in thinking about an ethical issue
or conflict is that of identifying all pertinent "patients"—that is, all affected parties
with a legitimate stake in the outcome of the dispute. Further, all protectable interests
of each stakeholder should be delineated and their relative weights carefully and
impartially assigned.

Key Concepts, Criteria, and Principles

A third kind of consideration is that of identifying the key concepts, criteria,
and principles in terms of which the ethical issue or conflict in question is formulated or debated. For example, the abortion issue hinges critically on the
protagonists' respective concepts of what it is to be a "human being" and a "person"
as well as what is meant by a "viable" fetus. The ethical (and legal) debate over the
withdrawal of technological life-support systems turns sharply on what is meant by
"killing" someone as well as on which criteria implicitly or explicitly govern
protagonists' use of the key terms "voluntary consent" (to withdrawal or withholding of treatment) and "death."

Ethical Theories and Arguments

A fourth kind of basic consideration to be kept clearly in mind is that ethical
disputes often involve two quite distinct kinds of decision-making theories and
arguments. *Consequentialist* ethical theories and arguments make determination of

the rightness or wrongness of actions and policies hinge exclusively on their estimated *consequences*. The most familiar consequentialist ethical theory is utilitarianism—the view that an action or policy is right if and only if it is likely to produce at least as great a surplus of good over bad, or evil, consequences as any available alternative. There are different versions of utilitarianism, depending on, among other things, what a given thinker understands by "good" and "bad," or "evil," consequences. For example, so-called hedonic utilitarians, of whom nineteenth century British reformer Jeremy Bentham is perhaps the best known, took pleasure to be the only good and pain the only bad, or evil. "Ideal utilitarians," such as the early twentieth century British philosopher G. E. Moore, construed "good" and "bad" quite differently, including things like friendship and beauty among goods and their absence or opposites, such as alienation and ugliness, among bads, or evils.[2]

The second kind of ethical theory and argument that often enters into ethical disputes is called deontological. *Deontological* ethical theories and judgments hold that certain actions or practices are inherently or intrinsically right or wrong—that is, right or wrong in themselves, independent of any consideration of their consequences. Different deontological theorists and thinkers point to different things about actions and policies, in light of which they are judged to be right or wrong. Some point to supposedly intrinsic moral properties of actions and policies falling into one or another category. For example, actions such as telling a lie or breaking a promise may be regarded as intrinsically wrong. Others emphasize that a certain course of action is obligatory or impermissible because it is approved or disapproved, or unconditionally mandated or prohibited by some authority, perhaps a deity. As we will see in this chapter, several of the most important kinds of ethical issues and conflicts engendered by developments in science and technology arise from or are exacerbated by the fact that partisans of one position on an issue are consequentialists while their opponents are deontological thinkers (for convenience, deontologists).*

KINDS OF SCIENCE- OR TECHNOLOGY-BASED ETHICAL ISSUES AND CONFLICTS

We now turn to examination of science- and technology-based ethical issues and conflicts. Given the purpose of this book, our objective here will not be to provide detailed discussions of—much less solutions to—even a select number of the long list of such problems. Rather, we will *identify and critically analyze the limited number of qualitatively distinct kinds of such disputes.* (Eight are considered here.) The aforementioned quartet of basic concerns—facts; patients and interests; concepts, criteria, principles; and ethical theories and arguments—will be used to shed light on the sociotechnical roots and intractability of many of these problems.

Violations of Established World Orders

Some ethical conflicts arise from the fact that scientific or technological breakthroughs make possible actions or practices that, in spite of what some see as their benefits, others believe violate some established order of things whose preservation

---

*In reality, the ethical thinking of denizens of contemporary industrial societies is rarely so black and white. It often incorporates consequentialist, deontological, and perhaps other considerations in uneasy or unstable combinations.

matters greatly to them. The order of things in question may be regarded as "natural" or as "sacred."

For example, much opposition to recent achievements in biomedicine and genetic engineering flows from beliefs that employing such techniques is *unnatural*. Thus some oppose the technique of *in vitro* fertilization as involving the unnatural separation of human reproduction from sexual intercourse. In a similar vein, the production of farm animals with genes from at least two different animal species ("transgenic animals") is viewed by some critics as a transgression of natural animal-species boundaries, while the use of genetically mass-produced bovine growth hormones to substantially increase the volume of milk produced by cows is opposed by some as "chang[ing] the natural behavior of animals" or as "interrupt[ing] the naturalness of [farmers'] environment."[3]

Opposition to technological violations of natural orders is, however, sometimes based on concern about the long-term consequences of intervention for human or other animal well-being or for ecosystem integrity. For example, some oppose the production of transgenic animals because they believe that the resultant animals will suffer physically as a result of being maladapted. Similarly, some critics of the use of bovine growth hormone to raise milk production levels are primarily concerned with the safety of such milk for young children. The plausibility of such consequentialist ethical thinking hinges on the details of the particular case under consideration, including the estimated magnitudes, likelihoods, and reversibility of the projected consequences of intervention.

Deontological ethical arguments against such intervention as intrinsically wrong take two forms. First, the intervention-free order of nature is regarded as natural and intrinsically "good," while technology is not viewed as part of the natural order but rather as artificial. Therefore, it is concluded, attempts to use technology to intervene in the natural order are improper. A second argument notes that something has existed or has been done in the so-called natural way from time immemorial and concludes that therefore it should be done or continue to be done in that same way—without technological intervention. Is either the "unnaturalness" or the "longevity" argument persuasive?

It is unclear why the development and transformative use of technology on nature should be seen as "unnatural." The claim that because God created the natural order it should not be "tampered with" by humans is suspect for two reasons. Those holding this idea presumably also believe that the human being was created by the deity, in which case the human is no less "natural" a creation than the "natural order" and indeed is properly regarded as part of that order. Moreover, they also presumably believe that God endowed humans with creative powers, including the ability to devise technics, thereby enabling them to intervene in the natural order. If so, why is it unnatural for natural creatures to use their God-given powers to intervene in the natural order? It seems implausible that the deity would endow its natural creatures with an unnatural power or with a power whose use was unnatural. If it is not the very use of technology to transform nature that is unnatural but only certain uses of it, then these opponents of technological violations of natural orders must clarify what it is that makes some technological interventions "violations" of those orders and others simply harmonious interventions in them.

As for the argument that the existing way of doing something is the proper way because of its longevity, it too fails to convince. That a practice is long-standing may make it familiar or seem natural. But long-standingness cannot by itself justify the view that the practice is proper. That would be drawing an *evaluative* conclusion from a purely *factual* premise. Conversely, a particular technological intervention in a long-established natural order might initially be resisted because it is unfamiliar or deemed unnatural. However, the fact that something runs counter to a long-standing practice does not suffice to show that it is improper. If that were so, then the abolition of slavery would have been improper. In fact, opposition to a practice initially regarded as unnatural because of its novelty or strangeness often diminishes over time as the new way becomes increasingly familiar. Some innovative technical practices eventually come to seem natural and quite proper, as has been the case with the use of antibiotics.

Is there, then, nothing to the concerns about technological violations of established orders as unnatural? Even if the deontological arguments examined here fail to hold water, the concerns they express still warrant serious consideration, for deontological thinking and argument are sometimes disguised or compressed versions of what are at bottom consequentialist thinking and argument. Reference to an innovative practice as unnatural and therefore as intrinsically wrong may be a powerful if deeply misleading way of expressing concern over its possible elusive long-term consequences.

Other scientific and technological developments have made possible practices that are seen by some groups as violations of world orders viewed not so much as natural but as *sacred*. Thus, in the Hasidic community centered in Brooklyn, New York, birth control is forbidden, supposedly on the basis of the Torah.[4] For the Wahabi, a fundamentalist Arabian Muslim sect, television, with its image-reproducing capacity, violates the sacred order related in the Koran. Opposition to certain technologies or technological ways of doing things as violations of sacred orders is less likely to ebb in the minds of such opponents, for the sacred way is apt to be regarded as God's way and, as such, as immutable and thus as something that ought not adapt itself to human technological change.

Violations of Supposedly Exceptionless Moral Principles

Other ethical issues arise from the fact that the use, failure to use, or withdrawal of particular scientific procedures or items of technology is seen by some as violating one or another important moral principle that its adherents believe to be exceptionless. For example, some people are categorically opposed to nuclear weapons on the grounds that their use will inevitably violate the supposedly exceptionless principle that any course of action sure to result in the destruction of innocent civilian lives in time of war is ethically impermissible.

Similarly, the supposedly exceptionless principle that "life must never, under any circumstances, be taken"—put differently, that "life must always be preserved"—is clearly an important ground of the categorical judgment that withdrawal of life-sustaining technologies, whether mechanical respirators or feeding and hydration tubes, is ethically wrong. A third example is the opposition by some to the "harvesting" of fetal tissue for use in treating Parkinson's or Alzheimer's disease, even in a relative. This opposition is often rooted in the supposedly exceptionless principle that "a human being must never be treated merely as a means to some other end, however worthwhile in itself."

Sociologically, opposition to certain scientific and technological developments on the grounds that they involve or may involve violations of some special order of things or some supposedly exceptionless moral principle, reflects a fundamental fact about modern Western industrial societies. While much has been written about their secularization, there remain in such societies significant numbers of people whose ethical thinking is deontological in character, whether or not religiously grounded.

The world views of such individuals contain categories of actions that are strictly forbidden or commanded. For them, the last word on a particular science- or technology-based ethical issue or conflict sometimes hinges solely on whether the action or practice in question falls into one or another prescribed or proscribed category. While deontological thinkers may resort strategically to consequentialist arguments in attempting to change the views of consequentialist opponents, the latter's arguments against their adversaries' deontologically grounded positions usually fall on deaf ears, however well documented the empirical claims brought forward as evidence. Deontological fundamentalists and consequentialist seculars are, in their ethical judgment and decision making, mutual cultural strangers.

An interesting consequence of deontological appeals to supposedly exceptionless moral principles in the context of potent contemporary technologies is the appearance of moral paradoxes. For example, Gregory Kavka has shown that the situation of nuclear deterrence undermines the venerable, supposedly exceptionless "wrongful intention principle"—namely, the principle that "to form the intention to do what one knows to be wrong is itself wrong."[5] Launching a nuclear strike might well be ethically wrong (because of the foreseeable loss of innocent civilian lives). But what about forming the intention to do so if attacked? According to the wrongful intention principle, forming the intention to carry out that wrong action would itself be *wrong*. However, since forming that intention might well be necessary to deter an attack and thus to avoid launching an impermissible retaliatory strike, it might well be ethically *right*. One and the same action—that of forming the intention to retaliate—is therefore both right and wrong, a moral paradox. Thus can technological developments compel reassessment of supposedly exceptionless ethical principles.

Distributions of Science- or Technology-Related Benefits

Some contemporary ethical issues and conflicts arise from the fact that the benefits of developments in science and technology are allocated in ways that do not seem equitable to one or another social group. This is particularly so with respect to medical benefits, whether they be diagnostic tests, surgical procedures, or therapeutic drugs, devices, or services.

Concerns over whether an allocation of such benefits is "distributively just" often emerge when demand for the benefit exceeds its supply and decisions must be made about who will receive the benefit and who will not—sometimes tantamount to deciding "who shall live and who shall die." For example, in the early 1960's, the supply of dialysis units available to the Artificial Kidney Center in Seattle, Washington, was insufficient to meet the needs of those with failed kidneys.[6] Criteria were selected to use in deciding who would be granted access to this beneficial scarce technical resource. Today, the demand for various kinds of human organs often exceeds available supplies. The criterion of "need" is thus by itself insufficient to make allocation decisions. Criteria such as "likelihood of realizing a physiologically successful outcome" seem promising, but are quite problematic, for, as Ronald Munson has argued,

[T]he characteristics required to make someone a "successful" dialysis patient are to some extent "middle-class virtues." A patient must not only be motivated to save his life, but he must also understand the need for the dialysis, be capable of adhering to a strict diet, show up for scheduled dialysis sessions, and so on. As a consequence, where decisions about whether to admit a patient to dialysis are based on the estimates of the likelihood of a patient's doing what is required, members of the white middle class have a definite edge over others. Selection criteria that are apparently objective may actually involve hidden class or racial bias.[7]

Other criteria, such as "probable post-treatment quality of life" and "past or likely future contribution of the treatment candidate to the community" are no less problematic. Hence, some believe that for such allocations to be distributively just, once need and physiological compatability have been established, a lottery should determine access to the scarce benefit.

On other occasions, it is not the shortage but the high cost of a medical treatment and the inability of all needy patients who want the treatment to afford it that engenders ethical conflict. Science and technology are often central factors in these high costs, for such costs may reflect the high purchase price of a machine or drug paid by a care unit, something which may in turn reflect the device's or substance's high research and development costs. Such situations help pose the contentious ethical issue of whether access to some needed expensive drug or procedure should be permitted to hinge on whether a prospective patient can afford to pay the going market price.

Deontological ethical thinkers who have come to think of medical care as a basic human right may find it morally unthinkable that a person be denied access to such treatment simply because of not being able to afford it (or because, for example, of being "too old"). In contrast, consequentialists, some of whom find the concept of an "absolute right" potentially dangerous, may believe that a particular technically exotic treatment is so expensive that granting everyone in life-or-death need unlimited access to it will effectively preclude many more individuals from getting less expensive, more beneficial, non-life-or-death treatments. Diverging accounts of "the facts of the matter" and different criteria for what makes a treatment "exotic" often bulk large in such judgments.

Consequentialists are apt to believe that individuals do *not* have a moral right to draw without limit on public or insurance-company funds to have their or their family members' lives extended regardless of the quality of the sustained life and the prognosis for its improvement. They may even hold that the financial and social consequences of doing so create a moral obligation to *terminate* such treatment, or at least to cease drawing on public funds to pay for continued treatment. In such ways have advances in science and technology as well as people's varying concepts (e.g., of a life worth living) and divergent ethical theories become intertwined in complex ethical disputes over distributive justice, rights, and obligations.

Infliction of Harm or Exposure to Significant Risk of Harm Without Prior Consent

A fourth category of ethical issues and conflicts engendered by developments in science and technology arises from activities that, while undertaken to benefit one group, inflict harm or impose significant risk of harm on another without the latter's prior consent. Examples of this sort of phenomenon abound and include some research on animals; production of cross-border and multi-generational pollution; the maintenance of carcinogen-containing workplaces; and the operation of "hair-trigger" military defense systems. As with earlier categories, the ethical issues and conflicts here have both technical and social roots.

Most parties to such disputes would agree that, other things being equal, it is always unethical to subject a morally pertinent party to undeserved harm or serious risk of same without the party's freely given prior consent. Let us examine how the consent issue plays out in the four above-mentioned kinds of cases.

In laboratory experimentation on sentient animals, the issue of consent bulks large in the persistent ethical conflict. Consequentialist proponents hold, on cost-benefit grounds, that activities that promise future benefits (including avoidance of suffering) for humans but that (supposedly unavoidably) inflict suffering on existing animals are ethically permissible, perhaps even obligatory. Those carrying out such activities may proceed because since animals cannot consent to anything, they are different in a morally relevant respect from human beings.[8] Hence the consent condition, precluding similar treatment of humans, is, in the case of animals, legitimately waived. Some opponents of such research, often deontologists, also subscribe to the prior-consent principle, but they see animals such as rabbits and monkeys as no less morally relevant patients than are humans. They draw a diametrically different conclusion: Since the consent of laboratory animals cannot be obtained, research activity that produces suffering for animals is ethically wrong or impermissible, even if the suffering is "unavoidable"—computer models that make animal tests unnecessary may not be available—and the benefits of the research could plausibly be shown to exceed its costs. It is not difficult to see why resolution of this disagreement is unlikely to be forthcoming.

Explanation of the rise of ethical conflict over cases of cross-border and multigenerational pollution (e.g., acid rain, dumping toxic chemical or metal waste into multinational bodies of water, and the possibly insecure disposal of nuclear waste), must heed technical factors as well as the problematic issue of consent. But for the capacity of contemporary scientific and technological activities to produce potent geographically and temporally remote effects, these ethical disagreements would simply not arise. Moreover, this "action-at-a-distance" capacity contributes to the tendency either to neglect or to assign modest weights to the legitimate interests of affected patients at considerable geographical or temporal remove. This in turn facilitates proceeding with the activities in the absence of consent of such endangered parties, or, in the case of not-yet-born members of future generations, impartial reflection on whether they would consent if they were informed and in a position to give or withhold it. The facts that the human capacity for empathy tends to diminish rapidly the more remote the injured or endangered party and that the world is organized into a weak international system of sovereign states both contribute to the genesis of such ethical conflicts.

In ethical disputes over workplaces made dangerous because of scientific or technological activities or products, the issue of consent rears its head in a different form. Historically, employers or their representatives argued that maintenance of a dangerous workplace was not unethical because a worker who accepted a job in one thereby voluntarily consented to exposure to all its attendant risks. To the extent that workplace hazards in the early industrial era were primarily threats to worker safety and that a worker had other less dangerous employment alternatives, such a viewpoint might seem at least minimally plausible. However, as twentieth century industrial workplaces became pervaded with thousands of industrial chemicals of uncertain bearing on worker health, the notion that workers could meaningfully consent to the imposition of any and all risks that their workplaces posed to their health began to ring hollow. Workers had to make decisions to take or keep jobs in ignorance of what, if any, risks they would be or were being exposed to. Put differently, management could proceed with its risk-imposing activities without their workers' informed consent.

This situation came to be viewed by some as a violation of the prior-consent principle, and hence as unethical. Others saw it as ethically permissible because the benefits (to both company and workers) of proceeding in this way supposedly outweighed the (typically undervalued) costs of doing so. The main attempt to mitigate this situation has taken the form of right-to-know legislation: Workers have a right to a safe workplace but not to a risk-free (in particular, carcinogen-free) one. They are, however, entitled to that which is deemed necessary for their giving informed consent to imposition of workplace risks; specifically, they are entitled to "be informed about" all carcinogenic and other toxic substances used in their workplaces. Whether the extensive technical information provided and the way in which it is communicated to workers suffice to ensure their "informed consent" remains an open factual and criteriological question at the core of a persistent ethical issue.

Ethical conflict over the operation of "hair-trigger" military defense systems is also driven by both technical and social factors. Such systems are called "hair-trigger" because they can be set to "fire" on being subjected to slight pressures. Their risk arises from the enormity of destruction that can be unleashed by slight pressure on the sensitive firing mechanism; such pressure can be brought by mistaken "sightings" or misinterpretations of data. The 1988 downing of an Iranian commercial aircraft by the high-tech-equipped U.S.S. *Vincennes* because of misinterpretation of radar and electronic data is a recent tragic case in point, albeit on a relatively small scale. There have been numerous occasions on which American retaliatory nuclear forces have been activated and on the verge of being unleashed because of what turned out to be mistaken technological indications that a Soviet attack had been launched.

While technological "progress" is partly behind such ethical conflicts, consent is also a factor. In the case of hair-trigger military defense systems (e.g., ones operating on a "launch-on-warning" basis), the public has not been afforded an opportunity to explicitly give or withhold its consent, informed or otherwise, to the imposition of such grave risks. For opponents of such systems, this alone makes them ethically objectionable. For proponents, the astonishing speed of current or emerging offensive military technologies makes the risk of *not* employing hair-trigger defense systems exceed the risk of relying upon them. Moreover, such systems are morally justified, proponents argue, since the people have indirectly consented to such risks by voting democratically for the government that imposes them. The fact that civilian aircraft are permitted to fly over populous areas without their residents having first voted on whether to accept the associated risks does not suffice to show that the people do not consent to the risks imposed on them by this practice. Hence, it would be argued, the consent condition has not been violated and ethical impropriety has not been demonstrated. The same would be true in the case of hair-trigger defense systems. However, the greater the magnitude of the danger involved—enormous in the case of the nuclear war—the lower the risk of its accidental occurrence must be if the explicit securing of consent is to be reasonably set aside as having been implicitly given. The upshot is that the lack of shared criteria for deciding whether citizen consent has been effectively obtained in such cases is central to this acute ethical dispute.

Two morals of this kind of ethical conflict deserve attention. First, the problematics of consent are, to a significant degree, science- and technology-driven. Second, the potency of much contemporary scientific and technological activity is pressuring sensitive ethical analysts to enlarge the domain of morally pertinent patients whose interests are to be taken into account in assessing the ethical propriety of current or proposed actions or policies. This situation is reflected in ongoing struggles over whether to include various kinds of previously excluded stakeholders, such as those far afield who are nevertheless deleteriously affected by potent "spill-over" effects and future citizens whose legitimate interests may be jeopardized by activities designed first and foremost to benefit the presently living. Here, too, the contours of the evaluative enterprise of ethics are being subjected to severe stress by developments in contemporary science and technology.

Science- or Technology-Precipitated Value Conflicts

A fifth kind of science- or technology-based issue or conflict arises when a scientific or technological advance allows something new to be done that precipitates a value conflict, not necessarily between the values of opposed parties, but *between two or more cherished values of one and the same party*. For example, life-extending technologies have engendered situations in which family members are compelled to choose between two values, to both of which they owe allegiance: human life preservation and death with dignity. The crucial point about this increasingly frequent kind of value conflict is that the parties plagued by such conflicts would not be so but for scientific or technological advances.

More recently, genetic tests allowing those with access to their results to know something of a sensitive nature about the health-related state or genetic predispositions of the person tested have proliferated. This has given rise to value conflicts between testers' or policymakers' concern for the protection of human *privacy* regarding disclosure of test results and their concern for *fairness* to one or another interested party other than the testee.

For example, in 1986 an adoption agency was trying to place a 2-month-old girl whose mother had Huntington's disease, a progressive, irreversible neurological disorder. The prospective adoptive parents indicated that they did not want the girl if she was going to develop the disease. The agency asked a geneticist to determine whether the child had the gene that would sooner or later manifest itself in the disease. The geneticist, while presumably sympathetic to the would-be adoptive parents' seemingly reasonable request, declined to do the testing. He reasoned that since many victims of the disease have claimed that they would have preferred to have lived their lives without knowing they had the "time-bomb" gene for the disease, it would be unethical to test someone so young that is, at a point before she could decide whether to exercise her right to privacy in the form of *entitlement not to know* that she had the fatal gene.[9]

Tests for various genetic disorders, such as Down's syndrome, sickle cell anemia, and Tay Sachs disease, have been available for some time. In the foreseeable future, however, it is expected that tests will become available for identifying genetic traits that predispose people to more common health problems, such as diabetes, heart disease, and major forms of mental illness: Thus, according to Dr. Kenneth Paigen, "We are going to be able to say that somebody has a much greater or much less than average chance of having a heart attack before age 50 or after age 50."[10]

The potential implications of such advances for matters such as employment eligibility, life insurance qualification, and mate selection are formidable. Will employers with openings for positions with public safety responsibilities (e.g., commericial airline pilots) be permitted to require that applicants take genetic tests that will disclose whether they are predisposed to heart disease or to a genetically based mental disorder such as manic depression? Will insurance companies be permitted to require applicants for life or health insurance to take genetic tests predictive of life expectancy or diabetes? Will prospective spouses come to expect each other to be tested to determine their respective genetic predispositions and whether they are carriers of certain traits of genetic diseases and to disclose the test results?

In the case of companies recruiting for jobs with public safety responsibilities, prohibition of such tests to protect applicant privacy could impose significant safety costs on society. In the insurance case, preventing mandatory disclosure of test results in the name of individual privacy would spread the cost of defending this cherished value over society at large in the form of increased insurance premiums for those *without* life- or health-threatening genetic traits or predispositions. In the case of mate selection, declining to pursue and disclose the results of reliable genetic tests could set up partners for severe strains on their relationship should presently identifiable genetic disorders manifest themselves in the partners or their offspring at a later date.

It remains to be seen how society will resolve the public policy questions raised in such cases by the ethical value conflict between privacy and fairness. However, it is already clear that advances in genetic science are going to pose powerful challenges to society's commitment to the right of individual privacy. The knowledge about the individual afforded by such tests is likely to be of such pertinence to legitimate interests of other parties that the protection afforded individual privacy may be weakened out of concern for fairness to those parties, perhaps to the point of recognizing that under certain conditions they have a right to that knowledge. Put differently, technology is here bringing micro, or personal, justice and macro, or societal, justice into conflict.

Science- or Technology-Engendered "Positive" Rights

Besides conflicts over the values of freedom and justice, issues of "rights," especially "human rights," bulk large in contemporary Western ethics. In recent decades, advances in science and technology have engendered a new ethical issue: that of how best to respond to newly recognized so-called *positive rights*.

In the modern era, some claims have come to be widely recognized as "human rights"—that is, as irrevocable entitlements that people supposedly have simply because they are human beings. Human rights are thus contrasted with civil or institutional rights—rights that people have because they are delineated in specific revocable legal or institutional documents. Among the most widely recognized human rights are "life" and "liberty."

These rights, and some derived from them—privacy, for example, is widely thought to be a kind of special case of liberty—have traditionally been viewed as what philosophers call "negative" or "noninterference" rights—that is, as entitlements *not to be done to* in certain ways. Thus, the right to life is construed as entitlement not to be deprived of one's life or physical integrity. The right to liberty is construed as entitlement not to have one's freedom of action physically constrained or interfered with, unless its exercise has unjustifiably harmed another's protectable interests (e.g., those in life, limb, property, reputation) or poses an unreasonable risk of doing so.

As scientific and technological progress has gathered momentum in recent decades, several rights traditionally viewed as negative have given birth to a number of correlative "positive" rights—in other words, entitlements *to be done to* in certain ways. Consider three examples. Many believe that the right to life, traditionally construed as a negative human right, must, *in the context of new life-preserving scientific and technological resources*, be regarded as having taken on a positive component: entitlement to be provided with whatever medical treatment may be necessary to sustain one's life (independently of ability to pay for it). According to this way of thinking, affirmation of the right to life in the contemporary scientific and technological era requires affirmation of a positive right of access to whatever means are necessary to sustain life. Thus, for example, denial of costly life-sustaining drugs to a patient in need of them on any grounds save scarcity, including concern over the aggregate high cost to society of providing them, is seen by many as a violation of the patient's right to life. Hence, depending on whether the ethical analyst is a deontological or consequentialist thinker, failure to provide these drugs would be deemed categorically or prima facie ethically impermissible.

The right to privacy has traditionally been viewed as a noninterference right, entailing, among other things, entitlement not to have one's home broken into by government authorities without a search warrant issuable by a court only upon proof of "probable cause." However, the computer revolution has put individual privacy interests at risk. To compensate for this, legislation in the United States and other countries entitles citizens to be provided with certain categories of information being kept on them in computerized files. For example, the U.S. Fair Credit Reporting Act of 1970 entitles each citizen to review and correct credit reports that have been done on them and to be notified of credit investigations undertaken for purposes of insurance, mortgage loans, and employment. Given the exceptional mobility of this information and the potential for severely damaging individual privacy that this creates, protection of the right of individual privacy in the computer era is held to require acknowledgement of countervailing positive rights: entitlement to know what exactly about oneself is contained in computerized government files and to have one's record rectified if it is shown to be erroneous.

A third, somewhat more speculative example involves a special case of the general right to liberty—namely, the traditional negative right of reproductive freedom: entitlement not to be interfered with in one's procreative undertakings, be they attempts to have or to avoid having offspring, including via "artificial" contraceptive means. It remains to be seen whether, in the context of the recent and continuing revolution in reproductive science and technology, the negative right of individual reproductive freedom will engender a positive counterpart: entitlement of those with infertility problems to be provided with (at least some) technical reproductive services enabling them to attempt to have offspring, where access does not hinge on a client's ability to pay or even perhaps on marital status.

As such scientifically and technologically generated positive rights expand, ethical tension will mount. Some deontologists, believing that human rights are "absolute," may conclude that their corresponding positive rights are likewise, hence inviolable. Others, including most consequentialists, while treating rights as claims that always deserve society's sympathetic consideration, may conclude that they cannot always be honored without regard to the social consequences of doing so. The most important consequence of this ethical tension may be that the day is drawing closer when society will have to come decisively to grips with the consequences of philosophical commitment to a concept of rights as "absolute" and "immutable." We shall return to this topic in Chapter 15.

Public Harms of Aggregation

Suppose that each of a large number of people carry out essentially the same action. Suppose further that, considered individually, each of these actions has at worst a negligible negative effect on a social or natural environment. Finally, suppose that the aggregated effect of the large number of people doing the same thing is that substantial harm is done to the environment in question. Let us call such outcomes *public harms of aggregation.* Many, if not most, such harms are possible only because, to an unprecedented degree, modern production, communication, and transportation methods have made many scientific and technological processes and products available on a mass basis. A curious moral aspect of such situations is that as the individual acts were assumed to be of negligible negative impact, they are typically regarded as being ethically unobjectionable. Hence, the aggregate effect of a mass of ethically permissible actions may nevertheless turn out to be quite ethically problematic. In ethics, sometimes numbers *do* count.[11]

Consider, for example, the pollutants emitted by each of the approximately 400 million automobiles in the world. The aggregate negative environmental effect of individually innocuous, hence seemingly ethically unproblematic, effects is known by now to be substantial. To the extent that this aggregate effect can be shown to harm people's health, particularly groups at special risk of being affected (e.g., the elderly, young children, and those with respiratory problems), the aggregate effect would begin to be judged as ethically unacceptable and unjust, and the individual pollution-emitting activities might begin to appear as something other than ethically neutral.

An analogy may help clarify this novel ethical situation. Suppose that a populous nation experiences a devastating depression in which many of its people suffer. Suppose that after the fact it is plausibly shown that an important contributing cause of the depression's occurrence was the fact that each family in the country had accumulated a substantial but individually manageable level of consumer debt. If the country was fortunate enough to recover its economic health, would not the new accumulation of a substantial but still manageable amount of consumer debt by an individual family be likely to be regarded as an ethically irresponsible thing to do? If so, the same could be said of an individual car owner's emission of pollution or an individual consumer's failure to recycle.

A somewhat futuristic example of the same pattern from the biomedical realm is that of predetermination of the sex of one's offspring. Given the fact that reproductive freedom is widely viewed as a human right, it is safe to assume that attempts of individual couples—at least married ones—to avail themselves of the latest scientific or technological means to determine the sex of their offspring will be regarded as ethically permissible. However, suppose that in a populous society with a culture biased in favor of male offspring a significant number of couples opt for predetermination and that a significant sexual imbalance of male over female offspring results. Suppose further that at least some of the ethically problematic consequences envisioned as resulting from this state of affairs come to pass (e.g., increased crime committed by men or heightened male aggressiveness in competition for scarcer female mates).

The upshot of this situation is that twentieth century science and technology may be pushing society toward reevaluation of "permissive" ethical judgments traditionally made about individual actions that are at worst "negligibly harmful." Consequentially speaking, the threshhold of harm necessary to activate negative ethical judgments may be in the process of being reduced by the aggregative potential of modern science and technology in populous societies.

Practitioner Problems

The kinds of science- and technology-based ethical problems considered thus far have something in common: While spawned by developments within the spheres of science and technology, the resultant issues and conflicts unfold, not primarily within those spheres, but in society at large. In contrast, problems in the final category considered here, while related to concerns of society at large, arise primarily *inside* the communities of practitioners of science and technology. They are ethical problems associated with the concrete processes and practices of scientific and technological activity, both those in which these activities unfold and those in which their results are communicated. Such problems are sometimes viewed as falling within the province of "professional ethics," meaning that they are ethical problems that arise in the course of professional practice.

Problems of Execution.   Edward Wenk has identified three kinds of ethical issues faced by practicing engineers in their work.[12]

(1) *Distributive Justice.*   The first is essentially an issue of distributive justice, involving as it does an allocation of costs, benefits, and risks. This kind of problem arises when an engineer must decide whether to embark upon or proceed with a feasible project that he or she recognizes is likely to expose people to a non-trivial degree of risk to their safety, health, or property without their consent. Beyond answering the question "Can it be done?" about the contemplated project, the would-be ethical engineer must confront the quite different question "Ought it be done?" For example, from an ethical point of view, should an engineering company accept a lucrative contract to erect a potentially hazardous structure, such as a hydroelectric dam, in a geologically unstable area near a rural village in the absence of the informed consent of its inhabitants?

Other things being equal, if the degree of risk—understood as a function of the estimated magnitude of the harm that could occur and the estimated likelihood of its occurrence—is substantial, then it would be ethically wrong to proceed. If it is negligible, then it would be ethically permissible, perhaps even obligatory, to do so. One problem with this kind of situation is that determination of what constitutes an "acceptable risk" is not a strictly technical question but a social and psychological one. Among other things, the answer to it depends on *what* members of the population at risk believe to be at stake, on *how highly* they value it at the time in question, and on *how seriously* they would regard its loss.

Meredith Thring has extended this analysis in the case of engineers who are independent operatives doing work in research and development. For years, Thring, a university professor of mechanical engineering, had been doing research on industrial robots. However, he eventually came to believe that "the primary aim [of such work] is to displace human labour." For this reason he abandoned work on industrial robots and decided to work only on applications where the aim is to help someone to do the job he does now without actually exposing his body to danger or discomfort; or where we need to amplify or diminish his skill and strength. A good example is "telechirics,"…artifacts that allow people to work artificial hands and arms and operate machines in hazardous or unpleasant environments as if they were there, while they are in fact in comfortable and safe conditions.[13]

Thring implies that it is also ethically incumbent on engineers to consider whether the work they contemplate—here, a research and development project—poses an unacceptable risk to any important nonsafety interest of patients likely to be affected by it—for example, that of not being rendered redundant. At bottom, this too is an issue in distributive justice. For Thring, the ethical engineer must first carefully estimate the costs, benefits, and risks likely to be associated with a possible technological endeavor and then ask "Are those benefits, costs, and risks likely to be allocated to the affected parties in a way that is distributively just?" The engineer may then proceed with the work only if he or she can answer that question in the affirmative.

Similar ethical constraints apply to the initiation or continuance of scientific experiments that pose significant undisclosed risks to the safety, health, or property interests of people participating in or likely to be affected by them. Three of the most ethically repugnant scientific experiments carried out in or on behalf of the United States during this century are of this character and warrant brief description.

Beginning in 1932, U.S. Public Health Service researchers administered placebos to 431 black men in Tuskegee, Alabama. Each experimental subject, induced to come in for blood tests supposedly as part of an areawide campaign to fight syphilis, was tested for and found to have syphilis. However, *the subjects were neither told that they had the disease nor treated for it.* The purpose of the experiment was to obtain scientific knowledge about the long-term effects of syphilis on mental and physical health. Nontreatment continued for 40 years, long after it became known that penicillin was a cure for syphilis and was widely available. Following press exposure in 1972, the experiment was terminated.[14] A Public Health Service investigation disclosed that of 92 syphilitic patients examined at autopsy, 28 men (30.4 percent) died from untreated syphilis—specifically, from syphilitic damage to the cardiovascular or central nervous systems. Hence, the total number of men who died as a result of nontreatment may have exceeded 100.[15]

In the 1950s, the U.S. Central Intelligence Agency solicited and funded a series of "mind-control experiments." Among the techniques used on experimental subjects were sensory deprivation, electroshock treatment, prolonged "psychological driving," and the administering of LSD and other potent drugs. By one estimate, at least 100 patients went through one series of brain-washing procedures.[16] Many participants in the experiments suffered long-term physical and mental health problems. In 1953, one subject was given a glass of liquor laced with LSD. He developed a psychotic reaction and committed suicide a week later.[17]

As part of its Biological Warfare program, the U.S. Army secretly sprayed bacteria and chemicals over populated areas of the United States (and Panama) during a 20-year period beginning in 1949. At least 239 such tests were carried out. The objective was to determine the country's vulnerability to germ warfare by simulating what would happen if an adversary dropped certain toxic substances on the United States. One frequently used microorganism was *Serratia marcescens.* Its safety was questioned prior to 1950, and strong evidence that it could cause infection or death existed in the late 1950s. Nevertheless, it continued to be used in tests over populous areas for the next decade. Four days after a 1950 spraying over the San Francisco Bay Area, a patient was treated at the Stanford University Medical Center for infection caused by *Serratia*, the first case ever recorded at the hospital. Within the next five months, ten more patients were treated at Stanford for the same infection. One of them died.[18]

Their ethically reprehensible character aside, such cases serve the useful purpose of showing that "freedom of scientific inquiry" is not an absolute, unconditional, or inviolable right. While clearly an important human value, "freedom of scientific inquiry" may, under certain conditions, have to take a backseat to other important values, such as protection of the dignity and welfare of each and every individual human being. We will return to the question of possible limits on scientific inquiry in Chapter 15.

(2) *Whistle Blowing.*   Wenk's second kind of ethical issue in engineering is that of "whistle blowing." Engineers—or scientists—may become aware of deliberate actions or negligence on the part of their colleagues or employers that seem to them to pose a threat to some component of the public interest (e.g., public safety, the effective expenditure of public monies, and so on). If the worried practitioner's "in-house" attempts to have such concerns addressed are rebuffed, then he or she must decide whether to "go public" ("blow the whistle") and disclose the facts underlying the concerns.

Problematic phenomena of the sort that impel some practitioners to consider such a course of action are often driven by the huge profits and professional reputations at stake in modern research and development activity. These phenomena can be associated with any of a number of phases of engineering or science projects. Consider, for example, misleading promotional efforts to secure public funding; cheap, unreliable designs; testing shortcuts; misrepresented results of tests or experiments; shoddy manufacturing procedures; intermittently defective products; botched installation; careless or inadequate operational procedures; or negligent waste disposal. A significant number of such cases have come to light in recent years, of which three follow.

At Morton Thiokol, Inc. (MTI), several engineers working on the *Challenger* space shuttle booster project tried to convince management that the fateful January 1986 launch should not be authorized since the already suspect O-ring seal on the booster rocket had not been tested at the unusually cold temperatures prevailing on the day of the tragedy. MTI senior engineer Roger Boisjoly testified before the presidential committee investigating the disaster about what led up to the decision by the company and the National Aeronautics and Space Administration (NASA) to authorize the launch, a process at whose turning point MTI's general manager told his vice president of engineering to "take off his engineering hat and put on his management hat."[19] For his candid testimony, Boisjoly was allegedly subjected to various forms of mistreatment within the company and was placed on extended sick leave.[20]

In 1972, three engineers employed by the San Francisco Bay Area Rapid Transit (BART) system, after receiving no response to their in-house memos of concern, went public about subsequently confirmed safety-related deficiencies that they had detected in the design of BART's Automated Train Control System. They were summarily dismissed for their trouble.[21]

A senior engineer at the Bechtel Corporation, part of a task force assigned to plan the removal of the head of the failed nuclear reactor vessel at Three Mile Island after the famous 1979 accident, became concerned about short-cuts allegedly being taken by his company in testing the reliability of the crane to be used to remove the vessel's 170-ton lid. When he protested the alleged shortcuts, he was relieved of many of his responsibilities. He then went public, was suspended, and later fired.[22]

Sociologically speaking, several things are noteworthy about such cases. Technical employees who find themselves in situations in which they are asked or required to do things that violate their sense of right and wrong are not an endangered species. Results of a survey of 800 randomly selected members of the National Society of Professional Engineers published in 1972 disclosed that over 10 percent felt so constrained. A "large fraction" were sufficiently fearful of employer retaliation that they acknowledged they would rather "swallow the whistle" than become whistle blowers.[23] A major 1983 study of technical employees found that 12 percent of respondents "reported that, in the past two years, they have been in situations in which they voiced objection to, or refused to participate in, some work or practice because it went against their legal/ethical obligations as engineers or their personal senses of right and wrong."[24]

For a number of reasons, engineers have traditionally been loath to criticize their employers publicly. Most obviously, those who feel compelled to "go public" enjoy precious little legal or professional-association protection against employer retaliation, often in the form of firing. However, as Wenk argues, some reasons that discourage whistle blowing are sociocultural in nature:

> For engineers, a problem arises because most work in large organizations and many find excitement of participation in mammoth undertakings. They learn to value formal social structures, an attitude akin to "law and order." They adopt the internal culture and values of their employer and are likely to be allied with and adopt the perspectives of the people who wield power rather than with the general population over whom power is held. As a consequence, there is less tradition and inclination to challenge authority even when it is known to be wrong in its decisions which imperil the public.[25]

Not without reason, engineers—and, increasingly, scientists in large industrial organizations—tend to see themselves as employees with primary obligations to their employers, not the public. Moreover, the notion that employees retain certain citizen rights—for example, freedom of expression—when they enter the workplace is a relatively new notion in American industrial history. In a classic 1892 opinion, Oliver Wendell Holmes, then Massachusetts Supreme Court justice, wrote:

> There are few employments for hire in which the servant does not agree to suspend his constitutional rights of free speech as well as idleness by the implied terms of the contract. The servant cannot complain, as he takes the employment on the terms which are offered him.[26]

Only in the late twentieth century has this traditional attitude begun to be reversed, partly because the costs of such enforced silence are now viewed as unacceptable to society.

Ethically speaking, the obligation of technical professionals to blow the whistle when it is appropriate to do so arises from several factors. First, much contemporary research and development is supported by public money, as is the graduate education of many scientists and engineers (through government fellowships and loans). Second, the scale of the possible harm to the public interest at stake in many contemporary technical activities is large. The third factor is the following ethical principle of harm prevention: "[W]hen one is in a position to contribute to preventing unwarranted harm to others, then, other things being equal, one is morally obliged to attempt to do so."[27] An engineer or scientist sometimes possesses personal, specialized, "insider" knowledge about a troubling facet of a technical activity or project. Coupled with the credibility attached to testimony provided by authoritative technical professionals (as opposed to claims made by nonspecialist activists), that knowledge puts the scientist or engineer in a special position to make a possibly decisive contribution to preventing unwarranted harm to others or at least to preventing its repetition. This gives rise to a moral obligation to blow the whistle—once all other reasonable steps to rectify the situation "in house" have been taken and failed.

Some have urged that the obligation to responsibly blow the whistle be emphasized during the formal education of scientists and engineers—by the use of actual case studies, for example.[28] Others have stressed the importance of effecting structural and policy changes in the organizations in which technical professionals work and in their professional associations so that whistle blowers are not required to choose between remaining silent and becoming self-sacrificing "moral heroes."[29] A third approach is that of legislation. A measure of protection for whistle-blowers has been built into some federal environmental and nuclear laws, and roughly half the states prohibit the firing of employees who have blown the whistle on their employers for practices violating existing public policies. However, some advocates for whistle-blowers see the need for comprehensive federal legislation allowing whistle-blowers who suffer reprisals to initiate legal action against their employers up to two years after such occurrences.[30]

(3) *Consideration of Long-Term Effects.*   Wenk's third and final category of ethical issues confronting engineers in daily practice involves "managing the future." He argues that engineers have a tendency to focus on designing, producing, or installing "hardware" without adequately "anticipat[ing]…longer term effects." This is an abdication of the engineer's "professional responsibility." In terms of the "quartet of basic concerns" that we have utilized in this chapter, given the scale and scope of the effects of many contemporary engineering products and projects, engineers who fail to scrutinize their projects with comprehensive critical vision, both with respect to its likely consequences (including possible longer-term ones) and its likely patients or "stakeholders" (including, where appropriate, members of future generations) are guilty of unprofessional and ethically irresponsible conduct. Uncritical allegiance to the deontological dictum "if it can be done, it should be done" no longer confers immunity from charges of ethical impropriety on technical practitioners.

Problems of Communication.   Other ethical issues faced by technical practitioners have to do not with possible effects of scientific and technological projects on the safety, health, or property of those who may be affected by them, but with problematic aspects of *practitioners' communication* of and about their work.[31] Issues in this category, most notably ones involving *fraud* and *misrepresentation*, pertain to publication or presentation of claimed findings and to work-related interactions with nontechnical funding or policy-making officials. Cases of fraud have come to light in recent years in which experiments reported on in published papers were in fact never carried out, crucial data were fabricated, and conclusions were drawn from data allegedly known not to support them.[32]

(1) *Fraud.*   Falsification of scientific data may not be as infrequent as normally supposed. June Price Tangney surveyed researchers in the physical, biological, behavioral, and social sciences at a large American university. Of 1,100 questionaires distributed, 245 were completed and returned. Half of the respondents were senior researchers with the rank of full professor. Not surprisingly, the survey revealed that 88 percent of the respondents believe that scientific fraud is uncommon. However, 32 percent reported that they had a colleague in their field whom they had at some time suspected of falsifying data.[33] This figure, while suggestive, must be interpreted cautiously. It is not proof that one third of all scientists engage in such misconduct, for not only may suspicions be mistaken, but multiple respondents could have had the same individual in mind.

Whatever the extent of fraud in science, scientists see a number of factors contributing to the phenomenon. Tangney's respondents identified the following as major motivations for fraud: desire for fame and recognition (56 percent), job security and promotion (31 percent), firm belief in or wish to promote a theory (31 percent), and "laziness" (15 percent).[34] Underlying many such factors, she contends, is *the highly competitive nature of contemporary science:* the pressure to publish, the shortage of desirable jobs, and the fierce competition for funds. Beyond contributing to fraud, Tangney argues that such pressures can negate "what might otherwise be a fairly adequate self-policing mechanism in the scientific community." Indeed, the results of her survey call into question the common wisdom about the self-correcting nature of science, via processes like refereeing and publication, for of the aforementioned 32 percent who had suspected a colleague of falsifying data, over half (54 percent) reported that they had taken no action to confirm or disconfirm their suspicions.[35] The competitive nature of contemporary science may have biased the reward system in the profession *against* undertakings aimed at uncovering fraud.

> In a highly competitive academic environment, many researchers may feel that, if they raise questions about serious misconduct, their own reputations will be tarnished and their own chances for resources and advancement will be diminished. A scientist may be rewarded for uncovering "legitimate" flaws or shortcomings in a rival's work. However, there generally is little to be gained and much to be lost by attempting to expose a fraud.[36]

(2) *Misrepresentation.*   Misrepresentation takes a number of forms in the communication of research findings, including both failure to credit or fully credit deserving contributors and crediting or overcrediting undeserving contributors. It might seem that such acknowledged species of misconduct, however regrettable, do not deserve to be called unethical, except perhaps by deontologists, for whom they fall into forbidden categories of actions regardless of the gravity of their consequences for science or society. However, consequentialists may also selectively regard such practices as unethical, since they can in fact result in serious public harm. In May 1987, a scientist was accused by an investigative panel of scientists appointed by the National Institutes of Health of "knowingly, willfully, and repeatedly engag[ing] in misleading and deceptive practices in reporting results of research."[37] The pertinence of these practices to consequentialist ethical judgment making becomes clear from the panel's finding that the scientist's publications had influenced drug treatment practices for severely retarded patients in facilities around the United States.

Presentations of research findings to groups of peers also offer opportunities for ethically problematic behavior. Such presentations are sometimes used to establish claims of priority in the conduct of certain kinds of research. However, given the intensely competitive nature of the contemporary scientific research enterprise, if the research work is still in progress, it is understandable that scientists may opt to disclose just enough of their findings to serve their priority interests but not enough to reveal their overall strategies or the next steps in their "battle plans." However, quests for priority and resultant recognition may go beyond being unprofessional and become unethical if deliberately misleading or outright false information is disseminated in hopes of sending rivals "off on wild goose chases," diverting them from paths believed potentially fruitful. While making such an ethical judgment may appear open only to a deontological thinker, doing so can also be defended on consequentialist grounds, by, for example, appealing to the harm that such deception can inflict on knowledge-sharing institutions like the peer seminar which have usefully served scientific progress and thus, indirectly, human welfare.

The interaction of scientists and engineers with public funding agencies or policy-making officials can also be ethically problematic. Institutional or organizational pressures to obtain funding for research and development ventures or units with significant prestige or employment stakes can induce applicants to resort to various forms of misconduct in hopes of increasing the chances of favorable action by a funding agency. Among these are use of false data, misrepresentation of what has been accomplished to date on a project in progress, and gross exaggeration of what can be expected in the grant period or of the scientific or social significance of the proposed work.

Dealings with makers of public policy often lend themselves to such hyperbole, for policymakers are typically individuals with nontechnical backgrounds who are unable to assess critically the plausibility of the claims made about current or proposed research or development projects. If a prestigious researcher deliberately misrepresents the potential or state of development of a pet project to an influential policymaker in order to enhance the project's funding prospects, then insofar as approval is secured through this deception and at the cost of funding for other worthwhile projects, consequentialist thinkers may join deontologists in judging the practitioner guilty of unethical conduct. This they may do not least on grounds of the long-term consequences for the welfare of society of undermining the integrity of the research funding process.

THE CHALLENGE OF CONTEMPORARY SCIENCE AND TECHNOLOGY TO TRADITIONAL ETHICAL THEORIES

The foregoing discussion of categories of ethical issues and conflicts engendered by developments in science and technology strongly suggests that these forces are putting growing pressure on traditional absolutistic ethical thinking. There are several reasons that the validity and utility of such thinking are being called into question in an era of rapid scientific and technological development.

As we saw, many such theories condemn or praise particular kinds of actions if they but fall into one or another category of supposedly intrinsically good or bad deeds. However, as noted, an action or practice condemned as "unnatural" can come to seem less so over time, especially if the original ethical judgment was predicated on the act's or practice's being unusual or unfamiliar when it first came to attention. Similarly, traditional absolutistic ethical outlooks are sometimes based on static world views born of their subscribers' limited experience. As a culture or subculture dominated by such a world view overcomes its geographical or intellectual isolation and interacts more with the rest of the world, supposedly immutable categories or rules pertaining to "sacred" things or ways tend to loosen up. Adherents of such world views may come to recognize that respectable members of different cultures or subcultures think and act differently than they do about the same matters. Further, new products, processes, and practices can, as noted, have long-term hidden effects. Their eventual eruption and empirical confirmation sometimes call for revision of ethical judgments made before recognition that such subterranean effects were at work. However, such reevaluation is not congenial to absolutistic thinking, which purports to base its unwavering ethical judgments and decisions on something other than consequences. Considerations such as these make it increasingly difficult to sustain absolutistic ethical theories and outlooks in contemporary scientific and technological society.

Besides challenges to its intellectual tenability, contemporary science and technology are calling into question the utility of traditional absolutistic ethical theories—that is, their ability to serve as intelligent guides to action in a world of rapid and profound technical and social change. Such categorical theories and outlooks are helpless when confronted with ethical issues and conflicts of the sorts discussed in the third section of this chapter. For example, such theories shed no light on cases involving the distribution of benefits, costs, and risks associated with scientific and technological developments; intrapersonal conflicts between two venerable ethical values; public harms of aggregation; or the situations of technical professionals torn between loyalty to employers, concern for their families' well-being, and devotion to promoting the public interest. Finally, traditional deontological approaches to ethical thinking offer no incentives to agents to consider whether, in the face of possible unforeseen effects of a technical innovation, expansion of the domain of pertinent patients or the list of their protectable interests might be in order.

This is not to imply that consequentialist theories and thinking are immune from difficulties when confronted by contemporary scientific and technological developments. For example, uncertainty about possible elusive or projected long-term consequences of scientific and technological innovations and developments makes ethical judgments based on such assessments provisional and open to doubt. However, that is a price that must be paid if ethical judgments and decisions are to be made on an empirical rather than an a priori basis and are to be focused on the bearing of scientific and technological developments on human harm and well-being.

One conclusion of this chapter, then, is that developments in contemporary science and technology call for revisions in traditional ethical thinking and decision-making. One kind of ethical theory deserving serious consideration we will call *qualified neo-consequentialism*. Under this theory, ethical judgments about actions, practices, and policies hinge first and foremost on assessments of their likely consequences. In particular, these assessments must have the following *neo-consequentialist* qualities. They should be

1. *Focused on harm and well-being*—directed to identifying and weighing the importance of consequences likely to infuence the harm or well-being of affected patients;*

---

*The reader will note that no account has been presented here of exactly what is meant by human "harm" and "well-being." That substantial task must be left for another occasion. Suffice it to say here that for this writer, "harm" is not reducible to considerations of physiological deprivation, physical injury, and property damage or loss; nor is "well-being" reducible to considerations of material abundance, financial success, and high social status.

2. *Refined*—designed to detect or at least be on the lookout for subtle effects that, although perhaps hidden or manifested only indirectly, may nonetheless significantly influence stakeholder harm or well-being;

3. *Comprehensive*—designed to attend to *all* harm- and well-being-related effects—social and cultural as well as economic and physical in nature—of the candidate action, policy, or practice on *all* pertinent patients, remote as well as present, "invisible" as well as influential;

4. *Discriminating*—designed to enable scientific and technological options to be examined critically on a case-by-case basis, in a manner neither facilely optimistic nor resolutely pessimistic, and such that any single proposal can emerge as consequentially praiseworthy and be adopted or as consequentially ill-advised and be rejected in its present form if not outright; and

5. *Prudent*—embodying an attitude toward safety that, as long as a credible jury is still out or if it has returned hopelessly deadlocked, is as conservative as the magnitude of the possible disaster is large.

Further, the assessments sanctioned by our proposed ethical theory must also meet certain conditions. If an action, policy, or practice is to earn our theory's seal of approval, its projected outcome must not only be likely to yield at least as large a surplus of beneficial over harmful consequences as that of any available alternative, but it must also meet certain additional *qualifications*, two of which will now be briefly discussed.

It is scarcely news that contemporary scientific and technological activities unfold in societies in which those who stand to benefit greatly from their fruits are rarely the same as those likely to bear their often weighty costs and risks. We therefore stipulate that to be ethically permissible or obligatory, the allocation of the scrupulously projected benefits, costs, and risks of a technical undertaking among the various affected stakeholders must also be *distributively just*.

Various criteria have been put forth for evaluating the justice of such distributions.[38] One that deserves serious consideration is John Rawls's famous "difference principle."[39] Imagine, says Rawls, a group of people in "the original position"—that is, convened to formulate from scratch the rules that will govern the first human society, one shortly to come into being. Suppose that these deliberations take place behind "a veil of ignorance"—that individual group members have no knowledge whatsoever of whom or what they will turn out to be (e.g., male or female, black or white, Asian or North American, physically handicapped or not) or of their eventual economic well-being or social status. Then, Rawls contends, the group would eventually reach agreement that it was in each member's best interest that the following rule of justice be adopted: an unequal distribution of any social or economic "good" will be permitted in the society-to-be only if there is good reason to believe that it will *make everyone, including the less fortunate, better off*. Indeed, Rawls eventually offered a stronger version of his principle according to which an unequal distribution of such a good is just only if there is good reason to believe that it will make everyone better off *and* that it will *yield the greatest benefit to those currently worst off*.[40] If either version of this rule is found compelling, it would have to be applied to each predominantly beneficial but unequal distribution of projected science- or technology-based benefits, costs, and risks before the conclusion could be reached that it was ethically permissible or obligatory to proceed with the action, project, or practice in question.

Our neo-consequentialist ethical theory has a second qualification. A science- or technology-related course of action may sometimes be denied ethical approval even if all of the foregoing conditions are met. Even then, it may be proper to withhold ethical approval if the projected harmful consequences (1) *exceed some substantial quantitative threshhold*—either in a single case or when aggregated over multiple cases of a similar sort—and (2) are not *greatly* outweighed by their positive counterparts. In such situations, the decision-making party may decide that it would be prudent to decline the admittedly greater projected benefits offered by the option under consideration.

Ethical decision making that takes no account of the absolute magnitude of an option's projected negative consequences even if they are outweighed by their positive counterparts, or of how the outweighed negative consequences of an individual course of action may aggregate over multiple instances, is deeply flawed. Indeed, allowing "yielding a positive balance of benefit over harm" by itself to compel ethical approval of individual courses of action may even be unjustified on consequentialist grounds, for following that criterion consistently in multiple instances may over time lead to unacceptable public harms of aggregation. For example, assessing the impact on traffic of individual proposed downtown high-rise office buildings solely in terms of the modest number of additional cars each structure may attract into the city may allow the aggregate effect on traffic of approval of a large number of such projects to go unreflected in individual decision-making processes.

CONCLUSION

Hopefully, the reader will find the qualified neo-consequentialist approach to thinking about ethical issues and conflicts just sketched more adequate to the realities of contemporary scientific and technological practice. In any event, in this chapter we have characterized a number of different kinds of science- and technology-based ethical issues and conflicts, indicated some noteworthy technical and social roots of such problems, and argued that important traditional ethical concepts and modes of thinking are being subjected to increasing pressure by scientific and technological changes in contemporary society. While this stress is being strenuously resisted in some quarters, it is likely in the longer run to lead to major transformations of ethical ideas and thinking.

ENDNOTES

1. I owe my initial awareness of this framework to a 1972 lecture at Stanford University by ethicist Dr. Karen Lebacqz.
2. See, e.g., William Frankena, *Ethics*, Foundations of Philosophy series, 2nd ed. (Englewood Cliffs, N.J.: Prentice-Hall, 1973), chaps. 2 and 3. See also Mary Warnock, *Ethics Since 1900* (London: Oxford University Press, 1960), chap. 2, pp. 48–52.
3. *Wall Street Journal*, May 4, 1989, p. B4.
4. Stephen Isaacs, "Hasidim of Brooklyn: Fundamentalist Jews Amid a Slumscape," *Washington Post*, "Outlook" section, February 17, 1974, Section B, p. 1.
5. Gregory Kavka, *Moral Paradoxes of Nuclear Deterrence* (Cambridge: Cambridge University Press, 1987), pp. 19–21.
6. Ronald Munson, *Intervention and Reflection* (Belmont, Calif.: Wadsworth, 1979), p. 398.
7. *Ibid.*, pp. 399–400.
8. For example, Carl Cohen argues that animals are not members of any "community of moral agents." Incapable of, among other things, giving or withholding consent, animals, unlike humans cannot have rights thereby precluding involuntary experimentation on them. See Cohen's "The Case for the Use of Animals in Biomedical Research," *New England Journal of Medicine*, 315, no. 14, 1986, 867.

9. Gina Kolata, "Genetic Screening Raises Questions for Employers and Insurers," *Science*, 232, no. 4748, April 18, 1986, 317.
10. *New York Times*, August 19, 1986, p. 21.
11. John M. Taurek, "Should the Numbers Count?" *Philosophy and Public Affairs*, 6, 1977, 293–316.
12. Edward Wenk, Jr., "Roots of Ethics: New Principles for Engineering Practice," American Society of Mechanical Engineers Winter Annual Meeting, Boston, Massachusetts, December 1987, 87-WA/TS-1, pp. 1–7.
13. Meredith Thring, "The Engineer's Dilemma," *The New Scientist*, 92, no. 1280, November 19, 1981, 501.
14. *New York Times*, July 26, 1972, p. 1.
15. *New York Times*, September 12, 1972, p. 23. For a detailed account of this episode, see James H. Jones, *Bad Blood: The Tuskegee Syphilis Experiment* (New York: Free Press, 1981).
16. Harvey Weinstein, *A Father, A Son, and the CIA* (Toronto: James Lorimer and Co. Ltd., 1988).
17. Leonard A. Cole, *Politics and the Restraint of Science* (Totowa, N.J.: Rowman and Allanheld, 1983), p. 111.
18. *Ibid.*, pp. 112–114.
19. Roger Boisjoly, "Ethical Decisions: Morton Thiokol and the Space Shuttle *Challenger* Disaster," American Society of Mechanical Engineers Winter Annual Meeting, Boston, Massachusetts, December 1987, 87-WA/TS-4, p. 7.
20. *Ibid.*, p. 11.
21. Stephen H. Ungar, *Controlling Technology: Ethics and the Responsible Engineer* (New York: Holt, Rinehart and Winston, 1982), pp. 12–17.
22. Rosemary Chalk, "Making the World Safe for Whistle-Blowers," *Technology Review*, January 1988, p. 52.
23. Rosemary Chalk and Frank von Hippel, "Due Process for Dissenting 'Whistle-Blowers'," *Technology Review*, June/July 1979, p. 53.
24. Chalk, "Making the World Safe," pp. 56–57.
25. Wenk, "Roots of Ethics," p. 3.
26. Chalk and von Hippel, "Due Process", p. 53.
27. Compare this principle with Kenneth Alpern's "principle of due care" and "corollary of proportionate care" in his "Moral Responsibility For Engineers," *Business and Professional Ethics Journal*, 2, Winter 1983, 40–41.
28. Boisjoly, "Ethical Decisions," p. 12.
29. Richard DeGeorge, "Ethical Responsibilities of Engineers in Large Organizations: The Pinto Case," *Business and Professional Ethics Journal*, 1, no. 1, 1981, 12.
30. Chalk, "Making the World Safe," pp. 55–56.
31. For a useful bibliography on this aspect of the problem, see Marcel Chotkowski LaFollette, "Ethical Misconduct in Research Communication: An Annotated Bibliography," published under NSF Grant No. RII-8409904 ("The Ethical Problems Raised by Fraud in Science and Engineering Publishing"), August 1988.
32. See, e.g., William Broad and Nicholas Wade, *Betrayers of the Truth* (New York: Simon & Schuster, 1982), pp. 13–15; and Nicholas Wade, "The Unhealthy Infallibility of Science," *New York Times*, June 13, 1988, p. A18.
33. June Price Tangney, "Fraud Will Out—Or Will It?" *New Scientist*, 115, no. 1572, August 6, 1987, 62.
34. *Ibid.*
35. *Ibid.*
36. *Ibid.*, p. 63.
37. *New York Times*, April 16, 1988, p. 6.
38. For cogent discussion of various criteria of distributive justice, see Joel Feinberg, *Social Philosophy*, Foundations of Philosophy Series (Englewood Cliffs, N.J.: Prentice Hall, 1973), chap. 7.

39. John Rawls, *A Theory of Justice* (Cambridge, Mass.: Harvard University Press, 1971), chaps. 1–3, especially pp. 75–78.
40. For discussion of alternate versions of Rawls's difference principle, see Robert Paul Wolff, *Understanding Rawls* (Princeton, N.J.: Princeton University Press, 1977), pp. 40–41.

CHAPTER 10
THE CHARACTER
OF EVERYDAY LIFE

INTRODUCTION

Thus far, in considering the influence of science and technology on modern society, we have explored phenomena that fall within the ideational and societal realms of the cultural system. We turn now to the personality and behavior sector of that system. Here too changes in modern science and technology have exerted a transformative influence. We will focus here on changes in one component of that sector: what we called in Chapter 4 the *behavior setting* of everyday life.

Everyday life in contemporary Western industrial society has a distinctive character or fabric that differentiates it from preindustrial or even early twentieth century industrial society in the West. Much of that character arises from the *nature and changing configurations of the human-made and natural objects and features that comprise the physical environments of contemporary life*. These environments are important because they influence and serve as backdrops for the behavior of everyday life. Our fifth influence component will therefore be at a microsocial level. We will identify, illustrate, and discuss the significance of a number of characteristic aspects of the behavior setting of everyday life in contemporary Western society. The aspects selected are ones that have been strongly influenced by developments in technology and science. Taken together, these aspects help constitute the fabric of everyday life in contemporary Western societies.

THE CHARACTER OF EVERYDAY LIFE

A preliminary caveat is in order. This chapter is more impressionistic than its predecessors, partly because reliable empirical knowledge about the everyday personal and social consequences of new technologies is quite limited.* Thus my

*After reviewing the literature devoted to characterizing the influence of the automobile and the telephone on everyday personal and social life, one scholar concluded: "That these sorts of unsystematized fragments of research...typify the literature on two of the most pervasive technologies of the twentieth century underlines the generally

personal experiences and subjective judgments have colored the content of this chapter more than they have in previous chapters. The reader is forewarned and invited to devise his or her own list of noteworthy technology- and science-influenced aspects of the environments of everyday life and compare it critically with what follows. Some aspects treated in this chapter, although of relatively recent vintage, are already widely taken for granted as characteristic features of the landscapes of contemporary industrial societies. Their linkages with technical changes are not always as widely appreciated, however. Other aspects, although not pervasive in all industrial societies, are widespread and important enough to warrant inclusion. We will discuss eight, sometimes closely related, dimensions of the character of everyday life in contemporary Western industrial societies:

multiplicity	transience
material abundance	scale
flow	mobility
pace	technicity

Multiplicity

The fabric of everyday life in contemporary society is characterized by *extraordinary multiplicity*. The number and variety of institutions, organizations, and kinds of material products (including food) and services, the number of options *within* many kinds of products, services, and institutional sectors (e.g., leisure), and the number and diversity of ideas, world views, moralities, and personal relationships is astounding, unprecedented, and in many cases still growing. For example, in 1986, 42,793 new books and 4,031 monthly periodicals were published. The following year, there were at least 1,860 mutual funds, 450 models of videocassette recorders, 203 new car models, 169 models of 19- and 20-inch color televisions, 60 models of can openers, 59 breakfast cereals, 50 brands of ground coffee, 42 laundry detergents, 27 brands of paper towels, and 23 brands of white caulking compound available in the U.S. marketplace.[1] Clearly, the multiplicity feature of the fabric of contemporary Western life—including, in urban areas, significant degrees of material and ideational cosmopolitanism—would be impossible without modern mass production and distribution technologies for both materials and information.

The popular notion that the new multiplicity is liberating has not gone unchallenged. For Ezra Mishan, the problem with the new options afforded by technological innovation is that "as the carpet of 'increased choice' is unrolled before us by the foot, it is simultaneously being rolled up behind us by the yard."[2] The possible hyperbole here not withstanding, it *is* misleading to represent, say, the automobilization of twentieth century society as having widened people's transportation options to include the car as well as the horse. Others have found the mushrooming multiplicity of modern industrial society psychologically problematic as well as deceptive. Already in the 1880s, Friedrich Nietzsche, in his role as critic of emerging industrial culture,

---

impoverished state of research on personal technology." To make the study of the influence of technology on everyday life more fruitful will require "rehabilitating the sociology of technology [through undertaking] full, detailed, painstaking study of specific technologies and their consequences, bringing to bear the widest array of social scientific techniques" (Claude S. Fischer, "Studying Technology and Social Life," in M. Castells, ed., *High Technology, Space, and Society* [Beverly Hills, Cal.: Sage, 1985], p. 294).

saw "... the abundance of disparate impressions" as being "greater than ever: cosmopolitanism in foods, literatures, newspapers, forms, tastes, even landscapes." The problem he saw was that because of the rapidity with which this influx was pressing itself in upon the modern psyche,

> the impressions erase one another; one instinctively resists taking in anything, taking anything deeply, to "digest" anything; a weakening of the power to digest results from this. A kind of adaptation to this flood of impressions takes place: men unlearn spontaneous action, they merely react to stimuli from outside. They spend their strength partly in assimilating things, partly in defense, partly in opposition. *Profound weakening in spontaneity.* Artificial change of one's nature into a "mirror"; interested but, as it were, merely epidermically interested.[3]

The multiplicity of modern industrial society requires that the individual acquire a more rigorous filter for choosing from among the expanded ranges of options if a productive path is to be steered between the paralysis of nonchoice and the dissipation of hyperchoice.

Material Abundance

Closely related to the great multiplicity characteristic of everyday life in contemporary industrial societies is another of its distinguishing features: *material abundance.* While this feature of contemporary Western societies is largely taken for granted, it should not be. The arsenals of material goods possessed by existing middle- and lower-class families make those of their preindustrial and even pre-twentieth century industrial counterparts seem Spartan by comparison.

Consider a few indicators of the level of contemporary material plenty. In 1984, of the 86.3 million households in the United States, 99.7 percent had refrigerators, 97.6 percent had full plumbing facilities, 73.1 percent had clothes washers, 61.5 percent had clothes dryers, and 59.5 percent had air conditioning (room or central).[4] In 1987, 99 percent of American households had at least one radio, 98 percent had at least one television, and 92.5 percent had telephone service.[5] In 1986, a record 16.3 million cars and light trucks were sold in the United States.[6] As of 1986, there were an estimated 135.7 million registered passenger cars and 40.9 million trucks and buses on American roads.[7] In 1986, there were 478 million radio receivers in American homes and, in 1984, 181 million telephones in American homes and offices.[8] But cars, trucks, and telephones, as well as other pervasive and often costly items like major kitchen appliances and clothes washers and dryers, have taken on the status of "needs" in American society. Perhaps material abundance would be better gauged by looking at non-necessities.

Television is an obvious choice. The story, however, is much the same. In 1985, there were 145 million televisions in roughly 87 million American households. As of January 1986, 91 percent of them had at least one *color* television, 57 percent had two or more sets, and roughly 30 percent had at least two *color* sets. In 1988, a record 20 million color television sets were sold in the U.S.[9] While this level of material abundance has been achieved over a period of 40 years since home televisions were first sold, the videocassette recorder is an even more startling indicator of contemporary material plenty. Over 13 million videocassette recorders were sold in the United States in 1986. The percentage of American households with this sophisticated electronic technic has surged from 1.1 percent in 1980 to 17 percent in 1985 to 68 percent in January 1990.[10] Regardless of which material products one focuses on, two things are clear: Contemporary material abundance in industrialized societies is formidable and unprecedented and would be inconceivable without their astonishing technology-based systems of mass production, marketing, and distribution. Not only are such systems capable of turning out enormous volumes of material goods, but the production efficiencies they embody enable purchase prices to be set at levels encouraging mass consumption.

However impressive and unprecedented the multiplicity and material abundance of everyday life in contemporary society, the benefits associated with these phenomena are unevenly spread across the socioeconomic spectrum. Increased multiplicity, in the sense of an expanded range of choices, is by and large a middle- and upper-class phenomenon. Moreover, as Mishan has observed, increased choice tends to be unevenly distributed by area, often available in less crucial realms, such as the number of kinds and models of cars and stereos from which to choose, while rarely available in areas traditionally regarded as being of central importance to human well-being, such as the conditions of work.[11] Similarly, material abundance, even with respect to quasi-necessary items like the telephone, has yet to reach millions of impoverished, unemployed members of the growing American "underclass." Such sobering observations qualify but do not invalidate the contention that unprecedented multiplicity and material abundance are characteristic aspects of the fabric of everyday life in contemporary Western society—ones that reflect the potent influence of technological and scientific innovations.

While multiplicity and material abundance are characteristic of the fabric of everyday life in contemporary industrial societies in the West, and while they may well continue to increase over time for the foreseeable future, there is nothing *intrinsically dynamic* about them. The extraordinary multiplicity and material abundance of contemporary life could in principle remain static from now on and be nonetheless characteristic of the fabric of everyday life. However, it is indisputable that an essential strand of the fabric of everyday life in most contemporary Western societies is its dynamism. The next three features we elaborate reflect that dynamic character.

Flow

An important feature of everyday life in contemporary industrial societies, and one that partly defines their distinctive character and feel, is the phenomenon of *enormous flow*. Put differently, we may say that contemporary industrial social systems have extraordinarily high levels of "throughput": Once obtained and "processed," energy, material, food, and informational resources flow into, through, and out of such systems in enormous, historically unprecedented amounts per unit of time.

Regarding material goods, many facilities, whether engaged in continuous or batch production, are organized—and periodically or continually reorganized—so as to augment the flow through their respective systems or increase the throughput of their respective products. Retail stores are similarly oriented. "Sales" are held, seemingly with ever-increasing frequency, to keep merchandise "moving," thus making room for the next batch being turned out and about to be shipped by producers. Other things being equal, realizing a substantial increase in sales each year has become a criterion for success in retail firms; similarly, a "flat" sales figure for a given year (in relation to the preceding year) is widely viewed in business as indicating an unsuccessful year. While the economic logic for this kind of thinking is no mystery, the point here is that generating an ever-increasing flow, or throughput, of goods has become the goal of producers and retailers alike. Ideally, producers and retailers strive to achieve ever-higher flow, or throughput, levels. The character or texture of the fabric of everyday life—and the behavior that unfolds in such a milieu—clearly reflects this dynamic situation.

A similar situation exists regarding the production, marketing, and consumption of informational goods. The amount of information generated, processed, distributed, "consumed," and "disposed of" each day by Western industrialized societies, including their respective publishing and broadcasting industries, is enormous. The throughput of information for individual household systems is also unprecedented, largely because of printing, bulk mailing, postal, and broadcasting technologies. These remarkable throughput levels are not only made possible but *mandated* by contemporary society's extensive and expensive production, transportation, and communications technologies and systems—ones *able* to produce, process, distribute, and dispose of informational and material goods rapidly and in enormous quantities.

The extraordinary throughput level of contemporary Western industrial societies is no less problematic than the great multiplicity just noted. Processing high levels of informational throughput requires people who wish to avoid inundation to use effective filters to screen for quality and importance. Indeed, the very generation of such levels of throughput exacts a steep environmental toll. As a 1970s bumper sticker put it, "Protect your national forest. Boycott the Sunday *New York Times!*" In 1970, printing the complete run of each Sunday edition of this newspaper consumed the product of 150 acres of forest.[12] As for the aggregate use of wood pulp, since 1960, U.S. consumption of newsprint has almost doubled, reaching in 1986 the stunning level of 11,936,000 metric tons.[13]

Pace

Although one does not logically imply the other, it would be surprising if, in light of the increasingly rapid energy, material, and informational flows through contemporary social systems, the *pace* of contemporary life had not also increased markedly in many areas. The ever-quickening pace of many mass production and production-related activities is indisputable, as with, for example, the decreasing time it takes manufacturers to produce complex products like cars and personal computers. The proliferation of information and its rapid diffusion in contemporary society has induced more and more people to try to pick up the pace with which they "process" the seemingly endless supply of it that is relevant to their professional activities ("speed reading"). Subsonic and supersonic jets have increased the speed of travel, while personal computers have increased the pace with which scholars can write and publish books and articles.

Activities of a more social nature have not escaped technological speedup. Aided and abetted by revolutionary food packaging, storage, and preparation materials and technologies, especially the microwave oven, leisurely meal-taking is an endangered species of activity and is beginning to resemble refueling. The traditional leisurely city stroll or promenade is fast becoming an anachronism in industrial societies. Indeed, it has been shown that the rate of pedestrian locomotion along city sidewalks is directly proportional to city population size.[14] This may reflect determination to have done with trying navigational tasks or the importance of meeting the schedules of the interlocking technical systems on which metropolitans depend. In any event, auto-infested streets scarcely create an ambience conducive to strolling.

More generally, the character of everyday life in contemporary industrial societies is not conducive to spiritual or emotional intimacy. Growing time demands on Westerners immersed in the increasingly rapid technology-based flows, or throughput levels, of contemporary life make regular, informal, relaxed encounters unstructured by role expectations—a prerequisite of intimate association—difficult to achieve.[15] As if adapting to this difficulty, personal relationships seem to have undergone developmental compression. Generally speaking, gestation—the progressive unfolding of a human activity at a slow or moderate pace—while not logically inconsistent with the character of the contemporary techno-economic order, is profoundly at odds with its ethos. The rapid-pace "ethic" which has taken hold in most spheres of contemporary life promotes receptivity to and use of the ever more efficient technologies developed and marketed by private enterprise. These technologies in turn reinforce this ethic, as any devotee of word processing compelled to fall back on pen, pencil, or even electric typewriter will readily confirm.

Transience

Another flow-related feature of the fabric of everyday life in contemporary Western industrial societies is *transience*. Evidently, a flow, whether rapid or slow, can be of either constant or changing composition. Transience exists when the composition of the flow through a system changes relatively rapidly over time. Crucial to the transient character of modern Western, especially American, life is the cultural notion that there are limits to the useful, legitimate, or worthwhile lifetimes of phenomena, such that phenomena outliving their respective designated lifetimes are "no good," uninteresting, or worthless. As with pace, the transient character of everyday life in contemporary Western society is made possible by modern mass production and construction technology. The former is able to turn out much more than would be consumed if people felt no need to have "the latest" model of a product, while the latter is able to transform the physical environment of a familiar locale in relatively short order.

The transience of everyday life in most contemporary Western industrial societies is reflected in numerous phenomena, such as annual models, planned obsolescence, the proliferation of products easier and cheaper to replace than to repair, outmoded ideas, "yesterday's news," ephemeral artistic and cultural trends, and, generally, a widespread cult of the new. Pop artist Andy Warhol's hyperbolic observation that in these days sooner or later everyone becomes a celebrity, at least "for fifteen minutes," points up yet another facet of contemporary transience.

Regarding rapid changes of fashion—"and this by no means applies only to fashions in dress"—Georg Simmel argued that they "interrupt the inner process of acquisition and assimilation between subject and object," something that makes any kind of personal relationship between the individual and the fashionable "product" virtually impossible.[16] The phenomenon of nostalgia crazes—possible only in an environment of transient character—and the widespread American interest in recent years in discovering various kinds of "roots" suggest that some individuals feel that the transience of the cultural and physical environment may be psychically debilitating. What makes the transience of contemporary life particularly problematic is the fact that the individuals exposed to it are living longer and longer and thus may in their later years find themselves at considerable remove from the cultural and physical environments of their youth or early adulthood. The much heralded sociological phenomenon of the "generation" gap is partly a culture gap born of the transient character of everyday personal and social life.

Mobility

Another distinctive technology-related feature of everyday life in the contemporary West—one that, while important in its own right, also fosters transience—is *mobility*. In the last century industrialized societies have developed remarkable abilities to move people, information, and materials in great numbers and amounts over great distances relatively quickly and easily.

This ability is reflected in diverse phenomena, such as "shuttle diplomacy," mass international tourism, "commuter marriages," instantaneous international stock- and currency-trading markets, same-morning international delivery of the *New York Times*, the *Financial Times* of London, and other "city" newspapers, and San Francisco restaurant menus reading "Maine lobster and Norwegian salmon, fresh daily." The development of the jet airplane and the telecommunications satellite have bulked large in producing such phenomena. The automobile and truck have also been powerful enabling factors for physical mobility. In the year prior to March 1986, fully 18 percent of Americans at least 1 year old changed residences, 6.7 percent moving to a different city.[17]

Unless one views them in historical perspective, it is easy to take such remarkable and unprecedented phenomena for granted. Consider, for example, that in April 1842, it took composer Richard Wagner five days to travel nonstop by coach from Paris to Dresden to attend rehearsals of his new opera. Of greater moment, consider the fact that the deadly Battle of New Orleans took place after the signing of the peace treaty of the War of 1812 because news of the armistice could not reach the battlefield on time.

The sociological significance of this mobility feature is complex and double-edged. For example, while mobility manifested in the form of international mass tourism has struck welcome blows against provincialism and xenophobia, it has also resulted in overloading or destroying some notable local cultural and natural environments, such as Florence, Paris, and certain historical sites and islands in Greece. Seemingly endless influxes of tourists have sometimes effectively denied indigenous inhabitants access to their own cultural patrimony. For example, San Francisco cable cars and the Uffizi Museum in Florence are continuously innundated with tourists in all but the depths of winter. It is, in fact, not much of an exaggeration to say that some of these treasures are maintained mostly for the sake of monied tourists. Similarly, while mobility in the form of rapid communication and train transport helped make India one country by "reducing the pull of local factors" and weakening the caste system,[18] high mobility in the United States has diluted citizens' psychic investments in and commitments to their often temporary neighborhoods and communities.

Scale

The scale of modern and contemporary life is a particularly distinctive aspect of its character. The scale on which modern Western industrial life is lived, whether in terms of the sizes of populations, human settlements, human gatherings, social organizations, or technics, is unprecedented. When William and Mary ascended the British throne after the Glorious Revolution of 1688, roughly three quarters of the British people lived in villages whose mean population was between 250 and 450— probably around 300. As Peter Laslett noted, much of the Stuart population lived out their lives in settlements so small that in the twentieth century they would be regarded as miniatures or curiosities.[19] In contrast, by 1950 over half of contemporary Englishmen lived in towns and cities of 50,000 or more, settlements "so vast that none of our rural ancestors would recognize his surroundings as human."[20] Settlements of people in cities with populations in the millions, gatherings such as the Normandy Invasion, the march on Washington, and the Woodstock music festival, and national and multi national corporations with multiple units, hundreds of facilities, and hundreds of thousands of employees, are to a significant degree distinctive creatures of the modern technological era.

Regarding technics, a contrapuntal trend has emerged: gigantism and miniaturization. Not long ago, the tallest buildings in the world were churches, on the order of several hundred feet high. Contemporary skyscrapers, using steel girders, rivets, and electric elevators, have reached 1,454 feet, with 2,000-foot-high structures already technically feasible. The evolution of earth-moving equipment also reflects contemporary gigantism. Not long ago, humans moved the earth with simple pickaxes and shovels. By 1917, the largest coal-burning steam shovels had a capacity of a few cubic yards per bite. Today, huge electric-powered dragline earth-movers are used, particularly in strip mining. As tall as 32-story buildings, their 220-cubic-yard-capacity buckets scrape up the earth at a rate of 4 million cubic yards per month as they are hauled toward the machine. Similar scale transformations are evident in the magnitude of many of the sociotechnical systems characteristic of contemporary society, such as long-distance telephone networks, enormous production facilities, and national highway, postal delivery, and air traffic control systems.

At the opposite end of the scale is an astonishing trend toward miniaturization, most evident in the evolution of digital computers. "The first truly electronic programmable digital computer was ENIAC (Electronic Numerical Integrator and Calculator), built at the University of Pennsylvania. The machine was completed in 1946."[21] It used 18,000 vacuum tubes, around 7,500 relays and switches, about 7 million resistors, occupied 3,000 cubic feet, weighed 30 tons, and used 140 kilowatts of power. Although huge in size, it had modest computing power.[22] Today, in the wake of the invention of the transistor and progressive advances in production technology, microprocessors—integrated circuits with tens or hundreds of thousands of components on tiny chips of semiconducting material and with the ability to carry out logic and arithmetic functions—have given rise to microcomputers with greatly increased computing power and virtual portability. This miniaturization trend has spilled over into a wide range of consumer products of greatly reduced scale and increased portability, from audio equipment and calculators to photocopiers and televisions.

Technicity

A facet of the character of everyday life in contemporary Western societies that is as important as it is easy to overlook is its unprecedented "technicity"—that is, the extent to which technics pervade everyday life. In recent decades, technology has penetrated virtually every nook and cranny of everyday existence, particularly outside the sphere of work, where it has long been entrenched. There is scarcely a sphere of activity, form of behavior, or facet of everyday life, no matter how intimate or mundane, into which technology—increasingly, *high* technology—has not insinuated itself, often to transformative, and sometimes to problematic, effect.

Consider, for example, familiar facets of everyday life like exercise, courtship, and death. Sophisticated and specialized athletic footware, high-tech workout apparatus, wrist chronographs, and portable stereos with headphones have altered the nature and conditions of exercise in everyday life. The automobile, motion pictures, and (personal ads in) printed media have transformed patterns of courtship. Medical science and technologies have radically changed the locus, meaning, and "timing" of "death." Whatever the desirability and broader social and cultural significance of such developments, the influence of technology and science on human behavior in everyday life has clearly been widespread and important.

In this connection, it is instructive to inventory one's everyday activities or behaviors during a typical 24-hour period, identify the technics involved in carrying out each of the activities or behaviors that use them, and ascertain which, if any, do not use or depend on contemporary technics in any direct or substantial way. One could start with the roles of the alarm clock, radio, thermostat, and automatic coffee maker in waking up, continue with the arsenal of technics used in personal hygiene and food-preparation and -consumption routines, move on to the technics used in one's work and leisure activities, and conclude with the roles of television, birth-control technics, "nite lights," and high-density anti-noise foam earplugs in routines associated with going to bed and going to sleep. By now, in even the most private sectors of their everyday lives, denizens of contemporary Western society are profoundly technological creatures.

Of sociological interest is the degree to which contemporary interpersonal relationships (nurse or physician to patient, teacher to student, retail clerk to customer) and the relationships of humans to nature (natural materials, animals, food) are coming increasingly to be *mediated* by contemporary technics, often in multiple layers. What portion of these mediators are "elegant instruments of...mutual estrangement"[23] and what portion truly enhance the human qualities of the relationships in question? To date, no systematic empirical studies of these difficult but important questions have been carried out.

CONCLUSION

The behavior settings and the character of everyday life in the industrial societies of the West have been profoundly influenced by twentieth century scientific and technological development. This transformation is the composite result of significant technology-based changes in each of the dimensions of the character that we have discussed here. The transformed character of everyday life is occasionally explored retrospectively.[24] With the exception of the scale dimension, however, it is rarely if ever taken into account in prospective social decision making. This is partly because of the difficulty of anticipating what changes in the character of everyday life will be engendered by some new technologies and partly because, even if anticipatable, it is unclear whether and to what extent they and similar outcomes should be regarded as blessings or curses. What *is* clear is that no account of the influence of scientific and technological change on Western industrial societies in this century can qualify as adequate or comprehensive if it fails to attend to this important, ongoing micro social revolution. Since the fabric of everyday life can influence behavior in ways that facilitate or impede the fulfillment of human needs, transformations of its character warrant careful study.

ENDNOTES

1. U.S. Bureau of the Census, *Statistical Abstract of the United States: 1988*, 108th ed. (Washington, D.C.: U.S. Government Printing Office, 1987), p. 528, and *Consumer Reports*, January–November, 1987.
2. Ezra Mishan, *Technology and Growth: The Price We Pay* (New York: Praeger, 1970), p. 52.
3. Friedrich Nietzsche, *The Will to Power* (New York: Vintage; 1968), p. 47.
4. *Statistical Abstract: 1988*, pp. 688 and 692.
5. *Ibid*, p. 523.
6. *New York Times*, January 6, 1989, p. C2.
7. *Statistical Abstract: 1988*, p. 576.
8. *1988 Britannica Book of the Year* (1988), p. 727.
9. *Ibid.*; *The World Almanac and Book of Facts: 1987* (New York: Pharos Books, 1987), p. 373; *New York Times*, January 9, 1989, p. C5.
10. *Statistical Abstract*: 1988, p. 523; *New York Times*, May 24, 1987, Section III, p. 1; *New York Times*, March 29, 1990, p. B1.
11. Ezra Mishan, "On Making the Future Safe For Mankind," *Public Interest*, no. 24, Summer 1971, p. 49.
12. Mishan, *Technology and Growth*, p. 16.
13. *Statistical Abstract: 1988*, p. 643.
14. Marc H. Bernstein and Helen G. Bernstein, "The Pace of Life," *Nature*, 259, February 19, 1976, 557–558.
15. Christopher Alexander, "The City as a Mechanism for Sustaining Human Contact," in W. Ewald, ed., *Environment For Man* (Bloomington: Indiana University Press, 1967), p. 62.
16. Peter Lowrence, ed., *Georg Simmel: Sociologist and European* (Surrey: Nelson, 1976), pp. 210–211.
17. *Statistical Abstract: 1988*, p. 20.
18. A. Rahman, "The Interaction Between Science, Technology, and Society: Historical and Comparative Perspectives," *International Social Science Journal*, 33, no. 3, 1981, 517.
19. Peter Laslett, *The World We Have Lost* (New York: Scribner's, 1965), p. 54.
20. *Ibid.*, p. 53.
21. Ernest Braun and Stuart Macdonald, *Revolution in Miniature*, 2nd ed. (Cambridge: Cambridge University Press, 1982), p. 32.
22. *Ibid.*
23. Mishan, "On Making the Future Safe for Mankind," p. 55.
24. In *Akenfield* (New York: Dell Pub. Co., Inc., 1970), Ronald Blythe evokes the relatively static character of everyday life in what was for all intents and purposes a preindustrial English village in the early twentieth century. In *The Americans: The Democratic Experience* (New York: Random House, 1973), Daniel Boorstin describes various aspects of the dynamic, rapidly evolving character of everyday life in the relatively affluent industrializing society of the United States in the period from 1880 to 1960. Comparing these works provides some idea of the profound transformation in the character of everyday life that has occurred in this century.

CHAPTER 11
THE FINE ARTS

INTRODUCTION

In pondering the influence of science and technology on modern society, the fine arts do not spring to mind as obvious candidates for consideration. Indeed, the evolution of the fine arts has mostly been viewed as independent of developments in the far-removed technical fields of science and technology. However, innovations in science and technology have made incalculable differences in the contours and courses of a number of the fine arts during the last 150 years. We will focus here on the visual art of painting and the performing art of music.

PAINTING

Developments in science and technology and the burgeoning industrial order that they made possible are among the formative influences on modern painting. Beginning in the late eighteenth century, painters were confronted by a rapidly changing society with whose dynamic, technological character they had to come to aesthetic terms. As they did so, painting underwent enormous changes. The range of its subject matter was greatly expanded, and generations of artists strove to find painting styles adequate to the unprecedented character of the new society.

Background

Consider the period and birthplace of modern painting: mid-nineteenth century Western Europe. As against the virtual absence of technological subject matter in pre-nineteenth century painting, factories, manufacturing processes, and various kinds of new transportation technics, such as trains and airplanes, began to appear with increasing frequency in the works of professional painters. While a number of pedestrian works offered detailed realistic depictions of technological subject matter, sometimes painters placed equal or greater emphasis on the inner spirit of or atmosphere created by a new technology or technological process. Such was the case in J. W. F. Turner's *Rain, Steam, and Speed* (1844), an evocation of a Great Northern Railroad train hurtling through the rain across the English countryside, and in Adolf Menzel's *Rolling Steel Mill* (1873), a depiction of the feverish activity inside a German steel mill shortly after that country had embarked upon industrialization.

The initial trickle of professional artists who attended to the new technology increased considerably over time. Renowned painters who executed works in which technological products, processes, or milieux bulk large include Henri Rousseau (*View of the Sèvres Bridge* [1908]), Fernand Léger (*Nudes in the Forest* [1908]), Umberto Boccioni (*The City Rises* [1910]), Robert Delauney (*Homage to Bleriot* [1914]), Francis Picabia (*Amorous Parade* [1917]), Charles Demuth (*Aucassin and Nicolette* [1921], Charles Sheeler (*Rolling Power* [1938]), and Joseph Stella (*The Brooklyn Bridge* [e.g., 1939]). In effect, between 1850 and 1950, painting underwent gradual socialization into the transformed way of life of modern industrial society.

Stylistically speaking, science and technology affected a number of modern art "movements," or "schools." Between 1910 and 1920, Italian artists working under the banner of futurism evolved painting styles aimed at capturing the dynamic spirit and celebrating the supposedly tonic effects of modern technology and industry. This they deemed crucial if Italy was to be shaken from nostalgic preoccupation with its glorious past, embrace industrialization, and thereby promote the greatness of vision and deeds that achieving the latter goal would require. On a different level, 1960s pop artists can also be said to have been responding to the stimulus of the new technological order. With his realistic renderings of Coca Cola bottles and Campbell's Soup cans, Andy Warhol used the august art form of painting to call attention to the pervasiveness—and aesthetic influence—of mass-produced technics in everyday personal and social life.

Impressionism

The influence of science and technology on modern painting was not limited only to schools and movements of secondary importance. Consider the case of French impressionism, which Bernard Denvir has called "the most important thing that has happened in European art since the Renaissance, the visual modes of which it supplanted."[1] Impressionism flourished in France in the 1870's and 1880's. Unlike the romantics, impressionists were not interested in painting idealized images of great historical or mythical figures or events. Rather, they aspired to capture their immediate visual impressions of everyday objects or scenes from contemporary life. The perceived colors and shapes of such objects and scenes, they realized, reflected the variable mediating influences of light and air (as well as the nature of the human sensory apparatus). Let us examine how science and technology affected impressionism.

Subject Matter.   Science and technology did not exert a profound influence on the subject matter treated in impressionist paintings. This is so in spite of the fact that in 1877, Claude Monet, one of the most famous impressionists, did twelve paintings of the great Saint-Lazare railroad station train shed in Paris. While selection of this subject matter reflected the transformed character of everyday life in European society, a positive value to all impressionists, Monet's choice was influenced primarily by the manifold, fleeting impressions engendered inside the transparent iron and glass train-shed structure through the interplay of changing patterns of sunlight and steam-engine emissions. The technologies of engineer Eugene Flachet's transparent shed structure and the steam- and smoke-emitting train engine may have been of some interest to Monet in connection with "his unstated ambition to be the painter of modern landscape."[2] However, their primary importance for him was that they provided an exceptional opportunity for a characteristically impressionist examination of transient patterns of light and air and their effects on the perceived colors and forms of objects of everyday life.

Pigments.   Reflecting the influence of light and air on visual impressions, the outlines of objects in impressionist paintings were often indistinct. Indeed, "the object tended to lose prominence and impressionist paintings became paintings of light and atmosphere, a play of direct and reflected color."[3] This impressionist obsession with light and atmospherics was facilitated by advances in pigments, the coloring substances that, finely ground and held in suspension in a medium, constitute paints.[4] In the mid-nineteenth century, the range and quality of pigments was substantially increased. New organic pigments became available through chemical research, into, for example, coal-tar dyes, while pigments more pure and more stable than their natural equivalents were chemically synthesized and manufactured.

Metal Tubes.   In order to render the actual transient effects of light and air on the objects of everyday life, many impressionist painters worked *en plein air*, in the open air, instead of in their studios. This option was greatly facilitated by a mundane technological innovation: the soft-metal tube. Until almost the mid-nineteenth century, oil painters had ground their own pigments in their studios to their preferred consistencies and kept them in pots. Beginning in the 1830s, however, ready-made oil paints became available in collapsible, screw-capped, tin tubes. Thus encased, paints could be conveniently transported, effectively preserved, and quickly deployed on the painter's palette for rapid outdoor use in capturing fleeting visual impressions. But the paint tube did more than facilitate painting *en plein air*. As Phoebe Pool has observed, impressionist canvases "often display visible, choppy strokes of paint applied with a hog's-hair brush, rather than the smoother surface achieved by Delacroix and Corot, whose work they admired...."[5] How is this to be explained? The answer seems to lie partly in the requirements imposed on the impressionists by their adoption of the metal tube for painting outdoors.

> [A] less fluid consistency had to be given to oil paints to make them suitable for packing in tubes, and other ingredients had to be added during manufacture to ensure that the pigments would stay suspended in the oil. Consequently manufactured paints do not flow from the brush as those of the Old Masters used to do and a stiffer shorter brush is needed for handling them or a dilutent must be used.[6]

Painting *en plein air* was also facilitated by the invention of a light, portable easel, available for use from about 1850.[7]

Transportation Technology.   The new technology of the railroad train exercised an important twofold influence on impressionism. First, the new mode of transport made it possible for impressionist artists, often based in or around Paris, to travel with relative ease to the lovely environments of southern France. As Denvir observes, the impressionists "traveled more extensively than any other group of artists had been able to in the past; their work was nourished by a greater variety of landscapes."[8] Second, the emergence and spread of the railroad in the 1830s and 1840s helped promote recognition of "the subjective nature of visual experience." Whereas prior to the arrival of the railroad, humans had not been able to travel faster than about 15 miles per hour, now they could travel at speeds of up to 50 to 60 miles per hour. "[T]he precise outlines [of objects and landscapes] to which post-Renaissance perspectival art had accustomed the artist's eye" were blurred, and the transitory nature of visual experience was underlined, affording a "larger, less confined view of landscape."[9]

The Camera. The growing use of the photographic camera in the period from 1840 to 1865 influenced impressionist painting in several ways. The recently invented device ("the pencil of nature") was used to obtain black and white 'sketches' of nature. As Josef Hodin pointed out, by furnishing "documents of momentary or 'candid' vision" that could be studied and referred to at length, the camera "facilitat[ed] the study in art of immediate sensory data," something which, as we have seen, was of great interest to impressionist painters.[10] In fact, actual photographs were used by some impressionists as a basis for some of their paintings. Moreover, the novel blurred manner in which tiny moving pedestrians were represented in street scenes painted by impressionists such as Monet may be indebted to familiarity with the similar way in which moving forms appeared on contemporary photographs including similar phenomena.[11]

The camera liberated painting from one of its traditional functions or obligations—namely, precise reproduction of external reality. The precision with which the camera could provide representations of external reality induced painters to move in directions in which they thought they would not be outdone by photographs as they knew them; they moved, for example, toward use of high-toned primary colors, greater focus on atmospherics, and experimentation with various kinds of nonillusionistic forms of representing reality. As the author of a prescient 1842 article in *The Spectator* put it:

> The artist cannot compete with the minute accuracy...of the Daguerreotype but...not all the delicate truth of photographic delineation can supply the want of colour. By imitating the local color and atmospheric effect alone can landscape painters hope to stand against such a formidable rival as Nature. Therefore it behooves them to study with redoubled assiduity the influence of atmospheric light upon the individual hues of objects and the general tone of the scene; and also to strive to imitate the appearance of movement in figures and foliage, water and clouds.[12]

Although there is no evidence that he did, one could be excused for wondering whether Monet might have read this article and taken it to heart.

The Science of Color. The efforts of impressionists to enhance the luminosity of their paintings were influenced by, among other things, the scientific research being done on light, color, and perception in the nineteenth century by investigators such as Maxwell, Fresnel, Helmholz, Rood, and, above all, Chevreul. The latter's *Principles of Harmony and Contrast of Colors, and their Applications to the Arts* was published in 1839.

Chemist Eugene Chevreul was appointed director of dyeing at the Gobelin Tapestry Works in Paris in 1824, a time when the firm was expanding to include the manufacture of carpets. As synthetic dyes were not discovered until the middle of the century, rugs were colored by using either natural dyes or hues obtained by mixing them. Troubled by complaints about the apparent darkness of some of his dyes and pigments, Chevreul undertook research into color harmonies, during which he discovered that colors in proximity alter each other's look. He also investigated what later came to be called "optical mixing." In experimenting with woolen threads, he found that two threads of different dye colors appear to have a single color when seen from a distance and that juxtaposing small patches of primary colors and allowing the eye of the viewer to do the "mixing" at a distance rather than by first combining them in dye vats—or, later, on a painter's palette—yielded enhanced luminosity.

Several impressionists were aware of and influenced by Chevreul's work, including Monet, Camille Pissarro, and, later, Georges Seurat.[13] The aims of the "neo-impressionists," Pissarro wrote to his art dealer in 1886, were

> to seek a modern synthesis of methods based on science, that is, based on M. Chevreul's theory of color and on the experiments of Maxwell and the measurements of N. O. [*sic*] Rood. To substitute optical mixture for mixture of pigments. In other words, the breaking-up of tones into their constituents. For optical mixture stirs up more intense luminosities than mixture of pigments does.[14]

The Art Dealer.   Allusion to Pissarro's art dealer brings us to another important, albeit indirect, way in which technology influenced impressionism. While the existence of the art dealer is today taken for granted, as a social institution it matured only in the nineteenth century. The onset of the industrial revolution had created much wealth in France, much of it possessed by people new to affluence. Unschooled in the traditional forms of artistic patronage, these newcomers provided a natural soil for the sudden flourishing in France around mid-century of the professional art dealer. The latter played several roles: adviser to artists, public relations specialist, and intermediary between artist and customer. To appreciate the importance of the art dealer to impressionism, one must remember that in 1873 the official, government-controlled, annual art exhibition, the Salon, rejected pictures by Monet, Pissarro, Pierre Auguste Renoir, Alfred Sisley, and Paul Cézanne. In Denvir's words,

> [The art dealer] liberated artists from their dependence on the annual official Salon; he opened up new outlets; without him the avant garde would never have existed. This effective influence was especially true for Impressionism, which owes an incalculable debt to the perspicacity, good sense, and loyalty of Paul Durand-Ruel and Ambroise Vollard, the movement's main dealers.[15]

Audience.   One other influence of technology on impressionism—for that matter, on painting in general—is worthy of note, even if it took effect only long after the movement had expired. Developments in technology have made possible the mass production and widespread diffusion of affordable, high-quality reproductions and museum posters of renowned impressionist works, particularly ones by Monet and Renoir, but also works of Edgar Degas and the neo-impressionist Seurat. The same is true of the mass production of exhibition catalogues containing color as well as black-and-white reproductions. Moreover, advances in transport technology in the twentieth century have enabled traveling exhibitions of great art works to be sent quickly and securely from one country or continent to another, thus affording millions of people direct access to works they would otherwise not see.

For example, in 1984 and 1985, "A Day in the Country: Impressionism and the French Landscape," an exhibition of 127 impressionist, neo-impressionist, or impressionist-related paintings on loan from public institutions and private collectors around the world, was on public view for two and a half months each in the cities of Los Angeles, Chicago, and Paris.[16] Over 820,000 people attended the exhibit during its stays in Los Angeles and Chicago.[17] Modern technology has democratized exposure to renowned paintings. In the case of impressionism, it has helped make a relatively short-lived, largely French movement a living part of contemporary Western culture for millions of people around the globe.

Conclusion

We have discussed the influence of developments in science and technology on aspects of impressionism pertaining to the ideational, societal, material, and behavioral sectors of the cultural system of late nineteenth century European society. In general, the impressionists' shift of European painting's focus from depicting traditional kinds of subject matter (e.g., mythical, historical, and heroic themes) to capturing the subtle effects of light on deformed objects of everyday life was an important step in a long revolutionary process, one in which developments in science and technology played important roles. This process culminated in the early twentieth century with the jettisoning of centuries-old painting conventions, such as the notion that the goal of painting was to achieve accurate and meaningful representations of external reality.

The episode of impressionism illustrates in subtle ways our earlier general contention that the evolution of Western painting in the last 150 years is to a significant degree the story of artists' efforts to come to aesthetic terms with, and to exploit the resources offered by, the new sociotechnical order, to probe their divergent attitudes toward it, and to express their responses in pictorial languages adequate to the unique character of the scientific-industrial era. In the words of Fernand Léger:

> [I]f pictorial expression has changed, it is because modern life has necessitated it...When one crosses a landscape by automobile or express train, it becomes fragmented; it loses its descriptive value but gains in synthetic value...A modern man registers a hundred times more sensory impressions than an 18th-century artist; so much so that our language, for example, is full of diminutives and abbreviations. The compression of the modern picture, its variety, its breaking up of forms, are the result of all this.[18]

MUSIC

Let us now turn to the performing art of music. We will first consider the influence of technology and science on modern classical music, and then, more briefly, on post-World War II popular music.

Classical Music

Two kinds of technological and scientific changes altered the contours of the classical-music enterprise in the modern period: innovations in musical instruments and advances in the transmission, recording, and reproduction of music. Changes in classical music engendered by the former developments were primarily aesthetic and will be discussed first. Then we will consider broader sociocultural changes in the classical-music enterprise occasioned by the latter technical advances.

Technological Changes.   Technology and, more recently, science have affected classical music by markedly improving the instruments used to perform it. When one thinks of modern classical music, the symphony orchestra and the piano come readily to mind. What is not often recognized is that both of these fixtures of classical music are relatively late products of complex evolutionary processes in which technological changes played important roles. For example, it was not until well into the nineteenth century that a series of ingenious technolgical innovations made possible the supple, sophisticated, well-tuned concert instrument known as the modern symphony orchestra. Consider the cases of the string, brass, and woodwind instruments.

The violin family of instruments had been highly developed in the late seventeenth and first half of the eighteenth centuries by great Italian craftsmen such as Nicolò Amati, Antonio Stradivari, and Giuseppe Guarneri ("del Gesu"). Toward the end of the eighteenth century, however, significant changes were introduced. For example, the violin's fingerboard and neck were lengthened and the latter's form altered. Traditionally, the surface of the neck was aligned with the edge of the body (soundbox). Now the neck was sloped back so that the strings formed a sharper angle when drawn over the newly heightened bridge. This arrangement, prompted by the kinds of attacks and strokes made possible by the introduction of the modern kind of bow, as well as by the need for stronger string resistance to the increased pressure exerted by such bowing, produced desired gains in power and brilliance of tone. The bass-bar, set inside the violin's body to provide structural support, was made longer and stronger, thereby enabling the instrument to bear the increased downward pressure from the changes just described. Able to transmit heavier vibrations, the new violin produced a larger tone. These improvements were sufficiently impressive that many already superb seventeenth and early eighteenth century violins were retrofitted to incorporate them.[19]

Before the nineteenth century, all brass instruments except the trombones were just tubes of brass and silver, sometimes coiled or bent in various shapes. Pitch was changed by use of breath and lips, and changes of basic keys were accomplished by physically inserting or removing additional lengths of tube into or from the main tube. Musical compositions for these instruments had therefore to avoid complicated key changes and chromatic pitches. This problem was solved around 1815 with the invention of valves. Depressing them enabled a player instantly to "cut in" extra lengths of tube coiled permanently alongside the main body of the instrument. Players could now play all the notes and every key with ease.[20]

As for the woodwinds, e.g., the clarinet, the problem was to cut finger holes which could be easily reached and effectively controlled yet also give accurate pitches, twin goals that had previously eluded simultaneous solution. After a long period, starting well back in the eighteenth century, during which the number of keys gradually increased, this problem was finally overcome in the 1830s with the perfection of covering and uncovering keys controlled by a set of levers, axles, and springs which acted as extensions of the player's fingers.[21]

The point here is not the accumulation of individually ingenious technical improvements, but the fact that by the 1830s composers had at their disposal an orchestra that could play a much more complicated and variegated series of pitches, a wider range of sounds, and do so *in tune*. This induced them to compose new works exploiting the greater flexibility of the modern orchestra. Technological change in instruments enlarged the sonic field on which composers could exercise their imaginations.* Romantic

---

*This situation echoes the discussion in Chapter 5 of technological determinism.

composers such as Berlioz, Wagner, and Mahler exploited these unprecedented technoaesthetic possibilities to revolutionary artistic effects.

The piano also underwent dramatic technological change.[22] Its predecessor, the harpsichord, was prominent as both a solo and an ensemble instrument from the sixteenth to the eighteenth centuries. As the orchestra grew in size during the 1700s, the accompanying harpsichord's characteristic light tone became increasingly difficult to hear. Moreover, its uniform timbre and inability to produce sounds of variable loudness limited the instrument's expressiveness. This dual situation provided impetus for the development of a louder, dynamically flexible keyboard instrument. As a percussive rather than a plucked instrument, the "pianoforte," invented by 1700 by Florentine craftsman Bartolomeo Cristofori, could play loud (*forte*) as well as soft (*piano*). It could thus stand up to the orchestra and not be overwhelmed.

Various figures helped move the instrument along the road to the contemporary grand piano. In 1821, the French craftsman Sebastien Erard patented an ingenious "double-escapement" keyboard action mechanism that enabled individual notes to be repeated in rapid-fire succession. As with the symphony orchestra, composers of piano music wrote within the constraints of the instruments available to them. Mozart composed for a piano of quite limited range with only a moderately loud and relatively thin tone. In contrast, the higher and lower notes, louder tones, and pyrotechnics called for in many Romantic piano compositions were realizable only with the expanded range, greater dynamic flexibility, and improved action of innovative early nineteenth century pianos.

Further along in the nineteenth century, the piano underwent additional revolutionary changes, ones that gave it the even greater range, power, and expressiveness we associate with contemporary grands. One way to make the piano louder was to make its string tension greater. But, as with wooden textile machinery driven to higher speeds by steam engines, then-standard wooden-framed pianos would collapse if string tension was increased enough to obtain desired loudness levels. A major step forward was taken by the American craftsman Alpheus Babcock. In 1825 he patented a full, one-piece, cast-iron frame for the "square" piano, significantly increasing the instrument's maximum loudness. In 1843, building on Babcock's achievement, Jonas Chickering, originally a cabinetmaker, secured a patent for a full, one-piece, iron-frame *grand* piano. Finally, in 1859, Steinway & Sons introduced a masterpiece of synthesis: a grand piano combining cross-stringing* (of the long bass strings at an angle over the shorter upper strings to a separate bridge) with a full, one-piece, cast-iron frame. The resultant instrument possessed enhanced richness and volume of tone.

Taken together, by the mid-1860s, these and other improvements (e.g., felt hammers and steel strings) yielded a grand piano of the sort that we now take for granted. They enabled the kind of pianism favored by legendary virtuosi from Franz Liszt to Vladimir Horowitz. Without these technological changes the familiar technosocial—and sociological—phenomenon of the awe-inspiring piano virtuoso's unamplified concert-hall performance of pieces of enormous dynamic range for audiences of thousands of "fans" would not have been possible.

Sociocultural Changes.   Let us now turn to some of the more important sociocultural changes in the total enterprise of classical music engendered by innovations in science and technology.

*Cross-stringing for upright pianos had been introduced in 1828 by Frenchman Henri Pape.

(1) *Audience.* One far-reaching influence of technological and scientific change on the classical-music enterprise has been the changed nature and scope of its audience. Socially speaking, in the eighteenth century, classical music in Europe was largely supported by, and performed for the pleasure and prestige of, the privileged few. Its characteristic performance in royal, religious, and private club locales reflected its primary sources of support and audience: royal courts, the aristocracy, the wealthy, and the Church. With the rise of the middle class in the late eighteenth and early nineteenth centuries, a phenomenon spurred by the economic consequences of the industrial revolution, the audience for classical music became less exclusive and more diverse in composition. The concurrent rise and flourishing of two new institutions, the permanent professional orchestra and the public concert—admission to the latter being open to anyone able to purchase a ticket—went hand in hand with this democratization trend. The desire of the new and rapidly growing middle class for access to classical concerts led to the construction of large halls in which to hold them, and hence to a significant increase in the size of concerts. Rarely accommodating more than 250 in the eighteenth century, new concert halls, such as London's Royal Albert Hall (1871) and New York's Carnegie Hall (1891), sometimes held considerably more than two thousand in the nineteenth. Audiences of twenty-five hundred and more are common in contemporary halls.[23]

In the twentieth century, the audience for classical music has grown exponentially, principally through a series of scientific and technological innovations. While the horizon-expanding effect on musical taste of the diffusion of the first mass-produced musical instrument, the piano, should not be forgotten, more important were new technologies of musical reproduction and transmission. Improved versions of Edison's primitive phonograph around the turn of the century provided the first practical reproduction of classical music. By 1930, improvements in recording quality—not least through the replacement of acoustical by electrical recording—and the diffusion of improved records and record players expanded the audience for classical music far beyond the level it had reached by the end of the nineteenth century.

Expanded radio transmission of classical concerts also played an important role. In 1937, the celebrated Italian maestro Arturo Toscanini accepted the invitation of General David Sarnoff, founder and president of the Radio Corporation of America (RCA), to become the conductor of a new ensemble created especially for him and staffed largely with virtuosi recruited from the country's leading orchestras. From 1937 to 1954, historic concerts of Toscanini and the "NBC Symphony Orchestra" originated in the National Broadcasting Company's state-of-the-art studios in the RCA building in Manhattan and were broadcast live nationwide and in Canada over the NBC radio network to audiences of millions.*

Further expansions in the audience for classical music were catalyzed by the introduction of the long-playing (LP) record in 1948, stereophonic records in 1957, and stereophonic audio cassettes in the late 1960s. Television also made a contribution. The first live broadcasts on American television of classical orchestral concerts took place in 1948. Live television broadcasts of Toscanini conducting the NBC Symphony occurred frequently between 1948 and 1952. In the 1960s, conductor Leonard Bernstein's popular "New York Philharmonic Young People's Concerts" introduced classical music to millions of viewers nationwide. Finally, exposure to classical music and opera has been increased in the 1970s and 1980s by long-running, distinguished

---

*NBC was a subsidiary of RCA throughout this period.

series on the national public television network, such as "Live From Lincoln Center" and "Great Performances." The upshot is that through a series of technological innovations, the audience for classical music has grown greatly in scope and diversity. Moreover, this enlarged audience has easy access to an unprecedentedly rich menu of recorded classical musical works.

The expanded, easier access enjoyed by a growing audience of listeners has had several interesting effects on classical music. Records and tapes have produced a more musically literate and demanding audience with high performance expectations, sometimes to the detriment of mediocre orchestras and performers. The advent of long-playing—initially up to 23 minutes per side—and quieter 33 1/3 rpm records in 1948 and the upgrading of home reproducing equipment to "high-fidelity" status to play the new LPs gave a great boost to classical record sales. This encouraged record companies to re-record the standard classical and romantic repertoire as well as to release hitherto unrecorded baroque rarities.[24]

The growing number of private individuals with substantial record collections of art music has given rise to an international canon of "classics" well known by concert goers, who feel virtually entitled to hear one or two of them at each live concert. Together with the important role of the middle-class audience in supporting the professional orchestra, this expectation has tended to circumscribe concert programming, thereby impeding the introduction of unfamiliar new music. Well-endowed technology firms, such as petroleum and telecommunications companies, have become important new patrons of classical music, while record companies have become valued institutional supporters of the orchestras whose performances they record and sell, often under exclusive contract. The contributions of such companies are undeniable. However, considerations of prestige and marketability tend to lend a conservative cast to recording agendas, thereby reinforcing the canon and indirectly constricting concert programmers.

(2) *Performers, Performance, and Technological Change.*   Technological changes played an important role in the evolution of the social status of the classical-music performer. From virtual royal or church servant in the days of Haydn and Mozart, the performer has in contemporary times attained the status of, at worst, respectable free-lance artist and, at best, virtuoso idol or superstar.

Their role in enhancing status and expanding and enriching audience access notwithstanding, some eminent artists, such as American march king John Philip Sousa and French composer and pianist Claude Debussy, disdained early phonograph records. Acoustic recordings were not only low in quality but inconvenient to make. Performers had to crowd around and concentrate their energy into a conical megaphone, at the bottom of which was a moving diaphragm with a needle attached which etched a wax-coated disc. (This is why performances by full symphonic orchestras are absent from early acoustic recordings: Their members could not all get sufficiently close to the megaphone.) Even when their sonic quality had improved somewhat, say by the end of World War I, many artists continued to resist or resent recording as then done, for since pre-LP records could contain only about 4 minutes of material per side, artists had only three choices, none ideal: limit themselves to short pieces, truncate longer pieces, or submit to the disconcerting "start-and-stop" method of recording longer pieces on multiple discs.[25]

Concern over sonic quality abated when, through research and development work carried out at Bell Telephone Laboratories, electrically recorded discs and an accompanying "exponential-horn phonograph"—dubbed the "Victrola" by the Victor Talking Machine Company—were introduced in 1925. (During the first week it was for sale, $20 million of orders for the new instrument were placed.) Substantial gains in fidelity were realized and, through use of the condenser microphone, invented in 1917 by Bell's E. C. Wente, performers no longer had to crowd around a megaphone. Recording full symphony orchestras was now feasible, and numerous classical works were issued beginning in July 1925. Many featured the Philadelphia Orchestra conducted by Leopold Stokowski, the foremost artistic champion of electrical recording.[26] The process by which classical musical artists adapted themselves to the new technology had received a powerful boost.

With the stunning improvements in recording and records in recent decades, the attitude of classical musical artists toward recording has changed radically; in at least one case, a full 180 degrees. The late Canadian classical pianist Glenn Gould completely abandoned concertizing in public in favor of making "perfect" recordings in the studio with the aid of sophisticated tape-splicing and mixing machinery. The orchestral conductor—itself a nineteenth century institutional innovation engendered by the increased size of the modern symphonic instrument—now routinely engages in postperformance manipulation of the balance among the different parts of the orchestra to obtain desired sonic effects. In recent years, the establishment of computer music research facilities "has made collaboration between composers, conductors, and instrumentalists on the one hand and scientists and engineers on the other less unusual."[27] Such perfectionistic, technology-intensive practices have raised questions about the future of the social institution of the live concert, the emergence of acoustically tunable concert halls notwithstanding. Will the fact that a concert scheduled for an acoustically mediocre hall is live remain a sufficient inducement to lure listeners accustomed to "perfect" recorded performances from the comfort and quality of their "private concert halls"?

(3) *Composers, Compositions, and Contemporary Society.* The relationship among composers, their compositions, and the classical-music-listening audience has also been transformed in this century. The social and intellectual upheavals spawned by the industrial and French revolutions of the eighteenth and nineteenth centuries encouraged artists—literary, visual, and musical—to go beyond traditional conventions of their respective arts. However, the early years of the twentieth century were a revolutionary era in their own right, both technologically and artistically. In 1913, the innovative Debussy expressed the challenge to create anew felt by many artists:

> Is it not our duty ... to find the symphonic formula required by our era and called for by its modern improvements, feats of daring, and victories? The century of airplanes has a right to a music of its own. Let the defenders of our art not be allowed to remain inert in the bottom ranks of the army of researchers. Let them not be outdone by the genius of the engineers.[28]

As in painting and architecture, twentieth century composers launched a search for music styles adequate to the new industrial era. As modern painters eventually abandoned the traditional conventions of perspective and representation, revolutionary twentieth century composers renounced the traditional musical conventions of tonality, the primacy of melody, and metrical rhythm. What they produced, however, was more complex, cerebral, and often dissonant music able to be appreciated only by a small cognoscenti of fellow musicians and the technically initiated.

The situation of the twentieth century composer has thus become poignant. With a potential audience of unprecedented magnitude and access to technological resources of enormous range, flexibility, and power—including the tape recorder, computer, and a growing battery of electronic music synthesizers—the contemporary composer has chosen to write "difficult" music, seemingly aimed at peers, that has attracted only a negligible fraction of the potential audience. Ironically, unlike the situation in modern painting, the huge new classical-music audience has largely rejected the music of contemporary composers and has embraced a repertoire of baroque, classical, and romantic works, supplemented by a few contemporary works written for the most part before 1920. Whether this situation is due more to the inherent character of the rejected music, to the now familiar, hence more intelligible, character of the canon, to the sense of cultural stability provided by its works in a time of increasingly rapid social (including musical) change, or to some other factor, is a matter of considerable controversy.

In any event, the upshot is that technological change, both in familiarizing a growing body of serious-music listeners with the traditional classics of the past and in precipitating a highly individualized search for music of intellectual complexity not beholden to traditional musical norms, has contributed to a breakdown in communication. Indeed, a condition of probably permanent aesthetic estrangement now exists between contemporary composers of art music and the overwhelming bulk of the classical-music-listening public. The contemporary composer, however highly regarded professionally, is at best a marginal figure, working in virtual isolation from the musical public and supported largely by orchestral and foundation commissions or by occupying a university teaching or research post, or both. It is unlikely that mushrooming advances in electronic music, however technically impressive and sonically innovative, will yield works that find abiding favor with even a significant fraction of the enormously expanded classical-music-listening public.

(4) *Interplay of Technological, Social, and Value Changes.*   In the spirit of remarks made earlier in this book (in Chapter 5) about the dangers of succumbing to belief in autonomous technology and technological determinism, it should be pointed out that while the influence of technological (and more recently scientific) change has been center stage in our discussion thus far, many of the technological innovations in question went hand in hand with important social changes. For example, it is one thing to talk about the musical influence of technological improvements in instruments. However, just as the technological innovations of the industrial revolution did not emerge in a vacuum, neither did these musical ones. While the internal "push" factor of performers' or artisans' drives to improve instruments is not to be discounted, the rise of the middle class was an important "pull" factor. The increasing number of people wanting to attend music concerts required larger listening halls, which (in the absence of electric amplification) required instruments able to generate sufficient sound to fill up those spaces. This provided an important impetus for many technological improvements in instruments. The same is true of the growing popularity of solo concerti, in which single featured instruments had to be able to be heard above accompanying orchestras of increased size.

In turn, the resultant technical ability of pianists or violinists to play solo concerts audible to large audiences of listeners helped pave the way for the musical version of the influential idea of the romantic hero: the virtuoso. Thus, the reader should be aware that changes in science, technology, and society often cannot be so neatly disentangled as the expressions "the influence of science and technology on society" and "the influence of society on science and technology" might suggest.

Popular Music

In many ways (e.g., improvements in and mass production of instruments and home playback equipment and the enormous expansion of audience), the influence of technology and science on popular music in the post–World War II period in the West resembles their influence on classical music. Here we will limit ourselves to brief comments on a few contrasting influences and their musical and social significance.

Modern technology is indispensible to much post–World War II popular music. Like its most characteristic institutional forms, the rock concert and festival, rock music could not have existed without the resources of contemporary technology (and science). These are used in a wide range of important electric and electronic technics, such as the electric guitar and bass, electronic keyboard instruments, microphones, amplifiers, and loudspeakers, and a host of recording, telecommunications, mass-production, and print technologies.

Many performers of pop music are themselves, as it were, creatures of technology. The distinctive "sounds" achieved on pop records often depend critically on the advanced technics and techniques employed by audio engineers and "sound mixers" in the recording studio, not just on the performer's unaided vocal and instrumental skills. While small groups could easily fill up the big spaces of rock concerts and festivals with the aid of the formidable technological arsenals at their disposal, the gap between the sound on a state-of-the-art, studio-produced recording and the sound that a performer or group could generate in concert was sometimes startling. Live television resorted to "lip synching" of studio recordings to bridge the gap, but discerning concert goers were sometimes disappointed.*

The sonic enhancement afforded by technology meant that performers could be chosen by the record industry at least as much for their star potential as for their musical talents, a development that increased the importance of charisma and sex appeal. The ability to mass produce, mass market, and give simultaneous mass media exposure to the technologically enhanced recordings of often modestly talented, unconventional, anti-bourgeois performers positioned them to be role models to youth who, for sociological reasons, lacked compelling familial or societal alternatives.

The generationally pitched content of its lyrics, simplicity of musical structure, and, not least important, amplified loudness and pulsating rhythmic beat help explain the reception of rock music by a musically unsophisticated audience of youth with abundant energy to expend and important developmental tasks of identity and affiliation to accomplish. The technological ability to record, enhance, mass produce, attractively package, and quickly and widely broadcast and distribute records and tapes of such music contributed to the rise in the 1960s and 1970s of an antiestablishment youth culture, national and partly international in scope. The economic impact of the pop music revolution has been enormous: In 1989, the record industry was a $23-billion-a-year business, the bulk of these revenues derived from pop music

---

*Compare pianist Glenn Gould's aforementioned dissatisfaction with and response to the sonic (and performance) imperfections of live concerts.

sales.[29] An account of its political importance must include pop music's central roles in campaign fund-raising and in the mobilization of antiwar and other kinds of social protest. In contrast, the sociological significance of pop music in recent decades is less clear. Whether, for example, pop music has been a causal factor in or merely a manifestation of the breakdown of traditional cultural values and behavioral norms remains an open question.[30]

CONCLUSION

Much of the influence of technology and science on modern painting and classical music can be summarized in three words: expansion, liberation, challenge. Technology and science greatly expanded the technical resources, tonal spaces, legitimate subject matter, and audiences of modern painting and music. These forces also contributed significantly to the gradual undermining of powerful aesthetic conventions that had long held sway: perspective and representation of external reality in painting, and tonality, primacy of melody, and metrical rhythm in classical music. In so doing, science and technology may be said to have placed the twentieth century painter and classical composer in a delicate position: It gave them unprecedented freedom to develop an individualistic style unfettered by convention and with a potential audience of unprecedented scope and magnitude, but it confronted them with the problem of communicating successfully with an audience that must either be won over to the artist's idiosyncratic approach or be forfeited. At this juncture, it would seem that, on the whole, twentieth century painters have been more successful in exploiting this opportunity than have their classical musical counterparts.

ENDNOTES

1. Bernard Denvir, *Impressionism* (Woodbury, N.Y.: Barron's, 1978), p. 3.
2. Robert L. Herbert, "Industry in the Changing Landscape from Daubigny to Monet," in John M. Merriman, ed., *French Cities in the Nineteenth Century* (London: Hutchinson, 1982), p. 150.
3. Harold Osborne, *The Oxford Companion to Art* (Oxford: Oxford University Press, 1970), p. 563.
4. *Ibid.*, p. 871.
5. Phoebe Pool, *Impressionism* (New York: Praeger, 1967), p. 7.
6. Osborne, *Oxford Companion to Art*, p. 1162.
7. *Ibid.*, p. 882.
8. Denvir, *Impressionism*, p. 11.
9. *Ibid.*
10. Josef Hodin, "Science and Modern Art," *Encyclopedia of World Art* (New York: McGraw-Hill, 1959), 5, 210.
11. Aaron Scharf, *Art and Photography* (Middlesex: Penguin, 1974), p. 170.
12. Osborne, *Oxford Companion to Art*, p. 865; and Scharf, *ibid.*, p. 169.
13. Pool, *Impressionism*, pp. 13–14.
14. *Ibid.*, pp. 243–244.
15. Denvir, *Impressionism*, p. 8.
16. Sarah B. Sherrill, "French Impressionism," *Antiques*, July 1984, 126, no. 1, 52.
17. Attendance figures provided by the Los Angeles County Museum of Art and the Art Institute of Chicago.
18. Fernand Léger, "Contemporary Achievements in Painting," in Leger, *Functions of Painting*, Edward F. Fry, ed. (New York: Viking, 1973), pp. 11–12.

19. *The New Grove Dictionary of Music and Musicians*, Stanley Sadie, ed. (London: MacMillan, 1980) 19, 831, and *The New Oxford Companion to Music*, Denis Arnold, ed. (Oxford: Oxford University Press, 1983), 2, 1931.
20. Michael Hurd, "Orchestra," *The New Oxford Companion to Music*, 2, 1333.
21. *The New Grove Dictionary of Music and Musicians*, 4, 437.
22. The following four paragraphs lean heavily on Edwin M. Good, *Giraffes, Black Dragons, and Other Pianos: A Technological History From Cristofori to the Modern Concert Grand* (Stanford, Cal.: Stanford University Press, 1982), especially chaps. 2, 5, and 7.
23. *The New Grove Dictionary of Music and Musicians*, 11, 206 and 13, 177.
24. John Borwick, "Recording and Reproduction," in *New Oxford Companion to Music*, 2, 1539.
25. See, e.g., the lament of pianist Ferruccio Busoni over the start-and-stop method of recording quoted in Robert E. McGinn, "Stokowski and the Bell Telephone Laboratories: Collaboration in the Development of High-Fidelity Sound Reproduction," *Technology and Culture*, 24, no. 1, January 1983, 73.
26. *Ibid.*, pp. 42-43, and Roland Gelatt, *The Fabulous Phonograph*, 2nd ed. (New York: Collier, 1977), pp. 230–231 and 235.
27. McGinn, "Stokowski and Bell Laboratories," p. 75.
28. Quoted in Claude Debussy, *Monsieur Croche et autres écrits* (Paris: Gallimard, 1971), p. 241 (English trans. by R.E. McGinn).
29. *New York Times*, March 15, 1990, p. A1.
30. For discussion of the sociological significance of rock music in the 1955–1975 period, see Todd Gitlin, *The Sixties: Years of Hope, Days of Rage* (New York: Bantam, 1987), especially pp. 37–44, 195–204, and 427–429.

CHAPTER 12
INTERNATIONAL RELATIONS

INTRODUCTION

The influence components examined in Chapters 6 through 11 were at the level of a single national or transnational society. However, as we saw in Chapter 3, contemporary science and technology are increasingly international in character. The same is true of their effects. Our seventh and last influence cut will therefore be at the *inter*national level. Science and technology have exerted a powerful transformative influence on international relations in the modern period, particularly in the twentieth century. As Otto Hieronymi contends, in the post–World War II period there has been a significant increase in "the relative weight of technology issues in virtually all aspects not only of intergovernmental, but also of the growing and increasingly complex web of private cross-border relations."[1] In spite of this, until relatively recently, academic works on international relations have paid modest attention to the roles of science and technology. International relations have many dimensions, but we will limit ourselves to discussion of influences of science and technology on three of them: the political, the economic, and the social.

TECHNOLOGY AND THE INTERNATIONAL ORDER

Arguably the most fundamental structural change in international relations in the modern period is one attributable in large part to advances in technology—especially in the military, communications, and transportation fields—and science, particularly physics. In the words of Warner Schilling:

> [A]s the industrial revolution transformed the bases of military power and increased its mobility, international relations became global rather than regional in scope, and the relations among the members of this global system became continuous, rather than episodic.[2]

An international relations system long characterizable for the most part in terms of *intermittent* and *local* interactions gradually gave way to a system of relations best described as *continuous* and *global* in character. This transformation has made international relations considerably more complex, creating myriad new opportunities for augmenting and challenging national political power and economic strength.

POLITICAL RELATIONS

Technology and Colonialism

The seeds of the globalization of international relations were sown centuries ago. Between 1500 and 1800, European colonialist inroads in Asia, Africa, and the New World were facilitated by the invention or adaptation of the clock, compass, gunpowder and cannon, as well as by improvements in ship design. However, the fact that European colonies were rarely located inland reflected limitations in available water transport and military technologies. In the nineteenth century, a new wave of European imperialism broke over Africa and Asia, one that achieved greater geographical penetration and exacted a greater toll of human destruction.

At the very least, this latter development was made possible by a host of nineteenth century technological and scientific advances. Daniel Headrick has advanced a stronger thesis. Rather than simply making pre-existing imperialist motives viable, these nineteenth century technical advances, by greatly facilitating military conquest, activated and may even have stimulated motivations to create far-reaching colonial empires. "[M]eans and motives were not rival but congruent causes of the new imperialism....[They] were interrelated, but not in a one-dimensional determinist way."[3]

Iron-hulled steam boats, unlike sail boats, could sail up and manuever in inland waterways, thereby opening inland areas to colonial domination. Iron steamers equipped with cannons devastated and were relatively immune to the use of fire by outclassed local naval resistance, for example, in China. The discovery of quinine prophylaxis overcame the obstacle to European domination of Africa previously presented by malaria. A series of improvements such as rifling, the percussion cap, the cylindrical-conoidal bullet, breechloading, metal cartridges, smokeless explosives, and the magazine and repeating mechanism, led to a revolution in guns in the nineteenth century. The muzzle-loading smoothbore piked musket was replaced by various automatic repeating rifles, culminating in the rapid-firing Maxim machine gun. (While declining to use them against their fellow Europeans, the British decimated determined African and Asian resisters with a notorious new invention: the mushrooming "dum-dum" bullet, specially designed to explode upon contact and tear gaping holes in the body.[4])

Ironically, technology eventually played an important part in the demise of political colonialism. The miniaturization and mobility of many modern weapons and weapons systems made it impossible to prevent their diffusion in the long run. Thus colonialist advantages in military technology proved relatively short-lived. (Similarly, the miniaturization and mobility of advanced weapons and weapons systems has in recent years been exploited for foreign-policy purposes by guerilla and terrorist groups in order to neutralize "superpower" advantages in large-scale weapons, systems, and logistics.) Moreover, mass communications technics, especially the transistor radio, facilitated the crystallization and growth of senses of identity and oppression among colonialized peoples, (for example, in Egypt) much as it did in the case of American blacks.

Technology and Contemporary Revolutions With International Components

In recent years, technology has been a critical factor in some important domestic revolutions with international components. Consider the cases of the Iranian revolution of 1979 and the revolutions in Eastern Europe in 1989.

In Iran, prior to 1979, the American-backed regime of Shah Mohammed Reza Pahlavi was firmly in control of the state radio and television networks. Dissident supporters of the exiled ayatollah Ruhollah Khomeini therefore turned to other technologies to transmit his messages from abroad to the disaffected masses at home. Long-distance telephone calls by Khomeini were recorded on tape cassette machines. The original tape was then duplicated, disseminated, and played over Shiite mosque loudspeakers around the country.[5] Thus, the dissidents created an effective new telecommunications network, something which proved to be an important weapon in their successful struggle against the shah.

While Soviet president Mikhail S. Gorbachev's program of *glasnost* and *perestroika* clearly played a central role in the occurrence of revolutionary change in Eastern Europe in 1989, technology was an important background factor. Consider, for example, the cases of East Germany and Romania.

The potency of the West German technoeconomic production system had long afforded West Germans material affluence and a much higher average standard of living than their East German counterparts. The reception of West German broadcasts on East German televisions vividly brought home to East Germans the relatively Spartan character of their way of life. This, along with long-standing political repression, had created a cauldron of discontent. Activated by the sudden availability of routes to the West via Czechoslovakia, Hungary, and Poland, and emboldened by Gorbachev's implicit support of substantial politicoeconomic change during his October 1989 visit to East Germany on the occasion of the Communist government's celebration of its fortieth anniversary, this discontent expressed itself in the forms of mass protest marches for democratic reform at home and large-scale emigration by train to the West, a dual development that led to the transformation of East German political life.

In Romania, technology played a critical foreground as well as an important background role. As in East Germany, by late 1989 foreign radio and television broadcasts accessible in Romania had made the populace aware of changes taking place elsewhere in Eastern Europe. However, what made the political role of technology different in the Romanian situation was television's contribution to the fragile struggle of dissidents against forces loyal to the recently ousted Ceausescu regime. Both sides fought to gain and keep control of the state television network headquarters in Bucharest. Once in control, the dissidents used television broadcasts to mobilize the public against the regime, to apprise the public of developments in the armed struggle (e.g., declarations of support for the dissidents by influential political, military, and cultural figures and repeated showings of the trial and execution of the Ceausescus), and to announce new policies adopted by the provisional government. The state television network was clearly a critical strategic tool in the struggle against the Ceausescu regime. Whether it was essential to the success of that struggle can never be known with certainty.

Science, Technology, and War in the Twentieth Century

From Einstein's demonstration of the interconvertibility of mass and energy and improved understanding of nuclear chain reactions, to development of more potent weapons and more rapid and accurate weapons-delivery systems, advances in science and technology have radically transformed the perennial international political problem of war and peace. While technological innovation has been a major influence on military power for millenia, in the twentieth century the relationship between science, technology, and national war-making reached a new stage.

With the successful development of poison gas, tanks, and fighter planes during World War I, major nation-states began to recognize the benefits of *institutionalizing* a network of relationships linking their national civilian scientific and technological enterprises with their respective military establishments. In World War II, that relationship was exploited in earnest. Thousands of German and American physicists and engineers were mobilized by their governments and at their behest developed, among other things, the V-2 rocket, the proximity fuse, and radar. In the United States, the development of the atom bomb by hundreds of civilian scientists and engineers mobilized by the military proved a historical watershed.

The postwar years have seen the further development and consolidation of that relationship in several forms, from substantial Department of Defense funding of "basic" research in the universities, to the issuance of lucrative government contracts to companies in the "defense industries," to the establishment of government laboratories, such as the Lawrence Livermore National Laboratory, devoted primarily to research and development of new weapons systems. The benefits of this new intimate relationship notwithstanding, it has also brought society to a point at which it is now possible to destroy world civilization and extinguish up to half of the living members of the species that created it.

The bomb dropped at Hiroshima in August 1945 had the explosive power of 12,500 tons of TNT and killed an estimated 66,000 people immediately.[6] However, many contemporary weapons make that bomb and those figures seem small. It is believed that Soviet SS-18 intercontinental missiles "carry 10 independently targetable warheads each with a payload of 750 kilotons"—that is, each possessing 60 times the explosive power of the bomb unleashed on Hiroshima.[7]

> Scientists studying the global effects of nuclear war have estimated that a large-scale exchange...would kill outright, by blast, heat, and radiation, about [a billion] people. About the same number would be seriously injured, and would be likely to die for want of medical attention. That would mean that up to half of the entire human race could be immediate victims of a nuclear war.[8]

Alexander King goes so far as to contend that "the nuclear bomb...has had more influence on international relations than any other single happening of the past century, including the rise of Marxism."[9]

Be that as it may, an undeniably potent influence of science and technology on international political relations in the post–World War II era has been the incessant development of an "arms race" of staggering proportions. Expenditures for national defense ($282.2 billion) accounted for 27.8 percent of the total U.S. budget ($1.015 trillion) for fiscal year 1987, while the Department of Defense spent about a third ($42.5 billion) of the total estimated 1988 federal research and development budget ($131.6 billion), much of it on work related to the development of new weapons of mass destruction.[10]

Ironically, as their unprecedented, horrific destructive power has made the use of nuclear weapons more "unthinkable," increasing reliance on sophisticated scientific and technological means of detecting the onset of a nuclear attack has made the chances of accidental initiation of hostilities seem less remote. On several occasions computerized

U.S. national defense systems have produced spurious indications that intercontinental ballistic missile attacks on the United States had been launched. Resultant maximum alerts of U.S. retaliatory forces were cancelled only upon discovery that the "sightings" were not incoming missiles but, for example, the rising moon (October 5, 1960) or due to failure of an integrated-circuit computer chip (June 3 and 6, 1980).[11] Indeed, the speed of nuclear weapons may reach a point in the not-too-distant future where computers will have to be programmed to trigger retaliatory strikes upon detecting an "attack" if the responding missiles are to have a chance to survive ("launch on warning"). In general, scientific and technological advances on a host of fronts have been widely deemed essential to remaining competitive in the arms race and to sustaining the viability of the theory of deterrence known as "mutually assured destruction" (MAD).

Given this sobering situation, the issue of arms control has been elevated in the post–World War II period to a position of top priority on national and international political agendas. Here too science and technology have assumed center stage. Possession of reliable technical means (e.g., seismic equipment and reconnaissance satellites), for verifying compliance with treaty terms is now viewed as indispensible for entering into an arms-control treaty with an adversary. Indeed, in recent years the hope of rendering nuclear weapons obsolete has been linked by some to the development of extraordinarily sophisticated systems of science- and computer-based space weapons that would supposedly provide an impregnable shield—at least for weapons installations—against enemy attack.

Geopolitically speaking, technological changes have transformed the political significance of particular territories around the globe. The existence of economies whose technological systems depend critically on petroleum has bestowed enhanced strategic value on the Middle East. The extended ranges of bombers and ships have done likewise to areas that are suitable candidates for refueling points. As Warner Schilling has pointed out, the advent of missile-firing nuclear submarines "endowed even the geography of the Arctic with strategic significance."[12] Consequently, remote areas, once of little consequence in the drama of international relations, have been drawn into the fray, often against their wills, and have sometimes been subjected to intervention by major powers in order to preserve or undermine their strategic value to one side or the other.

The social-opportunity costs as well as the financial burden of contemporary science-and-technology-intensive war-related activities are difficult to estimate with precision but must be assumed to be formidable. The mass production of new weapons of unprecedented destructive power has brought about a qualitatively new situation in international political relations: Not only innocent civilians but also nonparticipant nations, however neutral, have lost immunity from the effects and aftereffects of all-out war, as was graphically underscored in 1986 by the global reach of the Chernobyl nuclear power plant accident. The people of the world are now compelled to live, seemingly permanently, under a nuclear sword of Damocles, which could fall, intentionally or accidentally, at any time. To what extent this realization, even if suppressed from the conscious mind, manifests itself in a politics or economics of immediate hedonistic gratification is a matter of conjecture.

The Growing Pressure to Internationalize Political Decision Making

The arms race and its control aside, international government policy is being focused increasingly on issues engendered by scientific and technological activity.

Problems such as environmental alteration, population control, ocean resources, outer space, and food are perceived as being of increasing gravity and, as their effects often spread beyond national borders, of valid international concern. Such problems are not limited to activities characteristic of manufacturing-based economies. The emergence of a global information economy has given rise to sometimes troubling computer-and-telecommunications-based transborder information flows (e.g., the transfer of information about criminals and criminal activities, the Western-dominated gathering and diffusion of "news" about developing countries, and the movement of sensitive commercial information between branches of multinational corporations).

However, even as governments are coming to regard such problems as vital to their respective national interests, their ability to act unilaterally to protect those interests is decreasing. In Stanley Hoffman's words, "The vessel of sovereignty is leaking." According to Eugene Skolnikoff:

> [M]any technological developments today make [license for nations to do as they please] a partial truth at best. Self-interest in the use of many technologies makes it mandatory for nations to reach agreements that constrain their freedom of action, for to do otherwise would deny the use of the technology, or bring about various forms of retaliation. The constraints are usually freely entered into but they are nevertheless limitations on sovereignty....The growing constraints on freedom of national action, and the increased responsibility flowing to international organizations, will mean that the locus of decision-making will increasingly be forced from the national to the international arena.[13]

International pressure on nations to limit their freedom of action so as to mitigate serious environmental problems has already begun. For example, in 1987, 42 countries, negotiating under the auspices of the United Nations Environmental Program, signed the "Montreal Protocol." This treaty called for halving the production of five chlorine-based chemicals that deplete the atmosphere's protective ozone layer by 1998. When damage to the ozone layer exceeded expectations, in June 1990, 93 nations signed a second, more stringent treaty phasing out production and use of these chemicals by 2000. This landmark agreement was reached only after a new fund was created to help poor countries switch to chlorofluorocarbon-free technologies.[14]

The ozone-layer problem is but one of a family of serious science- or technology-related environmental problems of international scope. Thus, the acceptance of limitations on national sovereignty entailed by signing the ozone treaties set an important historical precedent. If anything is to be done to slow further global warming from the potentially catastrophic "greenhouse effect," binding international agreement, perhaps going beyond the voluntary modes employed to date, will be essential.

More generally, the extent to which the existing international system—"sovereign states vying for security and advantage, with the primary locus of decision-making within the states"[15]—can meet the increasing demands being placed on it by the proliferation of technology- and science-based issues, especially ones *not* generally perceived as posing grave threats to economic or medical well-being, is uncertain. Equally unclear are the specific feasible changes that, if made, would enable the system to grapple with such problems more effectively.

For Daniel Bell, the bearing of technology on contemporary politics is not limited to growing pressure to internationalize political decision making in the face of the transnational nature of many of the environmental problems engendered by contemporary science and technology. Bell acknowledges that there are forces requiring this internationalization. To him, however, they are primarily economic in nature, although each has an underlying technological source: "the problems of capital flows, commodity imbalances, the loss of jobs, and the several demographic tidal waves that will be developing in the next twenty years."[16] But, Bell argues, there are also factors demanding the *localization* of political decision making—namely, "the variety and diversity of local needs" and the loss by "local centers" of the ability to effectively control resources and to tailor resource decisions to those needs.[17] In a nutshell, according to Bell, the biggest political problem engendered by contemporary technology is structural: *"There is a mismatch of scale. The nation-state is becoming too small for the big problems of life and too big for the small problems of life."*[18] Technology has thus created a situation in which politics is out of synch with economic and social decision-making needs at both the international *and* local levels. The innovative federal-level institutions and regulatory mechanisms of Franklin Roosevelt's New Deal may be viewed as compensatory political responses to the mismatch in scale created by the emergence in early twentieth century America of markets and corporations on a national scale. However, resolution of the increasingly acute *dual*-scale mismatch will be more difficult. It will require new institutions at the international level and redefinition of government responsibilities and reallocation of government resources at sub-national levels.

ECONOMIC RELATIONS

As discussed in the section on technology and colonialism, science and technology have profoundly affected economic relations between nations. If anything, the economic importance of these forces seems likely to increase in the future. Contemporary technology-based international economic issues include economic competitiveness; the international mobility of capital, technical knowledge, and workers; and the global factory, office, and marketplace. While some such issues are primarily struggles between nations with highly developed economies, we will focus here on an important issue involving the economic relationship of the more developed to the less developed countries (LDCs).

Technology Transfer

Background.   Despite the gradual dissolution of the colonial power structure following World War II, the gap between the advanced industrial economies of the West and the economies of most African and Asian countries has persisted and, in some cases, widened. Belated acknowledgement of the economic and social injustices suffered by many LDCs at the hands of some highly industrialized countries gave rise to what Gunnar Myrdal calls "an entirely new concept." This was the notion that the latter, in their future dealings with the former, "should show a special concern for their welfare and economic development and should even undertake a collective responsibility for aiding them."[19] The key form taken by the aid that ensued was termed "technology transfer."

The assumption was that the injustice could be atoned for and the enormous gap in standard of living substantially narrowed if industrialized nations helped the underdeveloped countries "take over" the highly productive science and technology of the West. They would thus be spared the slow process of inventing and replicating it on their own. In this way the developing countries would gradually eliminate the economic (and sociocultural) dependence on the advanced economies to which they were reduced during the colonial era. In the event, the technology-transfer approach to international economic development, especially in the LDCs of Asia, Africa, and South America, has proven highly problematic. Let us consider some of the salient issues raised and alternate approaches proposed.

Problems with Technology Transfer. The very phrase *technology transfer* is profoundly misleading and potentially harmful. Given the widespread tendency to identify technology with technics, technology transfer has often been naively thought to involve merely the physical introduction into developing countries of various kinds of supposedly more efficient Western hardware. This assumption has obscured several important points that, although brought out in Chapters 2 through 5, merit reiteration in the present context.

(1) *Technology and Technics.* As was indicated in Chapter 2 when we discussed the different senses of the word *technology*, there is more to technology than its output (technics and related intellectual constructs). Hence, genuine "technology transfer" involves transmission of the complex of knowledge, materials, and methods pertinent to all activities associated with the production and use or operation of the technics or technical systems in question. In particular, genuine technology transfer includes transmission of the knowledge involved in undertakings like feasibility studies, market surveys, engineering design, detailed design, testing, plant construction, machinery installation, selecting and setting industrial processes, operation of production facilities, maintenance, training of personnel, and marketing.[20]

Initially, some petroleum-exporting countries of the Middle East into which numerous modern technics and technical systems were rapidly introduced in the 1970s (e.g., Saudi Arabia), relied heavily upon temporary skilled workers and management personnel from India, Pakistan, and the West to install and operate their new systems. In recent years, these developing countries have begun to insist on provisions in technology-transfer contracts stipulating that their nationals must work side-by-side with knowledgeable foreign technical professionals during construction and operation of new production systems and facilities to ensure *bona fide* technology transfer and movement toward greater autonomy. "Turn-key factories," which are essentially "black boxes" to locals are scarcely conducive to enhancing local technical innovativeness, entrepreneurship, or engineering and managerial expertise. They may even exacerbate technological dependence, as has sometimes happened in the case of imported computers.[21]

(2) *The Embeddedness of Modern Technics.* Contemporary technics are often embedded in complex technical or sociotechnical systems upon whose ongoing functioning their effective operation or use critically depends. Some technology transfers have foundered because although the transferred technics were compatible with the local cultural system, their embeddedness required infrastructure support systems either not available or staffable locally or not affordable by locals. To illustrate how failure to appreciate the implications of the system-embeddedness of many modern technics can threaten the success of a technology-transfer effort, consider the so-called Green Revolution in India.

The development of new high-yield strains of various domestic crops, especially wheat, rice, and corn, has greatly increased food production in tropical areas (e.g., in South and East Asia) since they were introduced in the late 1960s. There is, however, a less happy side to this development. After gaining its independence in 1948, India could not produce enough food to meet its growing population's minimum requirements. Importing more food increased the country's dependence. India escaped from this dilemma by introducing new high-yield varieties of wheat and rice developed in the Philippines and Mexico with philanthropic foundation support. Production increased radically and has made India tenuously self-sufficient in food. However, effective use of the new high-yield strains required intensive use of fertilizers and pesticides and associated infrastructure support systems: fertilizer plants, new roads to deliver the fertilizers, additional storage capacities for the increased yield, and new irrigation systems. Moreover, since the seeds were hybrids, new seed could no longer be grown by the farmer but had to be purchased annually at increased cost.[22]

"Buying into" the system-embedded, high-yielding seed varieties thus had hidden financial and unforeseen social costs. As they could better afford them, larger farmers tended to increase their holdings at the expense of smaller farmers. Many of the latter were forced out of business and joined the ranks of the urban unemployed unable to purchase the extra food. Indeed, some of the increased production had to be set aside for export to pay for the new infrastructure systems. The upshot was that India eliminated the gap between national food needs and production capacity only to enlarge the social gap between rich and poor Indian peasant farmers. It thereby nullified the egalitarian thrust of its postindependence land reform and redistribution program.[23]

(3) *Incompatability of Transferred Technic and Recipient Country's Social-Cultural-Environmental System.*   Technics are the creatures and expressions of complex social-cultural-environmental systems. As such, their designs are apt to reflect important characteristics of the societies that create them, including their values, social structures, employment and unemployment patterns, current scientific and technological bases, or abundant natural resources. Failure to consider possible incompatibility between any such characteristic and a corresponding one of the recipient society can seriously undermine or doom a technology-transfer effort, however well intentioned. Consider, for example, a case of value incompatibility. In the early 1970s, biogas installations were introduced in Papua New Guinea. Those at the village level failed miserably because they contravened traditional practices and beliefs. "Most Papua New Guineans have very strong superstititions concerning the use by others of their excrement in any form, and this cultural taboo mitigates against its collection for use in biogas production."[24]

(4) *Terms of Transfer.*   From the point of view of developing countries, the terms under which technology transfer is carried out often leave much to be desired. The commercial contracts involved may contain restrictive provisions, such as rules that prohibit making locally useful adaptations in the technology, selling the products produced to nonprovider companies or countries, and using the technology in different contexts for different purposes. To preserve the transferring company's hold on the technology and its market, the size of permitted production facilities is sometimes limited, desired technologies are sold only in "unbundleable" packages with undesired ones, and "tied purchases"—parallel purchases of raw materials, spare parts, or intermediate products from the same transferring company—are sometimes required. Such practices can be both technologically debilitating and economically devastating to developing countries.

New Technology Policies in Developing Countries

A fundamental conclusion about development drawn by many Third World countries in the past two decades is the necessity of creating "endogenous" (i.e., domestic) national capabilities in science and technology. This, however, is easier said than done. For example, a significant percentage of students from developing countries preparing to be scientists or engineers get their advanced education overseas in institutions designed, not surprisingly, to train people to work in advanced industrial economies. If such students return to their countries of origin—80 percent of Taiwanese students studying abroad in the early 1980s, for example, did not[25]—they often face a difficult dilemma.

On the one hand, the home institutions in which they work often appoint, promote, and bestow tenure for research publishable in international journals attuned to the research interests of the West. On the other hand, many scientists and engineers quickly recognize that most such research is at best marginally relevant to enhancing production and the standard of living in their own countries. Hence, many who initially return to their countries become frustrated and subsequently depart for positions in the West, where they can put their advanced learning to work. Studies by the Secretariat of the U.N. Conference on Technology and Development (UNCTAD) have estimated that between 1960 and 1975–1976, skilled migration—consisting of engineers, scientists, physicians and surgeons, and technical and kindred workers—from the developing countries to the United States, Canada, Great Britain, and Western Europe amounted to about 420,000 people.[26] Given its positive economic effect in consolidating or enhancing the research and development capability of the advanced countries, this migratory trend has come to be termed in some quarters a "reverse transfer of technology."[27] Direct economic loss via this "brain drain" to the developing countries has been estimated at $3.8 billion per year in the period from 1961 to 1972, more than their aggregate annual expenditure on research and development.[28]

The Western orientation of scientific practice in the developing world, the resultant marginalization of scientific research there, the brain drain phenomenon, and inadequate government funding for scientific research pose major obstacles to achieving endogenous, relevant scientific and technological research and development enterprises. A recent approach to both the problem of genuine technology transfer and that of institutionalizing relevant research in the developing world is that of trading off access to local markets or production facilities in return for establishment of local research and development facilities in which technological knowledge is transferred to scientists and engineers of the host LDC. "In July, 1985 Mexico allowed IBM to build microcomputers in that country, but among other things IBM promised to establish a semiconductor technology center to assist Mexico's electronics industry."[29]

Until endogenous scientific and technological capacities are attained, countries of the less developed world have little choice but to continue pursuing technological development, albeit in forms and under terms that avoid or minimize mistakes and disadvantages like those noted here. Three important trends in postwar development thinking and practice are aimed at doing precisely that: "appropriate technology" (AT), "intermediate technology" (IT), and the cultivation of indigenous technologies.

All three approaches emphasize the "development and use of technologies that make a more rational use of local resources, are suitable for decentralized use, are energy-saving, create jobs, and are environmentally sound."[30] There are subtle differences between them, however.

The essential idea of AT is that the production technologies and consumer products developed for Third World countries should be ones well adapted to the social, cultural, and economic facts of life of the milieux for which they are intended. Mindful of the radically inegalitarian structure of many developing countries and of the tendency of traditional capital-intensive technology transfer to reinforce or exacerbate this gap, proponents of AT focus on the development and transfer of labor-intensive, easy-to-understand-and-use technologies appropriate for improving the lot of the poor rural masses. In the words of Atul Wad:

> [T]he concept of "appropriateness" has more of a social flavor to it and even though the success in its implementation may have been far from satisfactory, the concerns with equity, self-reliance, environmental soundness, meaningful work, and decentralized operation that it espouses are valuable in and of themselves in the elaboration of science and technology strategies in the Third World.[31]

A major criticism of AT is that it tends to be preoccupied with developing gadgets that, while labor-intensive and small-scale, do not foster the development in the people of technological capacities "in the broad sense," including capital goods, engineering, and repair and maintenance capacities.[32]

In light of the "gadget" criticism, partisans of IT tend to favor taking a traditional labor-intensive technology through a series of modern capital-intensive innovations in such a way that the resultant technology still meets the criteria for AT. The goal is to "achieve a compromise that makes some use of the increased productivity offered by technological progress and simultaneously uses the cheap labor resources of the Third World."[33]

In contrast, concerned with enhancing the national technological capacities of LDCs, other thinkers emphasize the improvement of indigenous technologies, hoping in this way to foster broad-based participation by Third World peoples in the development of their own economies. The case for this approach has been put by Amadou-Mahtar M'Bow:

> [I]t is advisable to consider assigning a significant role to endeavors to reinstate technical traditions based on age-old skills which have long been neglected in the name of modernity. Because they tend to be regarded as a way of reasserting the cultural characteristics of a society, they can be an excellent means of winning the confidence of the whole population, and not just of an elite, so as to start a general movement towards a form of development benefiting widely from the participation and initiative of every individual. This approach is likely to prove successful in stimulating endogenous creativity.[34]

With regard to realizing improvements in the terms under which commercial technology transfers are carried out, one noteworthy development of the last 15 years is the attempt by UNCTAD to forge a Code of Conduct for Technology Transfer applicable to transnational enterprises that do the great bulk of the transmitting of technology to the developing world. Although this effort began in 1974 and the code has gone through a number of drafts, agreement had yet to be reached as of mid-1990. Given the deep disagreements and enormous financial stakes involved, this is not surprising.

Developing countries have argued that existing technology should be regarded as part of the common cultural heritage of humanity. Their hope is that acceptance of this proposition would result in placing substantial restrictions on the concepts of private ownership and control of technology, thereby facilitating its transfer to them on more favorable terms. Industrialized countries contend that the technologies and technological knowledge developed by firms in their countries fall under the category of private property. As such, they may be sold only at the developer's (or owner's) discretion. Moreover, they contend, restrictions on the ability of companies to dispose of their technologies as they see fit would actually diminish the amount of technology transferred by weakening their most powerful incentive—namely profit—for doing the costly work necessary to develop new technologies.[35]

Future Science- and Technology-Related Economic Problems of Less Developed Countries and Newly Industrialized Countries

The international economic problems of the LDCs are scarcely limited to the admittedly important issue of technology transfer. Let us briefly consider two other potentially crucial technology-related international economic challenges they will face in the future.

First, some of the success enjoyed by the newly industrialized countries (NICs) in the 1970s depended on their considerably lower unit labor costs compared with those prevailing in the highly industrialized countries. A good deal of manufacturing formerly done in the latter was for this reason transferred to NICs. Rather than investing heavily in state-of-the-art automated production facilites in their own countries, companies in various manufacturing sectors opted either to relocate production facilities abroad or to market imports made by foreign producers ("automate or emigrate").

In the 1980s, however, with advances in technology such as computer numerically controlled (CNC) machine tools and industrial lasers, as well as growing recognition that the emigrate-rather-than-automate strategy is conducive to declining manufacturing innovativeness, there are signs of automation initiatives in the more developed countries' traditional labor-intensive industries, including textiles, shoes, and garment making.[36] The goal of "bringing production back home" is to regain domestic and increase international market share. To the extent that this new "automate-and-repatriate" strategy succeeds, it would severely threaten the labor-cost advantages and thus the competitiveness of NICs, to uncertain, but potentially devastating, effect.

Second, with the microelectronics revolution in the process of transforming world industry, most LDCs, lacking the critical mass of scientific and technological resources to keep up with and implement these changes, are at risk of falling even further behind the highly industrialized countries (and the NICs). Assuming that the LDC's still aspire to industrialize, this confronts them with a difficult dilemma. In the words of Alexander King:

> [T]o continue with industrialization in the traditional sense is to industrialize to obsolescence; to seek to leap-frog the last 200 years of world industrial development by going directly to the most advanced automated industries may be beyond their capacity. It would demand an enormous capitalization and they have little capital; it would provide little employment where the provision of jobs is the highest priority; and finally it would be easily seen as a new phase of technological colonialism as the technology would be dominated completely by the North.[37]

Barring a sustained technoeconomic initiative of great magnitude and urgency by the highly industrialized societies, given the LDCs' lack of a critical mass of endogenous scientific and technological capacity, the microelectronics revolution is likely to force upon the world's poor nations a difficult choice: Either undertake to narrow the economic gap between themselves and the rich nations at the cost of becoming increasingly dependent upon the latter for vital scientific and technological resources (with all that that entails), or opt to become more independent of the richer nations at the cost of foregoing or substantially delaying any significant narrowing of the economic gap.

SOCIAL RELATIONS

International relations are not based solely on the political interaction of governments or the exchanges of goods or capital between national economies. There is also international interaction and exchange of people and ideas. This forms the basis for a third dimension of international relations: the social. As indicated by the previously described situations in international political and economic affairs, the current era is characterized by considerable and increasingly global interrelatedness. As interaction among the peoples of the world and their knowledge, institutions, and products has increased to unprecedented levels, in significant part because of scientific and technological change, it has become plausible to look at the world as a single society or social system. In this section we will explore two questions about the world order resulting from this development: First, what can one say about its *social structure*? And second, are the different national societies exhibiting increasing *similarity* to one another? If so, in what sense or senses and to what extent? In both cases we will pay special attention to possible influences of science and technology.

Social Structure

Alex Inkeles has proposed a set of seven concepts with which to characterize the emerging social structure of the contemporary world order in relation to that of earlier eras: autarky, interconnectedness, dependence, interdependence, integration, hegemony, and convergence.[38]

Autarky exists "when a set of people share a more or less completely self-contained and self-sustaining sociocultural system."[39] While a people such as the aboriginal Yir Yoront of Australia qualify—rather, once qualified—as autarkies, there are few if any such societies left in the contemporary world at the level of the nation-state. Albania, particularly under the four-decade iron rule of the late Enver Hoxha, was perhaps the last quasi-autarkial nation. Industrialization has proven a temptation that even the most isolationist national governments have been unable to resist. The more advanced and complex a social order, the less likely it is that the society in question will be able to provide on its own all requisite resources. Autarky thus becomes progressively less feasible with modernization.

Interconnectedness refers to "the volume or frequency of communication, interaction, or exchange between two sociocultural systems."[40] Twentieth century revolutions in communications and transportation have by themselves led to an exponential increase in worldwide interconnectedness, whether gauged by mail, trade, tourist flows, or the proliferation of international organizations.

Dependence refers to reliance on an item of exchange that is more or less indispensible to the survival of a system or, in the case of *interdependence* (i.e., mutual dependence), the systems party to the exchange. Evidently, interconnectedness does not logically entail dependence. Nor does dependence imply interdependence. Nevertheless, in the industrial era, both dependence and interdependence have grown enormously along with interconnectedness. This is not surprising, for "[i]t is the rare nation ... which can find within its boundaries all the material it needs, and it is the exceptional producer who can find a large enough market within one state's population to permit an efficient scale of production."[41]

At the same time, in the contemporary era, nation-states are actively attempting to reduce their sometimes fragile or debilitating dependency on others. Efforts are made to diversify suppliers of needed resources, stockpile or develop domestically available substitutes for currently imported raw materials, or build up viable endogenous scientific and technological capacities. Nevertheless, the rise of a global economy and the rapid growth in international trade make increased societal interdependence extremely likely. This is important because trade and interdependence between and among superpowers tend to exert a stabilizing effect on their political relationships. On the other hand, countries not blessed with abundant domestic supplies of vital material resources must generate large positive trade balances with their partners in order to import the needed resources. As seen in recent years, the inordinate dependence of such countries on their primary external markets may sour international political and economic relations.

Integration is a yet stronger mode of interrelatedness. It obtains to the extent that formerly autonomous units more or less permanently "surrender vital functions to another, more extended unit while still retaining a substantial number of other vital functions."[42] The difference between the degree of international integration required by the transnational character of certain science and technology problems and the degree of integration feasible under the current political system of sovereign nations is—and is likely to remain—a central problem of contemporary and future international relations.

Hegemony is forced, as opposed to voluntary, integration. Although the demise of colonialism marked the end of one species of hegemonic integration, the genus survives. The extent to which the apparently increasing technological dependence of the LDCs on the highly industrialized ones is tantamount to a new form of hegemony is a matter of more than semantic interest.

We will consider the idea of convergence and its applicability to the world social system in greater detail in a moment. For now, let us say that the emerging social structure of world society can be characterized as closely interlocked and increasingly so. Autarky is vanishing (although greater or total self-sufficiency through scientific and technological research and development remains an attractive ideal for some); interconnectedness and interdependence have increased greatly and promise to continue to do so; and a modest degree of integration has been achieved, some—perhaps an increasing amount—of which is hegemonic in character. An important social structural issue of the future, to which science and technology are of central importance, is the degree to which world society, facing grave transnational environmental and economic problems, can be effectively integrated in a non-hegemonic manner.

Sociocultural Similarity

Convergence refers to a process in which social units starting from different positions "on some scale of organization, sociopolitical structure, or culture,...move toward some more common form on the given dimension."[43] The issue of convergence is noteworthy in the contemporary era because of interest in whether the progressive industrialization of the countries of the world will homogenize the major dimensions of their respective cultural systems.

Inkeles has argued that discussion of the complex issue of convergence is apt to be more fruitful if, rather than being discussed *en bloc*, it is disaggregated. He therefore analyzes cultural convergence dimensionally—that is, as it unfolds along each of the following five dimensions or elements of a country's SCES:[44]

1. Modes of production and patterns of resource utilization
2. Institutional arrays, forms, and processes
3. Structures or patterns of social relationships
4. Systems of popular attitudes, values, and behavior
5. Systems of political and economic control

If consideration is limited to the industrial societies of the world—it is still too early for many LDCs to be exhibiting marked convergence toward characteristics of the highly industrialized countries—then, regarding dimension 1 on the list, there is strong evidence of international convergence. This is due mostly to increasing use in all such societies "of modes of production based on inanimate power, which rests in turn on modern technology and applied science."[45]

As for dimension 2 on the list, modern or highly developed societies possess "a fairly standard array of institutional structures" related to their modes of production. These institutions are organized in "rational-bureaucratic modes." Hence, social processes within these institutions tend to adhere to "standardized modes of nominally rational technical-bureaucratic procedure."[46] The primary factors lending impetus to this trend are intimately linked to technology: the size of modern nation-states and of the economic endeavors required to generate the goods and services demanded by their large populations. "In substantial degree, the world *is* being cast in the Weberian mold."[47]

On the other hand, the emergence in recent years of structural innovations in the production-related institution of work, ones associated with the movement known as "participative management," seems to pose a challenge to convergence theory. These innovations—including codetermination, works councils, partially decentralized decision making, worker involvement in job redesign, and the introduction of new technologies at the workplace—have emerged and been institutionalized in northwestern Europe, especially in West Germany and the Scandinavian countries.[48] These innovations owe their existence in significant part to particular local cultural traditions and historical circumstances. To date, only the fourth shows any signs of taking root in North America. The question, then, is whether such phenomena are transient or superficial, whether they or variants of them will eventually emerge in other industrialized countries, or whether they will prove distinctive institutional features of the landscapes of only a few industrial societies, thereby necessitating qualification of convergence theory on dimension 2.

Regarding dimension 3, "the basic issue for convergence theory is to assess how far the increasing similarity in modes of production and their associated institutional forms and processes encourages the development of concomitant similarities in sociocultural systems."[49] Substantial evidence of convergence, attributable in part to scientific and technological change, regarding such structural and pattern-related aspects of the cultural-environmental system (CES), already exists. For example, fragile, smaller-sized nuclear families, a social-stratification system reflecting the analytical-conceptual skills at a premium in an information- and knowledge-based economy, and leisure patterns oscillating between opportunities generated by technology-based leisure industries and attempts to escape or recover from the demands of the technoeconomic order by "returning to nature" seem to be increasing trends in all highly industrialized countries, including Japan.

However, convergence along dimension 3 may turn out not to be thoroughgoing. Structurally speaking, certain industrialized countries, such as Japan, Norway, and Sweden, are considerably less socioeconomically stratified than others, at least if gauged by the ratios of average incomes earned by the highest- and lowest-paid classes of workers. Moreover, not all institutions in industrialized countries exhibit convergence. The sociocultural subsystem of religion seems to be undergoing considerable bifurcation in recent years. In some but not all industrialized societies, orthodox practices and institutions have been and continue to be challenged by a strong wave of religious fundamentalism. This is particularly true in the United States. Unless this phenomenon proves ephemeral, it would seem to dim the prospects for confirming unqualified international convergence along this dimension.

As for dimension 4—of particular interest to some social critics—Inkeles has shown that there is significant but limited convergence with regard to attitudes and values in highly industrialized countries. However, the convergence in question is not toward a *single set* of values, attitudes, and behavior in all societies, but rather toward "a similar *structure* of attitudes and values manifested by the population of a diverse set of developed and developing countries."[50] In other words, convergence here takes the form of similarity in the structure of opinion. In each society studied, "certain views and orientations [became] either more or less frequent as one went up or down the scale of education, occupational prestige, and the like."[51] The differences of opinion within the structure supposedly arose from the diverse life experiences of people in different strata of large-scale complex societies. As industrialization advances and "human life experience becomes more alike, attitudes, values, and basic dispositions will also become more alike" *in a given social stratum across all industrialized societies.*

Inkeles and Smith examined six diverse developing countries and showed that "each increment of increasing contact with modern institutions"—especially the factory, school, and mass-communications media—"moved men a corresponding degree along a composite scale of modern attitudes and values."[52] While this contention does not bear directly on the issue of convergence vis-à-vis the countries of the more industrialized world, it is consistent with the claim of limited attitudinal and values convergence. The qualifier *limited* is included because Inkeles posits a convergence of opinion "only on certain aspects of modern industrial and organizational experience, as identified by the syndrome of individual modernity."[53] Thus, he acknowledges, there are realms of value and attitude far removed from the industrial organizational complex that will remain immune to pressures toward cross-societal convergence.

Two recent sociological studies support the limited attitude-values-opinion convergence thesis for industrialized countries. Ephraim Yuchtman-Yaar examined "popular economic culture"—"the patterns of economically related values, cognitions, and behavioral dispositions" of individuals—in six industrialized countries (the United States, the United Kingdom, West Germany, Sweden, Japan, and Israel).[54] He found that, with the possible exception of Japan, there is "a common pattern of orientation to economic growth, work, and technology." In particular, the bulk of his respondents displayed positive general attitudes toward economic growth, were strongly committed to their work, worked primarily to make a living or raise their standard of living, and felt that, on balance, technological changes had improved their jobs.

The fact that these views held across most of the six-country sample (Japan being the sole exception on some items) lends confirmation to the convergence hypothesis in dimension 4. The significance of Japanese attitudinal divergence is unclear. As Yuchtman-Yaar observes:

> [A]lthough Japan holds a prominent place among the small group of post-industrial nations, its sociocultural heritage sets it apart from the Western members of this group. It is possible, therefore, that the manifestations of malaise in the Japanese public stem from culturally rooted reaction to the intensity of Japan's effort at industrialization. Such feelings, however, may only reflect a transient phase of readjustment as Japan converges into the economic culture of the West.[55]

Were that to prove so, the dimension-4 limited-convergence thesis would be reinforced.

Interestingly, Yuchtman-Yaar found a "significant minority" of respondents in his survey who did not conform to the expected industrial values of support for economic growth, belief in the predominantly economic rationale for commitment to work, and positive evaluation of technological change. Some of this divergence appears to represent the rise of a "postmaterialist" or "postmodern" value syndrome, particularly in the case of self-actualization as the dominant work motivation of this minority. It could be, therefore, that complete attitudinal convergence, even in the limited domain of "economic culture," will not occur, or else that the convergence will be toward a value syndrome synthesizing selected modern and postmodern elements.

Shepherd, Kim, and Hougland studied blue-collar production workers in the oil and automobile industries in the United States and South Korea, one of the so-called NICs.[56] They found that, on average, the Korean workers were more alienated than their American counterparts. Nonetheless, there was a similarity in the *pattern* of reactions to technology. In both countries, workers in mechanized production situations were more alienated than those in either craft or automated systems. This "inverted U" finding—low followed by high followed by low alienation—suggests, in accordance with Inkeles's account of convergence along dimension 4, that as countries' production systems move toward similar patterns of craft, mechanical, and automated organization, worker attitudes will become more structurally similar.

It is in dimension 5 that the validity of the convergence hypothesis is most limited. The cases of the United States and the Soviet Union make it clear that quite different systems of political and economic control (e.g., ones that differ significantly in their degrees of centralization) are compatible with use of the same basic technological production system. Inkeles observes, however, that this important difference notwithstanding, a measure of political-economic convergence exists. All highly industrialized countries exhibit a common pattern: "the growing power of the state to control the lives of its citizens."[57] This tendency is fueled by modern science and technology in at least two ways. Contemporary technology and science make available to the state powerful and sophisticated technical means for interfering in the lives of its citizens. Moreover, the great bearing of modern technology and science on macroeconomic and general societal well-being seems to increase governments' inclination to use such means. The deregulatory political-economic impulses of the 1980s notwithstanding, these facts have inspired a wide range of governmental attempts to circumscribe the activities of individual and corporate actors by regulating or controlling scientific and technological activities as well as the diffusion and use of their products. We will return to the topic of the social control of science and technology in Chapter 14.

In sum, the homogenization of the global sociocultural system, while substantial in the highly industrialized countries, is far from total. Although evidence of convergence is likely to increase as developing countries increase their level of industrialization, considerable cultural divergence will persist for the foreseeable future for several reasons. First, in the more industrialized countries, the cultural convergence in progress is limited primarily to the first four dimensions noted earlier. Second, it is also limited in scope primarily to the technoeconomically related portions of each of the dimensional domains: Yuchtman-Yaar's evidence of values convergence is limited to the realm of "economic culture," and Inkeles posits "movement toward a common pattern [of] attitudes, values, and basic dispositions"[58] "only with regard to certain specific qualities identified as part of the syndrome of individual modernity, [a syndrome engendered by] the industrial organizational complex common to advanced nations."[59] Outside these realms— and perhaps sometimes inside—the different national historical experiences and sometimes strong and adaptable cultural traditions of countries may serve to prevent or delay convergence, and thus limit or retard homogenization.

If limited convergence seems a welcome projection, it is not without a problematic aspect. In the wake of dawning awareness in a modernizing society of the multiplicity of cultural traditions, and hence of recognition that one's culture is but one of many and not "made in heaven," inner allegiance to cultural heritage could become perfunctory, display of its outer trappings more a staged "performance" than a natural, spontaneous, un-self-conscious emanation. The quantity of residual cultural heterogeneity might be less important than its quality. Residents of small communities in countries relatively new to modernization, such as Italy and Greece, are apt to don their traditional peasant attire only on special occasions, such as for important religious feasts, historic rituals, or lucrative visits of curious tourists seeking "quaint" (read: premodern) experiences. An important question, then, is whether convergence is a *structural* and heterogeneity a *surface* phenomenon of late industrializing cultures, even for a country like Japan, whose culture is generally regarded, because of its distinctive values and institutions, as being fundamentally different from those of Western industrialized societies and likely to remain so.

CONCLUSION

We have explored the influence of science and technology on international relations in the modern and contemporary eras. Politically speaking, science and technology have had an unanticipated twofold restrictive effect on the political power of highly industrialized nations. While these nations acquired immensely more potent military forces with which to pursue state objectives, in the post–World War II period, use of these arsenals has been limited to conflicts with weaker adversaries or surrogates of major adversaries. Even in such cases, a sector of these arsenals—nuclear weapons— has remained unused, partly because of fear of unleashing their full destructive power.

Moreover, the transnational effects of certain environmental and economic problems—effects that would not have arisen without advances in science and technology—have exerted pressure on nations to acquiesce in the internationalization of political decision making, a second restriction on the free exercise of national political power.

Economically, excellence in science and technology has become a crucial factor affecting national competitiveness in the new international marketplace that these forces helped make possible. In addition, no issue is more important to the future economic relationship of the highly industrialized and the less developed countries than that of bringing about a more balanced international distribution of scientific and technological capacity.

Socially, science and technology are key factors fostering the emergence of an increasingly closely interlocked world social system, which is undergoing cultural convergence unprecedented in speed and scope. Well into the nineteenth century, people in many countries based their identities on the fact that they were residents of certain cities or, as remains true in Siena, Italy, of one ward rather than another. Nowadays, most people are apt to point to the states or countries of which they are resident citizens. The extent to which the international political-economic-cultural transformation now underway will result in grounding personal identity primarily on membership in some international region or in the emerging world social order—and, if so, to what effects—is an interesting, important, but as yet unanswerable question.

ENDNOTES

1. Otto Hieronymi, "Introduction," in O. Hieronymi, ed., *Technology and International Relations* (London: Macmillan, 1987), p. 5.
2. Warner Schilling, "Technology and International Relations," *International Encyclopedia of the Social Sciences*, 15 (New York: Macmillan, 1968–1979), 590.
3. Daniel Headrick, "The Tools of Imperialism", *Journal of Modern History*, 51, June 1979, 263–264.
4. Ibid., p. 256.
5. *New York Times*, December 28, 1989, p. A1.
6. David Fisher, *Morality and the Bomb* (London: Crook Helm, 1985), p. 1.
7. Anthony Kenny, *The Logic of Deterrence* (Chicago: University of Chicago Press, 1985), p. 1.
8. *Ibid.*, pp. 2–3.
9. Alexander King, "Science, Technology, and International Relations: Some Comments and a Speculation," in Hieronymi, *Technology and International Relations*, p. 13.
10. *Science and Technology Data Book: 1988* (Washington, D.C.: National Science Foundation, 1987), pp. 2, 7.
11. Severo M. Ornstein, "Computers in Battle: A Human Overview," pp. 8–9; and Alan Borning, "Computer System Reliability and Nuclear War," pp. 104–105; both in David Bellin and Gary Chapman, eds., *Computers in Battle—Will They Work?* (Boston: Harcourt Brace Jovanovich, 1987).
12. Schilling, "Technology and International Relations," p. 591.
13. Eugene Skolnikoff, "The International Functional Implications of Future Technology," in T. J. Kuehn and A. L. Porter, eds., *Science, Technology, and National Policy* (Ithaca, N.Y.: Cornell University Press, 1981), pp. 242–243.
14. *New York Times*, September 17, 1987, pp. A1, A12; and June 30, 1990, pp. 1, 2.
15. Skolnikoff, "International Implications," p. 227.
16. Daniel Bell, "The World and the United States in 2013," in *Daedalus*, 116, no. 3, Summer 1987, 14.

17. *Ibid.*
18. *Ibid.*, pp. 13–14.
19. Gunnar Myrdal, "The Transfer of Technology to Underdeveloped Countries," in Kuehn and Porter, *Science, Technology, and National Policy*, p. 215.
20. Tom Ganiatsos, "Transfer of Technology: Theory and Policy," in Krishna Ahooja-Patel, Anne Gordon Drabeck, and Marc Nerfin, eds., *World Economy in Transition* (New York: Pergamon Press, 1986), p. 237.
21. Stephen Hill, "Eighteen Cases of Technology Transfer to Asia/Pacific Region Countries," *Science and Public Policy*, 13, no. 3, June 1986, 165.
22. Robin Clarke, *Science and Technology in World Development* (Oxford: Oxford University Press, 1985), pp. 45–46.
23. A. Rahman, "Science, Technology and Society: Historical and Comparative Perspectives," *International Social Science Journal*, 33, no. 3, 1981, 518.
24. Ken Newcombe, "Technology Assessment and Policy: Examples from Papua New Guinea," *International Social Science Journal*, 33, no. 3, 1981, 501.
25. David Blake and Robert Walters, *The Politics of Global Economic Relations*, 3rd ed. (Englewood Cliffs, N.J.: Prentice-Hall, 1987), p. 158.
26. George Skorov, "Science, Society, and Endogenous Development," in *World Economy*, p. 257.
27. Blake and Walters, *Global Economic Relations*, p. 157.
28. Skorov, *World Economy*, p. 257.
29. Blake and Walters, *Global Economic Relations*, p. 157.
30. Atul Wad, "Science, Technology, and Industrialization in Africa," *Third World Quarterly*, 6, no. 2, April 1984, 338.
31. *Ibid.*
32. *Ibid.*, p. 340.
33. *Ibid.*, p. 339.
34. Clarke, *Science and Technology*, p. 57.
35. Blake and Walters, *Global Economic Relations*, pp. 159–163.
36. King, "Science, Technology, and International Relations," p. 23.
37. *Ibid.*, p. 24.
38. Alex Inkeles, "The Emerging Social Structure of the World," *World Politics*, 27, no. 4, July 1975, 469–472.
39. *Ibid.*, p. 469.
40. *Ibid.*, pp. 469–470.
41. *Ibid.*, p. 484.
42. *Ibid.*, p. 471.
43. *Ibid.*, p. 472.
44. *Ibid.*, pp. 489–490.
45. *Ibid.*, p. 494.
46. Alex Inkeles, "Convergence and Divergence in Industrial Societies," in Mustafa O. Attir, Burkart Holzner, and Zdenek Suda, eds., *Directions of Change: Modernization Theory, Research, and Realities* (Boulder: Westview Press, 1981), pp. 9, 12.
47. *Ibid*, p. 10.
48. See, e.g., Edward Cohen-Rosenthal, "Worker Participation in Management: A Guide for the Perplexed," in Daniel J. Skrovan, ed., *Quality of Work Life* (Reading, Mass.: Addison-Wesley, 1983), pp. 159–192.
49. Inkeles, "Convergence and Divergence," p. 10.
50. *Ibid.*, p. 10.
51. *Ibid.*
52. *Ibid.*, p. 11.
53. Inkeles, "Emerging Social Structure," p. 492.
54. Ephraim Yuchtman-Yaar, "Economic Culture in Post-Industrial Society: Orientation Toward Growth, Work and Technology," *International Sociology*, 2, no. 1, March 1987, 77–101.

55. *Ibid.*, p. 99.
56. Jon M. Shepard, Dong I. Kim, and James G. Hougland, Jr., "Effects of Technology in Industrialized and Industrializing Societies," *Sociology of Work and Occupations*, 6, no. 4, November 1979, 457–481.
57. Inkeles, "Convergence and Divergence," p. 12.
58. Inkeles, "Emerging Social Structure," p. 492.
59. Inkeles, "Convergence and Divergence," p. 11.

PART THREE
THE INFLUENCE OF MODERN SOCIETY ON SCIENCE AND TECHNOLOGY

CHAPTER 13

INFLUENCE AGENTS, TYPES, AND EFFECTS

INTRODUCTION

As argued in Chapter 4, a satisfactory account of the influence of science and technology on society requires setting these two forces in sufficiently broad context—namely, that of the social-cultural-environmental system (SCES). The same holds true for attaining an adequate understanding of the influence of society on science and technology. A number of societal factors external to science and technology, some from the immediate social system (ISS), others from the cultural-environmental system (CES), contribute in diverse ways to bringing about changes internal to these forces. Less attention has been given to the influence of society on science and technology than to the reverse influence relationship, partly because of the autonomy often mistakenly attributed to these forces. For better and worse, society gets the science and technology it nurtures and conditions.

In this chapter we will analyze the influence of society on science and technology, both the general *structure* of that relationship and important aspects of its *content*. We will begin by identifying and briefly discussing the major *categories of societal agents* that influence science and technology. Next, we will classify and illustrate the qualitatively different *types of influence* exercised by these agents. Then, we will explore the major *kinds of changes* in science and technology effected by agents that exert these types of societal influence.

CATEGORIES OF SOCIETAL INFLUENCE AGENTS

Four major areas or aspects of society influence its science and technology: government, the private sector, the public at large, and the cultural system of the society in question. Let us consider each in turn.

Government

Within the sphere of government, societal influence agents include the executive, legislative, judicial, and regulatory branches, the public as a political body, and independent government agencies. As usual, we will focus our discussion on the more developed Western democractic societies, with occasional reference, for purposes of contrast, to other societies.

Executive Branch.   The executive branch of government typically exercises a potent influence on the scientific and technological enterprises in modern societies. It does so most notably by priority setting—for example, establishing government budget priorities, proposing target areas for government-funded research and development work in the private sector, and setting priorities for government research laboratories. Sitting administrations also set science and technology policy for executive branch departments—for example, on matters such as scientific secrecy and export controls. They negotiate and sign international treaties affecting arms control and the conduct of various technical activities, empanel commissions to study science- and technology-related social problems, and decide whether to prepare for or wage war. The latter decisions can seriously disrupt national scientific and technological enterprises in various ways, from preoccupying research and development efforts to destroying adversaries' available technical resources. In totalitarian societies, the executive branch may be tempted to politicize scientific competition or compel science to serve reigning ideological biases, usually to the detriment of both the science and the society in question.

For example, consider the so-called Lysenko affair in the Soviet Union. In 1929, Joseph Stalin launched a campaign to reorganize the arable Russian countryside into massive, state-controlled collective farms. The campaign was vigorously resisted by peasant farmers, many of whom destroyed their crops and killed their animals when other forms of protest against forced, rapid collectivization failed. Against this turbulent political-economic backdrop, Stalin and his bureaucrats, eager to promote agricultural research oriented toward realizing immediate dramatic gains in crop yields, seized upon and supported the "progressive" agro-biology of the "peasant scientist" Trofim Lysenko. Thus encouraged, Lysenko conducted a protracted defamatory campaign against classical, neo-Mendelian genetics, some of whose practitioners paid with their lives for their opposition. Lysenko's effort culminated in 1948 at a session of the Lenin Academy of Agricultural Sciences, where he announced the support of Stalin's Central Committee of the Communist Party for the official condemnation of "bourgeois" neo-Mendelian genetics. Soviet biological sciences were seriously set back by this intrusion. In the words of Loren Graham:

> In the months following the 1948 conference, research and teaching in standard genetics were suppressed in the Soviet Union. The ban remained in effect until after Stalin's death in 1953. The recovery that occurred during the years after Stalin's passing was painful and fitful, and did not fully blossom until after Lysenko's downfall in 1965.[1]

Legislative Branch.   The main way in which the legislative branch affects science and technology is through its law-making functions. National legislatures shape and enact budgetary legislation, tax law, and trade bills, and establish independent science- or technology-related governmental organizations, all of which can foster or impede technical advancement. In the United States, organizations of the latter type established by Congress include the U.S. Geological Survey (1879), the National Bureau of Standards (1901), the National Advisory Committee for Aeronautics (1915),* and the National Science Foundation (1950). National legislatures also ratify or reject arms control treaties and occasionally enact laws aimed at protecting or compensating parties harmed by scientific or technological products or practices for which the federal government is deemed to have been at least partly responsible.

Judicial Branch. The judicial branch profoundly influences scientific and technological activities through courts' prohibitive, compensatory, and punitive decisions. Courts are frequently called upon to decide whether, given the existing legal framework, various proposed courses of technical action are permissible, or whether accomplished actions or existing practices are in compliance with various bodies of law (e.g., antitrust, patent, copyright, or product liability law) or with prevailing regulatory guidelines.

Regulatory Branch. During the last century, federal regulation has come to exert a powerful influence on scientific and technological activities in the United States. In this country, federal regulatory agencies are of two types. Some are parts of departments in the executive branch of the government. For example, among those dealing with scientific and technological affairs, the Occupational Safety and Health Administration (OSHA) is part of the Department of Labor, the Food and Drug Administration (FDA) is a unit of the Department of Health and Human Services, and the Federal Aviation Administration (FAA) is located within the Department of Transportation.

The second type of federal regulatory body is the so-called independent regulatory agency. Among those intimately involved in matters scientific and technological are the Federal Communications Commission (FCC), the Environmental Protection Agency (EPA), the Federal Trade Commission (FTC), the Nuclear Regulatory Commission (NRC), and the Consumer Product Safety Commission (CPSC). In accordance with a key 1936 U.S. Supreme Court decision, in which Franklin Roosevelt's attempt to remove a member of the FTC appointed by Herbert Hoover was blocked by the Court, regulatory agencies of the second type are not part of the executive branch of the government. Their heads are nominated by the president and confirmed by Congress but cannot be discharged by the president, as can the heads of executive-department agencies who serve at the chief of state's pleasure. This difference was meant to preserve the autonomy of politically sensitive regulatory bodies. Some opponents of the activities of the independent regulatory agencies view them as comprising "a new and politically unaccountable fourth branch of the national government."[2]

Regulatory agencies of both types are charged with translating legislative intent into detailed quantitative or qualitative guidelines or "regulations," and with ensuring that laws enacted by the legislative branch are enforced in the agencies' respective jurisdictional spheres. For example, the U.S. Department of Labor is charged with enforcing a 1988 federal law sharply restricting the use of lie detector tests at the workplace and can impose fines of up to $10,000 on a firm for noncompliance. Similarly, the "independent" EPA is responsible for monitoring and fostering compliance with quantitative guidelines designed to implement provisions of the 1970 Clean Air Act (periodically revised by the U.S. Congress).

*In the wake of the launch by the Soviet Union of *Sputnik I*, the first artificial satellite, this committee was succeeded by the National Aeronautics and Space Administration (NASA) in 1958.

The Public Referendum.   A fifth way in which government can influence science and technology is via the institution of the referendum. On occasion, sitting governments have decided to submit competing policy options directly to the electorate to obtain its binding or nonbinding judgment. Resort to national referenda on science- or technology-related policy issues has been more frequent in Western European countries than in the United States and has most often involved the nuclear industry. Occasionally, in the decision-making process for a particularly thorny technical policy issue, a government regulatory agency may resort to one or another form of referendum to obtain public reaction to alternative policy options, each with its own array of costs, benefits, and risks.

Independent Advisory Bodies.   Finally, some governments include prestigious independent advisory bodies that influence science and technology affairs. For example, in the United States, the National Academy of Sciences, the National Academy of Engineering, and the National Institutes of Medicine commission studies of and make recommendations on important science and technology policy issues. Among topics addressed by these bodies in recent years have been revised institutional guidelines for fostering ethical propriety in biomedical research, the advisability of proceeding with controversial science projects at one or another level of government funding, and mechanisms for prioritizing competing Big Science funding requests. These recommendations sometimes affect executive priority setting and legislative deliberations.

The Private Sector

In the major Western industrialized countries, the private sector's influence on science and technology is at least as important as that of the national government. The primary but not sole source of societal influence in the private sector lies in the sphere of business. Noncommercial private-sector influence agents include philanthropic foundations, labor unions, university associations, groups of technical professionals, and religious and public interest groups.

Business.   The influence exerted by business on science and technology stems largely from the institution of the market mechanism. The incentive of profit and the regulator of interfirm competition are behind a good deal of the effort expended by business to influence science and technology. Business influences science and technology by choosing directions for its research and product-development activities, lobbying government for favorable legislative and regulatory treatment, supporting scientific research and programs in universities, and adopting policies for dissemination of the intellectual property it has developed or otherwise acquired. Such policies include decisions about whether to enforce—and if so, how vigorously—its patents, copyrights, and trade secrets to gain or retain advantages over competitors.

The broadcasting sector of industry influences science and technology in an important way, albeit indirectly. Television is occasionally used to expose malfeasance in scientific and technological affairs and to provide background on socially controversial technically based issues. On the whole, however, the television industry has been content with reinforcing positive public attitudes toward scientific and technological endeavors. Society is continually bombarded with superficial, visually attractive booster reports on the latest "miraculous breakthroughs" achieved in research and development laboratories. This tendency serves the essential capital-raising and legitimacy-maintaining goals of scientific and technological organizations and institutions.

Not-For-Profit Groups and Organizations. In the not-for-profit sector, philanthropic foundations, such as those founded by Andrew Carnegie, Henry Ford, and John D. Rockefeller, have played and continue to play important roles in science and technology. Some such foundations have funded agricultural, population, and public health research projects and undertaken initiatives to recruit more women and members of minority groups into science and engineering. They have also established programs to enrich science and engineering education for students in technical majors, promote technical literacy for liberal arts majors, and enhance the competence of secondary-school science teachers.

Groups of technical professionals sometimes conduct research on or mobilize support for or opposition to controversial scientific or engineering projects. For example, Computer Professionals for Social Responsibility has sponsored research on the effects of computers in the workplace, while in 1988, 7,000 members of the American Mathematical Society, the national association of professional mathematicians, voted by a large margin to urge their fellow members to boycott the Pentagon's Strategic Defense Initiative (SDI) research program by not seeking or accepting research grants from the program.[3] Rarely are such expressions decisively influential. However, the support for undertaking the development of an atomic bomb, expressed in 1939 by eminent physicists who had emigrated from Europe and settled in the United States (e.g., Albert Einstein, Leo Szilard, and Eugene Wigner) is a noteworthy exception.

For about two centuries, unions of workers in the industrial West have used such tactics as the strike in attempts to prevent or impede employers from introducing technological innovations believed to pose a threat to their members' jobs or safety. For example, in the 1970s, printers' unions conducted a protracted strike against British newspaper publishers when the latter attempted to introduce labor-saving computerized typesetting technology.

In the modern period, some churches have sought to discredit or suppress selected scientific knowledge claims because of the threat that they were believed to pose to the credibility of traditional religious beliefs and the power of the authorities who defended them. The cases of Giordano Bruno, Galileo Galilei, and Charles Darwin are three of the more notorious instances of attempts by Christian churches and clergy to combat advances in modern Western science. More recently, fundamentalist Christian groups have threatened large drug companies with total economic boycotts if they market drugs, such as RU 486 and prostaglandin F2-Alpha, capable of, among other things, inducing abortions safely and easily.[4]

A fifth kind of not-for-profit entity that influences science and technology is the public interest group. Organizations such as the Sierra Club, the Foundation for Economic Trends, Public Citizen, and the Center for Science in the Public Interest engage in consciousness-raising activities and bring legal suits aimed at preventing, delaying, or terminating government or business technical projects or practices that they deem harmful to the public interest. They use as their weapons the Constitution, current legal statutes, or prevailing government rules and regulations. Some such groups, including Greenpeace and the Animal Liberation Front, have undertaken direct actions to throttle controversial practices and projects, such as atomic weapons tests, experiments on animals, and the release of genetically engineered microorganisms into the atmosphere.

The Public at Large

A third source of societal influence on science and technology is the public at large. Its role in influencing science and technology has expanded considerably in the last two decades and has served as a counterweight to the preponderant influences exerted throughout this century by government and business. The public at large influences science and technology in several ways.

The consuming public, although conditioned by corporate advertising, has the last word on which personal technics of what kinds are produced and used in society at a given time. The voting public, through the mechanism of the citizen initiative, can go over the heads of its governmental representatives and, within limits, effectively make technology policy in some areas by, for example, voting to shut down or restrict construction of controversial technological structures, such as power plants or freeways. It can also, of course, elect candidates partly on the basis of their stands on one or another weighty science or technology policy issue (e.g., toxic waste or arms control).

Public opinion, as determined through periodic surveys, provides important input for executives and legislatures as they consider what positions to adopt on science- and technology-intensive matters such as the patenting of genetically engineered animals, environmental protection, early worker notification of employer intent to close a plant, and weapons-research appropriations.

Culture

The societal influence agents that we have just considered exercise political or economic influence on science or technology. However, their respective agendas and tactics often reflect aspects of the background cultural context (e.g., the values of environmental groups and behavior patterns of union protesters). But culture exerts its own, often overlooked, influence on science and technology.

For example, it is hard to imagine that modern Western science could have come into being without the existence of cultural institutions such as the university and the library. Without the industrial research and development laboratory, a nineteenth century institutional innovation, many important twentieth century scientific and technological innovations, including the transistor, the telecommunications satellite, and the jet airplane, would not have been produced—at least not when and where they were. Characteristic modern Western cultural beliefs in freedom of inquiry, in the propriety of exploiting and mastering nature, and in the idea that advances in science and technology eventually yield societal progress are pillars of the modern scientific and technological enterprises.

At the level of the technical practitioner, ideational cultural elements exert important influences. Anachronistic conceptions of women's "proper" role in society, artificial ideas of "feminine" and "masculine" behavior, and stereotypical images of the personalities and abilities of minority-group citizens help account for the disproportionately low numbers of women and minorities in American science and engineering. Cultural phenomena such as anthropocentrism and the complementary view of animals as material resources for human exploitation have exerted subterranean influences on the practice of biomedical science (e.g., the sometimes cavalier treatment of animals in laboratory experiments).

SOCIETAL INFLUENCES ON SCIENCE AND TECHNOLOGY: A TYPOLOGY

It is one thing to identify the agents of societal influence on science and technology and to indicate which of them exercise the most potent, direct, pervasive, or subtle influences on science and technology. It is quite another, however, to elaborate the *qualitatively different types of influence* exerted by these agents. That is the task of this section.

As indicated in Figure 13-1, there are four pairs of general types of influence that societal agents exercise on science and technology: enabling and disabling, generative and terminative, helping and hindering, and determining and liberating. In the next section of this chapter we will delineate the kinds of effects on science and technology that these types of influence exercise may help bring about.

Enabling and Disabling

Some facets of a society's culture make it possible for scientific or technological activities to be carried out, in the sense that without them such endeavors would not be feasible. For example, the basic notion that pursuit of the truth about natural phenomena via scientific inquiry is a culturally legitimate form of endeavor is a condition without which modern science could not exist. It could be argued that even in the absence of such a notion—after a successful authoritarian political revolution, for example—scientific activity could continue "underground." However, given the nature of modern science, that activity would quickly atrophy under such a situation. Let us say, therefore, that such societal factors exert an *enabling influence* on science and technology. That people in Western industrialized countries take the enterprises of science and technology for granted tends to blind them to the profound dependence

Figure 13-1. The influence of society on science and technology: A typology of influence-exercises.

ENABLING	DISABLING

GENERATING	TERMINATING

HELPING	HINDERING
Species:	Species:
Sustaining	Preventing
Strengthening	Weakening
Furthering	Impeding
Means:	Means:
Inductive	Inductive
Facilitative	Obstructive
Prescriptive	Prescriptive

DETERMINING	LIBERATING

of their continued existence and vitality on widespread adherence to a number of basic underlying cultural institutions and assumptions.*

Other societal factors might be said to exert a *disabling influence* on science and technology. Evidently, one modern society can wage war on another and, by physically demolishing its institutional base, make its scientific or technological enterprises unable to function. Societal upheavals can sometimes produce a similar effect. For example, consider the "Great Proletarian Cultural Revolution" in China launched by Maoist forces in the mid-1960s. One of its professed goals was a more egalitarian social structure. To this end, many of the intellectual elite of Chinese society, including scientists, were sent away from the urban areas and universities—some of which were closed down for extended periods—to the countryside to engage in manual labor as agricultural workers. This development effectively disabled Chinese scientific activity during this era and dealt it a severe blow. Many Third World countries so lack the organizational, institutional, and ideational infrastructure of modern science that, shortfalls of skilled personnel aside, this absence might be said to constitute a disabling condition for the practice of modern science or engineering in these countries, at least by indigenous practitioners.

Generating and Terminating

A second pair of societal influences on science and technology might be called *generating* and *terminating*. As we have noted, enabling influences make certain phenomena possible. They do not, however, guarantee that what they make possible is actualized. A generating societal influence on a scientific or technological endeavor is one that, by providing an external social motive, goal, or rationale, ignites a process culminating in the birth of a technical endeavor or artifact. For example, while earlier achievements in physics and engineering were enabling conditions for NASA's Apollo program for landing on the moon, it was the launching of the Russian satellite *Sputnik I* in the midst of the Cold War (1957) that sparked or generated the Apollo effort; fears that the Nazis would achieve an atomic bomb had a similar effect vis-à-vis the Manhattan Project.

Terminating societal influences are ones that ignite processes leading to the effective "death" of an existing technical phenomenon, endeavor, or development (e.g., a project, proposal, theory, or system). A radical budget cut for an unfinished resource-intensive technical undertaking, an arms-control agreement to scrap an embryonic weapons research and development project, international revulsion over the use of chemical-warfare agents, and opposition by a politically influential group to the public funding or conduct of a scientific experiment that its members find offensive exemplify the sorts of societal developments that can exercise terminating influences on technical phenomena.

Helping and Hindering

A third important pair of types of societal influence on science and technology may be dubbed *helping* and *hindering*. Helping influences are those that favorably

---

*It should be noted, however, that it is not only the culture of a society that can exercise an enabling influence on science or technology. Political or economic decisions can provide a technical research project with the requisites it needs to "start up" (e.g., adequate personnel, equipment, materials, and money for salaries) as well as providing ongoing funding support.

affect the life or growth of science or technology in general or of a particular scientific or technological problem, project, activity, or field. There are several species of promotive influences, including sustaining, strengthening, and furthering. Societal forces may be said to exert a *sustaining* influence when they contribute to the continuance and a *furthering* influence when they contribute to the advancement of some scientific or technological activity or endeavor. Such influences are exercised by at least three major kinds of means: *inducements, facilitations,* and *prescriptions.*

Inducements are external means that incite potential agents to action. They may be positive or negative, monetary or nonmonetary. Positive inducements ("carrots") are ones the desire to realize which moves an agent to action. Negative inducements ("sticks") are ones the desire to avoid which moves an agent to action. Among the most potent and frequently employed positive inducements used by societal forces to sustain or nurture the development of scientific or technological activity are financial support and profit opportunities. These inducements may be direct, like the funding of academic research or awarding of lucrative government contracts to private firms, or indirect, like patent or trade laws that enhance the profit or prestige prospects of researchers or companies.

Negative inducements include the threatened withdrawal or withholding of funding; the threatened cancellation of, or decision not to renew, a contract; and the creation, maintenance, or expansion of obstacles to the initiation, continuation, or acceleration of scientific or technological work. The latter include laws increasing the maximum civil liability for businesses responsible for industrial accidents, laws holding responsible executives criminally liable for certain kinds of industrial misconduct, and complex bureaucratic procedures for obtaining government permission to carry out some scientific or engineering activity.

Facilitative means are those that make the furtherance of a scientific or technological endeavor easier by the removal or diminution of some sort of obstacle. The removal of a negative inducement, such as, say, a daunting government regulation previously discouraging a scientific or technological activity, may be regarded as a second-order positive inducement.

Other scientific or technological activities are promoted by *prescriptive*, rather than inductive or facilitative, means. Prescriptions are instructions to do or refrain from doing something, often backed up by authority and power to punish if the instructions are not followed. Perhaps the most important wielders of this kind of promoting influence are branches of national governments, in both the capitalist and noncapitalist world.

Given legislative approval of requested funding levels, the U.S. federal government can effectively order that certain projects be undertaken and carried forward, continued or discontinued, or accelerated or slowed down in its intramural research laboratories. Such, for example, is the case with certain weapons research and development projects in laboratories such as Lawrence Livermore and Los Alamos, and with AIDS research at institutions like the National Institutes of Health. While it would be misleading to claim that the federal government is able to influence prescriptively the scientific research it funds in universities, to the extent that the magnitude of that funding grows and dependence on its continuation becomes institutionalized, it is progressively more difficult for government funding inducements to avoid taking on a prescriptive character. Legislative, judicial, and regulatory branches of government can also exercise promotive influence on science and technology by prescriptive means—for example, by passage of a particular law, issuance of a binding legal decision, or establishment of a regulation obliging practitioners to behave as specified.

The antitheses of helping societal influences on science and technology may be called *hindering* influences. Hindering influences are those that adversely affect the progress or development of science or technology in general or of a particular project, problem, activity, or field. The situation here is largely the mirror image of that which obtains for helping influences. Species of hindering societal influences include ones that weaken, impede, or prevent the progress or development of the technical phenomenon in question. Such influences are effected by three sorts of means corresponding to those for promoting influences: inducements (positive and negative), obstructions, and prescriptions (orders to do and prohibitions against doing).

Determining and Liberating

A fourth pair of types of societal influence on science and technology may be called *determining* and *liberating*. A determining influence is one that helps establish the direction, nature, structure, or properties of its object—in the present context, technical enterprises, products, or processes. A liberating, or releasing, influence is one that loosens or removes one or more determinative constraints to which its object was previously subject.

The exercise of determinative influences on science and technology by public and government officials for the purpose of protecting or enhancing the welfare of society may be called *the social control of science and technology*. A particularly important species of such influence is *regulation*—the controlling or directing of a party or activity according to rules, methods, guidelines, or laws. Government regulation is clearly an important vehicle—arguably the *most* important one—for the social control of science and technology in the twentieth century industrialized world. We will have more to say of a historical-critical nature about government regulation of science and technology in particular and the social control of science and technology in general in Chapter 14. Suffice it to note here that in the twentieth century, in highly developed societies, the regulation of science and technology has become increasingly widespread; that is, such regulation is found in more and more *areas* of scientific and technological activity and extended to more and more *aspects* of scientific and technological activity, from their initiation to disposal of their waste by-products.

Regardless of type, societal influences on science and technology vary in importance. All contribute to one degree or another to bringing about some effect, but some such contributions are decisive to its occurrence. We will therefore distinguish societal influences that are *decisive* from those that are *contributory* (but not decisive). There are in turn two kinds of decisive societal influences: those that are *essential* (without which the effect in question would not have come to pass) and those that are *timely* (but not essential). For example, an effect on science or technology might occur only as the result of the cumulative pressure of many individually small societal influences. The last such influence might be decisive in the sense that its timely appearance happens to be "the straw that broke the camel's back," but not in the sense of being essential, for other influences could have appeared on the scene at the same time and produced the same effect.

Political and economic forces, individually or, more often, in combination, often exercise decisive influences on science and technology. However, cultural elements can do likewise. For example, society's aesthetic values sometimes exercise decisive influences on its technics. In Victorian England, prevailing aesthetic values resulted in the bedecking of many utilitarian objects (e.g., paperweights, telephones, steam engines) with lavish ornamental features having nothing to do with functionality. Contemporary high-fidelity audio components possessing myriad "bells and whistles," colorful plastic Swiss Swatch watches, and ubiquitous Japanese Casio timepieces, with their black plastic straps and cases and multiple buttons and informational and calculative functions, are among numerous contemporary "high-tech" technics over whose designs prevailing cultural tastes and "needs" have exercised decisive influences.

Of the types of societal influence on science and technology, enabling and disabling influences are the least frequently remarked upon, for they are often buried in society's cultural matrix. Yet, cultural factors can exercise contributory, even decisive, enabling and promotive influences on the enterprises and products of science and technology. However, a society's culture is not easily managed by inductive, facilitative, or prescriptive means—by, for example, simply adjusting economic incentives. If, as many scholars believe, Japan's excellence in technological innovation is to a significant degree attributable to its cultural system, America's response to this challenge has been largely political-economic in nature. The extent to which the Japanese economic challenge will serve to elicit changes in American culture of a sort conducive to improved manufacturing remains to be seen.

In contrast to the invisible hand of culture, government use of adjustable positive and negative economic incentives to promote science and technology in business and academia is no secret and has developed into an art form. However, use by the various branches of government and by the public of prescriptive means to influence science and technology has grown in recent decades, even though in most business and some academic circles this trend is strongly opposed. As science and technology become ever more potent and efficacious and research delves deeper into sensitive areas of the reproductive, genetic, and cognitive sciences, the strongest, most intrusive type of societal influence on science and technology, the determinative-prescriptive, seems likely to become more widespread.

EFFECTS ON SCIENCE AND TECHNOLOGY OF THESE TYPES OF INFLUENCE

The third facet of the societal-influence-on-science-and-technology relationship is not that of the "influencer" (i.e., the influence agent) or that of the types of influence exerted, but rather that of the "influenced" (i.e., the *effects* of the influences wielded). More precisely, we will now examine the *kinds of changes* in science and technology that can be and are effected by the exercise of one or another type of societal influence. We will delineate, illustrate, and briefly comment upon several such aspects, particularly ones not widely recognized.

In recent years, the range of aspects of scientific and technological activity affected by the exercise of societal influence has been expanding. This raises the question of whether any aspect of scientific or technological activities or practice is likely to remain immune from restrictive societal influence in the foreseeable future and, if so, why. If there is any such aspect, the most likely candidate is probably that of the freedom of scientists to choose *what subject* they wish to investigate, generate knowledge about, and come to better understand—as against *the means* used in their inquiries, something which, as we saw in Chapter 9, is already subject to societal limitation. As we will see in Chapter 15, however, even this seemingly compelling candidate has recently come under intense critical scrutiny.

Six major kinds of changes that societal forces have made in science and technology in the contemporary era will be considered here.* These changes have to do with

> direction selection,
>
> technic constitution,
>
> process specification,
>
> technic production,
>
> technic diffusion, and
>
> technic use.

Direction

Societal forces external to science and technology play an important role in determining the *directions* in which these enterprises move, thereby influencing the rates of progress in different areas of science and technology. They realize these directive effects by influencing which specific research and development projects, which general areas of research, and which general approaches to a given science- or technology-related social problem are furthered or opposed (via one or more of the available societal influence mechanisms). Depending on the attitudes of government, business, or the public, one or another project, area, or approach may be selected over another for sustained funding, benign neglect, or outright prohibition.

The U.S. government's long-standing support of development work on an artificial heart, its continued lavish support of particle physics research, the elimination by the Reagan administration of government funding for "soft energy path" research (e.g., on solar technologies), and the rapid increase in federal funding for AIDS research in the mid 1980s, all are cases in which various societal forces—the public, the particle-physics community (in concert with government representatives reflecting local economic interests), and vested private economic interests—exercised decisive directive or redirective effects on the enterprises of science and technology. A serious concern here is whether the increasing directive pressures on science and technology to serve short-term socioeconomic interests will dilute the long-term fruitfulness of these forces.

Constitution

Although it is not often recognized, societal forces sometimes influence the very make-up or constitution of the products—knowledge, individual technics, and technical systems—generated by science and technology. Let us begin with the design of technological items. Among the kinds of societal factors that sometimes influence technological design are political-economic power struggles, class and racial prejudice, and concerns over widespread social values.

---

*There are, of course, other important aspects of science and technology that are affected by social policies—the numbers of students and practitioners of science and engineering, the distribution of their fields of specialization, the representations of women and minorities in these professions, and the quality of the equipment available for use in research and development work.

For example, David Noble has argued that, technologically speaking, the development of automatically controlled machine tools in America could have gone in either of two ways. With the "record-playback" option, a machinist would "make a part while the motions of the machine under his command were recorded on magnetic tape. After the first piece was made, identical parts could be made automatically by playing back the tape and reproducing the machine motions."[5] Under this option, control of the labor process remains with individual machinists at their respective work stations.

Alternatively, with the "numerical control" (N/C) option, "[t]he specifications for a part—the information contained in an engineering blueprint—are first broken down into a mathematical representation of the part, then into a mathematical description of the desired path of the cutting tool along up to five axes, and finally into hundreds or thousands of discrete instructions, translated for economy into a numerical code, which is read and translated into electrical signals for the machine controls."[6] Here control of the labor process is removed from the shop floor and lodged with a centralized group of white-collar programmers presumably more amenable to managerial wishes.

Why did the N/C option eventually triumph? Noble acknowledges that extensive U. S. Air Force subsidization of the development of N/C technology (in hopes of meeting demanding aircraft performance specifications) and considerations of cost and profit in the aircraft industry played noteworthy roles in that triumph. However, he argues that the selection of the N/C design option was also influenced by the antagonistic nature of management-labor relations in the manufacturing sector. Management was predisposed in favor of a technological design that would enable it to capture control of the work process from recalcitrant machinists. Thus, for Noble, the political-economic power struggle between management and workers exerted an important influence on the constitution of the new automatically controlled machine tools.[7]

According to Robert Caro, New York City's legendary planning czar Robert Moses influenced the design of the numerous bridges spanning his Long Island parkways in the 1920s and 1930s. He knowingly prescribed arched bridges with clearance heights too low to accommodate public buses except in the centermost "fast lane" in each direction, thereby rendering bus use of the parkways impractical. Moses' design interventions were prompted by two considerations. First, he believed that arched bridges beautified—and the presence of buses uglified—his beloved parkways. Moreover, buses posed a threat to his long-held vision of a rural, parklike Long Island. Second, wishing to reserve the state parks and beaches that he had developed on Long Island for use by the prosperous white people who mostly traveled by private automobile, Moses specified bridge clearance heights that made it more difficult for poor, predominantly minority people, who tended to rely on public transportation, to reach these prime facilities. Thus was technological design shaped by invidious class and ethnic—as well as aesthetic—interests.[8]

Social values frequently shape technological design, particularly through government regulatory intervention. Invoking the social value of public safety, government regulations and contracts often specify required design or equipment features. For example, microwave ovens sold in the United States must have two inner door locks—one concealed—such that they shut off automatically when opened. Large-scale commercial aircraft must currently satisfy numerous safety-related design and equipment specifications: automatically deploying oxygen masks, automatically inflating emergency escape slides, center-aisle floor lights, smoke detectors and fire extinguishers in lavatories, and a prescribed minimum number of exits.

Besides required design elements or equipment, government agencies also often establish performance standards, sometimes on the very same products. For example, children's pajamas sold in the United States must meet a mandated flammability standard (i.e., they must not burn more quickly than at a specified rate), new microwave ovens must emit no more than 1 milliwatt of radiation per square centimeter at a distance of 5 centimeters, and, in certain states, the constituents of auto emissions levels may not exceed certain maximum levels.

As for science, societal forces have sometimes affected the very content of, among other things, the output of particular scientific activities (e.g., theories or knowledge claims). The substance of hypotheses, data, theories, and knowledge claims put forth or developed by certain practitioners has sometimes been affected by ideologies to which they subscribe or for whose promotion they are supported. The annals of the human sciences in the late nineteenth and early twentieth centuries, in both Europe and the United States, contain purportedly scientific claims affirming the alleged inherent intellectual superiority or inferiority of certain races of human beings.

For example, a team of American psychologists did extensive "intelligence testing" of "drafted recruits" into the U. S. Army in World War I. The test data supposedly revealed that recruits of different national origins exhibited different average shares of native mental ability. In descending order of "intelligence rating", the recruits' nations ranked thus: England, Holland, Denmark, Scotland, Germany, Sweden, Canada, Belgium, Norway, Austria, Ireland, Turkey, Greece, Russia, Italy, and Poland. The content of these claims—not to mention the inclusion in such a study of questions about the recruits' ethnic backgrounds ("nativity")—is partly a product of existing social prejudice, which may be said to have provided the nurturing atmosphere in which such investigations could be conceived and carried out and their findings be warmly received. Not coincidentally, the foregoing rank ordering is congruent with the stereotypes and prejudices of the day in the United States regarding "Slavic and Latin" peoples, millions of whom had in recent years emigrated to America.[9]

Such episodes notwithstanding, it is clear that societal influence on the content of specific scientific activities has been less frequent and invasive than in the case of technology. It is in shaping *process* specifications rather than *product* content that societal influence on science has become the rule rather than the exception in recent decades.

Process Specification

In recent years societal forces have succeeded in affecting not only some ancillary processes accompanying the carrying out of a piece of scientific or technological work, but also, in some cases, the very structure of the research process itself. For example, in the United States, research supported by the National Institutes of Health must obtain prior approval from a biosafety review board in the institution that houses the proposed project. Prior informed consent of any human subjects involved must also be secured. Similarly, according to the U.S. Animal Welfare Act, federally supported research work using animal subjects must adhere to certain guidelines governing the care and experimental use of animals.

Certain kinds of engineering projects, federally funded or not (e.g., nuclear power plants), may not commence normal operations without detailed testing having first been done and been scrutinized by appropriate governmental authorities (e.g., the

NRC). At the other end of science and technology processes, toxic waste by-products of various sorts (e.g., chemical and nuclear) are subject to a variety of informational and procedural regulations governing their storage, treatment, transport, and disposal. In short, the increasingly sensitive and potent nature of much contemporary scientific and engineering work has made the scrutiny accorded the processes of technical practice increasingly comprehensive and prescriptive. In recent years, this trend has generated frustration and resentment on the part of researchers and organizations accustomed to more autonomous modes of operation.

Production

Besides direction-setting, product-constituting, and process-specifying influences, societal forces, namely government, also affect the *manufacture* of certain products and materials. The reason society has undertaken to influence this phase of contemporary scientific and technological activity, one which many individuals believe should be left up to the firms and markets involved, is that the economic, political, and physical potency of many of the products involved is such that wider societal health and economic interests must be protected from the outset, not simply bandaged after the fact.

Within a narrow but important range of products, governments limit *who* can manufacture *what*, and under *which conditions*. Nuclear, chemical, and biological weapons are cases in point. No high school or college student, however brilliant or able to access the necessary resources, is free to produce an atomic bomb, mustard gas, or lethal virus. Synthetic hallucinogens and addictive, physiologically harmful drugs are also subject to strict production limits.

Diffusion

For political or economic reasons, governments sometimes attempt to foster or impose strict limits on the dissemination and diffusion of the products of scientific and technological activity (e.g., knowledge, technics, and technical systems).

Techniques used by governments to promote diffusion of favored technics include tax credits for consumer purchase and subsidization of purchase prices. A noteworthy example of government-fostered innovation diffusion at the national level is the case of "Minitel." Seeking to move its people and state-owned telecommunications industry into positions of leadership in the information era, since 1981 the French government, through its telephone monopoly, French Telecom, has loaned free over 4 million home computer terminals and keyboards at a cost to the government of $1.3 billion. The goal is to reach 8 million terminals, almost one third of French households. With the hardware, telephone users can access Minitel, a network that allows them to exchange messages with other users, carry out banking transactions, access an electronic telephone directory and train schedules, get stock market and weather reports, do home shopping, and use various other information services.[10]

Diffusion controls include banning the distribution of certain products outright or to specified parties, banning the diffusion of certain informational products through specified channels, and limiting product distribution to those who agree to abide by certain conditions regarding their use and possible redistribution.

For example, in the United States, prescription of the fetus-deforming drug thalidomide and sale of dangerous metal-tipped "lawn darts" and three-wheeled all-terrain vehicles have been banned outright or curbed by various government regulatory agencies. Alcoholic drinks, tobacco products, and firearms may not legally be sold to people under certain ages. Concerned about nuclear weapons proliferation, the U.S. government has long attempted to limit the diffusion of the technologies involved by requiring that recipients of American aid in building or running nuclear power plants adhere to strict conditions intended to prevent them from using such aid to develop nuclear weapons. A post-facto, increasingly important form of diffusion control in some contemporary industrial societies is that of "product recalls"—government orders to manufacturers to recall for repair, refund, or replacement products that a cognizant government agency has concluded pose a threat to consumer health or safety.

While some diffusion controls limit the domain into which a scientific or technological innovation may be disseminated, others limit the speed of the diffusion process. Normal Food and Drug Administration policy is to keep experimental drugs and new medical devices from the marketplace until they have passed tests deemed sufficient to prove their safety and efficacy. However, innovations that may pose a threat to public health and safety aside, the tendency of national governments in Western industrial societies has been to steer clear of limiting diffusion rates and leave that to the marketplace. Reflecting this laissez-faire tradition, a noted patent lawyer, responding to legislative and public concern over the 1988 United States Patent Office decision to grant patents for genetically engineered animals, observed incredulously:

> One of the most important aspects of the United States patent system is the implicit optimism that says, "Hey, a new invention, that's great."...What you have here is people saying we're scared. Nothing has been proven, we don't quite know why, but we're scared. Is Congress now going to say, *for the first time*, that here's *a new technology that we're going to delay* because we're going to presume it's bad until it's proven good?[11] [emphasis added]

Use

In recent decades governments have begun to increase regulation of the use of technics and technical systems. Rather than banning the diffusion of sometimes controversial technologies or products outright, thereby foregoing such advantages as they may offer, governments of industrialized countries have tended to impose selective limits on the use or uses of the products in question, in hopes of having it both ways.

In some instances, *specific uses* of technics or systems have been prohibited. For example, the U.S. postal service may not be used to defraud customers ("mail fraud"), and legislation has been proposed in some states to prohibit businesses from using the telephone network to offer pornographic-message services.

A different tack is that of restricting the *conditions under which a technology may be used*, regardless of the use or uses selected. For example, in 1988, the Legislature of Suffolk County, New York, enacted the first legislative regulation in the United States of the increasingly widespread technology of the video-display terminal (VDT). Henceforth in that county, use of VDTs by permanent employees who operate them more than 26 hours per week in companies with more than 20 such terminals will require special lighting, adjustable chairs and desks, detachable keyboards, 15-minute breaks for users every 3 hours, and annual user eye examinations, 80 percent of the costs of which are to be paid by employers.[12]

Other use conditions embodied in legislation include limits on *time* of use—some cities permit the use of certain technics, such as leaf blowers, only during certain hours of the day—on *days* of use—during a 1987 smog alert, Athens restricted private automobile use to either odd- or even-numbered days, depending on the vehicle's licence plate—and on *place and/or manner* of use—snowmobiles are barred from certain wilderness areas and portable "boom boxes" from some municipal beaches. Such examples and the familiar cases of passenger vehicles and guns notwithstanding, government regulation of the use of potent, mass-produced, privately owned technics remains rudimentary. It is, however, likely to expand in the future.

CONCLUSION

In a sense, this chapter has been an exercise in classification and delineation. The rationale for including it in this book is to promote enhanced awareness of the basic structure, complexity, and richness of the pivotal societal-influence-on-science-and-technology relationship, one which has thus far received less than its scholarly due.

We identified a wide range of societal influence agents vis-à-vis science and technology, characterized eight types of influence that such agents may exercise, and spelled out six kinds of effects on scientific and technological activity that such exercises can bring about. One conclusion suggested by our discussion is that in the late twentieth century, few if any aspects of science and technology remain beyond the reach of potent societal influences. This makes the quality and quantity of that influence matters of considerable importance for the prospects of human and other inhabitants of the earth. We now turn to analysis of the strongest and, in the contemporary era, arguably most important type of determinative societal influence action on science and technology: *control*.

ENDNOTES

1. Loren Graham, *Science, Philosophy, and Human Behavior in the Soviet Union* (New York: Columbia University Press, 1987), p. 124.
2. Edwin Meese, *New York Times*, February 28, 1986, section I, p. 20.
3. *New York Times*, May 31, 1988, p. A16.
4. *New York Times*, May 15, 1987, section II, p. 12; and February 22, 1988, pp. A1, A13.
5. David Noble, "Social Choice In Machine Design: The Case of Automatically Controlled Machine Tools," in *The Social Shaping of Technology*, Donald MacKenzie and Judy Wajcman, eds. (Milton Keynes, England: Open University Press, 1985), p. 111.
6. *Ibid.*
7. For discussion of the influences of different institutional settings and different cultural traditions on the development of NC machinery, see Håkon With Anderson, "Technological Trajectories, Cultural Values and the Labor Process: The Development of NC Machinery in the Norwegian Shipping Industry," *Social Studies of Science*, 18, 1988, 465–482.
8. See Robert A. Caro, *The Power Broker: Robert Moses and the Fall of New York* (New York: Knopf, 1974), pp. 318, 546, and 951–954.
9. National Academy of Sciences, *Memoirs of the National Academy of Sciences, Vol. 15: Psychological Examining in the United States Army*, ed. Robert M. Yerkes (Washington, D.C.: United States Government Printing Office, 1921), pp. 553 and 693–699.
10. *New York Times*, November 8, 1988, pp. C1, C4. See also Jeffrey A. Hart, "The Teletel/Minitel System in France," *Telematics and Informatics*, 5, no. 1, 1988, 21–28.
11. *New York Times*, April 13, 1988, p. A13.
12. *New York Times*, June 15, 1988, p. A1; and July 1, 1988, p. A14.

CHAPTER 14
SOCIAL CONTROL OF SCIENCE AND TECHNOLOGY

INTRODUCTION

Chapter 13 was devoted to analyzing the societal-influence-on-science-and-technology relationship. We explored a number of different modes of exercising influence on science and technology that are open to various societal agents as well as different kinds of effects on these forces that can be brought about by such exercises. This chapter will focus in greater depth on one kind of determinative societal influence on science and technology—what sociologists call the *social control of technology*, to which we will add "and science." We will begin by considering some popular arguments used to defend and oppose this important practice. Then we will examine six of its most influential forms: regulation, funding and management, liability litigation, prior assessment mechanisms, public participation, and legislative limitation.

JUSTIFICATION

The first issue that arises is that of the justification of this increasingly common practice, which we will refer to here as the social control of science and technology (SCOST). Is there a need for society to attempt to control its scientific and technological enterprises and activities? Let us canvas some major general arguments for and against the institutionalized practice of SCOST in twentieth century Western industrial societies.

One popular justification for SCOST appeals to the *unprecedented magnitude* of the potential effects or consequences of some modern scientific or technological innovations. A malfunctioning part in a commercial jet aircraft, an automotive design defect, an inadequately tested drug or medical device, or a slipshod nuclear plant installation can jeopardize the health or safety of hundreds or even thousands of people. Given the pressures of interfirm competition and the large, time-sensitive capital costs involved in such cases, some hold that there is need for an external check on the activities of firms involved with such potent products and practices.

One rebuttal to this argument is that firms responsible for such fatal flaws will pay the price in the marketplace in the form of lost customer patronage, hence losses of profit, as well as in the court room, through suits brought by injured parties or their kin. Hence, there is no need for the government to interfere. The usual response to this argument is that such intervention is aimed at *preventing* large-scale losses of such seriousness and scope from occurring in the first place. The issue then becomes an empirical one: Do the various forms of SCOST, all of which have nontrivial costs of various sorts associated with them, provide significant extra margins of safety beyond those offered by existing market forces?

A second important reason offered to justify SCOST appeals to the belief that, on balance, in the context of rapid scientific and technological change, *allowing the market free rein will exacerbate existing social inequalities*. That is, it is argued that permitting the free market to be the sole determinant of the allocation among affected individuals and groups of the (often weighty) costs, benefits, and risks of contemporary scientific and technological innovations, projects, and practices is apt to intensify existing social inequalities. Air, water, or noise pollution from refineries or manufacturing plants is apt to affect workers in the plants that generate it and nearby residents much more than it will the stockholders and the well-off residents on "the other side of the tracks." Thus, the argument goes, a society committed to promoting equality, or at least a more just distribution of such costs and benefits, needs to exercise a countervailing, corrective force to that of the free market. This may take the form of, among other things, issuance of prescriptive governmental regulations and provision of legal recourse for harm suffered from uses of products and exposure to scientific and technological practices and their by-products for which one cannot reasonably be held responsible.

Opponents sometimes argue that such intervention is, on balance, counterproductive, for, however well intentioned, it is apt to increase a firm's cost of doing business. These increases are ultimately passed along to the public, including the less well off—a group typically larger than that possibly benefiting from the government intervention. Yet it is precisely the less well off who may be hurt most by such increases.

A third major justification appeals to the importance of *fostering freedom in the form of voluntary consumer choices*. The consumer cannot make truly voluntary choices, it is argued, if those choices are made in ignorance of salient facts about the candidate product choices—for example, facts about a product's content, features, ingredients, performance, and possible effects on health and safety. Further, given the complexity of contemporary knowledge, the fact that all pertinent items of knowledge are usually not readily available to the would-be consumer, and the fact that firms often deliberately withhold some such information, it is held that there is a need for an external party responsible for combating this ignorance by ensuring that the consumer has ready access to all pertinent information.

A popular counterargument here is political-philosophical. Conservative libertarians view such government intervention as paternalistic, and hence as categorically unacceptable, and hold that in point of fact concerned citizens *can* obtain all pertinent information if they but make the effort. If they fail to do so, they have no one to blame but themselves. A second counterargument is economic. Providing such information may disclose proprietary trade secrets about the product and will surely increase the cost of the product. A third argument is that such regulation is unnecessary, perhaps even undesirable. For this information is often of such a technical nature that it cannot be understood by most consumers who bother to scrutinize it. Most consumers, for example, knowing little if any chemistry or nutritional science, do not in fact pay serious attention to labels that provide this sort of information. By its very presence such information may in fact evoke unwarranted alarm or anxiety rather than dissipate it.

A fourth major justification for SCOST has to do with the fact that so *much contemporary scientific and technological activity is funded, in whole or in part, with government money*, a significant part of which is ultimately derived from the taxpaying public. This argument is a variation on the theme of participatory democracy, whose cardinal principle is that all parties affected by a decision are entitled to play a meaningful role in the process of reaching it. Strictly speaking, this argument purports only to justify the public's (or its governmental representatives') exercising contributory but noncontrolling influence in the funding process (e.g., a role in determining directions of research and development work).

One counterargument here is a pragmatic one. If technically knowledgeable researchers were given total control over the allocation of government funding, better technical outcomes would result. But, it may be rejoined, scientific communities are themselves subject to the distorting influence of invidious competition and status-seeking, something which can, from the point of view of the paying public, "waste" some of its precious funds. Moreover, panels of technical specialists already exercise a potent influence over which research projects are funded by government monies and at what levels of support. However, when huge outlays of funds are requested, government is not obligated to write blank checks for projects independent of their possible connection to public welfare. In practice, a balance is struck between the priorities of technical specialists, often skewed by the commercial and professional interests of their firms and fields, and those of governmental officials, which more or less imperfectly mirror the wishes of the people they represent.

SIX INFLUENTIAL MODES OF SCOST

SCOST has undergone rapid development in the post–World War II period, especially in the last two decades. We will now discuss six important kinds of SCOST: regulation, funding/management, liability litigation, public participation, a priori evaluative mechanisms, and legislative control decisions. For each of these six modes of SCOST, we will describe a watershed or landmark in its historical development, relate some key aspects of the current situation with regard to the operation or status of that mode, discuss one or two pivotal cases from the last two decades, and, finally, analyze one or two contentious unresolved issues raised by ongoing use of that mode.

Government Regulation

Watershed.   By now, government regulation of scientific and technological activities in the private sector is a permanent feature of the landscapes of Western industrial societies. Government regulation has in fact become so institutionalized that it has become an integral element of contemporary industrial cultures. In the United States, government regulation of industry can be said to go back to the start of the republic. While Congress had long regulated interstate commerce, it limited itself to activities that either facilitated it (building roads, dredging canals, erecting lighthouses) or disburdened it (preventing duties and imposts on trade between the states).

Many believe that positive government regulation of private industry began with the establishment of the Interstate Commerce Commission in 1887 and its efforts to prevent unfair pricing practices by the railroads. This, however, is not the case.

It was the advent and flourishing of the high-pressure steam boat in the nineteenth century that gave rise to the first restrictive government regulation of a sector of private industry.[1] The problem was with exploding steamship boilers, whether from inadequate design, faulty manufacture, neglected maintenance, or unqualified engineer-operators. Between 1816 and 1851, over 235 steamboat explosions occurred in the United States—many on the Mississippi River—in which over 3,000 lives were lost. Although a weak law, full of loopholes and imprecision, was passed by Congress in 1838, only years later did Congress pass stringent and restrictive legislation. The law set a maximum allowable working pressure for any boiler, required that it undergo yearly tests at specified pressures, specified features of design and manufacture, outlawed other designs, required certification of engineers, prescribed penalties for violating boiler operation limits, and created a board of inspectors to investigate accidents.

Arguments in the U.S. Senate over the proposed bill revolved around a by-now familiar opposition: supposedly inviolable private property rights versus the duty of representative government to act in the public interest. The conflict took the form of a question: Should the lives and property of the steamboat-going public be allowed to be placed in jeopardy to preserve the traditional immunity of private enterprise from positive government regulation?[2] In 1852 Congress finally answered in the negative.

Current Situation. The 1852 law gave rise to the first of the many government regulatory agencies and positive regulatory activities that have come into being during the last 138 years. Important independent government agencies currently regulating scientific and technological endeavors are the Consumer Product Safety Commission (1972), the Environmental Protection Agency (1970), the Federal Communications Commission (1934), the Federal Maritime Commission (1961), the Federal Trade Commission (1914), the Interstate Commerce Commission (1887), the Nuclear Regulatory Commission (1974, successor to the Atomic Energy Commission), and the National Transportation Safety Board (1966). Cabinet-level executive departments with units that carry out important regulatory activities affecting science and technology are the Departments of Agriculture, Commerce, Energy, Health and Human Services, Interior, Labor, and Transportation.

It is generally believed that the decade of the 1970s witnessed "the most dramatic increase in federal regulatory activity ever."[3] One measure of this growth lies in the increasing size of the *Federal Register*, which publishes all proposed and final regulations. Its average yearly size grew from 9,562 pages in 1960 to 74,120 pages in 1980. The Center for the Study of American Business estimates that in 1986, about 112,300 people were employed full time in 54 government regulatory agencies at a cost of almost $9 billion.[4]

An Important Recent Case. Asserting in the presidential campaign of 1980 that the proliferation of government regulation was making American business less competitive, Ronald Reagan made "regulatory relief" a cornerstone of his new economic program. When he assumed office in 1981, Reagan took steps to ensure that cost–benefit–risk analysis bulked larger in the formulation and adoption of government regulations. He froze 172 pending regulations and appealed some legal cases that had grown out of them to the U.S. Supreme Court. One such case was that of the *American Textile Manufacturers Institute* v. *Marshall*.

This case revolved around the fact that, depending on the density of fiber particles in the air, workers in cotton textile factories were at risk for "brown lung disease" (byssinosis). The Occupational Safety and Health Administration (OSHA) had promulgated a maximum cotton particle density standard. The textile manufacturers association challenged a federal court of appeals decision upholding the OSHA standard in the U.S. Supreme Court, asking that the standard be set aside because it had not been shown that its benefits (to workers) exceeded its costs (to employers). Shortly after it took office, in a highly unusual action, the Reagan administration asked the Supreme Court to vacate the appeals court decision and send the case back to the Department of Labor for internal reconsideration in light of the president's new cost–benefit policy for government regulations. In a landmark decision, the Supreme Court held that the paramount value assigned to worker safety by the Occupational Safety and Health Act of 1970 made resort to cost–benefit analysis to disqualify such a regulation impermissible, unless the proposed standard was technologically infeasible or implementing it would effectively destroy the affected companies. This decision had the far-reaching effect of preventing demonstration that a proposed regulation's benefits exceeded its costs from being made a necessary condition for its adoption and implementation.

Outstanding Issues.   One problematic aspect of the entire governmental regulatory enterprise is the fact that executive agencies are subject to periodic politicization. The president of the United States appoints the heads of the independent agencies and of the cabinet-level executive departments involved in regulatory activity. Although these appointments must be approved by Congress, they are rarely turned down. Consequently, the possibility always exists that conflict may emerge between executive appointees with sharp ideological axes to grind and career civil service scientists and engineers who wish to preserve senses of personal and organizational integrity and make regulatory decisions on the basis of legislative intent and solid empirical evidence rather than on the grounds of political-economic expediency.

Echoing the 1852 Senate debate over the proposed steamboat law, regulators tend to fall into one of two categories: those for whom consumer, citizen, and worker interests are paramount, and those for whom corporate, national economic, or military security interests are always of primary importance in regulating matters scientific and technological. (On occasion, individuals are appointed who heed both sets of concerns and assign them weights on a case-by-case basis).

In the early and mid 1980s the regulatory agencies were largely populated by a business-oriented U.S. president with appointees of the second persuasion. An effort was made to remove or reduce regulatory restraints on business ("deregulation") in the name of enhancing competitiveness, profit prospects, and economic growth. This, it was argued, invoking the "trickle-down" theory, would in turn produce more jobs, income, and a higher standard of living for working people. Whatever the intended consequences of this process of unfettering, including less stringent information disclosure, easier licensing, and less rigorous performance standards, workplace safety and environmental protection regulations and their enforcement were significantly weakened.

The net effect of the Reagan administration's campaign against "excessive" regulation is a matter of controversy. Proponents claim that it is partly responsible for the extended period of economic growth enjoyed by the United States in the 1980s. Opponents argue that the politicization of regulatory appointments and decision making exacted a substantial toll: less safety for the consuming and working public (or a slowdown in the improvement of same) and diminished morale among the professional workforce of regulatory researchers and inspectors, something with disturbing long-term consequences. The issue of whether the primary role of government regulatory agencies is to remove impediments to increased industrial activity and profits or to protect workers and the public against harmful results of that activity by a combination of restraints and fines is yet to be resolved.

Government Funding and Performance of Science and Technology

Watershed.   A second important mode of SCOST is government extramural funding and intramural funding and performance of scientific and technological research and development activities. This qualifies as a mode of SCOST because through it the federal government can exert a decisive influence on the directions and speed of national research and development, whether such efforts are intended to reflect public opinion or serve the interests of one or another governmental bureaucracy (e.g., the military).

The undisputed watershed in the evolution of this mode of SCOST in the twentieth century is the research and development effort that the U.S. government undertook to build an atomic bomb. This six-year venture began with the carrying out of chain-reaction experiments at Columbia University in 1939 and concluded with the successful testing of the bomb at Alamogordo, New Mexico, in July 1945. The "Manhattan Project" is the name given to a crucial component of the overall A-bomb effort—namely, the intensive government undertaking between May 1942 and July 1945 to choose a method for producing fissionable material and to design, build, and test an atomic bomb.

The A-bomb effort was a watershed episode in the SCOST in two ways. First, it showed that the federal government could organize and successfully carry out an immense, complex, costly research and development project deemed essential to one of its missions: national defense. The Manhattan Project itself employed 120,000 people, brought into being 37 facilities in 19 states and Canada, and cost the unprecedented sum of approximately $2 billion.[5] At various points in its life, the project enlisted the participation of, and supported financially, a number of academic research facilities, including ones at Columbia University, the University of California at Berkeley, and the University of Chicago. New research and development facilities were constructed and dedicated to one phase or another of the project (e.g., plants in Hanford, Washington, and Oak Ridge, Tennessee, and a laboratory at Los Alamos, New Mexico). Thousands of technical practitioners were recruited for the effort. This was the birth of government-funded and -conducted Big Science projects. The huge, federally funded, mission-oriented Apollo and space shuttle programs of the 1960s and 1980s, projects which consumed enormous amounts of the nation's research and development resources, followed directly in the footsteps of the Manhattan Project.

A second, equally important way that the A-bomb project was a watershed for the SCOST in the United States lies in the fact that it led to the federal government's assuming a controlling position vis-à-vis basic scientific research in the postwar era. To understand why requires some historical background.

The U.S. federal government had long been involved in intramural scientific research. The U.S. Geological Survey was established in 1879, the National Bureau of Standards in 1901, the Public Health Service in 1912, and the National Advisory Committee for Astronautics in 1915. Moreover, the federal government had long provided funds, albeit at modest levels, for the Department of Agriculture's program of applied research aimed at helping farmers, work conducted at its network of experiment stations and land-grant colleges. However, when it came to *basic* research, prior to World War II the federal government had little to do with it, either its conduct in its own laboratories or its extramural funding. Basic research was done in the universities and supported intramurally or by philanthropic foundations and private benefactors.

The A-bomb project, however, depended critically on work done by basic researchers from academia. Besides the contribution of the Manhattan Project's head, physicist J. Robert Oppenheimer, eminent academics such as Enrico Fermi, Edward Teller, Hans Bethe, John von Neuman, and Ernest O. Lawrence played important roles in various phases of the effort. An Office of Scientific Research and Development list of the nation's leading nuclear physicsts, drawn up as a recruiting device in early 1943, designated 33 as "leaders in the field." Of these, 20 were working on the Manhattan Project. The same was true of 57 out of 150 physicists designated as "men of ability and considerable experience in the field."[6] The bulk of these physicists had been working in academia before the war. Afterwards, many of them left Los Alamos Laboratory and returned to the universities to pursue basic research problems.

However, given the success of the Manhattan Project and the fact that Europe, for the first time in American history, "could no longer be relied upon to send over a sufficient stream of basic research results relevant to the rapidly changing frontiers of science and technology,"[7] the U.S. government, particularly, but not only, the military, resolved not to lose its productive wartime partnership with science. Indeed, the success of the Manhattan Project led the government to believe that ongoing links with academic basic science would also yield peacetime fruit in areas of national interest other than defense, such as health.

The solution the government devised was to inaugurate in the postwar years the now familiar practice of government grants for basic research in the universities in the hope that the grantee's work would advance the grantor's mission. The government entities most centrally involved in this effort were the Office of Naval Research, the National Institutes of Health, the Atomic Energy Commission, and the newly created National Science Foundation (1950). The traditional independence of academic basic science from the federal government thus underwent a historic change. The key to the Manhattan Project's success, mission-related basic research, became the established pattern of government–university science relations in the postwar period.

Current Situation.   Federal government involvement in funding and performing work in science and technology in the United States has grown rapidly since World War II, until by now it plays a central, enormously influential role. With regard to funding, of the total amount spent on research and development work in 1989 ($130.8 billion [est.] in current dollars), the federal government accounted for almost one half (46.7 percent, or $61.05 billion [est.]). Of that total amount, about one seventh (14.5 percent, or $18.92 billion [est.]) was spent on basic research; over half of that ($10.23 billion [est.]) came from the federal government.[8]

The same holds true if one considers the traditional stronghold of basic research in the United States: the academic world. In 1989, the federal government provided about three fifths ($5,4 of $9.4 billion [est.]) of the money expended in academia on basic research, the rest coming from university and college funds, other nonprofit institutions, and private industry. As with academic basic research, so with academic research and development as a whole: In 1988, universities and colleges continued to be heavily dependent on the federal government for funding support (60 percent, or $7.8 billion of $13.0 billion [est.] of academic research and development funds were provided by the federal government).[9]

Not surprisingly, given these figures, the federal government exerts a powerful directive influence on both the total research and development and basic research enterprises in the United States. For example, about one third of the research and development monies expended in the private industrial sector in the United States in 1989 ($31.1 of $93.8 billion [est.]) came from the federal government, primarily in the form of contracts to carry out mostly applied research and development tasks that the government deemed high priority.[10] As for academia, in 1987 the National Institutes of Health and the Department of Defense were the top two government agencies in terms of amount of money obligated for academic research and development, the latter edging out the National Science Foundation for second place.[11] The focused missions of these two (and four other) government agencies thus powerfully shape the contours of U.S. academic research and development, a far cry from the pre–World War II situation.

While the federal government does not perform nearly as great a percentage of the country's total research and development work as it funds, it is still a major player and controlling influence. In dollar terms, in 1989 the U.S. federal government did about 11 percent ($15 billion) of the nation's research and development work.[12] This work was carried out in numerous mission-oriented government facilities, such as the Lawrence Livermore Laboratory, devoted to weapons research, the laboratories of the National Institutes of Health, and various NASA research and space-flight centers.

Recent Important Cases of Government Funding of Science and Technology.

Two of the most important government research and development undertakings of the last two decades are the Strategic Defense Initiative (SDI), or "Star Wars" project, and the Space Transportation System, or "Space Shuttle" project. The former, formally initiated by President Reagan in March 1983, is devoted to developing a space-based weapons system able to destroy thousands of enemy ballistic missiles shortly after launch. The latter, begun under President Nixon in 1972, was established to develop a means of routinizing transportation of people and cargo between earth and a projected future space station.

Both examples are typical of Big Science and Technology projects. Estimates of the amount of money required for research and development sufficient to establish the mere *feasibility* of a Star Wars system have run as high as $25 billion. The estimated $3 billion price tag for a new orbiter built in the wake of the *Challenger* disaster aside, NASA space shuttle–related expenditures between 1972 and 1986 have amounted to more than $31 billion.[13] The personnel- and resource-intensive nature of these multiyear projects, coupled with tightening federal budgets, has clearly exerted a focal influence on America's research and development activity. In the case of SDI, a substantial portion of the funding for research currently being done by academics in physics, electrical engineering, and computer science originates with the government's Strategic Defense

Initiative Organization and is funneled through the Departments of Defense and Energy. In industry the same focusing effect exists: In 1987, 59.2 percent of federal obligations for basic research in this sector came from NASA, followed by the Department of Defense which accounted for 14.1 percent.[14] The electrical equipment and aircraft and missile industries received most of these funds.[15]

Outstanding Issues and Problems. Issues under debate concerning government funding and performance of science and technology work in the United States include the skewing effect of the Big Science and Technology trend on American research and development as a whole; the relative portions of national research and development expenditures devoted to defense-related and nondefense-related efforts in different industrialized countries; the level of federal support for instrument and plant expenses associated with academic research and development activities; and the lack of a coherent, carefully prioritized government science and technology policy.

The number of exceedingly costly Big Science and Technology projects put forward and approved for federal funding or performance seems to have increased in recent years. In 1987 and 1988 alone, the U.S. government commenced funding a space station (projected cost: $13–$30 billion); a superconducting supercollider ($4–$6 billion); and a hypersonic jet aircraft ($3–$12 billion). Moreover, in 1988 the National Research Council, the operating agency of the National Academy of Sciences and the National Academy of Engineering, urged government funding for a 15-year effort to sequence the human genome ($3 billion), while other researchers proposed that a test reactor be constructed to explore the feasibility of practical nuclear fusion for the purpose of providing electrical energy ($1 billion).

Some observers hold that the enormous pricetags of such projects are not surprising given the extraordinary levels of complexity, performance, or scale involved in the projects. According to them, future megaprojects that aim to improve upon current or projected ones are likely to be even more costly. Others, including some eminent scientists, have criticized the trend toward megaprojects. They contend that given contemporary budgetary realities, federal science and technology funding is effectively a "zero-sum game." Funding such megaprojects has the effect of denying capital funding to less visible, less grandiose small projects. Nobel laureate Philip Anderson contends that "Science in the U.S. is dying of gigantism.... Big projects are the worst way to arrive at basic discoveries."[16] Yet, on occasion, the abstractions of theoretical physicists had as their points of departure data provided by large-scale particle accelerators and telescopes. Nonetheless, the suspicion is growing that science's drive to understand nature definitively may run into a stone wall in the form of budgetary rather than intellectual limits—a fate unimagined by Enlightenment optimists.

A second important issue concerning government's influence on science and technology revolves around the fact that while the percentage of the U.S. gross national product devoted to research and development (2.77 percent in 1987) is comparable to or exceeds the figures for its Western industrialized competitors, when one looks at *nondefense*-related research and development expenditures as a percentage of the gross national product, a less comforting result appears. The percentages for both the Federal Republic of Germany (2.6 percent in 1986) and Japan (2.75 percent in 1985) greatly exceed that of the United States (1.88 percent in 1987), a trend running back as far as 1971.[17] Indeed, this latter trend appears to be worsening. Whereas from 1972 through 1981, federal expenditures for nondefense research and development exceeded those for defense, since 1982 the reverse has been the case. Indeed, it is estimated that in 1988 fully two thirds of federal research and development spending was for defense-related projects.[18]

Some commentators believe that this situation bodes ill for future U.S. economic competitiveness and urge a substantial change in sectoral research and development allocations. Others argue that allies who benefit from U.S. defense capabilities should increase their own defense-related research and development expenditures and point to beneficial civilian economic "fallout" from military research and development work.

A third issue arising out of government's controlling influence on science and technology arises from the fact that contemporary research and development work, even if not part of any megaproject, is apt to be equipment-intensive. The issue in question involves the relation between the quality of the research and development work done in the academic sector and the spiraling cost of the infrastructure that makes that work possible (i.e., the instruments, equipment, and facilities with and in which research and development work is carried out on campus). The salient fact is that during the last 20 years, federal capital investment in academic science and engineering has declined greatly in relation to support for research projects. While federal expenditures for equipment used in academic research and development have risen somewhat since 1980, spending for academic science and engineering facilities has dropped dramatically and almost continuously since 1965—from over $360 million in 1965 to just over $52 million in 1984 (in 1986 constant-dollar terms).[19] This has generated acrimonious disputes between cognizant university and government officials over the "indirect cost rate" to be charged to the government by the institutions performing government-funded research and development—for example, for the depreciation of university-built and -maintained facilities in which federally funded research and development work is carried out.

Government has resisted the attempt by leading private universities to compensate for what they regard as infrastructural losses by negotiating ever-higher levels of indirect cost recovery. Congress has attempted to deal with the widely recognized inadequacy of facilities for research and development by launching a program of direct appropriations for specific facilities projects. It has done so, in the view of the major private research universities, on geopolitical grounds rather than on the basis of peer assessments of quality. For their part, government funding agencies wish to maximize the amount of research and development obtained from limited budgets and to avoid becoming more dependent on the leading research universities. The latter, however, contend that present government funding policies pose a threat to the quality of the research and development work they are able to produce. They are put in the position of having to choose between dipping deeper into their own institutional pockets or retreating from the forefront of research.

A fourth vexing issue about government funding of science and technology is implicit in some of the foregoing: the fact that the federal government seems to lack a coherent, long-term, carefully prioritized science and technology policy. Commentators of this persuasion contend that both science and government make up their wish lists in a vacuum and refuse to recognize the zero-sum consequences of proposing a proliferating number of costly ventures in the current budgetary environment. This "approach," they hold, vitiates the social control of science and technology, whether the would-be controller is the public, whose preferences are to be solicited and respected, or government decision makers, who have their own agendas.

Indicative of the federal government's loss of meaningful control over science and technology is the paltry state of advice-giving to the executive. The White House Office of Science and Technology Policy, a far cry from President Eisenhower's influential advisory committee of nonpolitical professional scientists, has in recent years exerted little influence on the executive branch's science and technology policy-making. Consequently, when diverse unprioritized megaprojects favored by the executive branch are presented serially to Congress for funding approval, all tend to be cut back instead of some being fully funded and others denied.[20]

Product Liability Litigation

Watershed.   A third important mode of societal control of science and technology is that of product liability litigation. Whether the product in question is a drug, an industrial chemical, a device, an appliance, or a building structure, under certain conditions its producers can be found liable for distributing or installing it and can be made to pay compensatory and, possibly, punitive damages. This form of societal control of science and technology does not affect only producers actually found liable. Through awareness of such suits and their outcomes, most producers have institutionalized safety concerns—most often assigning responsibility for product safety to a corporate "risk manager" precisely in order to avoid being the objects of such litigation.[21] In this way, the controlling influence of product liability suits has been greatly magnified.

At present, there are in the English-speaking world four generally recognized grounds on which a manufacturer can be found liable for one of its products: negligence, breach of warranty, misrepresentation, and strict liability. A manufacturer of goods is *negligent* when reasonable care is not taken in the design, production, assembly, or testing of a product that inflicts foreseeable harm on someone. A *breach of warranty* obtains when a product fails to fit the purpose for which it was intended (implied warranty) or fails to measure up to any explicit promise or claim made by the manufacturer (express warranty). *Misrepresentation* occurs when the manufacturer's advertising or promotion gives the buyer a false sense of security about the product, either by intentionally concealing potential hazards or by negligently failing to represent its hazards explicitly (e.g., by failing to provide appropriate directions and warnings on a medicine container's label). *Strict liability* obtains when a manufacturer, even though not guilty of negligence, is held responsible for producing a product that injures someone who comes in contact with it, where the injury is caused by a defect in the product that rendered it unreasonably dangerous.[22]

Strict liability represents a landmark in the evolution of product liability theory in the twentieth century. Prior to the industrial era, many product liability actions were ruled out by invoking the traditional doctrine of "privity"—"the rule that an injured person can sue the negligent person only if he or she was a party to the transaction with the injured person."[23] However, with the advance of the industrial era and greater circulation of mass-produced products, pressure grew to abandon the notion that negligent producers were immune to liability action simply because they had not had a direct transaction with the injured party.

While producers were held strictly liable in a few instances in the first half of the twentieth century—most involving food poisoning and inherently dangerous products like dynamite—a watershed case concerning strict liability was decided in 1963 in the California Supreme Court in the case of *Greenman* v. *Yuba Power Products, Inc.*

The plaintiff's wife had bought her husband a power tool as a Christmas present. Two years later he bought the necessary attachments to allow him to use the tool as a lathe. It was while Mr. Greenman was using the tool as a lathe that he was seriously injured. The wood on which he was working flew out and forcefully hit his head. He sued the manufacturer. In its decision the Court effectively gave plaintiffs a new ground for suing manufacturers for distributing defective products—that of strict liability in tort. The Court held that "a manufacturer [is] strictly liable in tort when an article he placed on the market, knowing that it was to be used without inspection for defects, proved to have a defect that caused the injury."[24] Thus, to be found liable, a manufacturer need not be shown to have been negligent or to have breached a warranty or to have misrepresented the safety characteristics of a product. Most states now recognize strict liability as a ground for holding a manufacturer liable, partly in the belief that such a ground will serve as an impetus to businesses to produce safer products.

Current Situation.   Product liability suits filed in U.S. federal courts have proliferated in recent years—from 1,579 in 1975 to 13,554 in 1985.[25] Plaintiffs' grounds vary considerably. A Conference Board poll of 232 major U.S. corporations revealed that of a total of 659 most recent product liability cases, defect in product design was the most frequent allegation (35 percent), followed by failure to warn (23 percent), defect in construction (22 percent), incorrect or insufficient labeling (18 percent), and foreseeable misuse (7 percent).[26] Significantly, however, of these 659 cases, 64 percent were settled out of court, and one quarter were either dismissed or settled in favor of the defendants. Moreover, the average settlement in favor of a plaintiff was on the order of $25,000. These figures suggest that the much-heralded "liability crisis" allegedly facing manufacturers and their insurers and threatening to drive them into insolvency is largely insurance industry hyperbole. Taking advantage of the relatively few highly publicized cases in which big product liability awards were made to plaintiffs, the industry has attempted to induce federal legislators—unsuccessfully as of late 1989—to change liability law so as to make successful suits even less likely than they are at present.[27]

Recent Noteworthy Cases.   Two important recent cases in product liability litigation are those involving the Dalkon Shield intrauterine birth control device and the Ford Pinto.

Between 1971 and 1974, some 2.7 million American women (and up to 1 million women in other countries) bought the A. H. Robins Company's Dalkon Shield intrauterine device (IUD). Subsequently, many of these women claimed to have suffered infertility, birth defects, spontaneous abortions, traumatic infections and other injuries from pelvic infections induced by the device (20 deaths have also been attributed to the Dalkon IUD). By 1985, about 9,500 women had filed and resolved product liability suits against Robins amounting to $530 million (an average settlement of about $55 thousand), more than 5,200 suits were still pending, and new suits were coming in at the rate of 400 per month.[28]

In August 1985, the company filed for protection under Chapter 11 of the U.S. Bankruptcy Code. As part of the bankruptcy reorganization process, supervised by a federal bankruptcy court judge, Robins was directed to conduct an international publicity campaign informing all potential claimants of their right to file claims and of the process for doing so. By June 1988, 330,600 domestic and international claims had been filed, of which about 200,000 included the completed forms required for eligibility. The judge then ordered that the company set aside a trust fund of $2.475 billion to be used to pay plaintiffs whose claims were deemed valid.[29]

The significance of this case is multifold. First, it is a mass-produced-product liability case with hundreds of thousands of claimants. As such, it poses threats to the viability of both the producing company and the legal system charged with handling product liability claims. Second, the case showed that resort to bankruptcy reorganization as a way of limiting a company's liability is not cost-free. Rather than face expensive litigation well into the future with untold thousands of claimants allegedly injured by one of its products, the company had sought to immunize itself by taking refuge in a bankruptcy proceeding. In this way it had hoped to short-circuit years of litigation and avoid incurring any punitive damages. However, the presiding judge required that the company set aside a trust fund he deemed adequate for pending cases and future claimants before the company's assets were distributed to its creditors and shareholders. A third significant aspect of this case is the company's controversial argument that since its IUD device was approved for marketing by the Food and Drug Administration (FDA), it should not be subject to punitive damages, since FDA approval supposedly shows that there was no evidence of the product's lack of safety at the time. Should that argument come to be accepted, no company marketing an FDA-approved product could be found liable for punitive damages. Given the often cozy relationship between the FDA and the industries it is charged with regulating, to give that principle legal force would be highly problematic.

A second noteworthy, relatively recent case is that of *Grimshaw* v. *Ford Motor Co.* In 1978, a California jury awarded a plaintiff $127.8 million in damages (reduced on appeal to $6.3 million) against Ford "as a result of an accident caused when a 1972 Ford Pinto stalled on a freeway and was hit from behind by another car. The gas tank exploded and the Pinto burned, killing the driver and seriously injuring her passenger."[30] In the trial it was brought out that in tests conducted by Ford before the Pinto model was first sold, the gas tank proved vulnerable to leakage when the car was backed into a wall at 20 miles per hour. In other words, the car was produced for sale with a fuel-tank design known to pose a serious risk of harm. It was also shown that the company considered—and rejected—installing a moderately costly safety device ($11 per car) on cost–benefit grounds. The jury, judging the cost of the safety device insignificant, imposed punitive damages on Ford for willful disregard of safety. Like the U.S. Supreme Court decision in the cotton-dust case discussed earlier in this chapter, this case is significant because it held that cost–benefit–risk analysis is not the last word in justification, either in regulatory implementation or in manufacturing decision making.

Outstanding Issues and Problems.   An important, perplexing, and unresolved issue in the field of product liability lies in the difficulty of establishing the cause or causes of certain harms suffered by humans—for example, harms attributed to toxic chemical substances. The difficulty may be one of determining (1) *whether* a given plaintiff or class of plaintiffs were in fact injured by a product to which they were exposed, or (2) *which* of several companies producing a generic product shown to have been harmful was responsible for the injury suffered.

The first kind of difficulty, involving determination of cause, is illustrated in the case of Agent Orange, an herbicidal defoliant containing dioxin to which hundreds of thousands of servicemen, U.S. and Vietnamese, were exposed during the war in Vietnam. Many American servicemen or their survivors claimed that they were killed or disabled as a consequence of their exposure to the toxin. In 1984, Vietnam Veterans Agent Orange Victims, Inc., filed a class action suit on behalf of as many as 250,000 Vietnam veterans and surviving family members against seven manufacturers of the herbicide. The suit ended in a $180 million out-of-court settlement without any admission by the manufacturers that their product had in fact caused the veterans' health problems. The federal district judge in whose court the original suit was litigated held that it was scientifically and legally infeasible to link the veterans' health problems to Agent Orange exposure. The judge decided that awards would be made on the degree of disability incurred, regardless of cause.

However, lawyers for some 300 of the plaintiffs sought and obtained a stay blocking distribution of the funds on the grounds that the plan "failed to connect the veterans' ailments to their exposure to Agent Orange,"[31] a key contention of their case. Eventually, appeals courts and ultimately the U.S. Supreme Court dismissed the veterans' lawsuits and let the distribution plan stand. The ironic upshot of this case is that causal "proof" is not necessary for a plaintiff to extract compensation in a product liability suit. Indeed, where the product is a chemical to which plaintiffs were exposed, and where plaintiffs' injuries emerged only long after the fact, scientific proof may well be less relevant than considerations of public relations and the terms of manufacturers' insurance policies.

The second difficulty arose in the case of diethylstilbestrol (DES), an FDA-approved drug prescribed from the late 1940s to the mid 1970s to prevent miscarriage. Today DES is held responsible for over 300 cases of cancer in daughters of mothers who had taken the drug while pregnant. Prior to 1980, in order to win a product liability suit, a "DES daughter" had to be able to show which company produced the DES her mother took while pregnant, something often impossible to do. In 1980, in California, in the DES case of *Sindell* v. *Abbott Laboratories*, in the absence of definitive proof that the plaintiff's injury had been caused by exposure to a particular company's DES product, a new "market share doctrine of product liability" was promulgated by the court. Under this doctrine, damages were apportioned among all companies manufacturing the drug at the time in accordance with their respective shares of the DES market at the time of injury.[32]

Mechanisms for Environmental and Technological Assessment.

Product liability litigation is first and foremost a post-facto form of SCOST. It is activated *after* alleged effects of products on people claiming to have been injured by them come to light. Some government regulations come into play before the fact—-for example, those that require that certain design criteria be met or testing provisions be carried out *before* a product or system is licensed to be sold on the market or allowed to commence operations. In the early 1970s, distinctive new forms of prior control were enacted. Unlike FDA and Federal Aviation Administration (FAA) regulation of new drugs, medical devices, and aircraft, these prior forms of social control did not rely upon experimental laboratory or field testing. They rely instead on nonexperimental projective studies and attend to concerns other than safety and health, including ones of a social and cultural nature.

Watershed.   In the closing years of the war in Vietnam, Congress passed a piece of landmark legislation aimed at fostering more environmentally sound decision making, including decisions about environment-related matters with significant scientific or technological components. A central purpose of the National Environmental Policy Act of 1969 (NEPA) was to "declare a national policy which will encourage productive and enjoyable harmony between man and his environment."[33] To that end, Congress directed that in "every recommendation or report on proposals for legislation and other major Federal actions significantly affecting the quality of the human environment," all cognizant agencies of the federal government must include a detailed account of the likely environmental consequences of the proposed action, specification of feasible alternatives to the proposed action, and projections of anticipated losses in natural resources.[34] Such mandated prospective analyses came to be referred to as *environmental impact statements* (EIS).

Of particular importance is the fact that the EIS of a government agency initiating or funding a project that might substantially alter the environment—human-made as well as natural—can be challenged in court as inadequate. If the court agrees with the plaintiff (e.g., a civic or environmental group), the proposed activity can be temporarily blocked until a satisfactory revised impact analysis is carried out and approved. If the EIS indicates that a creature currently on the government's "endangered species list" will be rendered extinct, then the project can be permanently prohibited.

For example, in 1972 the Tennessee Valley Authority's huge Tellico Dam project was challenged in court because the EIS disclosed that completion of the dam would have destroyed the only known habitat of the three-inch snail darter fish. After six years of litigation, the U.S. Supreme Court voted six to three in 1978 to bar completion of the $144 million dam. This decision would have permanently halted the project before the damming up of the Little Tennessee River had not Congress succumbed to political pressure and enacted *ad hoc* legislation permitting exceptions to the rule prohibiting projects that would extinguish an endangered species. Exceptions were permitted when "a project's benefits outweigh the value of preserving a species,"[35] a formulation conducive to contrived cost-benefit analyses.

Three years later, Congress passed a second, related piece of landmark legislation: the Technology Assessment Act of 1972. Its rationale lay in the recognition of a growing disjunction between the new technological reality and the old political order. Technology had undergone enormous expansion in the post-World War II era. Its pace of change and the scale and pervasiveness of its effects seemed to have markedly increased. In fostering and regulating that potent driving force, the executive branch, "resplendent in scientific resources," was confronting Congress with a "deluge of technological proposals," ones with which Congress felt itself unable to deal intelligently.[36] As Representative Charles Mosher observed during the 1972 debate preceding passage of the Act:

> [W]e in the Congress are constantly outmanned and outgunned by the expertise of the Executive agencies. We desperately need a stronger source of professional advice and information more immediately and entirely responsible to the demands of our own committees.[37]

Lack of an independent source of information about the proposals for science- and technology-related legislation put forward by the executive branch was crippling

Congress's ability to carry out its constitutional duty responsibly. Some in Congress even felt that the way Congress was forced to decide upon matters technological prior to 1972 constituted an unacceptable tilting of the balance of governmental power toward the executive branch. The problem faced by legislators and a solution for mitigating it were cogently put by Mosher:

> Nearly every congressional committee today is forced to make extremely important decisions which include significant technology components, and that will be increasingly so as we move ahead. We increasingly contemplate projects that require huge expenditures of public funds, projects that would have huge social, environmental, health, or economic impacts, not very readily evident to us. There is, therefore, a crucial need that we know better and assess more accurately those impacts, before we vote our decisions. We can accomplish that effectively only by the use of highly competent skilled systems analysis techniques—supplementing the common horse sense and practical instincts on which we traditionally depend.[38]

The passage of the Technology Assessment Act brought into being an Office of Technology Assessment (OTA) as an analytical, investigative arm of Congress. OTA's task was to identify existing and probable impacts, including unintended consequences, of technological innovations and developments, and policy alternatives to proposed or existing courses of technological action. With an OTA, members of Congress could "utilize this information, wherever appropriate, as one factor, in the legislative assessment of matters pending before the Congress particularly in those instances where the Federal Government may be called upon to consider support for, or management or regulation of, technological applications."[39] OTA does not make recommendations on technology policy. It is charged only with "disentangling knotty technical issues" with the aim of making Congressional debate on such complex matters more informed and rational.[40] OTA's creation was "a step toward matching changes in governance to the changes—both in *pace* of life and *scale* requirements—wrought by technology."[41]

Current Situation.   EISs continue to be required for all government projects that might substantially alter the natural or human-made environment. They are often challenged in court, sometimes successfully, by public interest groups that are concerned with the environment.[42] Given the time—sometimes years—necessary to complete a satisfactory EIS for some projects, temporary injunctions against proceeding on the basis of EIS inadequacies can assume the force of permanent prohibitions.

In 1988, OTA employed about 90 analysts and 60 support staff members to meet requests from Congress for analyses of the positive and negative physical and social consequences of and alternatives to existing or proposed courses of technological action. In addition, OTA's budget allows it to engage the services of several thousand outside specialists each year to work on commissioned projects. One important effect of the existence of OTA reports commissioned by Congress on controversial topics is that the executive branch no longer uniquely frames the terms of or monopolizes technical information sources feeding into government debates on such issues via release of the position papers generated by its own agencies.

Recent Noteworthy Cases.   One of the most influential government decisions revolving around an EIS in recent years occurred in the 10-year struggle over Westway, a proposed 4.2-mile, multibillion-dollar highway and real estate development project along the west side of Manhattan Island from 42nd Street to the Battery. The project was first proposed in 1974. Its path was complex and tortuous. However, a pivotal episode in its 11-year saga was the revocation in 1982 by a federal district court judge of a license, granted by the Army Corps of Engineers, to dredge and then fill the Hudson River to provide land for the project. The judge held that the EIS was deficient in not adequately assessing the impact of the landfill project on the river's striped bass population.

In an attempt to remedy its EIS, the Army Corps of Engineers subsequently carried out a 4-month study of this impact and concluded in a supplementary EIS that although there would be a "perceptible" impact on the fish, it would be "minor" and "[would] not threaten their survival." However, following a 1985 hearing on the Corps's revised EIS for the new landfill project permit it had issued, the same judge held that the revised EIS contained insufficient data to justify its analysis, that the projected impact on the fish forecast in the final version of the EIS was unaccountably weaker than that indicated in the draft version, and that the Corps had acknowledged that there were viable transportation alternatives to the project that would not exact the same environmental costs. The judge issued a ruling, later upheld unanimously by a U.S. appeals court, permanently barring the landfill permit from being granted, a step which ultimately led to cancellation of the project. The procedural safeguard of the EIS, institutionalized by the National Environmental Policy Act of 1969, thus proved pivotal in the fate of a huge urban transportation and real estate development project that would have transformed the face of the Manhattan waterfront.[43]

As for recent OTA analyses, none stands out as singularly or decisively influential. However, noteworthy OTA reports for Congress in recent years have included analyses of the effects of nuclear war, information technology and its impact on American education, applied genetics, technology and structural employment, hazardous waste, intellectual property rights in the age of electronics and information, manufacturing and the U. S. trade deficit problem, the feasibility and survivability of the SDI space-based ballistic missile defense system, the education of scientists and engineers in the United States, and government biotechnology funding.

Outstanding Issues and Problems.   One problem with reliance on an EIS as a way of promoting responsible forecasts of the effects of science- and technology-intensive projects is the same as the problem in the case of regulation. Government executives can instruct the heads of executive-branch or "independent" agencies sympathetic to the political agenda of those who appointed them to prepare truncated or skewed EISs in hopes of easing or blocking passage of environmentally disruptive projects. However, it is noteworthy that EISs must be available to the public and can be subjected to scrutiny in legal proceedings aimed at challenging their adequacy. Depending on the acumen and impartiality of hearing judges, this provision offers a measure of protection against efforts to manipulate the procedural safeguard of the EIS.

One problem voiced with the assessments and other studies produced by the OTA lies in the fact that they are devoid of recommendations, a feature that has contributed to OTA's nonpartisan image. A legislator-member of OTA's congressional board, while acknowledging that the agency provides Congress "with useful material, a distillation of the best knowledge on a subject and a list of policy options that Congress might adopt," contends that what Congress needs at least as much as information and alternatives is "clear strategic advice."[44] There is merit in this claim.

Even given OTA information and alternatives, the task of deciding upon a direction in which to proceed is left to Congress members and their nontechnical staff. However, providing advice would clearly be a difficult task and could put OTA's reputation for nonpartisan analysis at risk.

Public Participation

One of the most interesting developments in the SCOST during the past two decades has been the gradually increasing role of the public. This growing involvement has been brought about in several ways: first, by formal governmental efforts to inform the general public about specific, often contentious scientific and technological matters; second, by measures to better inform government about the views of the public on specific matters scientific and technological (e.g., through public participation in legislative hearings, government advisory boards, and commissions of inquiry); third, by ensuring that the views of the public are taken into account in processes of administrative and regulatory decision making involving science and technology; and fourth, by efforts to involve the public more directly in science and technology policy making (e.g., via referenda, citizen initiatives, and citizen review boards).[45]

Watersheds.   There have been noteworthy cases of public participation in each of the first three categories. However, the most striking developments pertain to the fourth: referenda, citizen initiatives, and citizen advisory boards, whether at the national, state, or local level. Most of the landmark cases of this sort in the last two decades concern technological developments, with nuclear power plants and high-rise buildings being the most popular targets.

In various states and countries, citizens have been asked to approve or disapprove of the start-up, continuation, expansion, or restriction either of nuclear power in general or of particular facilities. Two historically influential developments of this type were a 1978 national referendum in Austria and a 1976 citizen initiative in the state of California, both concerned with nuclear power. In the former, Austrian voters rejected government plans to put into operation the nation's first nuclear power plant, construction of which had begun in 1968. This vote, in the face of Chancellor Bruno Kreisky's threat to resign if the plant were not allowed to commence operations, dealt a death blow to the prospects for nuclear power in Austria for the foreseeable future.

In the latter, almost 4 million Californians voted two to one against "Proposition 15," a measure which would have required that California electrical utilities clearly demonstrate the complete safety of nuclear power facilities in the state *before* being allowed to operate. The Proposition 15 campaign, though unsuccessful, was an important development in SCOST in the United States. It launched a series of citizen initiatives in various states against nuclear power whose margins of defeat became smaller over time. This process culminated in June 1989, when residents of Sacramento, California, approved a landmark citizen initiative to shut down Rancho Seco, the city's problem-plagued, financially troubled nuclear power plant. This was the first time in American history that voters decided to close a working nuclear reactor.

A landmark series of citizen initiatives concerning high-rise office buildings also occurred in California. The first citizen initiative in U.S. history proposing to impose height limits on proliferating downtown high-rise office buildings ("Manhattanization") appeared on the San Francisco city ballot in 1971. However, while it, too, was resoundingly defeated—by about a four-to-one margin—it marked the onset of a process of slowly growing citizen discontent. After a series of five unsuccessful follow-up anti-high-rise initiatives, in which the margin of defeat became progressively slimmer, in November 1986 San Francisco voters passed the landmark "Proposition M," a citizen initiative which imposed the most stringent limitations on urban high-rise growth ever enacted in the United States, including an annual "cap" on the total amount of new office space permitted to be constructed in San Francisco.

As for science, a landmark episode involving the citizen-review-board form of direct public participation in science and technology decision making unfolded in the mid-1970s in Cambridge, Massachusetts. Some residents had become concerned over the implications for public health and safety of recombinant-DNA research being conducted within city limits at Harvard University and the Massachusetts Institute of Technology. The Cambridge City Council authorized its city manager to appoint a "Cambridge Experimentation Review Board" to assess the adequacy of the safety procedures then required by the government funding agency, the National Institutes of Health. The board, comprising eight nonscientist Cambridge residents, spent 4 months hearing testimony, visiting laboratories, reviewing published records, and holding a kind of "science court" in which teams of opposing scientists made their cases and responded to questions from review board members. The board concluded that the DNA research should be allowed to continue. In its final report to the city council, however, it recommended "broader public representation on the university biohazards committees required by [National Institutes of Health] guidelines" and that "a separate Cambridge biohazards committee be set up to oversee all research in the city."[46] The Cambridge citizen review board set a precedent for a number of similar entities empaneled in various communities around the United States.

Current Situation and Noteworthy Recent Cases.   At present, public participation in decision making involving science- and technology-related issues seems to have become institutionalized. For example, U.S. government guidelines on DNA research now require that existing "institutional biosafety committees"—required by the National Institutes of Health for all institutions that receive funds from it for DNA research—"draw 20 percent of their members from the general public having no connection with the institution where the research is being performed."[47] Similarly, in England, a national Genetic Manipulation Advisory Group was established by the government in 1977. Its membership of 19 represents a broad array of interests, including scientific and medical (8 members), employee (4 members), industrial (1 member), academic (1 member), and public (5 members).[48]

As regards forms of direct public participation, the California penchant for citizen initiatives, sometimes involving scientific and technological issues or developments, has continued apace. Referenda on nuclear power facilities continue to be held, and more are slated for the future. In the United States, the trend seems to be to oppose nuclear power in general by attempting to close particular facilities on grounds of safety and high cost of power produced. Internationally, part of the fallout from the Chernobyl disaster has been new national referenda on nuclear power. For example, in November 1987, Italian voters overwhelmingly approved three nationwide referenda designed to limit the development of nuclear energy. Local governments will no longer receive subsidies for allowing plants to be built in their areas, site selection will not be able to be unilaterally imposed by the central government, and Italy will no longer contribute money or personnel for nuclear energy development elsewhere in Europe.[49]

There has been one major recent science-related referendum in the United States. In November 1986, Californians overwhelmingly passed a far-reaching citizen initiative prompted by the widespread presence of synthetic chemical substances in contemporary industrial life. "Proposition 65" (the Safe Drinking Water and Toxics Enforcement Act) requires businesses either to prove that their products and emissions are safe or to provide "clear and reasonable [public] warning[s]" that they contain or emit chemical substances that may cause cancer, birth defects, or other reproductive harm. The law also prohibits any business from knowingly discharging into drinking-water sources chemicals not known to be safe or not proven to pose "no significant risk" of human cancer and to have "no observable effect" in promoting birth defects at 1,000 times the level of expected consumer exposure. Fines for violations of these provisions run up to $2,500 per day per exposure, and the law offers citizens who successfully sue violators 25 percent of the fines levied.[50]

Two things are striking about this citizen-initiative exercise in SCOST. First, control is exercised by shifting the burden of proof from "innocent until proven guilty" to "guilty until proven innocent." Manufacturers and would-be chemical waste disposers are required to do the work of self-control to serve the asserted social value of public health promotion or preservation. Second, it is evident that implementation of the law and the degree to which it imposes a burden on commerce will depend critically on the precise operational meanings given to vague phrases such as *"clear and reasonable* warnings" and "no *significant* risk."

Outstanding Unresolved Issues and Problems.   Citizen initiatives, particularly on the state level, are not without problems. Well-endowed private parties with vested interests in the outcomes (e.g., industry associations) can commit substantial amounts of money to support their side, typically many times more money than is available to the citizen groups who launched or support the initiative. Such tactics can sometimes effectively "buy" the desired outcome. Further, voters are called upon to vote simply "yes" or "no" on complex, multifaceted technical issues. Unlike legislative deliberations, opportunity for refining an initiative often comes only after its defeat. Supporters must once again undertake to get the revised version before the voters in a future election. Finally, some have expressed concern that the proliferation of citizen initiatives threatens to vitiate representative government. To this it may be rejoined that there are some issues for which, in the face of legislative diffidence or co-optation by vested interests, the citizen initiative is a valuable, if sometimes crude, tool of last resort. It may send a loud message to legislators about the depth of the public's concern and its wish that changes be made in the practices and priorities sanctioned by the reigning socio-technical paradigm.

Legislative Limits on Science and Technology

The sixth and last mode of SCOST we will consider is that of legislative limits on scientific and technological innovations. Such limits take a number of forms, from categorical or effective prohibitions on the undertaking or carrying through of certain scientific or technological developments to restrictions affecting whether or in what ways the products of certain scientific or technological research and development endeavors may be used.

Landmarks.   The last two decades have witnessed several landmark episodes in the history of legislative limitation of science and technology. The most striking American example of the federal government's deciding effectively to terminate a technological development of long standing—one widely viewed as a case of techno-logical progress—is that of the commercial supersonic transport (SST) aircraft. In 1971, in the face of strong pressure from industrial forces and appeals from the executive branch that American leadership in the aerospace industry was at stake, both houses of Congress voted against providing any more government money—beyond the $839 million already spent—for developing an American commercial SST. This decision left the area of commercial supersonic air transport for the foreseeable future to the Soviet TU-144 and the Anglo-French Concorde.

The watershed importance of this vote, later sustained against an effort to resurrect and extend government funding, is that the idea of the so-called technological imperative—that is, the idea that that which *can* be done, *will* be done—was revealed as a vulnerable social construct, not a true description of an immutable reality. Economic and environmental concerns—noise and alleged threats to the protective ozone layer—carried the day in the thinking of a sufficient number of legislators to override considerations of corporate profit and national prestige.

One of the most important post-World War II science-related legislative prohibitions is that mandated by a clause incorporated in three amendments to the Food, Drug, and Cosmetic Act approved by Congress between 1958 and 1968. The "Delaney clause," a provision introduced by Congressman James J. Delaney, forbids the inclusion in food, drugs, or cosmetics, of any additives shown to be carcinogenic in humans or laboratory animals.

The strict wording of the Delaney amendment—the FDA is required to ban ingredients containing even trace levels of carcinogens; that is, it must employ a so-called zero-risk standard—has been controversial. Considering the categorical wording of the Delaney amendment scientifically outdated, the FDA opted to reinter-pret the Delaney clause as containing an implicit minimal-risk exception. Thus products with trace levels of carcinogens were allowed to escape banning if they could be shown to pose "no significant risk" to humans.

This move generated intensive litigation by consumer and health groups seeking to enforce the strict wording of the Delaney amendment. Consider, for example, the case of color additives. Since 1960 the FDA has been considering a list of 200 manufactured color additives. By 1985 all but 10 either had been approved for use in foods, drugs, and cosmetics or had been banned from the market. However, the FDA had given the 10 remaining dyes numerous extensions—as many as 26 in 25 years—of the original dates set by Congress in 1960 for final resolution of their market status. During these extensions, these additives were permitted to remain on the market.

In October 1987, a federal appeals court, in a suit brought by Public Citizen Health Research Group, a consumer watchdog organization, ruled that the FDA's "no significant risk" standard was not in accord with the terms of the Delaney clause adopted by Congress. It thus prohibited further use, in food, cosmetics, or drugs, of 2 of the remaining 10 color additives known to be carcinogens but held by the FDA to pose minimal risk to humans.[51] The importance of this ruling lies, not in the barring of 2 more additives, but in upholding the letter of a rigorous legislative prohibition against a more permissive regulatory reinterpretation.

Current Situation.   Congress has traditionally been disinclined to categorically prohibit or terminate technological innovations. If anything, it has been even less inclined to prohibit the undertaking of particular scientific experiments. However, several things have combined to bring about important changes in these positions. Regarding technology, the enormous price tags and long times required to complete many contemporary technological endeavors, combined with competition from attractive, high-priority alternatives, have on occasion made midstream abandonment of some such projects seem advisable to the very legislative bodies that authorized their initiation.

An even more potent new factor has been the rise, growth, and sustained strength of the environmental movement. In trying to explain the unprecedented abandonment of the American SST project, the dawning recognition that such an aircraft was neither necessary nor particularly economical in its use of fuel was an important factor. Also contributing to its cancellation, however, was the heightened environmental awareness that had emerged by the late 1960s and perhaps also the increased sensitivity to unequal distributions of the benefits and costs of technologies engendered by the war in Vietnam. With consideration of such factors now legitimate in Big Technology decision making, such projects have become vulnerable in ways previously unthinkable.

Regarding science, as long as *science* meant *the physical sciences*, then prior to the dawn of the age of Big Science, categorical prohibition or forced discontinuation of scientific experiments by a legislature was inconceivable. However, with the rapid growth in the post–World War II era of the life sciences (particularly molecular biology and genetics), the explosion of biomedical research on new beginnings to life, and delicate experimentation involving human subjects, not only have government regulations for such science emerged but legislative bodies have been asked to seriously consider various kinds of bans or forced discontinuations of research. Such was the case in the late 1980s and will probably remain so for the foreseeable future.

Noteworthy Recent Cases and Developments.   Areas of scientific research that have elicited proposed legislative bans in the last decade are reproductive biology, embryology, and genetics. National government advisory committees, local legislative bodies, and private citizen and religious groups, both in the United States and in Western European countries, have in recent years proposed legislative bans on research into modifying human genetics in ways able to be passed on to future generations, certain embryo and fetal tissue experiments, the production of transgenic animal species via genetic manipulation, and surrogate motherhood.

Significantly, few, if any, of these proposed bans have been enacted on a national level. Local legislative bodies have, moreover, reacted in quite different ways. Even where bans have been enacted locally, to date none has been adopted in the categorical manner envisioned by some proponents. Typically, the kind of research at issue is not prohibited per se, but rather banned unless it meets certain specified conditions. Thus it is not surrogate motherhood per se that was the subject of a number of proposed and several enacted legislative bans in 1988, but *commercial* surrogate motherhood— cases in which money was paid to the surrogate by the commissioning parents. Similarly, Britain has not categorically banned research on "spare" embryos left over from in vitro fertilization treatments. However, Parliament has considered banning research on embryos beyond 14 days after fertilization, as recommended in a government-commissioned report.[52]

A similar trend is apparent in the case of a number of recent controversial technologies. For example, in 1988 the U.S. Congress enacted legislation restricting the polygraph device. The machine was not banned outright, but rather its use, particularly for screening job applicants, was restricted to situations in which certain specified conditions are met. For example, polygraph use for screening private-sector job applicants is permitted only if the firm is one of a number of particularly sensitive kinds of businesses specifically exempted from the ban (e.g., firms involved in intelligence work for the government, private security, drug manufacture, radioactive waste transport or disposal, and the like). Such exceptions aside, polygraph testing of private-sector job applicants is strictly prohibited.

As noted earlier, SCOST can take positive as well as negative forms. This is true in legislative as well as executive initiatives. The denial of further funding for an American SST was tantamount to banning its development. In effect, this was a negative, or "keeping from doing," form of control. However, the 1988 decision by the U.S. National Institutes of Health (NIH) to reverse its previously announced termination of its long-standing effort to develop a total, implantable artifical heart reflected a positive, or "compelling to do," form of SCOST. In the wake of the announcement by the NIH that it was terminating its 25-year-old, $239 million effort, influential senators from states that would have been affected economically by the discontinuation threatened to introduce legislation to block funding for all new programs at the National Institutes of Health until all long-term commitments to previous programs, including the artificial heart, had been fulfilled.[53] This threat compelled the NIH to reverse itself and agree to continue its $22 million per year artificial heart research and development program.

Outstanding Issues and Problems.   A number of important vexing issues raised by legislative limitations on science and technology remain unresolved. First, in the post–World War II period, tension has grown between academic freedom, including freedom of scientific inquiry, and the fact that science, particularly, but not only, the life sciences, is now entering domains of great social sensitivity, including the manipulation of human life. This has begun to put pressure on the right to freedom of scientific inquiry. At this juncture, the outcome and consequences of this budding struggle are as uncertain as they are weighty.

Some scholars hold that by now the only question is not *whether* scientific freedom of inquiry will be circumscribed, but *who* the participants in the control process will be, *what* control mechanisms will be used, and *to what effect*. The combination of the often culturally delicate subject matter of burgeoning and emerging fields of scientific research, the growing price tags of technology-intensive scientific research (not just megaprojects), and the resultant central role of government- (read: taxpayer-) provided funding makes the probability of imposition of limits even on basic scientific research increasingly likely. We will return to the contentious issue of freedom of scientific inquiry in Chapter 15.

Second, the interplay of annual legislative budget cycles, the changing memberships of legislative bodies, the vicissitudes of public opinion, and the long-term funding needs of Big Science and Technology projects has engendered a dilemma. If funding for Big Science and Technology projects is guaranteed only annually, then such projects are precarious until they are so far along that the "it-would-be-absurd-to-stop-now" argument can be invoked to carry the day, as it was in the protracted struggle over Tellico Dam. Moreover, to diminish that precariousness, project corners may be cut, thereby compromising safety, quality, or yield. The yearly funding-related pressure to choose a "cheap" orbiter design for the ill-fated space shuttle *Challenger* is a sobering case in point.

On the other hand, if funding for a whole project is to be "locked in" at the outset, then a legislature may be more reluctant to provide such a guarantee. Total a priori funding guarantees would preclude midstream changes of course reflecting subsequent shifts in societal priorities. Thus, the nature of much contemporary science and technology—the big scale and long duration of many of its projects—and the fact that research and development funding is so dependent on the federal government have combined to impale legislators on the horns of a dilemma: Keep long-lasting projects in a state of quasi-permanent insecurity or decide with fingers crossed on total funding needs at the outset, thereby compromising democratic decision making downstream.

Third, as the case of the Delaney clause illustrated, increasingly sophisticated scientific instrumentation can render categorical or crude legislative prohibitions problematic. This too can engender a dilemma. On the one hand, the scope of bans formulated at an earlier, more rudimentary stage of instrument development will increase—perhaps unreasonably so—as instruments become more sensitive and capable of picking up previously undetected phenomena that trigger the ban from a wider range of subjects. The alternative is to allow regulatory agencies to "reinterpret" or "update" legislative stipulations, thereby possibly vitiating the legislature's representative function. Potent pressures on regulatory agencies by corporate interests make this option difficult to resist.

Fourth, as noted, legislatures confronted with demands for unconditional bans of controversial technologies gravitate toward selective prohibition of use. (We will return to the question of whether modern industrial societies are even capable of categorical prohibitions—and if not, why not?—in Chapter 15.) It is a matter of opinion whether this tendency is best described as reflecting a mature capacity for discrimination of desirable from undesirable use or uses or as an arrogant or naive belief that through legislative stipulation one may enjoy the attractive benefits of a technology while simply filtering out its associated unwanted costs.

Fifth, to date, no consensus exists about the proper role of democratic legislatures in advancing or moderating the pace of developments in controversial new fields of science and technology. We noted earlier the chasm between those who would have potential agents of societal control over science and technology adhere to the traditional cultural attitude of "innocent until proven guilty" vis-à-vis new developments, and those who argue that this attitude should be replaced with one of "guilty until proven innocent." In fact, to some thinkers the proper role of legislatures is always to speed up developments in science and technology, with society adapting to their consequences along the way. For example, criticizing a congressman's request to the U.S. Patent Office to suspend temporarily the granting of patents for genetically engineered animal forms in order to give Congress time to consider the matter, a *New York Times* editorial asserted, in a tone of Cartesian certainty, that "Congress's duty is to keep up with technology, not slow it down."[54]

Others urge that society should *first* get clear about the general features of the way of life it wants, and *then* promote or restrict scientific and technological developments depending on the extent to which they are conducive or antithetical to the chosen goal. One would have thought that categorical positions such as these two might by now have yielded to one of a more discriminating character. For example, employing varying combinations of steering, accelerating, braking, shock absorbing, and other options, the legislative body's control of the high-powered vehicle of scientific and technological development should depend on how profound and disruptive a change in society's established way of life a particular development seems to promise. In Chapter 15, we will consider one reason that views on this question are so polarized.

CONCLUSION

We have examined a number of ways in which societal forces attempt to exercise control over science and technology. Our survey indicates that the SCOST mechanism evolved by modern industrial societies, particularly in the United States, is a complex, hydra-headed construct. Taken together, these modes of SCOST may be seen as potential parts of a kind of *comprehensive trial process* that all contemporary scientific and technological endeavors must undergo. At any stage of this process such an endeavor is subject to intervention by potent social forces attempting to shape its nature, channel its course, or modify its conditions and likely consequences.

Briefly, let us indicate at what (sometimes overlapping) stages in this distinctly nonlinear trial process social forces may intervene and attempt to exert their respective controlling influences. In *roughly* chronological order, important possible SCOST intervention points in the life cycle of a scientific or technological endeavor and, in parentheses, one or more modes of SCOST sometimes used to intervene at the point in question, are as follows:

1. Conception/initiation: contemplation about undertaking and decision to undertake a certain project or kind of project (government funding)
2. Prioritization: process during which relative priority of project is determined (public participation, legislative limitation)
3. Process of securing funding (public participation, government funding)
4. Early research and development work (government funding, legislative limitation)
5. Preliminary design specifications for an experiment, technic, or system (regulation)
6. Preliminary design approval (government funding)
7. Testing of product, apparatus, system, or process prior to final design approval (regulation)
8. Final design approval (regulation, government funding)
9. Ensuing experiment or development process (government funding)
10. Product-manufacturing or system-construction phase (regulation, a priori assessment mechanisms, legislative limitation)
11. Post-facto testing of product or system (regulation)
12. Diffusion of results—e.g., information, knowledge, products, or systems (regulation, legislative limitation)
13. Deployment and testing of distributed product or system (regulation)
14. Use or operation of product or system (regulation, public participation, legislative limitation)
15. Emergence of alleged consequences of product or system use (legislative limitation, product litigation, regulation)[55]

Of course, possible changes in society's dominant cultural values or in its reigning matrix of political, social, and economic forces and trends may be reflected in evolving legislative and legal actions bearing on science and technology. This, in turn, may mean that the best combination of SCOST mode and trial-process intervention point for a given kind of scientific or technological development will vary considerably over time. To conclude this book, we will briefly consider some remaining obstacles to improved social management of science and technology in late twentieth century Western society.

ENDNOTES

1. John G. Burke, "Bursting Boilers and the Federal Power," *Technology and Culture*, 7, 1966, 1–23.
2. *Ibid.*, p. 23.
3. Carolyn McGovern and Nancy A. Blanpied, eds., *Federal Regulatory Directory*, 5th ed. (Washington, D.C.: Congressional Quarterly Service, 1986), p. 3.
4. *Ibid.*, pp. 3–4.
5. Martin J. Sherwin, *A World Destroyed* (New York: Vintage, 1987), p. 42.
6. *Ibid.*
7. James L. Penick, Carroll W. Pursell, Morgan B. Sherwood, and Donald C. Swain, eds., *The Politics of American Science*, rev. ed. (Cambridge, Mass.: MIT Press, 1972), p. 21.
8. *Science and Technology Data Book: 1989*, (Washington, D. C.: National Science Foundation, 1988), pp. 2–6.
9. *Ibid.*, pp. 11, 15, 16.
10. *Ibid.*, p. 12.
11. *Science and Engineering Indicators: 1987* (Washingron, D. C.: National Science Board, 1987), p. 78.
12. *Science and Technology Data Book: 1989*, p. 4.
13. U.S. Bureau of the Census, *Statistical Abstract of the United States: 1988*, 108th edition (Washington, D.C.: U.S. Government Printing Office, 1987), p. 566.
14. *Science and Engineering Indicators:—1987*, p. 251.
15. *Ibid.*, p. 79.
16. *Newsweek*, April 18, 1988, p. 80.
17. *Science and Engineering Indicators: 1987*, pp. 236–237.
18. *Ibid.*, p. 265.
19. Rick Biedenweg and Dana Shelley, *1986–87 Decanel Indirect Cost Study* (Stanford, Calif.: Stanford University, 1988), p. 46.
20. William T. Golden, ed., *Science and Technology Advice to the President, Congress, and the Judiciary* (New York: Pergamon Press, 1988).
21. The Conference Board, *Product Liability: The Corporate Response*, report no. 893 (New York: Conference Board, 1987), p. v.
22. "Product Liability," in *The Guide to American Law* (St. Paul: West, 1984), vol. 8, pp. 318–324.
23. *Ibid.*, p. 19.
24. Derrick Owles, *The Development of Product Liability in the U.S.A.* (London: Lloyd's of London, 1978), p. 37.
25. *New York Times*, May 12, 1987, p. C9.
26. The Conference Board, *Product Liability*, pp. 10–11.
27. For discussion of the marked decline in the plaintiff success rate in federal district court product-liability cases between 1979 and 1988, see James A. Henderson and Theodore Eisenberg, "The Quiet Revolution in Products Liability: An Empirical Study of Legal Change," *UCLA Law Review*, 37, no. 3, February 1990, 479–553.
28. *New York Times*, December 13, 1987, section 3, p. 17.
29. *New York Times*, July 3, 1988, section 3, p. 4.

30. *The Guide to American Law*, vol. 8, p. 323. See also *New York Times*, February 8, 1978, p.8.
31. *New York Times*, August 26, 1986, p. 1.
32. Richard Gillam and Barton J. Bernstein, "Doing Harm: The DES Tragedy and Modern American Medicine," *The Public Historian*, 9, no. 1, Winter 1987, 60. In 1989, the U.S. Supreme Court let stand a New York State Court of Appeals ruling affirming a strong version of the market-share liability doctrine. See *New York Times*, October 31, 1989, p. D23.
33. Public Law 91-190, *United States Statutes At Large: 1969* (Washington, D.C.: U.S. Government Printing Office, 1970), vol. 83, p. 852.
34. *Ibid.*, p. 853.
35. *New York Times*, January 16, 1978, p. 1; September 26, 1979, p. 17; and November 30, 1979, p. 20.
36. U.S. Congress, Office of Technology Assessment, *1986 Annual Report to the Congress*, (Washington, D. C.: U. S. Government Printing Office, 1987), p. 5.
37. Anne Hessing Cahn and Joel Primack, "Technological Foresight for Congress," *Technology Review*, March/April 1973, p. 39.
38. Office of Technology Assessment, *1986 Annual Report*, p. 4.
39. Public Law 92-484, 92nd Congress, H.R. 10203, "Office of Technology Assessment Act", quoted in Office of Technology Assessment, *1986 Annual Report*, p. 132.
40. "When Decision Makers Turn To the Experts," *The Economist*, vol. 300, no. 7463, September 13, 1986, p. 95.
41. Office of Technology Assessment, *1986 Annual Report*, p. 5.
42. "Between 1970 and 1975, there were 332 suits filed against Federal agencies for inadequate EIS reports, of which 64 were sustained." K. Guild Nichols, *Technology on Trial* (Paris: Organization for Economic Cooperation and Development, 1979), p. 84.
43. *New York Times*, November 28, 1984, p. 1; January 25, 1985, section I, p. 1; February 26, 1985, section II, p. 3; July 4, 1985, section I, p. 12; July 23, 1985, section II, p. 3; August 8, 1985, section I, p. 1; and September 20, 1985, section I, p. 1.
44. *New York Times*, January 12, 1984, section II, p. 10.
45. Nichols, *Technology on Trial*, p. 20.
46. *Ibid.*, p. 99.
47. *Ibid.*, p. 101.
48. *Ibid.*
49. *New York Times*, November 10, 1987, p. A5.
50. *New York Times*, February 22, 1988, p. A11.
51. *New York Times*, October 24, 1987, p. 8.
52. *Report of The Committee of Inquiry into Human Reproduction and Embryology*—known as the Warnock Report, after committee chair Dame Mary Warnock (London: Her Majesty's Stationary Office, 1984), p. 84.
53. *New York Times*, July 3, 1988, pp. 1, 10.
54. *New York Times*, February 22, 1988, p. A18.
55. I owe the idea for developing such a scheme to anthropologist Pertti Pelto, author of *The Showmobile Revolution: Technology and Social Change in the Arctic*.

CHAPTER 15

SCIENCE, TECHNOLOGY, AND THE FUTURE: NEW MENTALITIES, NEW PRACTICES

INTRODUCTION

Thus far, the temporal focus of our study of science and technology in society has been primarily on the contemporary era, with occasional forays into the past. However, some of the unresolved problems associated with the social control of science and technology discussed in Chapter 14 point toward the future. We will conclude this work by considering several obstacles to realizing improved social management of science and technology in the future. In this chapter, unlike its predecessors, the obligations of comprehensiveness and objectivity assumed in writing a textbook will be set aside. What follows is highly selective and reflects my personal interests and biases.

APPROACHES TO THE STUDY OF SCIENCE, TECHNOLOGY, AND THE FUTURE

Approaches to the study of science and technology in future society are many and varied. To provide a contrast to my approach to this topic, let us briefly consider several kinds of such studies.

Some writers, often those of a technological-determinist bent, have authored what might be called *predictive-speculative* studies. They concern themselves with forecasting the content or timing of future technological or scientific innovations, either within a single technical field or across a wide spectrum of such fields, or within one or more spheres of everyday human activity. They sometimes supplement their predictions with speculations about the major social consequences deemed likely to flow from the innovations in question.[1]

Authors of *extrapolative-planning* studies project current science- and technology-related trends into the future and estimate what steps society will have to take to cope successfully with these outcomes. For example, in light of current facts and trends in telephone ownership and use, and of national economic and population growth rates, how much and what kinds of additional national and international long-distance telephone capacity will have to be developed in which countries if traffic is to be efficiently handled in 2025? Such studies are essential long-range planning documents for national governments and public and private entities charged with providing vital resources and services for citizens and organizations alike.

A third kind of approach to science, technology, and future society might be labeled *projective-cautionary*. Authors of such studies focus on what they see as looming threats to human survival—or at least to the kind of life to which the West has become accustomed—implicit in current practices and trends. Some, such as Donella Meadows and colleagues, base their projections on complex, dynamic, quantitative models of economic, technological, and environmental interactions.[2] Others rely upon less formal, more qualitative modes of analysis. For example, Robert Heilbroner has argued that the science- and technology-related ills of the arms race, overpopulation, and pollution are likely to lead to catastrophe unless draconian measures are taken to mitigate them.[3]

Daniel Bell has opted for what might be called a *structural-constraint* approach. Eschewing "gee-whiz" and "future-schlock" studies, Bell has limited himself to identifying and analyzing a number of emerging "basic structural frameworks" or transformations that, while not determining the future of the United States or the world in the year 2013, allegedly constrain possible scenarios for the future at that time. That is, for Bell, any plausible scenario for the future must be consistent with the emerging structural constraints he identifies. Among Bell's emerging structural transformations of the world are "the [economic] shift to the Pacific Basin," "the new international division of labor," the "third technological revolution" (the joining of computers and telecommuncations to produce a "wired nation" or even a "world society"), the fragmentation of national polities concurrent with a continuing trend toward international economic integration, and the growing international gap between the fractions of national populations consisting of people 15 years of age or younger (much greater in the less developed countries).[4]

A fifth kind of approach might be called a *change-prerequisite* approach. The focus here is not on probable social futures resulting from predicted technical innovations, but on changes that allegedly must take place if a desired social future is to come to pass. Among those taking this approach is the late literary critic and social theorist Raymond Williams. Having identified and analyzed a number of serious political-economic and environmental problems confronting contemporary industrial societies, Williams opted not to sound a Heilbronerian alarm or to concern himself with identifying emerging socioeconomic structural transformations à la Bell.

Finding that many of the ills of contemporary Western life were rooted in socially constructed mentalities, Williams articulated three fundamental "changes of mind" that he saw as prerequisites for "an alternative social order" that would overcome such problems. First, the established way of seeing the (human as well as physical) world as, at bottom, raw material for profitable exploitation must be replaced with a view of the world as a web of intricately interdependent and dynamically interactive "life forms and land forms." Second, the capitalistic—and Marxian—notion that (industrial) "production" is the sole realistic and useful form of societal "intervention" in nature can, and must, now be replaced by a broader notion of how society and its members may relate to nature—an orientation of "practical, self-managing, self-renewing societies in which people care first for each other in a living world." This new notion, which Williams called "livelihood," must build on the benefits of its unprecedentedly productive, historically conditioned predecessor but be rooted in a "broader sense of human need and a closer sense of the physical world." Third, the culturally reinforced dichotomy between "emotion" and "rational intelligence," the former dismissed by the dominant culture as inferior to the latter, must yield to a new concern with "forms of whole relationship"—ones adequately providing for the expression of the various facets of human beings and excluding the reigning specializing obsession with "production" per se as the alpha and omega of human existence.[5]

Of these approaches, the one adopted here most resembles that of Williams. We will now discuss several patterns of sociocultural practice rooted in attitudes, beliefs, and conditions characteristic of contemporary Western consciousness. My contention is that these patterns are problematic, even pernicious. If, however, the mentalities underlying them can be altered in appropriate ways, society's "management" of its increasingly potent scientific and technological resources can be significantly improved in the future.

FOUR CULTURAL OBSTACLES

Barriers to improved societal management of science and technology are of various kinds. We will not be interested here in obstacles that are primarily political or economic in nature or origin. Examples of this sort include the organization of the world into sovereign, economically competitive nation-states, the skewing of a nation's research and development activity by entrenched military interests, and the dependence of legislators needing funds for media-intensive reelection campaigns on contributions from powerful vested interests. Without intending to diminish the importance of such concerns, the obstacles analyzed in this chapter are primarily *philosophical-cultural* in character or origin.

Anachronistic Education

Contemporary undergraduate education in the Western industrialized countries, for students of liberal arts and science and engineering alike, remains to a significant degree under the sway of anachronistic notions of what it is to be an educated and cultured human being. These notions are residues of the ideals of nineteenth century European and American elite institutions. In European schools, these ideals reflected the highly stratified class structures of their respective societies. Whatever their merits and appeal, these notions continue to legitimize curricula that leave students ill prepared to function as "good citizens" of contemporary democratic scientific-technological societies.

Let us begin with liberal arts students. Most, even those in the elite colleges and universities, graduate with negligible, if any, understanding of the natures and functioning of science and technology. Yet such individuals often go on, after obtaining graduate professional degrees, to become leaders in their fields. As such, they are sometimes called upon to make or ratify decisions on private or public policy matters with significant scientific or technical components. Similarly, the production and reproduction of a public whose level of technical literacy is vanishingly small diminishes the prospects for improved social management of science and technology. In fact, regarding matters scientific or technological, this situation is conducive to insensitive technocratic rule over a largely acquiescent public, punctuated by occasional episodes of uninformed democratic participation amenable to monetary or demagogic manipulation. If it is unthinkable that a student majoring in a field in the humanities or social sciences graduate if he or she is illiterate in terms of the printed or written word, it is no less scandalous in today's world for a student to be allowed to graduate from a college or university if he or she is illiterate in science, technology, and mathematics. To allow such a student to graduate is to disenfranchise him or her and to jeopardize the prospects for meaningful democracy in contemporary or future society.

To gauge the social costs of technical illiteracy, consider the cases of judges and other public officials. David Bazelon, former chief justice of the Fifth Circuit Federal Court of Appeals in Washington, D.C., stated over a decade ago that

> some two-thirds of the D.C. Court's caseload now involves review of action by federal administrative agencies; and more and more of such cases relate to matters on the frontiers of technology. What are the ecological effects of building a pipeline to bring oil across the Alaskan tundra? How can society manage radioactive wastes from nuclear reactors, which remain toxic for two hundred centuries or more? Shall we ban DDT, or the Concorde SST, or lead in gasoline? These and many more such imponderables are now coming before our court, and the end is nowhere in sight.[6]

Acknowledging that he had no expertise in science or technology, Bazelon nevertheless rejected as "very harmful" two proposed solutions to this situation: providing "some sort of systematic instruction of the judiciary in the ways of science" and appointing "expert science advisers, to sit at the right hand of a judge when he is considering a case with scientific overtones." Bazelon viewed the former as unrealistic and the latter as running the risk of creating "surrogate judges." Courts should not get involved either in "assessing the merits of competing scientific arguments"—something for which they lack "knowledge and training"—or in "substitut[ing] their own value preferences for those of the agency" whose actions are under review. Rather than reviewing the *substance* of regulatory-agency decisions, appeals courts should limit themselves to examining the *processes* used by agencies in arriving at their decisions. That is, appeals courts should "scrutinize and monitor the decision-making process to make sure that it is thorough, complete, and rational; that all relevant information has been considered; and that insofar as possible, those who will be affected by a decision have had an opportunity to participate in it."[7]

Bazelon's proposal is unconvincing on three counts. First, it fails to address itself to the important and expanding range of cases with significant science or technology components that are *not* appeals of regulatory-agency decisions. For example, consider Bazelon's former appeals court colleague who presided over the trial and divestiture of the American Telephone and Telegraph Company (AT&T) in the early 1980s. Judge Harold Green had to assess the credibility of opposing claims about whether the technical integrity of AT&T's long-distance network would be compromised if it had to accommodate a number of competitor companies using different technologies. More recently, in 1988 a U.S. district court judge in San Jose, California, began hearing—without a jury—what he acknowledged was the most complex case he had encountered in 20 years on the bench: a suit brought by NEC Company of Japan against Intel Corporation of Santa Clara, California, over whether microcode—the instructions that run a microprocessor—can be copyrighted. The judge began the case by asking the opposing parties to provide a two-day courtroom tutorial for him on how computers work.[8]

Second, while Bazelon is probably right in saying that it would be futile to try to substantially raise judges' "scientific consciousness" at this late date, that is by no means the only option available. Instead of resorting to short, inevitably superficial tutorials, it makes more sense for the (preprofessional and professional) education of legal and other decision-makers-to-be to include courses aimed, *not* at bringing them to anything like the level of technical experts, but at making them technically literate in at least one field of science or technology. The individual who is technically literate in a field would have at least a basic grasp of the key terms, concepts, and principles of that field, enabling him or her to grasp, say, a typical *Scientific American* article on a subject in that field and to examine critically and ask pointed questions about position papers written by advocates on both sides of such disputes.

Third, assuming it were concluded that any attempt at realizing technical literacy in some field of science or technology were doomed to fail, appointment of "expert science advisors to sit at the right hand of a judge when he is considering a case with scientific overtones" is, again, not the only alternative. Some argue, for example, that for cases involving complex scientific or technological components, courts should be "give[n]...the ability to hire technical consultants who are not aligned with either of the parties in a case" and who would be able to subject the testimony of technical experts called by each side to critical courtroom scrutiny.[9]

Some observers believe that unless something is done to rectify this situation, "fair and honest justice [will be] at a large disadvantage in any case more complicated than a rear-end automobile collision."[10] The problem is no less serious when the outcome of such cases is decided by juries from whose potential ranks the technically trained or rare nontechnically trained but technically literate individuals with the ability to understand and assess technical evidence have been systematically purged by peremptory challenges.

Government officials and their constituents also pay a steep price for being technically illiterate. As we have seen, now, more than ever, science and technology are essential components of foreign as well as domestic policy. As noted, the U.S. Congress has seen fit to create an Office of Technology Assessment. Whether its reports suffice to compensate for the technical illiteracy of most members of Congress is open to question. With few exceptions—inventor Thomas Jefferson and engineers Herbert Hoover and Jimmy Carter—U.S. presidents have lacked the knowledge and training that would enable them to grasp or critically analyze issues or initiatives with substantial scientific or technological components. They are thus at the mercy of their possibly technically illiterate personal advisors, others reflecting the vested interests of entrenched bureaucratic forces, or their own uncritical ideological predispositions in favor of any seemingly plausible technical initiative.

Again, several alternatives to such a state of affairs suggest themselves: technical literacy on the part of elected public officials (and those in selected civil service posts) and the establishment of an appropriate governmental structure to ensure that the chief executive receives sound advice on science and technology issues. The latter would include issues of feasibility and funding priorities for scientific and technological research as well as broader social issues with important scientific or technological components.

Regarding the former alternative, recent history and the occupational and educational backgrounds of members of Congress offer little hope that high elected officials at the federal level will have any meaningful knowledge of science or technology. That leaves the issue of science and technology advice to chief executives.

Let us begin with some brief historical background. In 1951, Harry S. Truman became the first U.S. president to have a formal science advisory group consisting of eminent scientists. Innundated with proposals for meeting the challenge posed by the launch in 1957 of the Russian *Sputnik* satellite, Dwight D. Eisenhower appointed James R. Killian, president of the Massachusetts Institute of Technology (MIT) as his presidential science advisor. Killian then set up a President's Science Advisory Committee (PSAC). John F. Kennedy had a close relationship with his top science advisor, Jerome Weisner, also a former president of MIT. In 1973, President Richard M. Nixon terminated the presidential science advisor post and the PSAC group after some of its members made public their disagreement with his views on the merits of developing an American supersonic transport (SST) and new antiballistic-missile systems. Reacting to that move, in 1976 Congress mandated the creation of a White House Office of Science and Technology Policy (OSTP), and Jimmy Carter subsequently reinstated the post of presidential science advisor. In the 1980s, however, OSTP, with its small staff and modest budget ($1.89 million in 1988), had negligible influence on executive-branch science and technology policy, including the roughly $60 billion spent by the U.S. federal government on research and development in 1988.[11]

It has been suggested that presidential decision making involving science and technology would benefit if U.S. presidents had science *and technology* advisors whom they trusted and if the advisors had direct access to the president, rather than only through the president's senior staff.* Lacking such an arrangement, giving the office of presidential science advisor greater continuity by making it a civil service–type post, rather than having each chief executive appoint a new advisor, usually someone known beforehand to agree with the executive's views, might contribute to the provision of more objective advice. A relationship of greater trust might ensue, thereby effectively increasing the advisor's influence.[12]

However excellent from a technical point of view, in one sense the curricula currently prescribed for intending scientists and engineers is also curiously anachronistic. Such students can usually be safely assumed to be technically literate in their chosen fields. It is unwarranted, however, to assume that they also possess a second, equally important kind of science- and technology-based literacy. I will call this "STS literacy"—basic knowledge about the ways science and technology function in, affect, and are affected by society in general and their own society in particular. Technical virtuosity, while obviously necessary, is increasingly insufficient to ensure that engineers or scientists are adept practitioners of their art in contemporary society. Given the natures of contemporary science, technology, and society, it is important for would-be practitioners to understand the natures of and factors affecting scientific discovery and technological invention and innovation, the regulatory process, organizational behavior, the relationship of science and technology to economic growth and competitiveness, and professional ethics. In short, STS literacy is by now an essential element of scientific and engineering competence.

Courses providing STS literacy are no less important for liberal arts students, for they will also participate in decision-making processes about scientific and technological matters in the future. They should have a grasp not only of the natures and relationship of science and technology and of the basics of at least one field in these enterprises, but also of how science and technology function in, affect, and

___

*In April 1989, President George Bush named Yale University nuclear physicist D. Allan Bromley as the presidential science advisor, upgraded the position to Cabinet rank, and promised the advisor direct access to the president.

are affected by society in general and their own society in particular. Courses that provide such knowledge have begun to appear more widely in American colleges and universities in the last decade. Happily, they provide common ground on which both liberal arts students and engineering and science students can come together and learn synergistically.

Technological Maximality

A second obstacle to improved social management of science and technology involves a recurrent pattern of socio-technical practice characteristic of contemporary Western society, especially but not exclusively in the Untied States. The pattern in question involves the interplay of technology, rights, and numbers. While not without beneficial consequences, this pattern is a source of serious problems for the quality of life in societies in which it thrives. Unless appropriate changes are made, it promises to be even more destructive in the future.

In Chapter 9 we discussed public harms of aggregation—ones arising from the mass production of technological products, each of which seemed innocuous. This is a special case of the more general pattern in question here. I will describe the general pattern, clarify what it means, illustrate it, explain the cultural factors that foster it, and consider the general changes that will have to take place if the problematic pattern is to be brought under control. The pattern may be described as follows: "Technological maximality," practiced under the auspices of rights as traditionally understood and as (supposedly) held and exercised by increasing numbers of people, is apt to dilute or diminish the overall societal quality of life.

By *technological maximality*, I mean not only production or use of technics of enormous scale (Boeing 747s) or power (nuclear weapons). These are patent paradigms of "technological maximality." However, this concept is also intended to encompass other phenomena, such as the intensive use of a particular technic in a fragile environment or delicate situation; the extensive use of a technology in a relatively unrestricted or distinctive domain; and the diffusion, deployment, and inception of use of a technic as quickly as possible, even before adequate provision is made for its harmonious reception and debut.

Rights as traditionally understood refers to rights as they have long been construed in the modern West, including the belief that they may never morally be violated. Rights often interpreted in this absolutist way include the right to life, property rights, mobility rights, and procreative rights.

The *increasing numbers of people* factor refers to the presence in many kinds of situations of ever-increasing numbers of individuals who supposedly hold rights of the foregoing sort and who exercise them, among other ways, by using various technologies.

It is not technolgical maximality per se, but the *concurrence* of these three factors in repeated patterns of socio-technical practice—increasing numbers of individuals engaging in technologically maximalist practices as something they (supposedly) have an inviolable right to do—that is apt to put societal quality of life at risk, whether because of the aggregate fiscal, environmental, or other societal effects of such practice. Let us refer to these three interrelated factors as the "troubling triad."

This troubling triadic cultural pattern manifests itself in a variety of ways:

1. The intensive, sometimes extended use of life-prolongation technologies or technological procedures in treating thousands of terminally ill or irreversibly comatose patients, or

those needing an organ transplant or other life-support treatment, as supposedly sanctioned by the inviolable right to life;

2. The proliferation of mopeds, all-terrain, snowmobile, and other kinds of versatile transport vehicles in environmentally fragile or wilderness areas, as supposedly sanctioned by riders' mobility rights;

3. The proliferation of high-rise office buildings in downtown city centers, as supposedly sanctioned by developers' property rights; and

4. The proliferation of individuals with fertility problems seeking access to human reproductive technologies of various sorts, recourse to which is supposedly guaranteed by their procreative rights.

Other problematic phenomena exemplifying this pattern of socio-technical practice include the infestation of Grand Canyon National Park with over 50,000 tourist helicopter flights per year; the "Manhattanization" of urban environments (including human and vehicular gridlock and the progressive enshadowment of city centers); the depletion of ocean fishing areas with enormous, mechanically operated nets and high-speed, on-board fish-processing machinery; and the decimation of mature forests with power saws.

This pattern deserves to be called a cultural obstacle not only because it is characteristic of the Western cultural system, but also because some of its roots are cultural and pave the way for this pattern to exact its increasing financial and nonfinancial social tolls. While it is clear that economies and profits of large scale foster technological maximality, so too do certain ideas. For example, technological maximality is nurtured by American society's deeply entrenched "technological fix" mentality. Should anything go awry as a result of the practice of technological maximality, one can always, it is widely assumed, find a quick technological fix to remedy the situation in time. In American society, much prestige awaits the party who produces, possesses, or uses the biggest, fastest, or most powerful technic; more generally, the party who is "firstest with the mostest," technologically speaking. Influential sectors of American society also gauge progress and even civilization by the degree to which a country attains technological maximality. The absence in contemporary society of shared qualitative standards for making comparative value judgments also fuels technological maximality. The latter steps into the vacuum and becomes the new, quantitative standard of value: If a proposed building will be the tallest, then, we are told, it will surely be "the greatest"—a convenient confusion of quality and quantity.

As for rights, traditional natural rights are widely viewed in modern Western culture as God-given, individual, immutable, and inviolable. As we saw in Chapter 9, in the context of rapid scientific and technological developments, some such rights have been seen as taking on a positive status as well. That is, they are understood as encompassing entitlements to be *done to* in certain ways—to be provided, for example, with access to various kinds of life-sustaining medical technologies and treatments, such as renal dialysis, heart and lung transplants, medicines, and perhaps someday an artificial heart. Such positive rights often fuel technological maximality in both development and use.

As for the increasing-numbers factor, concern is often expressed in the United States about rapid population growth in the Third World. However, the cultural attitude that, when it comes to U.S. population, "more is better" is alive and well in America. Cultural phenomena such as the treatment of procreation as a sacrosanct right, strong support of international mobility rights, residues of the endless-frontier and land-of-unlimited-opportunity-for-the-world's-poor-and-oppressed myths, and belief that the United States has an unlimited spongelike capacity to absorb population increases without diminishing its quality of life make it unlikely that tough steps will be taken to curb further increases in American population levels and thereby avoid the steep environmental and social costs exacted by such increases. By fostering increasing numbers, such cultural phenomena fuel the pursuit of technologically maximalist practices to support the needs and desires of ever-increasing numbers of right holders.

Although the basic triadic pattern is well ensconced in American culture, it is not invincible. In fact, in recent years several exceptions to it have appeared. For example, several states have enacted laws that, under specified conditions, permit the withdrawal of all forms of mechanical life prolongation, including nutrition and hydration tubes. A few cities have enacted measures to limit automobility rights, while the property rights of owners who wish to construct high-rise office buildings in downtown city centers have on occasion been restricted. Nevertheless, the general pattern still prevails.

In the coming years and decades, Americans have some critical choices to make. If we continue to express our cultural propensity for technological maximality, unfolding under the auspices of anachronistic conceptions of rights supposedly possessed by ever-increasing numbers of people, we are likely to pay a steep price in the form of a diminishing quality of life. If this trend is to be checked, we will have to become more discriminating about our modes of socio-technical practice. We will have to accelerate the painful process of adapting our conceptions of rights to the full range of aggregated impacts of our increasingly potent technologies and associated maximalist practices. Finally, we should face up to the fact that the sheer number of people with access rights to these potent, often costly technologies must be stabilized. Failing that—a likely prospect—a proportionally tighter leash will have to be placed on technological practice, and increasingly radical adjustments will have to be made in our reigning permissive concepts of rights. The draconian approach to population control to which China has resorted in recent years is sobering in this connection. The consequences of technological maximality practiced by ever-increasing numbers of people may begin to suggest to society that continued affirmation of universal, unlimited individual rights of life, procreation, mobility, and property, as traditionally understood, raises serious problems in an age of mass-produced, potent, huge, or costly technics.

To paraphrase Lawrence Tribe, looming questions of survival aside, few tasks are more urgent for the future quality of life in the United States than that of sensitively using public policy to channel science and technology so as to enhance rather than degrade the fabric of our collective environment and ensure the dignity of the lives of all men and women.[13] Taming the "troubling triad" would be an excellent place to begin.

Freedom of Scientific Inquiry

Struggles over the two cultural obstacles considered thus far—anachronistic education and the troubling triad—are already with us. Debate over a third has emerged in the last decade, and the issue raised appears to be one with which society will have to come seriously to grips in the foreseeable future if it is to enhance, or at least prevent the deterioration of, its management of science and technology. The obstacle in question is related to a belief deeply held within (and to a lesser extent outside) the scientific community: *that freedom of scientific inquiry should be unrestricted by society.*

This belief is variously regarded as a precious, hard-won social treasure or as a potential threat to society (or both). Whether or not the reader regards this belief as an obstacle to improved social management of science and technology, it is clear that the gathering conflict over whether that belief will continue to serve as a cornerstone of public policy on scientific research is itself a formidable cultural obstacle. It has already consumed considerable time and energy on the part of government, industry, and the informed public in, for example, extended debates over government funding or authorization of certain recombinant-DNA research projects.

To discuss this topic fruitfully, an important clarification must be made at the outset. Earlier in this book, we noted two senses in which scientific inquiry is *already* subject to societal limitation. First, many science projects that investigators wish to carry out remain undone because proposals for funding are denied. Thus, selective funding, whether because of limited available resources or political considerations, is one societal limitation on science. Second, in Chapter 9 we noted several scientific experiments that, because of the ethically offensive means they employed, were terminated (the Tuskegee syphilis study) or would have been had they come to light before their completion (the CIA mind-control and Army biological-warfare experiments). Thus, accepted standards of ethical treatment of human beings, including those affected by scientific experiments, constitute a second existing societal limitation on science.

However, neither of these is the sense in question here. The issue is this: Will societal restriction of science ever take the form of *limiting the scope of permissible scientific inquiry*—that is, prohibiting the pursuit of selected scientific projects, not because of the ethical impropriety of the means used or the lack of available funding, but because the knowledge sought is believed to be *socially undesirable*? This issue was joined a decade ago in influential essays written by two eminent biologists: Robert Sinsheimer, formerly professor of biology at the California Institute of Technology and chancellor of the University of California at Santa Cruz, and Nobel Laureate David Baltimore, formerly professor of microbiology at MIT and, since late 1989, president of Rockefeller University.[14] Before we examine their arguments, note that a pattern is at work here that is analogous to that associated with "technological maximality." The pattern might be described as one of "scientific maximality"—the domain of subject matter open to being investigated scientifically is unbounded—occurring under the auspices of a right—freedom of scientific inquiry—represented as inviolable, where this right is exercised by an ever-increasing number of practitioners (scientists) who believe that they clearly have and may legitimately exercise that right. Is this pattern problematic in any sense? If so, in what sense and how seriously? To answer these questions, let us consider the views of Sinsheimer and Baltimore in some detail.

Sinsheimer's case for selectively restricting scientific inquiry has three parts. First, he offers several examples of research, pursuit of which he regards as "inopportune" and "of dubious merit." He hopes that the reader exposed to them will at least be willing to consider the case for selectively restricting scientific inquiry. Next, he attempts to show that his position cannot be dismissed out of hand on the grounds that its implementation is infeasible. Finally, Sinsheimer attempts to make "the case for restraint" philosophically.

Sinsheimer's first example is research aimed at making the separation of isotopes easier and less expensive, something which if successful would quickly be applied to facilitate separation of U-235 from U-238, thereby "[breaching] one of the last defenses against nuclear terror." Second is "the proposal to search for and contact extraterrestrial intelligence." His concern here is not an increased likelihood of nuclear war, but the "cultural shock" or "psychological impact upon humanity" that such contact would supposedly engender. Third is research into the aging process, which, if successful, would have a "devastating" impact on "the carrying capacity of a planet already facing overpopulation."

We will not explore in detail Sinsheimer's arguments aimed at showing that restriction of the scope of scientific inquiry is feasible. However, two important points about his treatment of this question must be noted. First, he has nothing to say about *who* would make the decisions to restrict, and second, he acknowledges that restriction may be feasible only in a weak, fallback form: "[E]ven if, at best, we can only slow the rate of acquisition of certain areas of knowledge, such a tactic would give us more time for social adaptation—if we mobilize ourselves to use that time."[15]

Sinsheimer's case for the philosophical justifiability of selective restriction of science rests on five main arguments, all of which are at bottom consequentialist in nature. First, the likely applications of the results obtained from certain lines of scientific inquiry would be "incompatible with the maintenance of other freedoms," such as freedom from nuclear destruction (see his first example) and freedom to reproduce and live in an environment not plagued by overpopulation (see his third example). Hence, foregoing such lines of inquiry may be part of the price that society will have to pay to preserve those other valued freedoms.

Second, given human frailty and the fact that human rationality, foresight, adaptability, and good will are distinctly limited, it is naive to expect that the human race can survive and thrive *regardless* of what knowledge is generated by unrestricted scientific inquiry and diffused in contemporary society.

Third, failure to selectively limit scientific inquiry could so destabilize society that the latter would become unable or unwilling to continue to support "the scientific enterprise."

Fourth, the idea, espoused by Baltimore, that the restriction of science should be limited to the level of the *application* of knowledge rather than to the level of its acquisition fails to reflect the difficulty inherent in trying to limit applications of new knowledge "once that knowledge has become available in a free society." This is particularly true in societies with powerful organizations dedicated to the rapid translation of scientific knowledge into profit-making technological products and processes.

Fifth, changes in "the nature of science or technology or in the external society—in either the scale of events or their temporal order—can affect the preconditions, the presumptions, of scientific activity." Thus, while "long- cherished rights of free inquiry" may have been perfectly appropriate in the cultural and social contexts prevailing from the seventeenth to the mid- twentieth centuries, that right requires reevaluation in the radically different context of contemporary Western society, for that context is one in which the continued exercise of that traditional right, viewed as unconditionally binding, is dangerous to society. This is so partly because "the exponential growth of scientific activity and the unprecedented magnitude of modern industrial ventures permit the introduction of new technologies (e.g., fluorocarbon sprays) on a massive scale within very brief periods often with unforeseen consequence."[16] Put differently, a right reasonably proclaimed under one set of sociocultural circumstances can become socially dysfunc-tional at a later point in time if the activities initially covered by it or the contexts in which those activities are carried out undergo substantial change.

Such are Sinsheimer's arguments for countenancing selective limitation of scientific inquiry. In my view, he makes several cogent points in attempting to justify selective restriction, particularly that concerning the dangers of regarding rights as immutable when the conditions that gave rise to them change. However, without specification of a viable decision-making mechanism for determining which inquiries will be limited by society, the case for selective restriction remains incomplete.

Now let us examine Baltimore's case against any such restrictive undertaking. He is opposed to limiting scientific inquiry in any way other than "determin[ing] the pace of basic scientific innovation." Focusing on biological research, Baltimore offers five reasons for thinking that limiting the domain of permissible research "because of the danger that new knowledge can present to the established or desired order" is ill advised.

First, he contends that "the criteria determining what areas to restrain inevitably express certain sociopolitical attitudes that reflect a dominant ideology."[17] That point is not applicable to Sinsheimer's argument, however, for the only criterion underlying the examples Sinsheimer offers as candidates for restriction is that of *survival*, whether physical (the first and third examples) or psychic (the second example). Sinsheimer's criterion scarcely seems an example of what Baltimore terms "sociopolitical attitudes" and "a dominant ideology."

Second, Baltimore opposes selective restriction of scientific investigation be-cause of what he calls "the Error of Futurism"—that is, "the fallacy that one can predict what society will be like even in the near future." He asks the following: What would happen if, to keep people from living longer and thereby exacerbate the population problem, research into the biology of aging were restricted, birth rates happened to fall substantially, and world population stabilized? While a quite palatable prospect to some, Baltimore responds as follows:

> We might welcome a readjustment of the life span....In any case, we have built a world around a given human life span; we could certainly adjust to a longer span and it would be hard to predict whether in the long run the results would be better or worse.[18]

But this scenario misinterprets what Sinsheimer has in mind. He is urging that research on aging be prohibited not unconditionally and in perpetuity, but only under the present conditions of population growth. That is precisely why Sinsheimer uses the word *inopportune* to refer to certain kinds of knowledge. The opportuneness or inoppor-tuneness of such knowledge is, for Sinsheimer, a function of social context, and hence of time. If means became available for sending the entire human race to live on other planets and half the race opted to emigrate, this would surely cause Sinsheimer to revise the conditional judgment that the knowledge resulting from research on aging would be inopportune.

Third, Baltimore argues that while partisans of selective restriction of scien-tific investigation express concern over the socially disruptive effects of some research, "in fact societies need certain kinds of upheaval and renewal to stay vital." Sinsheimer would not disagree. However, as with sex and food, so also with upheaval and renewal: There can be too much of a good thing. Upheaval taken to extremes can be destructive. The issue thus reduces to a question: Can the results of a scientific research project be so disruptive as to undermine rather than sustain social vitality and engender chaos or destruction? Sinsheimer apparently can imagine some scientific research projects capable of producing destructive upheaval and chaos. In contrast, Baltimore seems to believe that *any* social disruption or upheaval capable of being caused by any scientific research project will *always* eventually reinforce or enhance social vitality. The disputants thus have different assessments of the disruptive potential of scientific research and of the adaptability of the human race, as well as different timeframes of analysis.

Baltimore's fourth argument is that "scientific orthodoxy is usually dictated by the state when its leaders fear that truths could undermine their power." Their "repressive dicta" are interpreted as evidence of insecurity, which may lead to "unrest requiring further repression." A social system that leaves science free to explore "transmits to members of society strength, not fear, and can endure." This argument hinges on Baltimore's implausible equation of *any* limitation on scientific inquiry with the ominous imposition of "scientific orthodoxy." Criticizing the proposed establishment of a National Commission on Recombinant DNA Research, considered (but abandoned) by the Senate in 1977, Baltimore claimed that the long-term success or failure of such efforts, involving, among other things, pondering whether any DNA research is dangerous or controversial enough to be proscribed, would determine whether the United States continues to have "a tradition of free inquiry into matters of science or *falls under the fist of orthodoxy*" (emphasis added). We will have either unrestricted freedom of scientific inquiry or, eventually, a fist of orthodoxy. Baltimore apparently sees no defensible ground whatsoever between these extremes.

This version of the "slippery-slope argument"—if one takes but a single step down a slippery slope, one will inevitably wind up at the bottom—is not compelling. It assumes that the combination of the slope's steepness and slipperiness and society's fragile braking and other control systems will invariably lead to the bottom of the slope, regardless of how carefully society steps onto and positions itself on the slope. This assumption is open to serious doubt for contemporary American society. For example, restricting "freedom of expression" in the United States in cases in which its exercise would pose a clear and present danger to other people, or restricting "property rights" where their exercise would harm protectable interests of other parties or the commonweal, has not led to wholesale loss of free speech or property rights. Brakes can be applied to some liberty-limiting endeavors even after cautious first steps have been taken. Such is also the case, it can at least be argued, with judiciously chosen limitations on freedom of scientific inquiry. The burden of proof would then be on the party invoking the slippery-slope argument in the present context to show why societal brakes that have been effectively applied on other slopes cannot be on this one.

Baltimore's fifth argument against selective limitation—or, as he prefers to characterize it, the "imposition of orthodoxy on science"—is the "practical impossibility of stopping selected areas of research." His main line of argument is that "major breakthroughs cannot be programmed" and often come from outside an area of fundamental research for which they prove seminal. Hence, if society wanted to "cut off an area of fundamental research," it would have to "shut down...all scientific research" to "guarantee" such an outcome. This is crude hyperbole. Moreover, Sinsheimer expects no "guarantees." What he has in mind is withdrawing or withholding financial support and instrument access from those research projects that are *aimed* at generating knowledge that would, it is widely believed, manifestly threaten physical or psychic survival under present social conditions. That Sinsheimer does not have the shutting down of the scientific enterprise in mind and recognizes that unwanted knowledge could flow from unexpected sources is suggested by his statement that the best that might be done in certain cases is to *slow down the rate of acquisition* of certain knowledge to give society more time to "prepare for social adaptation."

Baltimore concludes his case by quoting approvingly the following remarks of Dr. Lewis Thomas:

> Is there something fundamentally *unnatural*, or intrinsically wrong, or hazardous for the species, in the ambition that drives us all to reach a comprehensive understanding of nature, including ourselves? I cannot believe it. It would seem to me a more *unnatural* thing, and more of an offense against nature, for us to come on the same scene endowed as we are with curiosity, filled to overbrimming as we are with questions, and naturally talented as we are for the asking of clear questions, and then for us to do nothing about it, or worse, to try to suppress the questions. This is the greater danger for our species, to try to pretend that we are another kind of animal, that we do not need to satisfy our curiosity, exploration, and experimentation, and that the human mind can rise above its ignorance by simply asserting that there are *things it has no need to know.*[19] [emphases added]

Two points about this quote deserve attention here. First, it is sheer a priori prejudice to assume that doing what is alleged to be "natural" will *always* turn out to be best for the human species or for the ecosystem as a whole, regardless of the scientific and technological powers at hand at a given time. Second, while Baltimore may believe that partisans of selective limitation hold that the human mind can rise above its ignorance by arrogantly asserting that there are "things it has no need to know," Sinsheimer's point is quite different—namely, that at this point in its evolution the species may have to try to compensate for the gap between its all-too-human frailties and its potent technical resources by adopting the prudent position that, for the time being, there are *things it needs not to know*, a quite different proposition. For Sinsheimer, such an "unnatural" position may be temporarily necessary to preserve or promote a human condition worth living and fighting for.

Such, in any event, is Baltimore's case against selective restriction of scientific research. Clearly, as with the case of Lysenko discussed in Chapter 13, the crude politicization of science is to be avoided. However, Baltimore's arguments against any form of societal limitation rely on exaggeration and misattribution and are not persuasive. Those in search of a strong case against selective restriction must turn elsewhere.[20]

One conclusion suggested by the foregoing exchange is that, like some other sacred cows—private property, for example—freedom of scientific inquiry may eventually have to be stripped of its long-standing status as an absolute or inviolable right. In its place, society could adopt a general *presumption in favor of scientific research*. Scientific inquiry would then be regarded as something whose unrestricted pursuit is always a good thing and as an activity that society will always allow to unfold—*unless* there is a strong societal consensus (based on a compelling case of substantial expected social harm) against respecting that presumption *in a particular case*. However rare such overridings might be under this presumption, it would be genuinely possible for such a case to be brought forward, considered, and accepted or rejected on its individual merits, not summarily dismissed a priori.

The basic ground for this possible change in the liberty status of scientific inquiry is that in its funding, execution, and influence, science is less and less a private affair and more and more a public one. The major supporting and affected party—society—should have a say in whether an area of scientific research widely regarded as a potential threat to societal survival or well-being is restricted, either permanently or temporarily, while, for example, social conditions remain as they are at the time of the perceived threat.

The significance of the debate over limits to scientific inquiry extends beyond science. As with technological maximality, so with scientific inquiry: The power and pervasiveness of contemporary science and technology are resulting in mounting pressure on a traditional form of Western individualism—that is, individual rights, here in the form of individual freedom of scientific inquiry. It remains to be seen whether the collision between social pressure and the exercise of this traditional right will occur and, if it does, what the long-term fates of the parties involved will be.* To suggest, as Baltimore does, that enacting *any* restriction on the domain of scientific inquiry would jeopardize the entire scientific enterprise is needlessly alarmist. In fact, by inviting quick dismissal, such a position could be counterproductive to his own interest. A position that acknowledges that society may legitimately impose limits on the scope of permissible scientific inquiry under certain extreme and rare circumstances, but couples that acknowledgement with a counsel of extreme caution in the use of those restrictive powers, might well prove more effective in protecting the integrity of and maintaining social support for scientific inquiry.

Neglected Intangibles

The last obstacle to realizing improved management of science and technology in the future discussed here has to do with barriers to incorporating consideration of certain kinds of intangibles into decision making regarding controversial scientific and technological innovations.[21]

Many disputes over the pursuit or proposed introduction of scientific or technological innovations exhibit a common pattern. Proponents argue that a given innovation or development will *definitely* yield *direct, concrete, quantifiable* benefits—economic or medical benefits, for example—realizable in the *short to intermediate term.* Opponents often counter that proceeding with the innovation or development in question *may* produce serious "costs," albeit ones that are *indirect* results of the proposed undertaking, *intangible* in nature, *nonquantifiable*, and ascertainable only in the *long run.* This pattern has characterized disputes over innovations as diverse as in vitro fertilization, nuclear power, and integrated computerized government files on citizens.

At least two problems make such disputes difficult to resolve rationally. The first is the *responsibility-feasibility dilemma of innovation.* On the one hand, the longer a conscientious decision maker wishing to be socially responsible holds off making a decision in order to ascertain the full range of likely impacts, including intangible ones, of the innovation or development at issue, the stronger the body of evidence may become weighing against approving or supporting it. Yet a variety of factors makes deciding to reject or abandon such an undertaking at a later date proportionally less feasible. Such factors include the enormous human and capital investments typical of

---

*One field in which a collision may be inevitable is embryology. There have already been calls for categorical or conditional bans on human embryo research. In the future, another area of research that could precipitate such a struggle is human germ-cell genetic therapy or enhancement.

many modern technical projects and the national prestige and current or future jobs dependent on staying the course.

On the other hand, the earlier one can convincingly portray an innovation or development as deleterious to human well-being, the more feasible it is to alter or stop it. Yet, precisely at such times of maximum vulnerability, it is especially difficult to acquire compelling evidence of long-term effects that, although intangible in nature, pertain to making a socially responsible decision to proceed.

The upshot, then, is that the requirements of social responsibility are most likely to be satisfied when it is least feasible to reject or substantially modify the innovation or development and, conversely, least likely when it is most feasible to do so. This dilemma between responsibility and feasibility makes it extremely difficult to reach decisions about technical innovations and developments that are rational, responsible, and honest.

However, even if evidence about the bearing of the innovation or development in question on intangible concerns were to become available early on, a second problem often rears its head. In the highly pluralistic culture of the United States, it is relatively easy to make a persuasive case for the concrete, short-term, direct benefits claimed for an innovation or development. However, it is difficult to forge a consensus about possible deleterious, intangible effects.

Consider the following imaginary but not very far-fetched example. Suppose a firm petitioned the FDA to allow it to market an artificial womb that it claimed is superior to the natural model; it is safer, the firm says, and so advanced that fetuses can be housed in it directly after in vitro fertilization. Suppose further that the cognizant government decision maker asked teams of government analysts to develop the strongest cases for and against giving the firm permission to market the system. It is unlikely that a society as culturally heterogeneous as that of the United States could bring itself to decide to prohibit or rigorously restrict even such a controversial technological innovation.

Many concrete benefits would undoubtedly be cited in the innovation's favor: It will save fetuses that would otherwise die from uterine disorders of some would-be mothers; it might well be less expensive or more reliable than artificial chemical stimulation of pregnancy; it would save the lives of mothers who now die in childbirth; it would eliminate the health problems of babies of mothers addicted to alcohol, drugs, or tobacco; and it would yield valuable knowledge of embryonic development, something likely to eventually pay handsome medical dividends.

What sorts of arguments could be marshalled against approval? It might have long-term, spiritually dehumanizing effects on the "sacredness of life" by rationalizing childbirth; it might dilute mother–child bonding, with whatever long-term consequences that might have, if any; use of the device would be a "cop-out," enabling individuals and society to avoid coming to grips with the environmental and behavioral problems that give rise to less healthy babies carried to term in utero; and, finally, if healthier children were in fact to result from use of the artificial womb, then access to it should not be limited solely to those able to pay the going market price; to do so would be unjust—better to forego the innovation's benefits than to exacerbate social injustice.

It is unlikely that such ethical and ethereal concerns over possible, long-term, indirect, intangible effects would carry the day over the concrete benefits cited. Moreover, it is doubtful whether access to such an innovation would be limited to those with a physiological need for it, as against reasons of economic need or personal preference.

One problem in cases with this structure of disagreement lies in the diversity of world views, philosophical and religious outlooks, and value and moral systems active in the U.S. public policy arena. Consequently, it is difficult to achieve cultural consensus on the *reality and importance* of unquantifiable intangibles that could serve as a basis for moderating or rebuffing controversial innovations or developments. Unlike in certain relatively homogeneous traditional societies, such as those of the Yir Yoront and the Hasidic Jewish community, there is no shared sacred world view in the larger U.S. society that certifies the reality and importance—and hence promotes the preservation—of intangibles like *community, character, intimacy, spirit, harmony, self-respect, tranquillity, treating someone like a person, or preservation of valued aspects of a threatened lifeway.* Those opposed to a particular innovation or development because they believe that it may undermine or destroy some valued intangible phenomenon are like runners who begin a race laps behind their opponents. Those so handicapped must exert themselves strenuously to catch up quickly before it is too late, that is, before rejection or serious modification becomes economically or politically infeasible.

Short of a technical innovation's or development's seeming to pose a serious threat to public health, military strength, or the economic well-being of the politically influential, as happened in the case of the American SST and as seems to be happening in the case of commercial nuclear power, contemporary American society is quite unlikely to rebuff any concrete-benefit-bestowing innovation—however bizarre—on the flimsy grounds that its adoption might put valued intangibles at risk. And yet, in the words of Friedrich Nietzsche, "[A]n interpretation [of existence] that permits counting, calculating, weighing, seeing, and touching, and nothing more—that is a crudity and naïveté, assuming that it is not a mental illness, an idiocy."[22]

Is there any prospect of counterbalancing the culturally rooted a priori advantage enjoyed in the West by controversial innovations and developments whose direct, concrete, short- to intermediate-term benefits are widely acknowledged? To answer this question, let us distinguish three broad, ideal-type evolutionary stages in the relationship between technical innovations and developments on the one hand and intangible-protecting world views on the other.

In a society in stage 1, its members share a sacred world view that protects the status of certain valued intangibles only by being inflexibly resistant to and categorically dismissive of significant, possibly beneficial changes with which it is confronted. Let us call such societies "singular traditional" cultures. Such was the case with the Yir Yoront and is still largely the case with the American Amish and Hasidic Jewish peoples.

The members of a society in stage 2 possess no shared intangible-protecting world view that can be mobilized and used to rebuff admittedly beneficial technical innovations and developments on the horizon. Certain subcultures within the society may, however, have such shared world views and may attempt, by political or economic action, to pressure society as a whole to adopt restrictive or prohibitive policies on particular technical undertakings consistent with their respective world views. They are rarely successful, however. Let us call such societies "pluralist modern" cultures. To a significant degree that is the stage in which the United States currently finds itself, where the only possible candidate for a shared world view is quite materialistic in nature. Nevertheless, opposition to certain biomedical innovations is centered in certain religious groups whose members may share a certain nonmaterialistic element.

Stage 3, as I conceive of it, is a kind of Hegelian synthesis of its antithetical predecessors. To date it has shown only faint signs of emerging. A society in stage 3 resembles one in stage 1 in that it *is* able to selectively reject or restrain benefit-bestowing innovations, even when they are not economically, militarily, or medically damaging to society. It is unlike Stage 1 in that its resistance is *not* based on a shared totalistic religious world view that dictates categorical opposition to substantial lifeway changes, including ones spawned by technical innovations. Stage 3 is like stage 2 in that its members subscribe to a variety of world views, but unlike it in that it *is* able to be discriminating about technical innovations and developments. This it can do because, in spite of its cultural pluralism, a core of intangibles has come to be recognized, to whose protection an influential, culturally heterogeneous, minority sector of the society is dedicated, on grounds that differ from person to person and range from religious to secular humanistic. Let us call stage 3 societies "discriminating sentinel" cultures. In its general posture toward technical innovations and developments, a stage 3 society would embody Aristotle's notion that moral virtue is a kind of mean between extremes of deficit and excess.

The "discriminating sentinel" posture of stage 3 attempts to navigate between undiscriminating and, for contemporary industrial societies, unworkable extremes: the (selective) categorical rejection of technical innovations characteristic of some static traditional societies—at least of our possibly oversimplified historical images of them—and the sometimes facile and unbridled scientific and technological optimism of more developed industrial societies.

Thus, in some cases, a partial solution to the disregard of intangibles in technical decision making may lie in the emergence of a critical mass of "stage 3" individuals. Such persons would be capable of making discriminating judgments about technical innovations. They would freely acknowledge and take seriously into account the substantial benefits often yielded by such innovations. The stage 3 individual would undertake to serve, together with like-minded individuals from diverse cultural and religious backgrounds, as a cultural sentry, ever alert and determined to protect valued intangible aspects of the societal way of life from risks posed to them by otherwise beneficial developments in science and technology. Stage 3 societies would find merit in Thoreau's radical contribution to a more comprehensive kind of cost–benefit–risk analysis: "The cost of a thing is the amount of what I will call life which is required to be exchanged for it, immediately or in the long run."[23]

CONCLUSION

A key challenge for industrial societies in the coming decades is to transcend the youthful, productive, but increasingly dissipative and destructive Faustian culture characteristic of the West during the last 200 years and attain a more mature, discriminating, and conserving "sentinel" culture. In such a culture, technical innovations and developments would be assessed by society not just in narrow economic, military, and medical terms but also on the basis of their likely bearings on human spiritual and physical health and well-being. Whether such a new, ultimately more adaptive stage of modern cultural development will emerge is as yet unclear. Time, however, is of the essence: Can the destructive consequences and ominous potentials of our astonishingly and unprecedentedly fruitful and rapidly developing scientific and technological resources *as exploited by entrenched forces* be alleviated and brought under effective social control in time by what Ezra Mishan calls "the slow-gathering forces of sanity and understanding"?[24] Unmasking the often destructive cultural mentalities and practices that we have considered here can contribute to this vital struggle.

ENDNOTES

1. See, e.g., Theodore J. Gordon and Robert H. Ament, "Forecasts of Some Technological and Scientific Developments and Their Social Consequences," in Albert H. Teich, ed., *Technology and the Future*, 4th ed. (New York: St. Martins's Press, 1986), pp. 141–153.
2. See Donella H. Meadows, Dennis L. Meadows, Jørgen Randers, and William W. Behrens, *The Limits to Growth* (New York: Universal Books, 1972).
   Some writers have criticized the grim conclusions about human survival and quality of life drawn by authors of certain projective-cautionary studies. For example, in *The Resourceful Earth* (New York: Basil Blackwell, 1984), Julian L. Simon and Herman Kahn rebutted the findings of *The Global 2000 Report to the President: Entering the Twenty-First Century* (New York: Pergamon, 1980)—prepared by the U.S. Council on Environmental Quality and the U.S. Department of State, under the direction of Gerald O. Barney—and argued for their own more optimistic projections.
3. Robert L. Heilbroner, *An Inquiry Into The Human Prospect* (New York: W.W. Norton & Co., Inc., 1974).
4. "The World and the United States in 2013," in *Daedalus*, 116, no. 3, Summer 1987, 1–31.
5. Raymond Williams, *The Year 2000* (New York: Pantheon, 1983), pp. 260–267.
6. David L. Bazelon, "Coping With Technology Through the Legal Process," *Cornell Law Review*, 62, no. 5, June 1977, 817–818. © Copyright 1977 by Cornell University. All rights reserved.
7. *Ibid.*, p. 823.
8. *San Jose Mercury*, April 25, 1988, p. D1.
9. *New York Times*, January 21, 1988, p. 26.
10. *Ibid.*
11. William Golden, *Science and Technology Advice to the President, Congress, and the Judiciary* (New York: Pergamon Press, 1988).
12. *New York Times*, June 10, 1988, p. A10; and August 26, 1988, p. A10; and *Scientific American*, September 1988, p. 144.
13. Lawrence Tribe, *Channeling Technology Through Law* (Chicago: Bracton Press, 1973), p. i.
14. Robert L. Sinsheimer, "The Presumptions of Science," and David Baltimore, "Limiting Science: A Biologist's Perspective," in Gerald Holton and Robert S. Morison, eds., *Limits of Scientific Inquiry* (New York: W.W. Norton & Co., Inc., 1980), pp. 23–35, 37–45. The material used from these essays is reprinted by permission of *Daedalus*, Journal of the American Academy of Arts and Sciences, "Limits of Scientific Inquiry," Spring 1978, vol. 107, no. 2.
15. *Ibid.*, p. 33.
16. *Ibid.*, p. 26.
17. *Ibid.*, p. 41.
18. *Ibid.*, p. 42.
19. *Ibid.*, p. 44.
20. See, e.g., Carl Cohen, "When May Research Be Stopped?" *New England Journal of Medicine*, 296, no. 21, 1976, 1203–1210; and Dagfinn Føllesdal, "Some Ethical Aspects of Recombinant DNA Research," *Social Science Information*, 18, no. 3, 1979, 401–419, especially 402–412.
21. For a fuller account of the argument sketched here, see Robert E. McGinn, "In Defense of Intangibles: The Responsibility-Feasibility Dilemma in Modern Technological Innovation," *Science, Technology, and Human Values*, no. 29, Autumn 1979, pp. 4–10.
22. Friedrich Nietzsche, *The Gay Science* (New York: Vintage, 1974), p. 335.
23. Joseph W. Krutch, ed., *Thoreau: Walden and Other Writings* (New York: Bantam, 1962), p. 128.
24. Ezra Mishan, "On Making the Future Safe For Mankind," *The Public Interest*, no. 24, 1971, p. 61.

THE CURRENT STATE OF THE STS FIELD: A BRIEF OVERVIEW

COURSES, PROGRAMS, DEPARTMENTS, AND DEGREES

The field of science, technology, and society (STS) is still relatively young. The first STS courses and programs appeared on the academic horizon in the late 1960s. While hundreds of such courses are currently given in North American, West European, and Australian colleges and universities, relatively few are offered in autonomous STS programs or departments. Most are housed in established disciplinary departments in the social sciences (especially economics, political science, and sociology), humanities (especially history and philosophy), and occasionally science or engineering. As is the case in fields such as religious studies, American studies, and international relations, STS teachers and researchers come from a wide variety of disciplinary backgrounds.

A relatively small number of undergraduate STS departments and programs exist, some of which confer their own degrees. Degree-granting STS-type programs are somewhat more numerous on the graduate level, however, partly because of the widespread faculty belief that those contemplating graduate work in STS would benefit from undergraduate work in a standard discipline, particularly in the social, biological, or natural sciences, or in engineering. Most undergraduates who major in STS do not do so with the intention of going on to graduate work in this field. Rather, they do so as an interesting form of undergraduate liberal arts education that fosters responsible citizenship in the contemporary era and that will prepare them for graduate work—perhaps with an STS slant—in professional schools such as law, business, education, government, and journalism, fields in which issues of science and technology in society bulk ever larger.

PROFESSIONAL ASSOCIATIONS AND SCHOLARLY JOURNALS

There is no single professional association with which all or most STS teachers and researchers are affiliated. Many STS practitioners see themselves as members of a national or international "invisible college." Organizationally, however, they divide up into a number of subfields of established disciplines. Thus, there is a Society for Social Studies of Science (4S) in which sociologists predominate, a Society for Philosophy and Technology dominated by philosophers, societies populated primarily by historians of technology and historians of science, and societies of technical professionals with STS interests, such as Computer Professionals for Social Responsibility, Physicians for Social Responsibility, the Union of Concerned Scientists, and the Committee on Social Implications of Technology of the Institute of Electrical and Electronics Engineers (IEEE).

If there is currently one nationwide organization with which a substantial number of U.S. STS practitioners are formally or informally affiliated and whose annual meetings serve as vehicles of STS scholarly exchange, it is the American Association for the Advancement of Science (AAAS). In 1988, however, a National Association for Science, Technology, and Society (NASTS) emerged, with the objective of becoming the main society for scholars and other professionals active or interested in the STS field, including teachers of technical-literacy courses.

A growing number of professional journals and annuals publish scholarly STS articles or items of STS interest. Some are disciplinary in orientation, including *ISIS* (published by the History of Science Association), *Research in Philosophy and Technology* and *Philosophy and Technology* (the latter published by the Society for Philosphy and Technology), *Social Studies of Science*, and *Technology and Culture* (published by the Society for the History of Technology). Others are more multi-disciplinary in character, including *Issues in Science and Technology* (published by the National Academy of Sciences), *Science, Technology, and Human Values* (published by 4S), *Science and Public Policy*, and *Technology in Society*. *Science*, the weekly for professional scientists (published by the AAAS), and *Scientific American*, the monthly magazine for the lay public interested in science, occasionally contain articles of STS interest.

STS ACTIVITY BEYOND ACADEME

STS activity is not limited to the academic world. Various branches of government do work focusing centrally on science and technology in society. For example, some U.S. governmental agencies, in both the executive and legislative branches, do policy research on issues involving science and technology in society. As discussed in Chapter 14, numerous federal laws have been passed and regulations issued affecting scientific and technological practice. Precedent-setting legal decisions have been issued to adjudicate disputes over science and technology in society.

As for society at large, increasing attention has been paid in recent years to matters involving science and technology in society. Several distinguished television series have been produced ("The Ascent of Man," "Nova," "Connections," "The Day the Universe Changed") and several monthly magazines have appeared that are devoted in part to covering STS subject matter for the general public (*New Scientist*, *Discover*). Newspapers have given STS topics expanded coverage in recent years (e.g., the weekly "Science Times" section of the *New York Times*). On occasion, hundreds of U.S. newspapers have simultaneously offered government-sponsored, university-coordinated "Courses by Newspaper" on STS topics, such as "Technology and Change" and "Working: Changes and Choices."

In sum, discussion and study of STS issues has become a seemingly permanent part of the contemporary public and academic landscapes.

GLOSSARY

(N.B.: Terms printed in **boldface** within a definition are defined elsewhere in the glossary.)

appropriate technology. The idea that the design and selection of technologies should reflect the social, economic, cultural, and ecological conditions of the society into which they are to be introduced. The phrase is most often used to refer to low-energy, labor-intensive, easy-to-understand-and-use technologies conducive to local, independent use in energy-poor, labor-rich, less developed countries.

autonomous technology. The theory that **technology** has a life of its own and develops independently of human control.

behavior setting. The natural matter and **technics**, and their configuration, that constitute the material environment for human behavior and sometimes influence it.

big science. A phrase used to point up the fact that since World War II, scientific research has increasingly involved money, personnel, organization, and equipment on a large scale. Without such resources, much such activity would have been impossible.

big technology. A phrase that points up the fact that since about the mid-nineteenth century, technological activity has increasingly involved money, personnel, organization, and equipment on a large scale. Without such resources, much such activity would have been impossible.

chain-linked model of innovation. A model of the **innovation** process that stresses the existence of diverse starting points for and multiple indirect pathways with feedback loops to technological innovation.

character of everyday life. The general texture or fabric of everyday existence that confronts and affects individuals living in a particular society and is substantially influenced by scientific and technological innovations and activities.

consequentialist ethical theories. Ones in which the rightness and wrongness of actions and policies hinge exclusively on their estimated consequences.

context of science and technology. The social-cum-natural setting in which scientific and technological activities unfold and that affects and is affected by their processes and products.

cultural convergence. A process in which two or more cultures exhibit increasing similarity of content or structure in some or all dimensions of social life.

cultural system. A society's **culture** viewed as a complex of interacting background factors or elements. These are often grouped into four sectors: the ideational, societal, material, and personality behavioral subsystems.

culture. A group's or society's total inherited and transmitted way of life, comprising its characteristic ideas, values, world views, institutions, roles, social structure, material artifacts, ways of making things, personality traits, and behavior patterns and settings. Behavior unfolding in a social unit both influences and is influenced by its culture.

cumulative synthesis theory of invention. The theory that **invention** is a cumulative, synthetic, social process involving a genetic sequence of four stages of novelty: the perception of a problem, the setting of the stage for the solving of the problem, the occurrence of a critical act of insight, and critical revision. These stages apply not only to the process of breakthrough that issues in a particular notable invention, but also to the processes involved in realizing each of the prior strategic inventions that set the stage for its realization.

deontological ethical theories. Ones in which the rightness and wrongness of actions and policies hinge on considerations other than their estimated consequences, e.g., on their allegedly intrinsic properties, the intentions or motives of their agents, or their being approved or disapproved by some authority.

deskilling effect. A result of a new work situation in which a worker, partly because of technological change, is no longer called upon to exercise previously utilized skills. The term is sometimes used to claim that because of the introduction of new workplace technologies workers must, on balance, utilize fewer or "lower" skills than under the previous regimes.

engineering. That professionalized branch of technological activity devoted to organizing the design, production, and operation of **technics** and technical systems in order to meet practical human needs.

enskilling effect. A result of a new work situation in which a worker is called upon to develop and exercise new skills not required under the previous work regime.

environmental impact statement. A systematic estimation of the possible and likely effects of a proposed technological initiative on the natural and human-built environment.

equilibrium-disequilibrium model. A model of the process of technically induced cultural change that stresses the disruption by a technical innovation of the prior equilibrium of society's cultural system, the fall of that system into a state of dissonant disequilibrium, and its eventual return to a new equilibrium state because of changes enabling the (possibly altered) cultural system to accommodate the (possibly revised) innovation.

formalized technical procedures. Intellectual constructs, often in the form of computer programs, that indicate or direct in a definite and precise manner how some **technic**-related task is to be carried out.

heroic theory of invention. The idea that **inventions** are created by single individuals who succeed by sheer genius, resolve, and hard work.

high technology. Late twentieth century **technics** and **technologies** heavily dependent on or embodying advanced scientific or **engineering** knowledge, e.g., many of those produced by and used in the microelectronics-based, biotechnology, aerospace, and instrumentation industries. High technology is often indirectly characterized as the product of that industrial sector whose companies employ substantially higher than average percentages of scientists and engineers and have substantially higher than average ratios of research and development expenditures to sales.

IDUAR model. A model of the technical-change-ensuing-social-change (**TCESC**) relationship in which the social change outcome of a technical change is a joint product of the nature of the technical change realized and the interplay of the **SCES** (at the time the technical change is introduced) with five interacting intervening variables: the particular **innovation** (I) into which the technical change is turned, the **diffusion** (D) it attains, the pattern of use (U) of the innovation that emerges, the adaptation (A) made by innovation users and nonusers, and the societal resistance (R) elicited by the innovation and its patterns of diffusion, use, and adaptation. Cf. **technological determinism**.

indigenous technology.   **Technology** native to a particular place, people, or region.

influence agent.   A social actor, e.g., a government agency, business firm, union, or public interest group, that exercises some type of influence on scientific or technological activity or products or on some aspect of the total societal enterprise of **science** or **technology**.

influence effect.   A change in some aspect of scientific or technological activity or products or of the total societal enterprise of science or technology brought about through some type of **influence exercise**.

influence exercise.   Any of several qualitatively different types of influence on **science** or **technology** that can be exerted by an **influence agent** in trying to bring about some kind of **influence effect**.

innovation.   A new intellectual, material, or social product or process ready for practical use, or the process involved in arriving at one from, e.g., an **invention**.

innovation diffusion.   The process by which an **innovation** is disseminated in a social group.

innovation system, the Western.   The complex of specific dispositions, values, and political and economic institutions and rewards that, taken together, enabled and fostered technological **innovation** in modern Western society.

institutionalization of science and technology.   The process by which the fledgling endeavors of **science** and **technology** take on established forms of organization and practice in a society, eventually to the point of becoming recognized as abiding constituent elements of the society's **culture**.

intermediate technology.   A **technology** resulting from taking a traditional technology through a series of incremental modern **innovations** that make it much more productive yet leave it still able to meet the criteria for **appropriate technology**.

invention.   A substantially original operational device or process—or the process of conceptualization and experimental testing by which one is realized—that achieves a desired result, often in an ingenious manner.

ISS.   The Immediate Social System, i.e., the **system** of foreground factors consisting of the reigning political, economic, and social forces and interests of the day in the society in question.

LDCs.   Less Developed Countries, often referred to collectively as the so-called Third World.

legislative limitation of science and technology.   Activities undertaken by legislatures to restrict scientific and technological developments, ostensibly to serve what is held to be in the public interest.

linear model of the innovation process.   A model of the **innovation** process that represents technological innovation as due, at bottom, to basic scientific research, followed in order by development, production, and marketing phases.

MDCs.   More Developed Countries, often understood as referring to those of Western Europe, North America, and Japan.

modern business firm.   An organizational **innovation**, consisting of the large-scale, multiunit, hierarchically organized, professionally managed firm, that arose in the second half of the nineteenth century as a response to technologies that made business on a national and international scale technically feasible.

NICs.   Newly Industrialized Countries; often used to refer to countries such as Taiwan, South Korea, Singapore, Thailand, and Malaysia.

outputs characteristic of scientific and technological activity.   Well-founded knowledge of the natural world (**science**); **technics** and **technic-related intellectual constructs** (**technology**).

paradigm.   The set of intellectual commitments common to most practitioners of a given discipline or field of intellectual or practical activity. Such commitments may include beliefs about how work in the field is properly conducted, about what phenomena deserve attention by practitioners, about what counts as high achievement in the field, and, in the case of natural **science**, about what exists and is fundamental.

polymorphism of contemporary science and technology.   The idea that scientific activity and technological activity each take many coexisting forms in the contemporary era.

product liability litigation.   Legal proceedings aimed at resolving a claim that a product's manufacturer or distributor is legally responsible for the harm incurred by a product user because of some defect in the product or deficiency in the way in which it was represented.

public participation in science and technology.   Involvement by the public at large or its representatives in advisory or legally binding decision making intended to affect scientific or technological affairs.

purposes or functions characteristic of scientific and technological activity.   To attain an enhanced understanding of the natural world, including human and social phenomena (**science**); to expand the realm of practical human possibility (**technology**).

rationalization.   A process whereby practice in a sphere of human activity proceeds decreasingly on the basis of "tradition, sentiment, and rule-of-thumb" and increasingly on the basis of "explicit, abstract, and intellectually calculable knowledge, rules, and procedures."

regulation of science and technology.   A social control mechanism whereby a government body elaborates and enforces the terms and conditions under which scientific and technological activities may be carried out, ostensibly in the name of protecting or promoting what is held to be the public interest.

resources for scientific and technological activity.   Supplies of available means with which such activities are carried out. Transformative resources (knowledge, **technics**, labor power, and methods) are brought to bear on input resources (money, materials, and natural phenomena) to produce the respective characteristic **outputs** of scientific and technological activities.

responsibility-feasibility dilemma of modern technical innovation.   The dilemma often faced by public decision makers who must decide whether to approve a technical **innovation** either at a point when it is late enough for a socially responsible decision to be made but too late for it to be feasible to reject or substantially modify the innovation, or at a point when it is early enough to be feasible to reject or substantialy modify the innovation but, since all relevant information about possible long-term effects is not yet available, too early for the decision to be socially responsible.

SCES.   The Social-Cultural-Environmental **System**, the general **context** in which scientific and technological developments should be situated if thinking about their causes and consequences is to be systematic and comprehensive.

science.   A term that can mean any of the following: the organized, well-founded body of knowledge of natural phenomena; a field of systematic inquiry in which such knowledge is sought; a distinctive form of human cultural activity whose practitioners include professional scientists; and the total societal enterprise devoted to the study and understanding of the natural world.

scientific management.   A phrase that refers to techniques devised for the systematic analysis and specification of work tasks and for the evaluation of worker performance, and to policies adopted for the selection, training, motivation, and compensation of workers, all with the goal of increasing productive efficiency. (Also called "Taylorism," after the American engineer, Frederick Winslow Taylor, usually credited with inaugurating this managerial tradition.)

SCOST.   The Social Control Of **Science** and **Technology**.

social constructivism.   The theory that apparently naturalistic or objective phenomena, e.g., aspects or products of scientific and technological activity such as scientific facts and technological inventions, are actually, in whole or in part, the outcomes of often complex, extended, and conflictive social processes.

sociotechnical system.   A **system** of interacting social and technical elements.

STS.   A expression meaning "science, technology, and society" or "science and technology studies."

system, concept of. The idea of a complex of elements viewed with respect to possible interactions between or among them and their possible interactions with the system's environment.

system-embeddedness of technics. The phenomenon of the dependence of **technics** on complex sociotechnical support systems for their design, production, use, operation, and maintenance.

systems analysis. The usually quantitative analysis of systems to determine how they behave or would behave under certain conditions or assumptions.

task orientation toward work. A traditional cultural orientation toward work, in accordance with which it is done when and to the extent required to complete a particular task at hand. Work thus conceived is intermittent and often related to irregular natural and human processes and rhythms. Cf. **time orientation.**

TCESC relationship. The relationship between a Technical Change and the Ensuing Social Change it initiates. See **equilibrium-disequilibrium** and **IDUAR model.**

technicity. An aspect of the character of everyday life in a society that refers to the extent to which **technics** pervade everyday existence.

technic-related intellectual constructs. Any mental conception devised to assist in the design, production, operation, use, or maintenance of **technics** and technical systems.

technics. Material products of human fabrication.

technological determinism. The general theory that society is determined in some sense by its **technology.** In hard technological determinism (HTD), society's technical base fixes the form or configuration of all patterns of social existence. In soft technological determinism (STD), changes in technology are the single most important source of social change.

technological maximality. The quality, often exemplified in technological endeavors, of doing or striving to do something technology-related to the greatest degree possible, e.g., producing the largest or most powerful technic possible, producing or selling as many units of a given sort of technic as possible, diffusing or deploying a technic as rapidly and widely as possible, or using a technic as quickly, intensively, or extensively as possible.

technological unemployment. The idea that technological change, especially automative technology, causes unemployment.

technology. A term that can mean any of the following: the material products of human fabrication (**technics**); the complex comprising the knowledge, materials, and methods used in making a particular kind of technic (a technology); a distinctive form of human cultural activity whose practitioners include engineers, machinists, and many craftspeople; and the total societal enterprise devoted to the research, development, production, operation, and maintenance of technics and **sociotechnical systems.**

technology assessment. Systematic estimation of the possible and likely social, economic, health, and environmental consequences of the introduction of new technologies or the implementation of new technology policies.

technology transfer. The conveyance of **technics** and technical systems and the transmission of various kinds of **technology**-related knowledge from one organization or society to another.

themata. Nonscientific, culturally generated and transmitted suppositions about nature that can inform or otherwise influence a scientist's theoretical or empirical work.

time orientation toward work. A modern cultural view of work as fungible labor carried out for the duration of the set workday—viewed as comprising regular, equal, abstract units of time—whether or not the assigned task is completed. Cf. **task orientation.**

troubling triad. Technological maximality, traditional rights, and increasing numbers viewed as a triad; patterns of sociotechnical practice embodying this interactive triad are often problematic for the quality of life in a society.

whistle blowing. Public charges, often by a scientist or an engineer, of hitherto hidden misconduct in the accuser's organization that he or she contends has harmed, jeopardized, or unjustifiably risked damaging the public interest.

BIBLIOGRAPHY

Adler, Paul S., "New Technologies, New Skills," *California Management Review*, 29, no. 1 (Fall 1986), 9–27.

Alexander, Christopher, "The City as a Mechanism for Sustaining Human Contact," in *Environment for Man*, ed. William R. Ewald, pp. 60–109. Bloomington: Indiana University Press, 1967.

Andersen, Håkon With, "Technological Trajectories, Cultural Values, and the Labour Process: The Development of NC Machinery in the Norwegian Shipbuilding Industry," *Social Studies of Science*, 18, 1988, 465–482.

Arkell, V. T. J., *Britain Transformed: The Development of British Society Since the Eighteenth Century*. Harmondsworth: Penguin, 1973.

Ashton, T. S., *The Industrial Revolution: 1760–1830*. Oxford: Oxford University Press, 1968.

Austin, Benjamin G., *Lewis Terman and the Genetics of Genius: The Rise and Fall of Intelligence Testing: 1879–1940*. Stanford, Calif.: Honors Program in Values, Technology, Science, and Society, 1988.

Baron, Ava, "Contested Terrain Revisited: Technology and Gender Definitions of Work in the Printing Industry, 1850–1920," in *Women, Work, and Technology: Transformations*, ed. Barbara Drygulski Wright, Myra Marx Ferree, Gail O. Mellow, Linda H. Lewis, Maria-Luz Daza Samper, Robert Asher, and Kathleen Claspell, pp. 58–83. Ann Arbor: University of Michigan Press, 1987.

Bacon, Francis, *The New Organon*, in *Francis Bacon: A Selection of His Works*, ed. Sidney Warhaft. New York: Odyssey Press, 1965.

Barber, Bernard, "The Sociology of Science," *International Encyclopedia of the Social Sciences*, ed. David L. Sills, vol. 14, pp. 92–100. New York: Macmillan, 1968–1979.

Bazelon, David L., "Coping With Technology Through the Legal Process," *Cornell Law Review*, 62, no. 5 (June 1977), 817–832.

Bell, Daniel, *The Cultural Contradictions of Capitalism*. New York: Basic Books, 1976.

———, "The World and the United States in 2013," *Daedalus*, 116, no. 3 (Summer 1987), 1–31.

Bellin, David and Gary Chapman, eds., *Computers in Battle: Will They Work?* Boston: Harcourt Brace Jovanovich, 1987.

Bell Telephone Laboratories, Inc., *A History of Engineering and Science in the Bell System*, vols. 1–8. New York: Bell Telephone Laboratories, Inc., 1975–1985.

Bernstein, Helen G., and Mark H. Bernstein, "The Pace of Life," *Nature*, 259 (February 1976), 557–558.

Bijker, Wiebe, and Trevor Pinch, "The Social Construction of Facts and Artifacts: or How the Sociology of Science and the Sociology of Technology Might Benefit Each Other," *Social Studies of Science*, 14, 1984, 399–441.

Blake, David, and Robert Walters, *The Politics of Global Economic Relations*, 3rd ed., pp. 151–170. Englewood Cliffs, N.J.: Prentice-Hall, 1987.

Bloch, Erich, "Basic Research and Economic Health: The Coming Challenge," *Science*, 232, no. 4750 (May 1986), 595–599.

Blythe, Ronald, *Akenfield*. New York: Dell Pub. Co. Inc., 1970.

Boisjoly, Roger, "Ethical Decisions: Morton Thiokol and the Space Shuttle *Challenger* Disaster," American Society of Mechanical Engineers Annual Meeting, December 1987, 87–WA/TS-4, 1–13.

Boorstin, Daniel, *The Americans: The Democratic Experience*. New York: Random House, 1973.

Bose, Christine, Philip Bereano, and Mary Malloy, "Household Technology and the Social Construction of Housework," *Technology and Culture*, 25, no. 1, 53–82.

Brannigan, Augustine, *The Social Basis of Scientific Discoveries*. Cambridge: Cambridge University Press, 1981.

Braun, Ernest, and Stuart Macdonald, *Revolution in Miniature*, 2nd ed. Cambridge: Cambridge University Press, 1982.

Briggs, Asa, *Mass Entertainment: The Origins of a Modern Industry*. Adelaide, Australia: Griffin Press, 1960.

Broad, William, and Nicholas Wade, *Betrayers of the Truth*. New York: Simon & Schuster, 1982.

Brock, W. H., "Liebigiana: Old and New Perspectives," *History of Science*, 19, part 3, no. 45 (September 1981), 201–218.

Butterfield, Herbert, *The Origins of Modern Science*. New York: Free Press, 1957.

Burke, John G., "Bursting Boilers and the Federal Power," *Technology and Culture*, 7, 1966, 1–23.

Bynum, W. F., E. J. Browne, and Roy Porter, eds., *Dictionary of the History of Science*. Princeton, N. J.: Princeton University Press, 1984.

Cahn, Anne Hessing, and Joel Primack, "Technological Forecasting for Congress," *Technology Review*, March/April 1973, 39–48.

Chalk, Rosemary, "Making the World Safe for 'Whistle-Blowers,'" *Technology Review*, 91, 1 (January 1988), 48–57.

Chalk, Rosemary, and Frank von Hippel, "Due Process for Dissenting 'Whistle-Blowers,'" *Technology Review*, June/July 1979, 49–55.

Chandler, Alfred D., *The Visible Hand: The Managerial Revolution in America*. Cambridge, Mass.: Harvard University Press, 1977.

———, "Technology and the Transformation of the Industrial Organization," in *Technology, Economy, and Society*, ed. Joel Colton and Stuart Bruchy, pp. 56–82. New York: Scribner's, 1987.

Clark, Ronald W., *Edison: The Man Who Made the Future*. New York: Putnam's, 1977.

———, *Works of Man*. New York: Viking Penguin, 1985.

Clarke, Robin, *Science and Technology in World Development*. Oxford: Oxford University Press, 1985.

Cohen, Carl, "When May Research Be Stopped?" *New England Journal of Medicine*, 296, no. 21, 1976, 1203–1210.

———, "The Case For the Use of Animals In Biomedical Research," *New England Journal of Medicine*, 315, no. 14, 1986, 865–870.

Cohen-Rosenthal, Edward, "Worker Participation in Management: A Guide for the Perplexed," in *Quality of Work Life*, ed. Daniel J. Skrovan, pp. 159–192. Reading, Mass.: Addison-Wesley, 1983.

Cole, Leonard A., *Politics and the Restraint of Science*. Totowa, N.J.: Rowman and Allanheld, 1983.

Coleman, Alice, "High Rise," *Science and Public Policy*, 15, no. 2, April 1988, 99–107.

Comstock, George A. et al., *Television and Human Behavior*. New York: Columbia University Press, 1978.

Conference Board, *Product Liability: The Corporate Response*, Report no. 893. New York: Conference Board, 1987.

Cowan, Ruth Schwartz, "The Industrial Revolution in the Home: Household Technology and Social Change in the 20th Century," *Technology and Culture*, 17, no. 1 (January 1976), 1–23.

————, "From Virginia Dare to Virginia Slims: Women and Technology in American Life," *Technology and Culture*, 20, no. 1 (January 1979), 51–63.

DeGeorge, Richard, "Ethical Responsibilities of Engineers in Large Organizations: The Pinto Case," *Business and Professional Ethics Journal*, 1, no. 1, 1981, 1–14.

Djerassi, Carl, "The Making of the Pill," *Science 80*, 5, no. 9, 1984, 127–129.

Durbin, Paul T., ed., *A Guide to the Culture of Science, Technology, and Medicine*. New York: The Free Press, 1984.

Easlea, Brian, *Witch-Hunting, Magic, and the New Philosophy*. Atlantic Highlands, N.J.: Humanities Press, 1980.

Ellul, Jacques, *The Technological Society*, trans. J. Wilkinson. New York: Knopf, 1964.

Ferguson, Eugene S., "The Mind's Eye: Nonverbal Thought in Technology," *Science*, 197, no. 4306 (August 1977), 827–836.

Fischer, Claude S., "Gender and the Residential Telephone, 1890–1940," *Sociological Forum*, 3, no. 2, 1988, 211–233.

————, "'Touch Someone': The Telephone Industry Discovers Sociability," *Technology and Culture*, 29, no. 1 (January 1988), 32–61.

Fisher, David, *Morality and the Bomb*. London: Crook Helm, 1985.

Føllesdal, Dagfinn, "Some Ethical Aspects of Recombinant DNA Research," *Social Science Information*, 18, no. 3, 1979, 401–419.

Fores, Michael, "Scientists on Technology: Magic and English-Language 'Industrispeak,'" in *Research, Development, and Technological Innovation*, ed. Devendra Sahel, pp. 239–250. Lexington, Mass.: Lexington Books, 1980.

Form, William, *Blue-Collar Stratification*. Princeton, N. J.: Princeton University Press, 1976.

————, "Technology and Social Behavior of Workers in Four Countries: A Sociotechnical Perspective," *American Sociological Review*, 37, December 1972, 727–738.

Freiberger, Paul, and Michael Swaine, *Fire in the Valley*. Berkeley: Osborne/McGraw-Hill, 1984.

Friedland, William H., Amy E. Barton, and Robert J. Thomas, *Manufacturing Green Gold: Capital, Labor, and Technology in the Lettuce Industry*. Cambridge: Cambridge University Press, 1981.

Gabor, Dennis, *Innovations: Scientific, Technological, and Social*. London: Oxford University Press, 1970.

Ganiatsos, Tom, "Transfer of Technology: Theory and Practice," in *World Economy in Transition*, ed. Krishna Ahooja-Patel, Anne Gordon Drabeck, and Marc Nerfin, pp. 229–251. New York: Pergamon Press, 1986.

Gelatt, Roland, *The Fabulous Phonograph*, 2nd ed. New York: Collier, 1977.

Gillam, Richard, and Barton J. Bernstein, "Doing Harm: The DES Tragedy and Modern American Medicine," *The Public Historian*, 9, no. 1 (Winter 1987), 57–82.

Gitlin, Todd, *The Sixties: Years of Hope, Days of Rage*. New York: Bantam, 1987.

Golden, William T., ed., *Science and Technology Advice to the President, Congress, and the Judiciary*. New York: Pergamon Press, 1988.

Good, Edwin M., *Giraffes, Black Dragons, and Other Pianos: A Technological History from Cristofori to the Modern Concert Grand*. Stanford, Calif.: Stanford University Press, 1982.

Graham, Loren, *Science, Philosophy, and Human Behavior in the Soviet Union*. New York: Columbia University Press, 1987.

Gunn, A. D. G., *Oral Contraception in Perspective: Thirty Years of Clinical Experience With the Pill*. Park Ridge, N.J.: Parthenon Publishing Group, 1987.

Harman, P. M., *The Scientific Revolution*. London: Methuen & Co., Ltd., 1983.

Hart, Jeffrey A., "The Teletel/Minitel System in France," *Telematics and Informatics*, 5, no. 1, 1988, 21–28.

Headrick, Daniel R., "The Tools of Imperialism," *Journal of Modern History*, 51 (June 1979), 231–263.

Heilbroner, Robert L., *An Inquiry Into the Human Prospect*. New York: W. W. Norton & Co., Inc., 1974.

———, "Do Machines Make History?" *Technology and Culture*, 8, no. 3 (July 1967), 335–345.

Heilbroner, Robert L., and Aaron Singer, *The Economic Transformation of America: 1600 to the Present*, 2nd ed. New York: Harcourt Brace Jovanovich, 1984.

Herbert, Robert L., "Industry in the Changing Landscape from Daubigny to Monet," in *French Cities in the Nineteenth Century*, ed. John M. Merriman, pp. 139–164. London: Hutchinson, 1982.

Hieronymi, Otto, ed., *Technology and International Relations*. London: Macmillan, 1987.

Hill, Stephen, "Eighteen Cases of Technology Transfer to Asia/Pacific Region Countries," *Science and Public Policy*, 13, no. 3 (June 1986), 162–169.

Hobsbawm, Eric, *Industry and Empire*. Harmondsworth: Penguin, 1969.

Hodin, Josef, "Science and Modern Art," in *Encyclopedia of World Art*, vol. 5, pp. 210–214. New York: McGraw-Hill, 1959.

Holton, Gerald, and Robert S. Morison, eds., *Limits of Scientific Inquiry*. New York: W. W. Norton Co., Inc., 1980.

Hughes, Thomas P., ed., *The Development of Western Technology Since 1500*. New York: Macmillan, 1964.

Inkeles, Alex, "Convergence and Divergence in Industrial Societies," in *Directions of Change: Modernization Theory, Research, and Realities*, eds. Mustafa O. Attir, Burkart Holzner, and Zdenek Suda, pp. 3–38. Boulder, Col.: Westview Press, 1981.

———, "Linking the Whole Human Race: The World as a Communications System," in *Business in the Contemporary World*, ed. Herbert L. Sawyer, pp. 133–174. Lanham, Md.: University Press of America, 1988.

———, "The Emerging Social Structure of the World," *World Politics*, 27, no. 4 (July 1975), 467–495.

———, *What Is Sociology?* Foundations of Modern Sociology Series. Englewood Cliffs, N.J.: Prentice-Hall, 1964.

Jones, R. V., "How Far Has Twentieth-Century Physics Changed Man's Concept of the Universe?" in *Proceedings of the Fifth International Conference on the Unity of the Sciences*, pp. 913–922. New York: International Cultural Foundation Press, 1977.

Kavka, Gregory, *Moral Paradoxes of Nuclear Deterrence*. Cambridge: Cambridge University Press, 1987.

Kenny, Anthony, *The Logic of Deterrence*. Chicago: University of Chicago Press, 1985.

Kerker, Milton, "Science and the Steam Engine," *Technology and Culture*, 2, no. 4 (Fall 1961), 381–390.

Kline, Stephen J., "Innovation Is Not a Linear Process," *Research Management*, 28, no. 4 (July/August 1985), 36–45.

———, "Innovation Styles in Japan and the United States: Cultural Bases and Implications for Competitiveness," Report INN-3. Stanford, Cal.: Thermosciences Division, Department of Mechanical Engineering, Stanford University, 1989.

Kolata, Gina, "Genetic Screening Raises Questions for Employers and Insurers," *Science*, 232, no. 4748 (April 1986), 317–319.

Kranzberg, Melvin, and Carroll W. Purcell, eds., *Technology and Western Civilization*. Oxford: Oxford University Press, 1967.

Kuehn, T. J., and A. L. Porter, eds., *Science, Technology, and National Policy*. Ithaca, N. Y.: Cornell University Press, 1981.

Kuhn, Thomas S., "Historical Structures of Scientific Discoveries," *Science*, 136, no. 3518 (June 1962), 760–764.

———, *Structure of Scientific Revolutions*, 2nd ed. Chicago: University of Chicago Press, 1970.

Kumar, Krishan, "The Social Culture of Work: Work, Employment, and Unemployment as Ways of Life," *New Universities Quarterly*, 34, no. 1 (Winter 1979/1980), 5–28.

LaFollette, Marcel Chotkowski, "Ethical Misconduct in Research Communication: An Annotated Bibliography," published under NSF Grant No. RII-8409904 ("The Ethical Problems Raised By Fraud in Science and Engineering Publishing"), August 1988.

Landes, David S., "The Industrial Revolution," in *Encyclopaedia Britannica*, 15th ed., Macropaedia, vol.6, pp. 229–242, Chicago, 1979.

———, *The Unbound Prometheus: Technological Change and Industrial Development in Western Europe From 1750 to the Present*. London: Cambridge University Press, 1969.

Laslett, Peter, *The World We Have Lost*. New York: Scribner's, 1965.

Latour, Bruno, *Science In Action*. Cambridge, Mass.: Harvard University Press, 1987.

Latour, Bruno, and Steve Woolgar, *Laboratory Life: The Social Construction of Scientific Facts*. Beverly Hills, Cal.: Sage Publications, 1979.

Laudan, Rachel, ed., *The Nature of Technological Knowledge*. Amsterdam: Reidel, 1984.

Lawick-Goodall, Jane van, *In the Shadow of Man*. Boston: Houghton Mifflin, 1971.

Léger, Fernand, "Contemporary Achievements in Painting," in *Functions of Painting*, ed. Edward F. Fry, pp. 11–19. New York: Viking, 1973.

Lenehan, Michael, "The Quality of the Instrument," *Atlantic Monthly*, August 1982, 33–58.

Lindberg, David C., ed., *Science in the Middle Ages*. Chicago: University of Chicago Press, 1978.

Linder, Staffan B., *The Harried Leisure Class*. New York: Columbia University Press, 1970.

Lloyd, G. E. R., *Early Greek Science: Thales to Aristotle*. New York: W. W. Norton Co., Inc., 1970.

MacKenzie, Donald, "Marx and the Machine," *Technology and Culture*, 25, no. 3 (July 1984), 473–502.

MacKenzie, Donald, and Judy Wajcman, eds. *The Social Shaping of Technology*. Milton Keynes, England: Open University Press, 1985.

Malcolmson, Robert W., *Popular Recreations in English Society: 1700–1850*. Cambridge: Cambridge University Press, 1973.

McGinn, Robert E., "In Defense of Intangibles: The Responsibility-Feasibility Dilemma in Modern Technological Innovation," *Science, Technology, and Human Values*, no. 29 (Autumn 1979), 4–10.

———, "Prestige and the Logic of Political Argument," *Monist*, 56, no. 1 (January 1972), 100–115.

———, "Stokowski and Bell Telephone Laboratories: Collaboration in the Development of High-Fidelity Sound Reproduction," *Technology and Culture*, 24, no. 1 (January 1983), 38–75.

McGinn, Robert E., and N. Bruce Hannay, "The Anatomy of Modern Technology: Prolegomenon to an Improved Public Policy for the Social Management of Technology," *Daedalus*, 109, no. 1 (Winter 1980), 25–53.

McGovern, Carolyn, and Nancy A. Blanpied, eds., *Federal Regulatory Directory*, 5th ed. Washington, D.C.: Congressional Quarterly, 1986.

McKelvey, John P., "Science and Technology: The Driven and the Driver," *Technology Review*, 88, no. 1 (January 1985), 40–47.

Meadows, Donella H., Dennis L. Meadows, Jørgen Randers, and William W. Behrens, *The Limits to Growth*. New York: Universal Books, 1972.

Merrill, Robert S., "The Study of Technology," in *International Encyclopedia of the Social Sciences*, ed. David L. Sills, vol. 15, pp. 576–589. New York: Macmillan, 1968–1979.

Merton, Robert, *Science, Technology, and Society in Seventeenth Century England*. New York: Howard Fertig, 1970.

————, *The Sociology of Science*. Chicago: University of Chicago, 1973.

Mesthene, Emmanuel, *Technological Change*. New York: Mentor, 1970.

Meyrowitz, Joshua, "The Adultlike Child and the Childlike Adult," *Daedalus*, 113, no. 3 (Summer 1984), 19–48.

————, *No Sense of Place: The Impact of Electronic Media on Social Behavior*. Oxford: Oxford University Press, 1985.

Mills, Herb, "The San Francisco Waterfront: The Social Consequences of Industrial Modernization I: The Good Old Days," *Urban Life*, 5, no. 2 (July 1976), 221–250.

————, "The San Francisco Waterfront: The Social Consequences of Industrial Modernization II: Modern Longshore Operations," *Urban Life*, 6, no. 1 (April 1977), 3–32.

Mishan, Ezra, "On Making the Future Safe for Mankind," *Public Interest*, no. 24, 1971, 33–61.

————, *Technology and Growth: The Price We Pay*. New York: Praeger, 1970.

Morgan, Jane, *Electronics in the West*. Palo Alto, Calif.: National Press Books, 1970.

Mumford, Lewis, *Technics and Civilization*. New York: Harcourt Brace & World, 1963.

Munson, Ronald, *Intervention and Reflection*. Belmont, Calif.: Wadsworth, 1979.

National Science Board, *Science and Engineering Indicators—1987*. Washington, D.C.: U.S. Government Printing Office, 1987.

National Science Foundation, *Science and Technology Data Book: 1988*. Washington, D.C.: National Science Foundation, 1987.

National Science Foundation, *Science and Technology Data Book: 1989*. Washington, D.C.: National Science Foundation, 1988.

Nelson, Daniel, *Managers and Workers*. Madison: University of Wisconsin Press, 1975.

Nichols, K. Guild, *Technology On Trial*. Paris: Office of Economic Cooperation and Development, 1979.

Noble, David, *Forces of Production: A Social History of Industrial Automation*. New York: Knopf, 1984.

————, "Social Choice in Machine Design: The Case of Automatically Controlled Machine Tools," in T*he Social Shaping of Technology*, ed. Donald MacKenzie and Judy Wajcman, pp. 109–124. Milton Keynes, England: Open University Press, 1985.

Owles, Derrick, *The Development of Product Liability in the U.S.A.* London: Lloyd's of London, 1978.

Parker, Stanley, *The Sociology of Leisure*. London: George Allen and Unwin, 1976.

Pelto, Pertti J., *The Snowmobile Revolution: Technology and Social Change in the Arctic*. Menlo Park, Calif.: Cummings, 1973.

Penick, James L., Carroll W. Purcell, Morgan B. Sherwood, and Donald C. Swain, eds., *The Politics of American Science*, rev. ed. Cambridge, Mass.: MIT Press, 1972.

Perrow, Charles, *Normal Accidents*. New York: Basic Books, 1984.

Pollard, Sidney, "Factory Discipline in the Industrial Revolution," *Economic History Review*, 2nd series, 16, 254–271.

————, *The Idea of Progress*. Harmondsworth: Penguin, 1971.

Pollock, J. C., *Where Does the Time Go?* New York: Newspaper Enterprise Association, 1983.

Pool, Phoebe, *Impressionism*. New York: Praeger, 1967.

Postman, Neil, *The Disappearance of Childhood*. New York: Dell Pub. Co., Inc., 1982.

————, *Amusing Ourselves to Death: Public Discourse in the Age of Show Business*. New York: Penguin, 1986.

Price, Derek J. deSolla, *Little Science, Big Science*. New York: Columbia University Press, 1963.

Reti, Ladislao, *The Unknown Leonardo*. New York: McGraw-Hill, 1974.

Rieff, Philip, *The Triumph of the Therapeutic*. New York: Harper & Row, Pub., 1968.

Roberts, Kenneth, *Leisure*, 2nd ed. London: Longman, 1981.

Robinson, Thomas F., Stephen M. Factor, and Edmund H. Sonnenblick, "The Heart as as Suction Pump," *Scientific American*, 254, no. 6 (June 1986), 84–91.

Rogers, Everett, *Diffusion of Innovations*, 3rd ed. New York: Free Press, 1983.

Rohan, Paul C., and Bernard Brody, "Frequency and Costs of Worker Accidents in North America," *Labor and Society*, 9, no. 2 (April/June 1984), 165–176.

Rosenberg, Nathan, *Inside the Black Box: Technology and Economics*. New York: Cambridge University Press, 1982.

Rosenberg, Nathan, and L. E. Birdzell, Jr., *How the West Grew Rich*. New York: Basic Books, 1986.

Roy, Robin, and Nigel Cross, *Technology and Society*. Milton Keynes: Open University Press, 1975.

Scharf, Aaron, *Art and Photography*. Middlesex: Penguin, 1974.

Schilling, Warner, "Technology and International Relations," *International Encyclopedia of the Social Sciences*, ed. David L. Sills, vol. 15, pp. 589–598. New York: Macmillan, 1968–1979.

Schon, Donald A., *Technology and Change*. New York: Delacorte, 1967.

Scientific American, *The Mechanization of Work*. San Francisco: Freeman, 1982.

Shepard, Jon M., Dong I. Kim, and James G. Hougland, Jr., "Effects of Technology in Industrialized and Industrializing Societies," *Sociology of Work and Occupations*, 6, no. 4 (November 1979), 457–481.

Simmel, Georg, *Georg Simmel: Sociologist and European*, ed. Peter A. Lawrence. Surrey: Nelson, 1976.

Simon, Julian, and Herman Kahn, *The Resourceful Earth*. New York: Basil Blackwell, 1984.

Singer, Charles, E. J. Holmyard, A. R. Hall, and Trevor I. Williams, *A History of Technology*, vols. 1–8. Oxford: Oxford University Press, 1954–1978.

Street, James H., *The New Revolution in the Cotton Economy: Mechanization and Its Consequences*. Chapel Hill: University of North Carolina Press, 1957.

Tangney, June Price, "Fraud Will Out—Or Will It?" *New Scientist*, 115, no. 1572 (August 6, 1987), 62–63.

Taylor, Frederick Winslow, *Principles of Scientific Management*. New York: W. W. Norton Co., Inc., 1967.

Teich, Albert H., *Technology and the Future*, 4th ed. New York: St. Martin's, 1986.

Terkel, Studs, *Working*. New York: Ballantine, 1985.

Thompson, E. P., "Time, Work Discipline, and Industrial Capitalism," *Past and Present*, no. 38, 1967, 56–97.

Thring, Meredith, "The Engineer's Dilemma," *New Scientist*, 92, no. 1280, November 19, 1981, 500–502.

Traweek, Sharon, *Beamtimes and Lifetimes: The World of High-Energy Physicists*. Cambridge, Mass.: Harvard University Press, 1988.

Tribe, Lawrence, *Channeling Technology Through Law*. Chicago: Bracton Press, 1973.

————, "Towards a New Technological Ethic: The Role of Legal Liability," *Impact of Science on Society*, 21, no. 3, 1971, 215–222.

Truxal, John G., "Learning to Think Like an Engineer: Why, What, and How?" *Change*, 18, no. 2 (March/April 1986), 10–19.

Turkle, Sherry, *The Second Self: Computers and the Human Spirit*. New York: Simon & Schuster, 1984.

Ungar, Stephen H., *Controlling Technology: Ethics and the Responsible Engineer*. New York: Holt, Rinehart and Winston, 1982.

U.S. Bureau of the Census, *Statistical Abstract of the United States: 1988*, 108th ed. Washington, D.C.: U.S. Government Printing Office, 1987.

U.S. Congress, Office of Technology Assessment, *Life-Sustaining Technologies and the Elderly*. Washington, D.C.: U.S. Government Printing Office, 1987.

————, Office of Technology Assessment, *1986 Annual Report*. Washington, D.C.: U.S. Government Printing Office, 1987.

U.S. Employment Service, *Dictionary of Occupational Titles*, 4th ed. Washington, D.C.: U.S. Government Printing Office, 1977.

Usher, Abbott Payson, *A History of Mechanical Inventions*. Cambridge: Harvard University Press, 1954.

Vincenti, Walter G., "The Air-Propeller Tests of W. F. Durand and E. P. Lesley: A Case Study in Technological Methodology," *Technology and Culture*, 20, no. 4 (October 1979), 712–751.

―――, "Technological Knowledge Without Science: The Development of Flush Riveting in American Airplanes," *Technology and Culture*, 25, no. 3 (July 1984), 540–576.

Wad, Atul, "Science, Technology, and Development," *Third World Quarterly*, 6, no. 2 (April 1984), 327–350.

Wallace, Michael, and Arne L. Kallenberg, "Industrial Transformation and the Decline of Craft: The Decomposition of Skill in the Printing Industry, 1931–1978," *American Sociological Review*, 47, June 1982, 307–324.

Warnock, Mary, *Report of the Committee of Inquiry into Human Reproduction and Embryology*. London: Her Majesty's Stationary Office, 1984.

Weber, Max, *Weber: Selections in Translation*, ed. W. G. Runciman. Cambridge: Cambridge University Press, 1976.

Wenk, Edward, "Roots of Ethics: New Principles for Engineering Practice," American Society of Mechanical Engineers Annual Meeting, December 1987, 87- WA/TS-1, 1–7.

Williams, Raymond, *Keywords*. Glasgow: Fontana, 1976.

―――, *The Year 2000*. New York: Pantheon, 1983.

Williams, Tannis MacBeth, ed., *The Impact of Television: A Natural Experiment in Three Communities*. Orlando, Fla.: Academic Press, 1986.

Winner, Langdon, *Autonomous Technology: Technics-out-of-Control as a Theme in Political Thought*. Cambridge, Mass.: MIT Press, 1977.

―――, "Do Artifacts Have Politics?," *Daedalus*, 109, no. 1 (Winter 1980), 121–135.

Winograd, Terry, and Fernando Flores, *Understanding Computers and Cognition: A New Foundation for Design*. Reading, Mass.: Addison-Wesley, 1987.

Wrong, Dennis, "Introduction," in D. Wrong, ed., *Max Weber*. Englewood Cliffs, N.J.: Prentice-Hall, 1970.

Yuchtman-Yaar, Ephraim, "Economic Culture in Post-Industrial Society: Orientation Toward Growth, Work, and Technology," *International Sociology*, 2, no. 1 (March 1987), 77–101.

Zilsel, Edgar, "The Sociological Roots of Science," *American Journal of Sociology*, 47, 1942, 544–562.

Ziman, John, *The Force of Knowledge*. Cambridge: Cambridge University Press, 1976.

INDEX

PRENTICE HALL
FOUNDATIONS OF MODERN SOCIOLOGY SERIES

Alex Inkeles, Editor